WILLIAM LLOYD GARRISON AND GIUSEPPE MAZZINI

Conflicting Worlds: New Dimensions of the American Civil War

T. MICHAEL PARRISH, *Series Editor*

WILLIAM LLOYD GARRISON

ABOLITION, DEMOCRACY, AND RADICAL REFORM

AND GIUSEPPE MAZZINI

ENRICO DAL LAGO

LOUISIANA STATE UNIVERSITY PRESS BATON ROUGE

Published by Louisiana State University Press

Manufactured in the United States of America
FIRST PRINTING

DESIGNER: *Mandy McDonald Scallan*
TYPEFACE: *Calluna*
PRINTER AND BINDER: *Maple Press*

Library of Congress Cataloging-in-Publication Data

Dal Lago, Enrico, 1966–
William Lloyd Garrison and Giuseppe Mazzini : abolition, democracy, and radical reform / Enrico Dal Lago.
pages cm. — (Conflicting worlds : new dimensions of the American Civil War)
Includes bibliographical references and index.
ISBN 978-0-8071-5206-5 (cloth : alk. paper) — ISBN 978-0-8071-5207-2 (pdf) — ISBN 978-0-8071-5208-9 (epub) — ISBN 978-0-8071-5209-6 (mobi) 1. Garrison, William Lloyd, 1805–1879. 2. Abolitionists—United States—Biography. 3. Antislavery movements—United States—History—19th century. 4. United States—Politics and government—1815–1861 5. Mazzini, Giuseppe, 1805–1872. 6. Statesmen—Italy—Biography. 7. Democracy—Italy—History—19th century. 8. Nationalism—Italy—History—19th century. 9. Italy—Politics and government—1815-1870. I. Title.
E449.G25D35 2013
326′.8092—dc23
[B]

2013001846

The paper in this book meets the guidelines for permanence and durability of the Committee on Production Guidelines for Book Longevity of the Council on Library Resources. ∞

CONTENTS

PREFACE

This book is about two prominent nineteenth-century radicals, one American, the other Italian: William Lloyd Garrison and Giuseppe Mazzini. Both were born in 1805, but from different family backgrounds—one poor, the other privileged—in different parts of the Euro-American world. They lived entirely different lives, Garrison as a citizen of an American democratic republic, Mazzini as an exile proscribed by most European monarchies. Their lives covered parallel chronological spans, which embraced the majority of the nineteenth century—a time of profound economic, social, and political transformations in both America and Europe—and in that period they both made their mark, though in different ways and contexts. In fact, Garrison's and Mazzini's lives are particularly representative of two specific egalitarian ideologies, American abolitionism and Italian democratic nationalism. The two figures came to be practically identified with the causes related to those ideologies, the struggle for the abolition of slavery and the creation of an Italian democratic nation.

A comparative biographical study of Garrison and Mazzini, therefore, is as much a study of American abolitionists and Italian democratic nationalists, and of the American and Italian nineteenth-century contexts to which the two belonged, as it is a study of their lives and achievements. Nineteenth-century America and Italy were profoundly divided societies, but for different reasons. In the American case, the flourishing slave system of the antebellum U.S. South, based primarily on cotton production and export to the textile mills of Britain and New England, was tightly tied to the incipient Industrial Revolution, and yet it was at odds with the republican ideals on which the United States was founded and with the religious conscience of many evangelical Christians. Italy at the time was not a nation; the Italian national territory had been carved into multiple dynastic states, most of them absolute monarchies and some of them ruled by foreign powers. This situation was increasingly in conflict with the ever-growing popularity of national sentiment within large sections of the elites and of the educated middle class, both of whom longed for better opportunities of political participation within more liberal forms of rule. In the United States, the single most important divisive national issue was the power of the slave system in the South; in Italy the single most important divisive national issue was the fragmentation of the nation into small states ruled by absolute systems of power.[1]

It is within these contexts that we must see the parallel novelties represented by the creation of movements carrying radical messages such as the immediate abolition of slavery in the United States and the creation of a democratic nation in Italy. Garrison and Mazzini were hardly the only ones who put forward these messages, but they were the ones who worked more tirelessly than anybody else, throughout their lives, toward the achievement of the two objectives of an American nation free from slavery and of a unified Italian republic free from foreign rule. Initially unaware of the parallels in the passionate single-mindedness they showed in the dedication to their life causes, Garrison and Mazzini gradually began to see there was much common ground in what was, effectively, in both cases a struggle for national freedom, whether from slavery or from foreign oppression. By the time they met in London, in 1846—both forty-one years old—they had developed a mutual admiration based on this common ground, and from then on, they shared a long-lasting friendship. Garrison wrote the introduction to a collection of some of Mazzini's autobiographical writings shortly after Mazzini's death, in 1872, and there he explained simply and straightforwardly the reason for this unusual friendship: "We cherished the same hostility to every form of tyranny."[2]

I believe we cannot consider it coincidental that Garrison and Mazzini found such a profound affinity—one that was based first, but not solely, on hostility to tyranny—and that, when they actually met, this affinity developed into enduring friendship and collaboration. Parallels between the two men, between the ways they lived their lives and between the general principles to which they committed themselves, are numerous and are also relatively easy to draw.

A short treatment of some of the most striking parallels and, indeed, similarities between Garrison's and Mazzini's lives has to focus on their absolute, uncompromising, and enduring commitment to the abolition of American slavery in both Garrison's case and to the creation of an Italian republic in Mazzini's case. Strikingly, such commitment assumed highly religious tones in both men: Garrison talked of a "holy struggle" against slavery, thinking of a Protestant type of God, who did not condone sin or injustice and punished them with damnation; Mazzini, instead, talked of an "apostolate," thinking of a common God of humankind, whose plans for uplifting oppressed men and nations ought to be fulfilled. Either way, the religious tones Garrison and Mazzini gave their two life causes had the effect of transforming their struggles into no less than true "missions" of "redemption" of their nations. This approach set the two men apart from many radicals and revolutionaries of the time.[3]

Remarkably, it was in the same year, 1831, and with a similar idea of working toward the aim of a moral regeneration of the nation, that in Boston Garrison began the publication of his radical paper the *Liberator,* with which he began his struggle for the immediate abolition of slavery in the United States, and in Marseilles Mazzini founded Young Italy, which was the first revolutionary society that publicized its republican program of Italian national unification. Each revolutionary in its own terms, these two foundational acts were both radical departures from previous practices and beginnings of movements whose developments were bound to change forever the course of events in the two countries to which they related.[4]

Thereafter, for the next thirty to forty years, facing and surviving different types and degrees of opposition and persecution, at home and abroad, Garrison and Mazzini gave most of their inexhaustible energies to the two causes to which they had sworn to dedicate their lives and with which they gradually became identified wherever they went. By 1846, when the two men finally met at the London home of their mutual friend William Henry Ashurst, Garrison, as the head of the American Anti-Slavery Society, the most radical antislavery association in the United States, had managed to transform the *Liberator* into the most prominent abolitionist paper in the Atlantic world, while Mazzini was known all over the European continent and also in America as the most prominent Italian nationalist, as well as for having founded, several years earlier, the radical democratic association Young Europe.[5]

It appears that, even though they fought for different causes, Garrison and Mazzini acknowledged the extraordinary parallels in their commitment to their respective missions and also saw many connections between them. Not even the fact that, for the most part, they were convinced of the necessity of opposite means prevented the two men from supporting each other at different times in what they clearly saw as related struggles, no matter how different their endeavors might seem to us now. In fact, Garrison's strategy was mostly nonviolent pressure on American public opinion toward the objective of legal abolition of slavery, while Mazzini's strategy for achieving Italian unification focused on revolutionary deeds by force of arms and on projects of insurrection. Yet, in the words of Aida Audeh and Nick Havely, "whether or not the causes were identical is beside the point. Both Garrison and Mazzini believed they were." Perhaps even more significant is that several of their contemporaries who were involved in or sympathized with the radical activities of both, starting with their friend Ashurst, saw Garrison's and Mazzini's two different missions and battles as having more than one characteristic in common. The most important one was that they stemmed, as Garrison himself wrote, from "the same hostility to every form of tyranny."[6]

This book, then, is a comparative study of the parallel lives of William Lloyd Garrison and Giuseppe Mazzini and also, in a smaller but very important measure, of the contacts between the two men as emblematic representatives of American abolitionism and Italian democratic nationalism, firmly contextualized within their two nineteenth-century historical milieus. Applying a quote from John Stauffer's seminal parallel biography of Abraham Lincoln and Frederick Douglass, we can say that by placing Garrison's and Mazzini's "lives side by side, reflecting the one off the other, we gain a fuller picture of each man's career and character. . . . We also acquire a richer sense of the nature of personal transformation and its limitations." This is the general aim of my comparative study: a better understanding of Garrison and Mazzini when seen in light of each other. Yet, my study also has a specific aim, which is to understand how Garrison and Mazzini came to see their different struggles for freedom as both linked and similar in some ways.[7]

In other words, employing a comparative method, but also taking into account the importance of connections, the present study aims at understanding, through the analysis of Garrison's and Mazzini's lives and their particular modes of "thought and action" (Mazzini's famous slogan), why the two men saw the issues of liberation from slavery and liberation from national oppression as both related and parallel. In this sense, the parallels between Garrison's and Mazzini's thoughts and activities epitomized the existence of wider parallels and connections between a host of different, but very much related, struggles for freedom in the nineteenth-century Atlantic and Euro-American world. Such struggles often took on a particularly moral, if not religious, dimension, and they became, then, movements aiming at the "redemption" of races, populations, and nations from oppression in any form.[8]

The book is organized in the following manner. The introduction briefly reviews the historiography of American abolitionism and Italian democratic nationalism as parts of a wider nineteenth-century Euro-American world of radical ideas. Each of the chapters that follow opens with a brief explanation of the wider international context during the time period covered by the chapter. Chapter 1 is about Garrison's and Mazzini's early lives and their cultural background. Chapter 2 treats Garrison's and Mazzini's first autonomous stands in fighting against American slavery and for Italian freedom, respectively, in 1831–32, with Garrison's publication of the *Liberator* and Mazzini's founding of Young Italy. Chapter 3 compares Garrison's and Mazzini's thought, focusing specifically on the two radical activists' sense of moral mission and the pervasive religious dimension of their struggles. Chapter 4 shows how, in the late 1830s and early 1840s, Garrison and Mazzini found themselves challenged in their strategies and tactics. Chapter 5 recounts the momentous events of the late 1840s and early 1850s, which forced Garrison and Mazzini to take even more radical stances, and the two agitators' first meeting in London. In chapter 6 Garrison and Mazzini react to the rise of moderate political forces—the Republican Party in the United States and the moderate liberals in Italy—that took the lead in the crisis that brought about the American Civil War and in the process of Italian unification. Chapter 7 deals with the events of the 1860s, when the abolition of American slavery led to Garrison's consecration as an initiator of slave emancipation and when the establishment of an Italian kingdom led to Mazzini's exile. The conclusion explains how, despite these very different outcomes in their lives, both Garrison and Mazzini became objects of cults of a sort for having represented the hidden radical souls of the nations to which they belonged.

~

In the course of the research and writing of the present book, I have been very fortunate in receiving help from numerous scholars, institutions, and friends. My first thanks go to Mike Parrish, who encouraged me to submit my book manuscript to Louisiana State University Press and who has been extremely supportive and encouraging about my work; I cannot thank him enough.

The research I conducted to write this book was funded by the Irish Research Council for the Humanities and Social Sciences (now simply Irish Research Council), which granted me a Research Fellowship for 2007–8. At my home institution, the National University of Ireland–Galway, I wish to thank especially the History Department and all my colleagues, as well as the past and present heads of the History Department, Daibhi O'Croinin, Steven Ellis, and Caitriona Clear, and also the past and present heads of the School of Humanities, for providing the ideal environment for me to work and write my book. Particularly warm thanks go to Gearoid O'Tuathaigh, for his help and enthusiasm for my book project, and to the Moore Institute's former director, Nicholas Canny, for his continuous support. In the course of my research, I received invaluable help from the staff at the Office of Interlibrary Loan, James Hardiman Library, NUIG; at the Rare Book Division, Boston Public Library; at the Manuscript Section, Massachusetts Historical Society; at the Manuscript Section, Houghton Library, Harvard University; at the Library of the Domus Mazziniana in Pisa; at the Van Pelt Library, University of Pennsylvania; at the Biblioteca Nazionale in Turin; and at the Biblioteca Comunale in Ivrea. In the present book, all translations from Italian documents and publications, unless otherwise stated, are mine.

Preliminary and somewhat different versions of a few sections of the book have been published in the following two articles: "'Condividevamo la stessa ostilità verso ogni forma di tirannia': William Lloyd Garrison, Giuseppe Mazzini e la lotta contro la schiavitù tra Europa e America," *Il Pensiero Mazziniano* 67, no. 1 (2012): 9–26; and "'We Shared the Same Hostility to Every Form of Tyranny': Transatlantic Parallels and Contacts between William Lloyd Garrison and Giuseppe Mazzini, 1846–1872," *American Nineteenth-Century History* 13, no. 3 (2012), 293–319. I also presented parts of the research conducted for this book in numerous papers, most recently "Mazzini, Slavery, and the American Civil War: Transnational Perspectives on Republicanism, Nationalism, and Emancipation," presented at the annual meeting of the American Historical Association, New Orleans, January 2013.

I wish to thank colleagues and friends from different countries who have helped in different ways, all important. Some read my drafts and offered comments, suggestions, or criticisms; others simply asked me about my project or allowed me to talk about it. Particularly warm thanks go to Caleb McDaniel, who generously shared his book manuscript with me before it was published and who, equally generously, read my own entire book manuscript (and very fast! on my request), making extremely helpful comments, at least some of which I have done my best to address. I also wish to thank Norwood Andrews, Manuel Barcia, Gearoid Barry, Cristina Bon, Richard Carwardine, Catherine Clinton, Paolo Colombo, Don Doyle, Ferdinando Fasce, Roisin Healy, Maurizio Isabella, Peter Kolchin, Axel Korner, Bruce Levine, Rafael de Bivar Marquese, Margot Minardi, Giuseppe Monsagrati, Lucy Riall, Tim Roberts, Maria Pia Roggero, Ed Rugemer, Ricardo Salles, Roland Sarti, Martin Thom, and Dale Tomich. At Louisiana State University Press, I wish to thank especially the anonymous reader of my manuscript, who provided extremely enthusiastic and positive comments, and Rand Dotson for all his help. Very special thanks go to Madeleine, who has helped me throughout with her warm, special friendship and her unwavering belief in my abilities as writer and scholar. Finally, I wish to thank my parents, Olinto and Rosa Dal Lago, for their continuous enthusiasm and patience, and my brother Stefano, who provided crucial criticism at an important stage and helped me formulate the titles of the chapters. Ultimately, this book is about two men who met only a couple of times in their lives and yet managed to keep, somewhat effortlessly, an exceptionally strong and warm friendship, as happens between true friends. Therefore, I dedicate my book to all my true friends—those whose friendship I have treasured throughout the good and bad times, even if, like Garrison and Mazzini, we have not seen each other as often as we had hoped.

WILLIAM LLOYD GARRISON AND GIUSEPPE MAZZINI

INTRODUCTION

Garrisonian Abolitionism, Mazzinian Democratic Nationalism, and Transnational Comparisons

Nineteenth-century American abolitionism and Italian democratic nationalism were radical movements put forward by activist minorities who hoped to decisively influence the public opinions of their respective countries. Both movements used the enormous power of the press to reach their aims, but Italian democrats were far more prone than American abolitionists to make widespread use of violence. Both were also diverse movements within which different ideas and currents existed, but each movement had a single general aim that bound those currents together, although the differences in strategies and tactics determined permanent divisions. For American abolitionists, the aim was the immediate abolition of slavery in the United States; for Italian democrats, it was the establishment of a free Italian republic. Between the 1830s and 1860, in the decades that preceded the American Civil War and Italian national unification, American abolitionists and Italian democrats established themselves as the proponents of the two most radical solutions to the two crucial problems of the existence of slavery in the United States and national oppression in Italy. Even though scholars have not usually put nineteenth-century American abolitionism and Italian democratic nationalism in relation with each other, there is much to learn from comparing them and discovering their similarities and differences.

Such a comparison must start with the two historical characters who were foremost within the two movements: William Lloyd Garrison and Giuseppe Mazzini. It is of paramount importance to remember that, despite being often identified with American abolitionism and Italian democratic nationalism, Garrison and Mazzini represented very much their own versions of the two movements, while their followers, the Garrisonians and the Mazzinians, were particular groups within those movements. And yet, Garrison and Mazzini and their followers were the most convinced advocates of the universal character of their battles, which they saw as struggles that asserted the resilience of liberty against all forms of tyranny, including slavery and national oppression. Thus, as they acted within the American abolitionist movement and the Italian democratic movement, Garrison and Mazzini also acted within wider, Atlantic and Euro-American contexts as proponents of the universal rights of humankind. Though long aware of the importance of the international dimension in Garrison's and Mazzini's ideas and activities, only recently have scholars begun to analyze the implications of this dimension for American abolitionism and Italian democratic nationalism. The two movements have come to be seen as parts of a much wider nineteenth-century Euro-American world of radical reform and revolutionary action—a world in which the transnational debate on the relationship between democracy, nation-building, and slavery was fervent on both sides of the Atlantic.[1]

To understand the wider context in which the two men operated, Garrison as a representative of American abolitionism and Mazzini as a representative of Italian democratic nationalism, it is useful to utilize the socioeconomic framework of the "second slavery," as it has been described by Dale Tomich and other scholars. According to Tomich and Michael Zeuske, "the concept of second slavery calls attention to the world-historical processes that transformed the Atlantic world between the 1780s and 1888," and specifically the mass "redeployment of slave labor as a productive force" in those areas, such as the U.S. South, Cuba, and Brazil, where cash crops provided a crucial link with the world market, fulfilling the needs of the growing Industrial Revolution in Britain and the market revolution in the northeastern United States. At the same time, those same world-historical processes led, first, to the making of movements of opposition to slavery aiming at either gradual or immediate slave emancipation, and then to the eventual demise of slave systems in the entire Atlantic world. The era of the "second slavery," in fact, was also an era of abolition, which started with the Haitian revolution (1791–1804) and ended with the emancipation of slaves in the United States (1863–65) and then in Cuba and Brazil (1886–88). It was also an era when abolitionist networks characterized a transnational sphere of activity populated by radical antislavery agitators on both sides of the Atlantic.[2]

We can usefully compare the momentous changes related to the rise and fall of the "second slavery" with the equally momentous and contemporaneous changes that stemmed from the legacy of the "Era of Atlantic Revolutions," specifically the American and French Revolutions and the Napoleonic period (1776–1815), and focused on the definition of citizenship rights and the recognition of oppressed nationalities. Largely as a consequence of the definition of liberal and democratic forms of citizenship elaborated during the French revolutionary period and as a result of the tradition of resistance to Napoleonic rule in large areas of Europe, in the Atlantic world the nineteenth century saw the emergence of a large number of movements of nation-building, beginning with the Latin American wars of independence (1808–25) and culminating with the 1848 European revolutions, and then again with the making of Italy (1859–70), mostly in reaction against empires and absolute monarchies, and with a crucial component of support for constitutional rights at their core. Against all forms of autocratic rule, most European liberal and democratic activists and revolutionaries demanded nations founded on "freedom of the press, the rule of law, constitutional governments, and greater participation in the affairs of the state," claiming that these were the principles that made the nation a voluntary community of responsible citizens, whose basic rights ought to be protected by the state. It is no coincidence that the era of abolition in response to the rise of the "second slavery" in the Americas and the era of constitutional nation-building in response to autocratic rule in Europe and the Americas occurred at the same time. As studies by Robin Blackburn and other scholars have clarified, the struggle against slavery and the struggle for citizenship rights were related, and both struggles had to do with the definition of modern nationality. This was the nineteenth-century Euro-American world context in which Garrison and Mazzini operated, the context that influenced them and came to be influenced by them.[3]

Therefore, the rise of the "second slavery" in the U.S. South, from the start of the nineteenth century, and the reaction to it, helps us understand better the reasons for the birth of a new, radical, and "immediatist" form of American abolitionism from the late 1820s onward—the type of abolitionism that Garrison epitomized from 1831. At the same time, the legacy of Atlantic revolutionary doctrines of participant and responsible nationality and citizenship and of recognition of constitutional rights helps us understand better the reasons for the rise of new, radical forms of resistance to political oppression and denial of national self-determination such as Mazzini's democratic republicanism, also from the early 1830s. In general, in the period 1830–60, the United States and Italy were profoundly divided societies in ideological and political terms. In both cases, a "national question" dominated the thoughts and activities of the most prominent intellectuals and politicians. In the United States, the divisive issue was slavery, and consequently the "national question" focused on bringing together, as a true nation, the free North and the slave South that were joined in a loose confederation of states. In Italy, where political division prevailed in different dynastic states and foreign oppression was ongoing, the "national question" focused on bringing the country together by freeing it at the same time. Seen within these frameworks, Garrisonian abolitionism and Mazzinian democratic republicanism—which, within their respective contexts, assumed definite national characteristics—appear as two radical initiatives, both progressive and revolutionary at the same time, with parallel aims. Those aims were to provide two particularly radical solutions to the two most pressing national questions in the United States and Italy, with a view to extending the solutions' benefits to the wider world—in Garrison's case through the abolition of American slavery and possibly also Atlantic slavery, and in Mazzini's case through the creation of a democratic republic in Italy and then also democratic governments in the whole of Europe.[4]

For a long time, American scholars considered Garrison and his Garrisonian abolitionists as part of a radical movement, partly because of how they considered themselves and partly because of how the majority of their contemporaries viewed them. Early scholars of abolitionism, such as Gilbert Barnes and Dwight L. Dumond, between the 1930s and the 1950s, made a clear distinction between radical Garrisonians and the other abolitionists. Then the new "neoabolitionist" scholarship that flourished in the wake of the civil rights movement in the 1960s and up to the 1970s—from the studies of James McPherson and Aileen Kraditor to those of Lewis Perry—proudly considered Garrison and his followers as radical initiators of opposition to violence through nonresistance; they saw his influence in the battles for racial and gender equality and even in anarchist pacifism. This was especially true of those scholars—such as Russell Nye, John L. Thomas, and Walter

Merrill—who wrote biographies of Garrison and were determined to show how all of the above were clearly evident features in Garrison's thought and activity from the early 1830s onward. In all these studies, at the heart of this view was the idea that what made Garrison a true radical was first and foremost his "immediatism," his advocacy of immediate emancipation, which he embraced beginning in 1831 with the publication of the *Liberator*.[5]

In recent years, though, studies on American abolitionism have multiplied and have greatly expanded our understanding, not just of the leading individuals who advocated immediate abolition, but also of several different groups of abolitionists, which most previous scholars had largely overlooked; notable exceptions were Benjamin Quarles, Jane and William Pease, and Richard Blackett. Therefore, recent studies have focused largely on "rank and file" abolitionists, on African American abolitionists, on abolitionist women, and, more recently still, on those non-Garrisonian abolitionists who advocated either violence or outright political action for the immediate resolution of the slavery issue—clearly in contrast with Garrison, who rejected both. The result of this new wave of scholarship has been the creation of a much more complex picture of American abolitionism and of the different groups within it than we had previously thought. As a consequence, scholars have begun also to advocate a different view of radicalism, one that now emphasizes the roles of the first African American immediatists in the late 1820s, of the more politically oriented abolitionists in the 1840s, and of the more militantly violent abolitionists in the 1850s—as in the works, particularly, of Richard Newman, Bruce Laurie, and John Stauffer.[6]

Yet, as Caleb McDaniel has argued in a recent reappraisal of the definition of radical abolitionism, nonresistance "still qualifies as 'radical'—its adherents [Garrison and his followers] were a minority, many of whom were certainly 'extreme' in their degree of personal commitment; it represented an especially uncompromising version of key principles . . . of a 'radical' tradition, like individualism and the equal worth of all human beings." But there was more to it than that. Partly following the early studies by Gilbert Barnes, contemporary scholars such as Robert Abzug have identified how a great deal of that "radical tradition" descended from ideas and attitudes related to the Second Great Awakening. In the 1820s and 1830s, thanks to the tireless work of particularly charismatic revivalist preachers, such ideas, and especially the idea of the individual's need to fight only through "moral suasion"—that is, by appealing to people's consciences—the sin of slavery and all the other social evils in order to achieve salvation, became commonplace in the United States, influencing especially Garrisonian abolitionists. As James B. Stewart has noticed, "embedded in these abolitionist appeals [to moral suasion] were attitudes and values that marked the movement as an unprecedented step in the direction of ideological modernity." Such "modern" attitudes and values included specifically a widespread empathy for the weak, the suffering, and the exploited—whether they were slaves or other categories of people—and a willingness to engage in the struggle for "making the 'black race' equal to the 'white.'" To be sure, the nature of the relationship between abolitionism and modernity in general is still open to debate, especially if we think of the latter as particularly represented by the modern type of industrial capitalism that had begun to characterize the antebellum northern United States; different scholars have seen abolitionists, at different times, as either opponents or supporters of individual freedom in economic terms as well, or else as rather ambivalent in their attitudes. It is also known that Garrison, in particular, paid little attention to problems related to class exploitation. However, in several other realms—not just in relation to slavery and race issues—Garrison and the Garrisonians proved not just to be radical, but to be extraordinarily ahead of their times: this was certainly the case in regard to both their idea that dissent was necessary to safeguard democracy and their support for women's rights.[7]

One realm, also related to support for women's rights, in which Garrison and the Garrisonians were both radical and ahead of their time was the international dimension of the abolitionist struggle, which they wholeheartedly embraced and which became a hallmark of their universalism in advocating radical reforms. Although there were earlier pathbreaking studies by a few historians, including David Brion Davis, Betty Fladeland, and Robin Blackburn, scholars have only recently begun to investigate this very important aspect of Garrisonian abolitionism. The recent studies by Thomas Bender, Ian Tyrrell, and Carl Guarneri—who have placed American abolitionism in the context of a "transnational" narrative of American history—and the latest scholarship on "Atlantic history" have done much to emphasize the international connections between American and English abolitionist activists. More than anything, the recent wave of new scholarly studies that have investigated and reevaluated the different facets of American abolitionism has led to a renewed focus particularly, but not exclusively, on Garrison's and the Garrisonians' contacts with other abolitionist groups and reform movements also outside the United States. This latest trend in scholarship is well represented by the work of Richard Blackett, Edward Rugemer, and Caleb McDaniel.[8]

In particular, in *The Problem of Democracy in the Age of Slavery* (2013), McDaniel has shown how crucial were transatlantic links and exchanges with British and European reformers and agitators for Garrison's and the Garrisonians' reconceptualization of that same American democracy that they sought to improve at home with their dissent and with their influence on political institutions through extraparliamentary abolitionist activities. Even though this approach to American abolitionism has taken only its first steps, it already illustrates a new way to look at American abolitionism's radical features within a "transnational" context. Moreover, the new approach is also clear in the latest studies on Garrison himself. The most recent biographical study of Garrison, Henry Mayer's *All on Fire* (1998), pays much more attention to the international context of Garrison's abolitionist ideas and activities than the previous biographies of him. The new transnational approach is also particularly significant in James B. Stewart's edited collection *William Lloyd Garrison at Two Hundred* (2008), which celebrated the two-hundredth anniversary of Garrison's birth; in that work, attention to Garrison's activities within the Atlantic and international realm is clearly evident and forms a major focus of investigation and reappraisal.[9]

In contrast with Garrison and the Garrisonians, Mazzini and his followers underwent a type of scrutiny by early Italian scholars of the Risorgimento period that mostly tended to overlook the radical features of their republican ideal and, instead, accentuated their nationalism; this was certainly the case of scholars of the Fascist period—from the 1920s to the 1940s—such as Giovanni Gentile and Arturo Codignola. Conversely, following Antonio Gramsci's interpretation of Italian unification and the Risorgimento as a "passive revolution," Marxist scholars accused Mazzini and the Italian democrats of having failed to lead the masses in a true popular national movement. Yet, many among the Italian Left and anti-Fascists, from Nello Rosselli to Piero Gobetti, felt the fascination of Mazzini's radical ideas of democracy. By the second half of the 1940s, with the creation of the Italian republic, and up to the 1970s, several leftist scholars—among them especially Giuseppe Berti, Alfonso Scirocco, Giuseppe Galasso, and Franco Della Peruta—published studies that reevaluated the revolutionary character of the actions conducted by both Mazzini and the Italian democrats, even though they did not ignore either the divisions within the democratic movement nor their ultimate defeat at the hands of more conservative liberal forces. At the same time, scholars such as Emilia Morelli and Salvo Mastellone produced the most detailed studies yet of some of the most important Mazzinian activities. At the heart of all these positive evaluations, which were also included in important conference proceedings and collections of essays, were two assumptions holding little in common with Gramscian historiography. The first assumption was that, despite their misunderstandings, Mazzinian democrats were the first to attempt to create a genuine Italian national movement on democratic bases; the second was that the deep roots of the post–World War II Italian republic—seen as a positive outcome, rather than as an instrument of bourgeois "hegemony"—lay in those attempts.[10]

In Italy as in the United States, more recent years have seen a crescendo of historiographic "revisionism," which questioned old assumptions and focused on previously overlooked issues. However, unlike what happened with American abolitionism, Italian "revisionist" studies focused neither on Risorgimento politics nor on Mazzinian democratic nationalism, aside from a few notable exceptions, such as, for example, Clara Lovett's critical treatment of the nineteenth-century Italian democratic movement as a whole. In fact, the main emphasis of these studies was on deconstructing both the Gramscian view of the Risorgimento's "passive revolution" and the opposite, teleological, view of Italian unification inherited by liberal historians such as Benedetto Croce and Rosario Romeo through the investigation of a number of micro case studies in the economy and society of different Italian regions and the consequent reevaluation of preunification Italian states. Ultimately, "revisionist" scholars have argued for the existence of complex factors that led to the formation of the Italian nation. Consequently, not only did great historical figures such as Mazzini—already considered rather irrelevant in previously strictly Marxist views based on structures rather than individuals—lose, for the most part, their central role in history, but also politics and political movements such as Italian democratic nationalism lost their importance, since their actual contribution to the Risorgimento paled in comparison with much more relevant economic and social changes. In this respect, it is very significant that, until very recently, the two most acclaimed recent biographies of Mazzini—both written at the height of the popularity of Italian "revisionist" historiography—were the product of an

English scholar and an American scholar, Denis Mack Smith and Roland Sarti.[11]

Only very recently have historians of Italy turned their attention back to Risorgimento politics and to Mazzini himself, both analyzed with novel perspectives. In fact, as Lucy Riall has pointed out, some of the latest scholarship—particularly the studies focusing on Italian culture in the age of Risorgimento—may very well contain within itself the reasons for a new reevaluation of nineteenth-century Italian nationalism and Mazzinian democratic nationalism in particular. Studies by Albert Russell Ascoli and Krystyna Von Henneberg, Alberto Banti, Silvana Patriarca, Lucy Riall, and Paul Ginsborg have posed the question of what nineteenth-century national Italian culture actually consisted of. Thanks to these studies, we are now much more aware of the symbols, the metaphors, and the common language that formed an established repertoire that Italian patriots utilized consistently in order to describe themselves and the national Italian culture to which they belonged—and the nation they sought to create. In this context, Mazzini's relevance becomes clear when one realizes that he utilized these symbols, metaphors, and common language more often and better than any other; thus, in him, in the words of Lucy Riall, "we can locate the connecting point between nationalism as cultural identity and nationalism as a political movement." But what sort of political movement? Certainly one that, in terms of its own characteristics, we can only describe as radical in its doctrine of universal participatory democracy and revolutionary in its aims of overthrowing kingdoms and empires in order to establish republics, first of all an Italian democratic republic.[12]

In their edited collection of essays *Il Risorgimento* (2007), Alberto Banti and Paul Ginsborg have made a provocative plea for the reevaluation of the Risorgimento as a "mass movement," rather than a movement that a few upper-class noblemen and bourgeois revolutionaries guided and used for their own sake—as both the old liberal and the Marxist historiographies maintained. In making their plea, Banti and Ginsborg have written that they do not refer to Mazzini's view of the Italian people awakening after centuries of decadence to fight against the foreign oppressor—since this is historically untrue—but rather to the fact that "many tens of thousands of people took active part in the Risorgimento, understood as a political movement whose aim was the formation of a nation-state in the Italian peninsula," while many others sympathized in different ways with that same movement.

In this respect, without regard to his misunderstandings, Mazzini certainly had a fundamental role in inspiring a national movement that included also "the educated strata of the urban popular classes," as Silvana Patriarca and Lucy Riall have pointed out in *Il Risorgimento Revisited* (2012). In this sense, some of the new biographical and historiographic studies of Mazzini, such as Giovanni Belardelli's monograph *Mazzini* (2010) and an important article by Roberto Balzani, and especially Anna Arisi Rota's study on the impact of Mazzini's novel ideas and strategies on the nineteenth-century Italian youth, have shed much light on Mazzini's contribution to the Risorgimento and also on the problems related to the interpretation of his thought and activity.[13]

Equally, C. A. Bayly's and Eugenio Biagini's edited volume *Giuseppe Mazzini and the Globalization of Democratic Nationalism* (2008) has illuminated important aspects through an innovative approach to both his personality and his legacy. In many ways, the essays gathered in this collection show the way forward in understanding Mazzini and Mazzinian democratic nationalism within the transnational context of the world around them. Like Garrison, Mazzini was always concerned with universal issues, and his radical ideas about democracy and republican government—no less than his actions to support revolutionary national movements and also progressive causes such as the abolition of slavery and women's rights—can be understood completely only within the nineteenth-century Euro-American milieu in which he moved and operated, as studies by Roland Sarti, Salvo Mastellone, Maurizio Isabella, and Timothy Roberts have recently shown.[14]

It is vitally important, then, in a comparative study of Garrison and Mazzini, to situate the two men not just within the historical contexts of American abolitionism and Italian democratic nationalism, but also within the much wider contexts of which they were part: "Atlantic abolitionism," the Anglo-American and French movements for immediate and worldwide slave emancipation, in Garrison's case, and European nationalism, especially the democratic and revolutionary type of nationalism spread in continental Europe, in Mazzini's case. Even though these two different contexts came in contact only on a sporadic basis, they were both parts of an encompassing nineteenth-century Euro-American world of radical reform and change—change that often drifted toward outright revolution—which gathered within itself all the progressive spirits of the age. Indeed, the existence of this transcontinental progressive milieu was the very reason why many reformers and revolutionaries in the Americas and Europe, including Garrison and Mazzini, even though fighting for different causes, came in contact with one another and recognized a commonality in their struggles. In this respect, it is fair to say that the international dimensions and ramifications of Garrison's and Mazzini's struggles to "redeem" their nations are so important that it is virtually impossible to understand the true meaning of the radical, and to a certain extent also revolutionary, movements that they headed without constant reference to the wider Atlantic and European milieus and to the events and historical figures that characterized them. The present study, therefore, follows in the footsteps of some of the recent scholars on the Atlantic world—according to which the transnational flow of goods, people, and ideas that characterized the early modern period continued, and even intensified, in the course of the nineteenth century—and also, in a similar vein, the recent pleas for building a transnational scholarship of the Civil War era. Within both views, there is much room for a comparative analysis of both general movements and specific individuals, such as Garrison and Mazzini, that takes into account the crucial links and connections that developed on both sides of the Atlantic Ocean and, more generally, of the Euro-American world.[15]

Thus, on one hand, a study of Garrison and Mazzini is necessarily comparative, given that the study's primary objective is to discover the similarities and differences between the two men's struggles for the cause of freedom and for the "redemption" of their nations. But on the other hand, such a study necessarily also has an element of "transnational history," since it must acknowledge the paramount importance of the wider contexts in which Garrison and Mazzini lived, by making constant reference to what transnational historian Ian Tyrrell has termed "international connections." In practice, the present book is a case study that aims also to prove what Daniel Rodgers has claimed in his synthesis of American reform in transnational perspective: that all the great nineteenth-century reform movements in the United States were related to equally important, or even more important, movements happening elsewhere. In this sense, complementing the studies of McDaniel and others, the aim of an analysis of Garrison and Mazzini in comparative perspective is to study through a specific example the effects of what several scholars have referred to as one of the primary objectives of "transnational history": the circulation and flow of ideas—

which in turn was one of the factors that created connections and relationships between different parts of the world. In the present case study, the ideas that circulated and created connections as a result of the transnational activities of Atlantic progressives and radicals such as Garrison and Mazzini led many to consider all struggles against slavery and against national oppression as intimately related issues, even though, in practice, the situations in which these struggles occurred varied greatly from place to place.[16]

It is then within a world context characterized both by transnational support for civil liberties and, at the same time, by specific local struggles of national regeneration that we should situate a comparison between Garrison and Mazzini—an example of what George Fredrickson has termed "cross-national comparative history"—as a way to understand better the connections between the movements and milieus to which the two activists belonged. The present study, though, owes an even greater intellectual debt to a few scholars who have attempted, with their wide-ranging efforts, to connect ideologies and movements and compare them on a cross-continental "world history" scale within the long nineteenth century. Among these scholars, especially important are Eric Hobsbawm, with his trilogy *Age of Revolutions* (1962), *Age of Capital* (1975), and *Age of Empire* (1983), and, more recently, C. A. Bayly's *The Birth of the Modern World, 1780–1914* (2004) and Robin Blackburn's *The American Crucible* (2011). In particular, Bayly's "world history" approach, with his focus on investigating the "rise of global uniformities in the state, religion, political ideologies," and the connections that created "hybrid polities, mixed ideologies" but could also "heighten a sense of difference," seems very much the perfect point of departure to understand Garrison's thought and activities, representative of radical American abolitionism, and Mazzini's thought and activities, representative of radical Italian and European democratic nationalism, as parts of a nineteenth-century transatlantic exchange of ideas. Even though the points of origin of this exchange necessarily related to different local, regional, and national contexts, throughout the best part of the nineteenth century the effects of continuous transatlantic connections often led to the development of perceived global uniformities in the ideas of freedom that characterized the United States and Europe, and even other parts of the world beyond the Atlantic Ocean. As a result of these perceived uniformities, as Paola Gemme has noted in her *Domesticating Foreign Struggles* (2005), "Abolitionists often went further than merely juxtaposing political oppression and American slavery and openly equated the conditions of persecuted Italian patriots with those of the domestic bondsmen."[17]

In this perspective, I propose that a comparative study of William Lloyd Garrison and Giuseppe Mazzini as foremost representatives of the radical traditions of American abolitionism and Italian democratic nationalism is an example of how we can tie together the local and the global through a comparative investigation that includes "transnational" elements and points out their clear significance on a world history scale, given the impact on the nineteenth-century Euro-American world of both Garrison's and Mazzini's thought and activities. In fact, the starting point of my study is the transnational dimension of the American abolitionist movement, as it is clearly seen in the activities of Garrison and his followers. McDaniel has shown at length in his study that, as an abolitionist editor and the leader of the American Anti-Slavery Society, Garrison related his program for the regeneration of the United States on moral and religious grounds to a wide-ranging campaign of support for progressive causes and libertarian movements and collaboration with other radical projects of humanitarian reform in the entire Atlantic world, specifically in both the United States and Europe. During his quest, Garrison met Italian democratic nationalist Giuseppe Mazzini, who, with his own involvement in antislavery activities, provided the American abolitionist movement with an important link to the progressive and radical ideas that agitated the European continent.[18]

It is well known that Mazzini felt a particular affinity with Garrison. Convinced that they were fighting for similar ideals—the acknowledgment of oppressed nationalities and the liberation of slaves from exploitation—Mazzini and Garrison developed a mutual admiration and friendship and also engaged in occasional collaboration. While Garrison spread Mazzini's fame in the American abolitionist circles, Mazzini, as the main advocate for the creation of an Italian democratic republic and for a Europe of free nations, contributed articles for Garrison's antislavery journal the *Liberator*—a title that, perhaps not coincidentally, resonated with the nicknames of both Latin American nationalist leader Simon Bolivar and Irish Catholic reformer Daniel O'Connell. It is certainly no accident that Garrison and Mazzini considered themselves universal radical reformers who supported the common cause of humankind. Both were imbued with romanticism's ideals and with the legacies of the Enlightenment, among which the most important was the belief in the universality of natural rights, and each of them saw abolition of slavery and national regeneration as crucial steps in humankind's march toward progress. This common belief makes comparison between these two historical figures possible, while the difference in the ways they expressed this belief and acted upon it makes the comparison between Garrison and Mazzini worthwhile.[19]

All in all, in analyzing these specific similarities and differences, and also the modes of specific transatlantic collaboration between Garrison and Mazzini, my study aims at establishing a first example of cross-continental comparison between American abolitionism and the Italian democratic nationalist movement, following many of the ideas of the different "transnational methods" but privileging at the same time a comparative historical methodology. In fact, only by both focusing on comparison and looking at the contacts and collaboration between these two great figures and the wider contexts they belonged to, is it possible both to highlight Garrison's and Mazzini's radical convictions and to investigate American abolitionism and Italian democratic nationalism as parts of a global, transcontinental movement for the affirmation of liberty over oppression and slavery in all forms.

Therefore, a cross-continental comparative analysis of Garrison and Mazzini has a clear "world history" dimension, because it has the potential to lead us to a better appreciation of how the categories of slavery and freedom were understood in the wider nineteenth-century Atlantic and Euro-American milieu. More importantly, by implementing a cross-continental approach in a comparative study of two major radical advocates of abolitionism and democratic nationalism, we might be better able to understand how, in the course of the nineteenth century and on a world scale, the discourses of slavery and of the fight against it were utilized in the most disparate contexts—especially contexts related to nationalist movements—as immediately recognizable metaphors for all self-evidently justified radical struggles against oppressive institutions.

1

EARLY ATTEMPTS AT DEMOCRATIZATION

The Making of Two Radical Leaders, 1805–1830

The world in which William Lloyd Garrison and Giuseppe Mazzini were born, in 1805, was a world in turmoil: it was an epoch that Robert Palmer appropriately described fifty years ago as the "Age of Democratic Revolution" and that recent scholarship, following Palmer's lead, has treated fruitfully in comparative perspective. Starting in the late eighteenth century, from one side of the Atlantic to the other, revolutionary movements shook the foundations of the old European and colonial American orders, with indelible repercussions on the struggles to abolish slavery and to liberate oppressed nationalities. Long before they became the two life causes of Garrison and Mazzini, the abolition of slavery and liberation from national oppression reached the height of their popularity, as a result of the increasing democratization of society brought about by the American, French, and Haitian revolutions. Those revolutions were consequences both of the spread of Enlightenment ideas about human rights' inalienability and universality and of incipient romantic notions about individuals' and peoples' entitlement to self-fulfillment.[1]

By 1805 the successful conclusion of the Haitian revolution in the former slaveholding French colony of Saint Domingue and the 1804 formation of the free Haitian republic had come at the end of a process of dissolution of the old system of colonial slavery in the New World; it was a period that had seen the implementation of antislavery measures all over the Americas, especially in Revolutionary and post-Revolutionary North America. The Haitian revolution had become not only a positive paradigm for a possible world without slaves, but also a negative paradigm for what the world would become if whites did not proceed to abolish slavery before being forced to do so. In Europe, the Napoleonic Empire was at its height by 1805, spread as it was over the breadth and length of Europe, as a result of an almost continuous state of war between expansionist Napoleonic France and Europe's reactionary powers, supported especially by Britain. The Napoleonic Empire had had a fundamental role in spreading to other European countries French revolutionary ideas—the same ideas that had sparked the initial revolt and then the Haitian revolution in Saint Domingue. However, the spread of revolutionary ideas by force of arms had prompted in response a surge of protonationalist movements in those same European countries, including Italy—and that fact led to unforeseen and devastating consequences for the French armies of occupation.[2]

If this was the situation in 1805, in the following ten to fifteen years, the period of early youth for Garrison and Mazzini, the revolutionary thrust died out and a renewed version of the "Old Order" seemed to grip the entire Euro-American world. Despite the momentous abolition of the Atlantic slave trade implemented by the British Empire in 1807 and by the U.S. Congress in 1808, the end of Saint Domingue's economic hegemony in the Caribbean had led to a restructuring of the entire slave system in the New World and to the rise of a new, aggressively capitalist and more exploitative "second slavery" in the U.S. South, Cuba, and Brazil. At the same time, with the Congress of Vienna, Napoleon's final defeat at Waterloo, and the creation of the "Holy Alliance" between Russia, Prussia, and Austria in 1815, even though French occupation ended throughout Europe, the national aspirations of several European peoples were sacrificed in favor of the restoration of former polities headed by reactionary rulers. This happened in both Italy and Germany, and both were divided into multiple dynastic states. The world in which Garrison and Mazzini made their early acquaintance with the issues that occupied them for their lifetimes—slavery and national oppression—was thus a world in which conservatism and reaction, as opposed to reform and revolution, were the norm; and yet the legacy of the immense changes resulting from the revolutionary period on both sides of the Atlantic had not been lost but was dormant underneath a veneer of order and immobility.[3]

In fact, from 1816 on, there were telling signs of change in the Americas and Europe, either open or hidden, in regard to opposition to slavery and national oppression. In the British Empire in particular, abolitionists, led by William Wilberforce, had become progressively stronger in Parliament and—also helped by the public uproar caused by large-scale slave rebellions in the West Indian colonies of Barbados (1816) and Demerara (1823)—had managed to build consensus around the issue of gradual emancipation. By 1823 they had founded the Society for Mitigating and Gradually Abolishing Slavery throughout the British Dominion, which came to be known as the Anti-Slavery Society (ASS), headed by Thomas Fowell Buxton, while British prime minister George Canning had called for "ameliorative measures" regarding slavery in the British colonies. By contrast, in continental Europe, opposition to the policy of Restoration and its reactionary violation of the principle of nationality coalesced around the creation of secret societies, given the presence of police regimes in most European countries. In the period 1816–25, the influence of possibly the largest among these secret societies, the Carboneria, reached its peak, having gathered thousands of adherents among the young middle class both in Italy and in other countries such as Spain, where it was at the origin of the 1820–21 constitutional revolution, and in France, where, led by university student Philip-Joseph-Benjamin Bouchez, it was instrumental in revolutionary conspiracies against the restored Bourbon king Louis XVIII.[4]

If we place these developments within their Atlantic context, we will notice that they appear to be elements of a long wave of movements that, at the beginning of the postrevolutionary period, shook the foundations of the restored Old Order throughout the Atlantic. This wave culminated with the ten-year struggle for Greek independence (1821–30) from the Ottoman Empire and with the successful Latin American revolutions, which in the early 1820s defeated the Spanish Empire and birthed several countries in Central and South America. Significantly, secret societies played a leading role in both the Greek and the Latin American struggles, and those struggles mostly led to the foundation of new nations. More significant still is that there was also an antislavery element within the Latin American revolutionary movements: the most famous revolutionary hero there, Simon Bolivar, acquired the nickname "The Liberator" both as a redeemer of peoples or nations and as a supposed liberator from slavery. In fact, at the 1819 Congress of Angostura, Bolivar pleaded with the Creole elite to do away with what he called the "dark mantle of barbarous and profane slavery." Despite his later ambiguous attitude toward the issue, Bolivar became a model and a paradigm for both Garrison and Mazzini; thus, the example of Bolivar's rhetoric shows well how, by the 1820s, the common language spoken by radicals and revolutionaries on both sides of the Atlantic identified liberation from national oppression with liberation from slavery as if the two were intimately linked struggles for the common benefit of humankind.[5]

Religious Influence and Ethical Commitment in Garrison and Mazzini

Born at the beginning of the nineteenth century, Garrison and Mazzini took their first steps in the postrevolutionary and Restoration Euro-American world. In that world, as they knew it in the United States and Italy, religion played a very important role in the daily life of the people. On one hand, each of the two men was subject to the influence of his own family environment, and in both cases the mother played a crucial role in the religious education of her son. On the other hand, particular religious movements and strains, which reached the peak of their activity in the 1820s and 1830s, contributed crucially to forming the character and the worldview of both Garrison and Mazzini in their youth. Specifically, in Protestant New England, and particularly in Massachusetts, where Garrison grew up, evangelical Christianity—through two consecutive reform movements, the latter of which was the Second Great Awakening—had increasingly assumed a militant tone, calling on believers to purge their sins in this life, so as to amend their personal relationship with God. Italy was dominated by the Catholic Church, and yet, in the city of Genoa, where Mazzini was born, the influence of Jansenism was particularly strong and had contributed to the spread of ideas close to those of Protestant Christianity, including the paramount importance of a personal relationship with God.

The influence of these parallel varieties of Christianity had an incalculable weight on the formation of Garrison's and Mazzini's young minds and left indelible traces that, in time, combined with other influences no less important to stir the course of the two youths toward their life causes. Both Garrison and Mazzini had early experiences of acquaintance with oppression, though in different forms; Garrison experienced it directly when working as an apprentice and growing up in poverty, while Mazzini experienced it indirectly through his meeting with a political exile and patriot who was reduced to poverty. As Garrison and Mazzini came of age, the combination of religious influences with libertarian ideals marked the thought of both to such an extent that, though in different contexts and in different ways, they became similarly convinced of an ethical "mission" that they had been called to fulfill: the extirpation of slavery in Garrison's case, the liberation from national oppression in Mazzini's case. And as their two missions became ethical to them in an almost absolute sense, with highly religious tones attached, their commitment to what became their life causes grew to be equally absolute and uncompromising.

The United States in the early decades of the nineteenth century, the setting of William Lloyd Garrison's youth, was a country undergoing tremendous transformation. In the North, in particular, the changes that accompanied the spread of the "market revolution"—that is, early industrialization and the workers' exploitation it generated, expansion of communication and transportation, and the spread of mass culture and popular publications—influenced almost every aspect of social life. Understandably, people struggled to make sense of these momentous transformations and of the improvements and strains they had brought for individuals and families. As this happened, several morally committed individuals dedicated themselves to showing Americans the contradictions of the society in which they lived and called for a variety of social reforms. From the beginning, the reformist impulse became associated with religious principles; as a consequence, reform movements—the most important being the temperance movement, which fought against alcohol consumption—sprang up, claiming to fulfill American society's urgent need for moral change and acting as much for religious as for economic reasons.[6]

In New England, and especially in Massachusetts, where early industrialization was more pronounced than elsewhere and thus had led to earlier and more substantial changes, the reformist impulse was especially strong. Together with the temperance movement, already in the early nineteenth century religious associations had appeared, calling for moral reform through a stricter adherence to Christian principles. The most important of these associations was the New England Tract Society, which in 1825 converged into the American Tract Society, based in New York, whose wealthiest sponsors were future abolitionists Arthur and Lewis Tappan. Both springing from and causing the reformist ferment was a wave of evangelical revivalism—the Second Great Awakening (the First Great Awakening had occurred in the eighteenth century)—that swept across the United States with particularly radical effects in New England and in the region between the state of New York and the Great Lakes area, the "burned-over district," in the 1820s. In this region, charismatic preaching, spontaneous mass meetings, and voluntary conversions involved thousands of people in an ecstatic experience of faith that, like a spreading fire, enveloped everybody it encountered on its path. At its heart, the revivalist message was one of radical opposition to the more conservative established church; people were taught that they could personally experience God through charismatic services and by achieving a moral redemption that focused, first and foremost, on abandoning their sinful way of living and the particular established social norms that caused it. As Robert Abzug has explained, responding to America's religious crisis, evangelical revivalism provided a powerful cosmological view, filled with millennialism and alternative to the dominant religious tenets, within which reform activities were as much a sign of religious as of social protest.[7]

Thus, as Methodist and Baptist preachers embraced enthusiastically and in increasing numbers the practices and messages of the new evangelical wave, through their work they became instrumental in laying the foundations for an overall change in attitude in the public that ultimately favored the spread of an abolitionist movement—the most radical expression of both religious and social protest in nineteenth-century America. Famous preachers such as Charles G. Finney and Lyman Beecher urged individuals to abandon their sinful lives and obtain redemption through radical changes that would lead to a substantial moral improvement in the society they lived in. They focused their attacks on the slave system that oppressed the South as the main moral problem and the biggest sin from which American people ought to free themselves—since, the preachers believed, they had the capacity to free themselves if they were persuaded to do so—in order to start on their path toward redemption and thus salvation. Thus, both evangelical ministers and evangelical converts who were touched by the revivalist wave constituted an extremely important influence on the abolitionist movement. Moreover, several abolitionist leaders were educated in New England by those same evangelical preachers, who gave them a strong sense of moral and religious commitment and a will to fight moral degradation and the evil that sins brought with them. And slavery, doubtless, represented the greatest sin of all.[8]

The family William Lloyd Garrison was born into in Massachusetts was one of many whose members had, in different ways and degrees of intensity, a personal experience of the evangelical revivalism that sprang from the Second Great Awakening. His mother, Frances Maria (Fanny), had a very strong influence on young Garrison in religious matters. After the death of her eldest daughter Caroline and her husband Abijah's departure from the family household, in 1808 Fanny was left alone to provide for the remaining three children, James, Lloyd, and Elizabeth, in the small seaport of Newburyport, Massachusetts. Doubtless, Fanny's deep "belief in the redemptive power of Jesus, expressed in a consuming Baptist piety," in the words of James B. Stewart, was her way of fighting against life's difficulties, but there was more to it than that. Following a rather common pattern among the "new-born" Christians who joined the huge camp meetings and gatherings addressed by the great evangelical preachers, Fanny was converted from a strict, conservative Anglicanism, of which her father was a typical representative, to a revivalist and even revolutionary Baptist faith, and as a consequence, she was banished from her family. From that moment on, Fanny's life moved firmly within the boundaries set by the two main and opposite evangelical concepts of sin and redemption.[9]

After failing to redeem her husband—a seafarer with too much of an aptitude for drinking and good company—from his sins, Fanny set about to prevent her children from falling into their father's ways; in the process she provided young Garrison with the strongest possible moral example of living, an example that was decisive in forming Garrison's uncompromising stance against the sin of slavery. Even when Fanny, unable to support all her children, moved to Lynn with her eldest son James in 1812, she made sure that Garrison would continue to have a proper Christian education; she left him with the strongly religious family of Ezekiel Bartlett, the deacon of her church. For three years young Garrison was schooled in the scriptures and in sermons and hymns, and he kept the role model of his mother constantly in mind; the force of his mother's influence may have been even stronger now, because he missed her and longed to be with her and to have his behavior approved by her. Young Garrison learned well the importance of conscience, piety, and the redeeming power of Christian love, as well as the devastating power of sin, which, it seemed to him, had irremediably affected his brother James. Then in 1815–16, Fanny was briefly able to live again with all her children, first in Lynn and then in Baltimore, where it quickly appeared that the conflict between Garrison's dissolute brother James and his mother was escalating. After working first as a shoemaker and then as a cabinetmaker, Garrison decided to leave, at only eleven, to escape Baltimore and return to Newburyport, with Fanny's blessing and a growing sense of his own moral role in a world in which the Christian God he had learned to love and respect seemed to him an increasingly crucial influence.[10]

Garrison would not see his mother again. Fanny died in 1823, following the death of his younger sister Elizabeth and seven years after his departure from Baltimore. During those years, Garrison worked as an apprentice to Ephraim W. Allen at the *Newburyport Herald* and discovered his talent and passion for what became his life activity: journalism. By 1823, although he was only eighteen, and although his education was largely self-taught, Garrison was already writing pieces under different names, commenting on politics in both the United States and Europe and appearing, at this date, a man of staunch Federalist principles and unquestionable morality. Recent scholarship has assigned a great deal of importance to Garrison's time at the *Herald,* and there is little doubt that Allen's particular combination of Federalism and antislavery sentiment must have made a deep impression on the young apprentice. In this connection, Matthew Mason has argued that "Garrison's Federalist heritage stands as but one example, for many white abolitionists besides Garrison had deep roots in New England Federalism and the religious and political culture for which it stood." Thus, it is entirely possible, as both Mason and Mark Arkin have maintained, that the influence of Federalism on abolitionism—and particularly on the New England brand of abolitionism typified by Garrison—might still be little understood and might reveal a particularly important factor to investigate and take into account.[11]

Moreover, as Caleb McDaniel has shown, it was largely as a result of his period of apprenticeship at the *Herald* that Garrison gained his appreciation for viewing the news from the angle that Allen had adopted for his paper—one that emphasized the struggles for freedom throughout the Euro-American world. The *Herald* reported at length about both the Latin American wars of independence from Spain, in which Simon Bolivar played a particularly significant role, the Greek revolution against the Ottoman Empire, and Italy's 1820–21 revolutions against the peninsula's autocratic regimes. In McDaniel's words, "these reports charged Garrison's imagination with the idea that a new age of liberty was underway." If in Latin America the opponent to the peoples' liberty was the Spanish Empire, in Europe the great reactionary power was represented by the "Holy Alliance" of Russia, Prussia, and Austria. In the first articles he published, signed "An Old Bachelor," or simply "A.O.B.," starting in 1822, Garrison showed that he already interpreted the events happening in his lifetime as if they proved the existence of a global struggle between those he called in an 1823 article "the friends of reform throughout Europe and America" and the forces of reaction, determined to suppress the people's demands for freedom.[12]

As Garrison moved through these crucial experiences during his apprenticeship years at the *Herald,* he kept looking for his mother's approval and, through her, for God's moral approval of his actions. In May 1823, Garrison wrote Fanny: "Thus you perceive, my dear mother, that my leisure moments have been usefully and wisely employed;—usefully, because it is beneficial in cultivating the seeds of improvement in my breast, expanding the intellectual powers and faculties of my mind; wisely, because it has kept me from wasting time in that dull, senseless, insipid manner, which generally characterizes giddy youths." As a result of the crucial influence of his mother, young Garrison already had clear in his mind the two principles that guided him in his life mission: a constant exercise of intellectual questioning and a moral sense of purpose in his life. Doubtless, it was Garrison's attitude toward questioning, together with his high Federalist beliefs, that led him to oppose both Democrat Andrew Jackson and National Republican John Quincy Adams, despite the latter's closeness to the Federalist ideas, in the 1824 presidential election. In the end, Garrison supported Georgia senator William Crawford, presumably because Crawford had an idea of Federalism, as Garrison wrote to the *Salem Gazette,* "worthy of its great leader, the immortal WASHINGTON." Washington was Garrison's favorite revolutionary hero, together with the French Marquis de Lafayette and the romantic English poet Lord Byron. In the meantime, Garrison went so far as directly attacking Andrew Jackson's perceived antilibertarian spirit and dubious moral standing from the pages of the *Herald.* A year later, in 1825, Garrison had completed his apprenticeship. Though devastated by the two tragic deaths in his family, he wasted no time and set out to use his journalistic experience to communicate his ideas, keeping faithful to his principles. At this point he had not yet established a clear focus for his activity, but even so, in his two editorships—first of the *Free Press,* and then of the *National Philanthropist*—Garrison brilliantly expressed his opinions on a wide range of moral issues, including slavery and temperance.[13]

Unlike Garrison, who was born and lived his early years in an independent republic, Giuseppe Mazzini was born in a country that was technically under foreign occupation. In 1805 Napoleon had incorporated Genoa, Mazzini's birthplace, and its region, the Liguria, into the Kingdom of Italy, which included northern Italy and part of central Italy. For the following ten years (1805–14), Napoleon's rule, centered on the capital, Milan, proceeded to create a homogeneous administrative structure and to transform the economic and social system that had characterized the previous Old Order. Napoleon first abolished feudalism and confiscated church property and then promoted a class of bourgeois landowners, who competed with the old landed aristocracy for the public offices. Moreover, the establishment of the first large unified Italian state in almost one thousand years—even though it was hardly an independent entity, being governed by Napoleon through the Italian kingdom's capital Milan—had incalculable consequences for the creation of an Italian nationalist consciousness in the early nineteenth century. This consciousness first became apparent in the years after 1815, even though in that year, after Napoleon's fall, Europe's reactionary powers, gathered at the Congress of Vienna, had decided the shape of Restoration Europe, attempting to turn the clock back to pre–French Revolution times. In Italy, after the dismemberment of the Kingdom of Italy, the old dynasties were reassigned their former states. Thus, most of northern Italy was divided between Lombardy and Venetia under the Habsburg Empire and the Kingdom of Piedmont-Sardinia under the House of Savoy, which now included also Genoa and the surrounding region of Liguria.[14]

It is important to understand, though, as a number of recent studies (notably those by Marco Meriggi) have highlighted, that, once back in power, the old dynasties did not erase the important economic and social reforms that had characterized the Napoleonic period. Instead, they ruled through a "hybrid" system, the "administrative monarchy," that combined reactionary absolutism with administrative and economic modernization and also promoted bourgeois landownership and efficient service to the state. To be sure, northern Italy did not experience a "market revolution" as the northern United States did; yet, especially in Piedmont and Lombardy, but also in Emilia, then under the pope's rule, agricultural production, especially of wheat and rice, was more advanced than in other parts of Italy, with large farms and fields located in the fertile Po Valley. A system of domestic industry—termed protoindustrialization by scholars—which focused on textile manufacturing had also started to appear. These phenomena were tightly linked with the rising power of progressive landowners, both noble and bourgeois, and of the professional and educated bourgeoisie; however, even though these classes supported the modernizing aspects of the administrative monarchies, they found the lack of freedom of expression, and of channels through which to voice their opinion and exercise their influence for or against the government, increasingly difficult to cope with in a strictly absolutist system. Thus, unlike what happened in the early-nineteenth-century northern United States—where the economic and social transformations led to a large-scale cultural and religious ferment that offered solutions to the strains brought by early industrialization—in northern Italy the reaction to the economic and social transformations, on a different scale, led to a political ferment that offered solutions to the strains brought by the disconnection between rulers and subjects in the modernization process.[15]

Politics was central, and the main avenue of expression of discontent, even though it was covert and conspiratorial politics, given the repressive character of the Restoration regimes, so similar to Napoleon's rule. However, at the time of Napoleon's first Italian campaign, in 1796, the French Republic had been based on the principles affirmed in the French Revolution, and paramount among them was the novel concept of a democratic nation as the expression of the people's free will. The 1796 campaign had given origin to "sister republics," with various degrees of dependence on France but self-governing to a certain extent during the entire Jacobin triennium (1796–1799). In northern Italy, along with establishing the Cisalpine Republic based in Lombardy and the Cispadan Republic based in Emilia, in 1797 Napoleon had reorganized Genoa—which itself had been an independent republic ruled by a merchant patrician elite since the Middle Ages—into the Ligurian Republic, which lasted for the best part of eight years. Ruled by a government that agreed with the French Revolution's democratic ideals, it produced an important radical document: "a Declaration of Rights and Duties, which," according to Harry Hearder, "seemed to imply that among a citizen's rights was that of education." Although the "sister republics" eventually fell, the republican and democratic tradition of Jacobin nationalists such as Melchiorre Gioia—who was the first to argue in favor of a unified republican Italy—was still very much alive at the time of Napoleon's Kingdom of Italy and equally so at the beginning of the Restoration, despite the change of times and regimes. In both cases, it was former Jacobins who provided the backbone of the opposition to absolutist rule.[16]

Even though religion in Italy was fairly static—at least compared to the varieties of American Protestantism and the sweeping influence of the Second Great Awakening—oppositional politics in Italy also had an important religious dimension. In fact, the presence of the papacy as a source of not only spiritual but temporal rule—its temporal rule included parts of northern and central Italy under the Papal State—created an anomalous situation, since the Catholic Church represented the ultimate reactionary power that opposed both modernization and national unity. At the beginning of the nineteenth century, in northern Italy, there were some influential Protestant communities, traditionally associated with the mercantile and entrepreneurial bourgeoisie; there is no doubt that these groups, particularly through their contacts with English and Swiss evangelicals, had an important influence, though fairly small, on the anticlericalism of a several Italian nationalists, including Mazzini. However, by far the most diffused source of anticlericalism in northern Italy was Jansenism. Originally coming from France, Jansenism had spread in northern Italy as early as the eighteenth century as a reform movement within Catholic Christianity and had met with particular favor in Genoa, likely because, as Eugenio Biagini has noticed, "Jansenism's critique of papal power and its identification between the church and the people had potentially radical implications"; therefore, it seemed close to the Ligurian city's republican tradition.[17]

The family into which Mazzini was born in 1805 as the only son out of four children was immersed in an anticlerical and Jansenist atmosphere and belonged to the Genoese middle class. Thus, in contrast to Garrison's, Mazzini's family was a stable one, with a house and the means to provide him with a sheltered life in his early years. Mazzini's father, Giacomo, had been a Jacobin and had participated enthusiastically in the democratic experiment of the Republic of Genoa. After the republic's fall, he had left politics and exercised the profession of physician; this profession took him to Genoa University, and eventually he obtained a chair there. Despite Giacomo's disenchantment, his "hidden" Jacobin beliefs certainly had an influence on Mazzini, and so did his vocation and his disinterested passion for his work as a physician. However, it was Mazzini's mother, Maria Drago, who had a much more crucial influence on him, in part because she was the one who took charge of his education. Indeed, according to Ros Pesman, it was Mazzini's mother "who gave him his sense of messianic mission, told him that he was one of 'God's elect' and inculcated him with her rigorous Jansenist religious outlook."[18]

Already from Mazzini's early years, Maria, noticing the extraordinary intelligence of the boy (whom she and Giacomo called "Pippo"), did everything in her power to nurture it. She read him stories taken from literary works and in the process created a strong and special bond with her only son. Mazzini's relationship with his father, on the other hand, was full of conflict, and he was really fond of only one of his three sisters, Cichina. As a result of his childhood experiences, Mazzini assigned a central role to his family, and to the women within it, in the formation of his later views. For her part, Maria, whose beliefs were very close to Jansenism, stressed the importance of experiencing God individually through conversion and of following one's conscience, even if it meant challenging the authorities. Yet, according to Francesco Landogna, Jansenism also "portrayed life as a mission and taught the virtue of sacrifice . . . faith in the regeneration and infinite progress of humankind, freedom and equality of the human race." All these themes became central in Mazzini's thought. Moreover, by the time he was five, Mazzini had as a private tutor a Jansenist priest, Luca Agostino De Scalzi, who in 1817 was followed by another Jansenist priest, Stefano De Gregori, who taught him humanities and literature.[19]

Thanks to his intelligence and the extraordinary private education he had enjoyed, Mazzini became a student at the University of Genoa, then part of the elite educational institutions of the Kingdom of Sardinia, when he was only fourteen. He began by studying law, then moved to medicine, which he left soon afterward because his great interests were literature and history. History became particularly important for Mazzini, since it was the discipline that gave him a crucial, well-rounded general knowledge of the world and the means to understand the causes of events. He followed a quest for knowledge parallel to the one Garrison sought through his journalistic apprenticeship. As Franco Della Peruta and Tiziano Tussi have written, in this period Mazzini was "eager to learn and build a historical vision as complete as possible." However, the atmosphere at the university was very repressive and under close scrutiny by the Restoration Sardinian government, especially since university professors were routinely suspected of holding liberal beliefs. Only a year after his registration, in 1820, Mazzini defended the students' right to a free education against the Jesuits' attempt to control it; he was arrested for a short while and achieved early fame as agitator. In that year he also became acquainted with his long-term friends Giovanni and Jacopo Ruffini, who nicknamed Mazzini "Fantasio."[20]

In 1820 revolution broke out in different parts of Europe, including Italy, and news of it traveled as far as Massachusetts and was reported by the *Newburyport Herald,* where Garrison worked at the time. The revolution reached the Kingdom of Sardinia and then Genoa in March 1821. There, it transformed into a republican revolt supported by the students against Sardinian rule and led to the closing of the university for two and a half years, until 1824, and to a harsh repression that forced several of the agitators to leave the city in exile. Mazzini did not participate in the revolt, although he supported it, but the memory of meeting one of many impoverished and exiled revolutionaries who had fought against the reactionary forces with the aim of creating a free Italian nation made a lasting impression on him. Years later, in 1861, Mazzini remembered the encounter with the famous words, "That day was the first in which a confused idea presented itself to my mind—I will not say of country or of liberty—but an idea that we Italians could and therefore ought to struggle for the liberty of our country." In other words, that early experience of acquaintance with a political exile fighting for freedom led Mazzini to believe that the struggle for a higher ideal of liberty was going to be a defining one in his historical period and one worth embracing. It was during those same years that Garrison was coming to a similar conviction.[21]

The difference between the milieus in which Garrison and Mazzini were born and raised heavily conditioned the years of their early youth and the choices the two men made. Born and raised in poverty, Garrison was very much a self-educated man, one who had to struggle to create his own role as a knowledgeable opinionist. Mazzini, whose origins were fairly privileged compared to Garrison's, had a classical intellectual education, and even though he talked about "the people," his knowledge of the real world remained scanty at best in his early youth. Also, Garrison finally achieved in his adult life the familial stability that he had missed and craved in his childhood, while Mazzini had no stable family life of any type after his youth.

Despite these differences, after a certain point, Garrison's and Mazzini's paths began to follow comparable and parallel trajectories, as they both struggled to find sense in their lives. Though in different ways and in different contexts, they both looked for ways to acquire a knowledge of the world that would help them make sense of the momentous events occurring all around them, as a new wave of revolutions engulfed Europe and the Americas. Garrison sought this knowledge through understanding and interpretation of the news in his journalistic apprenticeship, and Mazzini sought a comparable knowledge through his eagerness to read history texts at the university. Ultimately, and more importantly, this was a major reason, together with the legacy of crucial religious and family influences, why Garrison and Mazzini, as they came of age, began to be vaguely aware that they had an irrepressible moral urge to fight for the improvement of the world and of the societies in which they lived—the very same idea, although at this time still in embryonic form, that formed the basis of their life struggles for different but related types of liberty.

Apprenticeships to Radicalism: Antislavery and Secret Societies

At the time of Garrison's and Mazzini's youths, in both the United States and Italy the forces of conservatism and reaction had to confront staunch opposition, though poorly organized and not very effective, in the shape of more or less radical agitators and societies—organizations that gathered, in the open or in secret, according to the degree of democracy of the place, those who intended to challenge the status quo. It was by their contact with these organizations, specifically the American Colonization Society (ACS) and the Carboneria, that Garrison and Mazzini gained their first knowledge of what fighting against slavery and fighting for national liberation really meant in practice. It was also as a result of these experiences of apprenticeship to radicalism that they decided to part ways with their fellow agitators, after it became clear to them that they (Garrison and Mazzini) wished to engage in much more radical sorts of struggle for the causes they had identified with and to establish much more radical organizations, organizations through which they could make a real difference in American and Italian lives. Yet, however personal, these developments in the two men's lives did not happen in a vacuum but took place within the contexts of the first two major crises that the conservative regimes faced in the United States and

Italy almost contemporaneously, at the beginning of the 1820s—and thus they are somewhat connected to them. The two events were the Missouri crisis and the 1821 revolution. With these two crises, slavery in America and democratic reform in Italy for the first time became issues to be reckoned with on a national scale. They constituted a warning of a sort that Garrison's and Mazzini's life causes were to be taken seriously.[22]

In the United States, the ACS had started its activity already in 1816, and despite its mild and substantially racist antislavery program, it went on to gain the support of radical antislavery activists such as Benjamin Lundy and Garrison himself. More important, though, was the crucial opposition to the society staged by free African American activists, such as David Walker, in favor of an abolitionist alternative. Such activities showed to most Americans that the American antislavery milieu of the 1810s and 1820s was a world in flux and transition, one whose rapid growth in importance would lead slavery to quickly become a dominant national issue. In marked contrast with the American republic, from 1815 on, divided Italy suffered under the constant policy of oppression implemented by the restored dynastic regimes. Yet, several activists who sought to overthrow both foreign and reactionary rulers in the peninsula gathered in secret societies—most famous among them the Carboneria—which, even though characterized by the scarcity of success in their aims and actions, nonetheless offered important experiences to innovative revolutionaries committed to programs of national liberation. Among those revolutionaries were Mazzini and, more important at this stage, Filippo Buonarroti.[23]

In the 1820s United States, Massachusetts was a society that acknowledged its attachment to freedom and equality by celebrating its revolutionary legacy on the fiftieth anniversary of the American Revolution. But Massachusetts was also in turmoil; cultural changes, reflecting the economic and social transformations, were constant. There, according to James B. Stewart, "the powerful combination in the 1820s of Yankee conservatism, revivalist benevolence, New England upbringing, and social unrest was leading young Evangelicals toward a radical religious vision, out of which a militant abolitionist movement began to take shape." Yet, during the period in which Garrison came of age, the leadership of the most radical forms of the fight against slavery was not in the hands of white New England evangelicals. It is one of the great achievements of contemporary historiography on abolitionism to have shed light on the process that led to the making of what Richard Newman has called "the second wave Abolitionism." It is now clear that, before the 1830s, there was a complex tradition of abolitionist movements, at whose heart was the Pennsylvania Abolition Society (PAS), led by Quaker activists, which called for gradual abolition of slavery. At the same time, the crucial, indispensable role of free African Americans in influencing the transformation of this early abolitionist tradition into the more familiar, radical, immediatist stance epitomized by Garrison is now wholly acknowledged by historians.[24]

African Americans were at the forefront of reform and antislavery activities, both within and outside the PAS in Pennsylvania and, later on, the Massachusetts Anti-Slavery Society (MASS), in Boston. According to Richard Newman, they "pressed for equality in the workplaces, courts of law, and schools" and even "sought legal aid from white abolitionists." Moreover, African Americans held their own celebrations of freedom by commemorating the end of the Atlantic slave trade (1 January 1808), significantly on 14 July, the French Revolution's Bastille Day. Out of this cultural milieu came David Walker, the greatest black activist of the 1820s and the author of the first "modern" abolitionist pamphlet—*Appeal to the Colored Citizens of the World* (1829)—in which he called for a continent-wide revolt of black slaves against their white oppressors. It is undeniable that Walker and other African American activists, together with associations and events related to the early abolitionist movements of the 1820s, had a crucial influence on young Garrison and contributed to the shaping of his radical views. However, not until he met Quaker abolitionist Benjamin Lundy, in 1828, did Garrison begin to appreciate the importance of the antislavery struggle in the battle for reform and the crucial roles that both Quakers and African Americans played in it.[25]

In many ways, Garrison's path to abolitionism was typical of radical white New England reformers in the 1820s. Deeply grounded in the revivalist message and open to battles for justice that ranged from libertarian politics to temperance and embraced freedom struggles against oppression in the four corners of the world, Garrison's convictions naturally veered toward addressing the big issue that loomed over America's conscience at the time: the injustices, the suffering, and above all the sin represented by slavery. As Henry Mayer has suggested, Garrison's increasing concern over slavery was also a response to the effects of the slaveholders' relentless expansionist attitude in the United States. In 1820–21, the Missouri crisis had made manifest the power of slaveholding interests in Congress. Even though the 1821 Missouri Compromise, with the confinement of slavery below the 36°30' line, had temporarily settled the sectional conflict over slavery's expansion, by the late 1820s the slaveholders' expansionist policy, focused on the settlements in the western territories, had led to the creation of a slaveholding enclave in the territory of Texas, in northern Mexico.[26]

Garrison's 1828 meeting with Benjamin Lundy, who was also a member of the powerful ACS, and his subsequent collaboration with Lundy as co-editor of the abolitionist newspaper the *Genius of Universal Emancipation* in Baltimore, provided Garrison with the opportunity to experience firsthand what slavery really meant—through meetings with runaway slaves and free blacks and witnessing the horrors of the slave trade. Garrison also had a true role model in Lundy, with his libertarian interpretation of world events and his determination not to allow any "opposition or adversity to deter him from pursuing the antislavery goals of his youth," in the words of Merton Dillon. As Caleb McDaniel has shown, Lundy, like Ephraim Allen with his *Newburyport Herald,* used his paper the *Genius* to report about and support the struggles for liberty that occurred in Europe and Latin America against reactionary powers; in addition, Lundy showed Garrison for the first time how those struggles for liberty were tightly linked to the fight against slavery, since many of the best-known figures—starting with Garrison's heroes Lafayette and Bolivar—were involved in both. At the same time, Lundy was instrumental in convincing Garrison that slavery was an embarrassment and a disgrace that weakened the influence of American republicanism in the global struggle for freedom and that it was a major source of shame for American reformers abroad. This was a crucial theme in Garrison's later abolitionist career.[27]

It was also during this period that Garrison started to develop his doctrine of "immediate emancipation," as opposed to the gradual abolition advocated by Lundy and by most Quakers from the founding of the PAS. To be sure, Garrison's changing views had a great deal to do with the fact that, at the end of his coeditorship of the *Genius,* in March 1830—not yet twenty-five years old—he underwent a deep personal crisis, from which he emerged strengthened and even more radicalized in his abolitionist and immediatist convictions. Garrison's crisis originated when he was condemned to spend almost two months in the Baltimore jail for libeling merchant Francis Todd with the accusation of slave trading in his editorials. From jail, on 13 May 1830, Garrison wrote Todd very significant words: "As a New-England man . . . I am ashamed. . . . How could you suffer your noble ship to be freighted with the wretched victims of slavery? Is not this horrible traffic offensive to God, and revolting to humanity? . . . What language would be strong enough to denounce the abettor? . . . I denounced your conduct in strong language—but did you not deserve it? . . . I am in prison for denouncing slavery in a free country!" Besides the fact that these words show the depth of Lundy's influence on Garrison, one cannot help but notice that many of the themes that resurfaced less than a year later in the *Liberator* were already present in this letter. They included the idea of slavery as an offense to God and humankind, the true meaning of freedom in a country that protected slavery, and the need for a new, strong, language to shake the consciences of New Englanders.[28]

When Garrison was released from jail, with the help of fellow New York abolitionist Arthur Tappan, he was in many ways a changed man. It was not just that the time in jail and the time Garrison had spent pondering had strengthened his abolitionist convictions; he had also elaborated his own ideas about how to better deal with what had become, by then, his life mission of achieving the emancipation of the slaves in the United States. After the end of his collaboration with Benjamin Lundy, Garrison moved to Boston, where he embarked on a series of efforts to publish his own abolitionist paper. By that time Garrison had become thoroughly convinced that his program for emancipation was going to be more immediatist than that of most of his abolitionist contemporaries; he also realized, more crucially, that he would have to publicly reject colonization as a viable solution. This was significant because, at the time, the ACS was the most influential antislavery organization in the United States; it had attracted prominent abolitionists such as Benjamin Lundy, Theodore Weld, Arthur Tappan, Gerritt Smith, and James G. Birney. Founded in Washington, D.C., in 1816, under the sponsorship of future Whig statesman Henry Clay, the ACS encouraged manumitted slaves and free blacks to emigrate to West Africa, where, by 1822, the United States had acquired the territory that was to become the nation of Liberia specifically as a home for these migrants.[29]

The ACS supporters claimed that by returning African American slaves to their original homeland, they would be acting out of humanitarian interests, but only those few who were abolitionist at heart were genuinely convinced of this. Most simply wished to be rid of free blacks, because they feared the possibility of a racial war, or at the very least they did not welcome any challenge to white supremacy. As a consequence, the ACS garnered most of its support from racists of both the North and the South. There is no doubt that, besides being racist, the plan for colonization had little practicality: in forty years, the total number of African Americans shipped to Africa was only nine thousand. Like Benjamin Lundy and the other ACS abolitionist members, though, Garrison had initially been sympathetic toward colonization, perhaps as a means to avoid a future racial conflict and also as a way for the African American individual to uplift himself or herself—but certainly not as his own preferred way to bring about the abolition of slavery. Thus, on 4 July 1829, when he was asked to deliver his first public antislavery speech, sponsored by the ACS and on behalf of colonization, in front of Park Street Church, Boston, Garrison expressed this still somewhat ambiguous attitude. According to Henry Mayer, Garrison spoke "on the necessity of abolishing slavery in the name of equal rights, not racial separation," while he also "deliberately slighted colonization in his remarks." But, agitating the specter of "the horrors of St. Domingo"—referring to the Haitian revolution—Garrison also called "upon . . . citizens to assist in establishing auxiliary colonization societies in every State, county, and town." A year later, however, after his spell in jail and as a result of his closer contacts with free African Americans, Garrison changed this ambiguous attitude into a wish for a direct attack both against the ACS and against the practice of colonization and the racist philosophy behind it.[30]

Similarly to Garrison's Massachusetts, Mazzini's Genoa was a milieu in the midst of cultural turmoil. But rather than expressing itself through evangelical reform, in Genoa as in most of Italy, the drive toward change that found particularly fertile soil in the minds of idealistic youngsters such as Garrison and Mazzini led to a proliferation of romantic literature that extolled the virtues of great ideals and noble sacrifices—a clear indication that, in Mazzini's Italy, the ultimate radical change was identified with the self-sacrifice necessary to achieve the creation of an Italian nation. While he was studying law (he eventually graduated from the university in 1827), Mazzini was already inclining toward literature; he read the great romantic poems of Ugo Foscolo, with whom he empathized deeply, as Garrison loved Byron's works. In 1826 Mazzini wrote an essay, "Sull'amore di Dante per la patria" (On Dante's love for his country), in which he argued that romantic literates, unlike classicists, ought to possess a significant amount of civic commitment, especially in Italy. In 1828 he began the publication of a journal called *L'indicatore genovese,* which quickly became devoted to literary critique and to his passionate defense of romantics against classicists. When the authorities forbade the publication of the journal, Mazzini went to Livorno, in Tuscany, to publish a new version under the name *L'indicatore livornese* (1829).[31]

Also in 1829, Mazzini collaborated with the prestigious literary review *L'Antologia,* based in Florence, for which he wrote an important essay, "D'una letteratura europea" (About a European-wide literature). There he argued, "The events, the institutions, the new beliefs, the changed customs, and the passions differently expressed have created the need for a new type of literature that represents . . . modern civilization," a literature he thought would be capable of expressing the deepest feelings and needs of the people, and a literature he conceived of—ahead of his times—as European. This essay is important for another reason, too. In a section of the essay, Mazzini made perhaps his first documented reference to his abolitionist convictions, when he rejoiced in stating, "The evil [slave] trade has been abolished, and the world's condemnation follows the traders of [human] blood." The reference was to the abolition of the Atlantic slave trade and to Mazzini's feelings of contempt for the slave traders, which he was convinced he shared with the majority of the people. Thereafter, as Steven Epstein has effectively remarked, "Mazzini remained an abolitionist for the rest of his life."[32]

But there were other ways for young romantic revolutionaries such as Mazzini to express their ideas. Many joined one of the several secret societies that represented the most extreme degree of political dissent in repressive regimes such as those of Restoration Italy. Secret societies had flourished in Italy during the Napoleonic era, which had led to the foundation of the unified Masonic Lodge Grande Oriente d'Italia in 1805, also as result of Napoleon's support of Freemasonry. Within Italian Freemasonry, there was a distinction between a more conservative Masonic constituency, tied to the state, and a more libertarian and republican Masonic constituency, whose ideals were inspired by the eighteenth-century Illuminati movement of Bavaria. From this latter group derived the secret societies of the Restoration period, such as the Adelfia and the Filadelfia, which in 1818 radical Jacobin Filippo Buonarroti grouped under the name Sublimi Maestri Perfetti

(Sublime perfect masters). The origins of the famous Carboneria can also partially be traced to both Freemasonry and the Illuminati. The center of activity of the Carbonari (Charcoal burners) was actually in the Bourbon Kingdom of the Two Sicilies in southern Italy, where the Carboneria might have been present since 1810, deriving from the French Charbonniers; there it represented mainly the interests of the landed bourgeoisie in transforming the absolutist Bourbon monarchy into a constitutional kingdom. There is no doubt that the same was true for the larger section of the Carboneria that had spread to northern Italy, but it is also true that its more radical members were Jacobin and republican, as indicated in a document called "Patto sociale costituzionale dell'Ausonia" (Ausonian social and constitutional agreement) and written by a committee of Carbonari between 1815 and 1820; according to the document, the Carboneria was to free Italy by leading a popular upheaval and establish the federal republic of Ausonia, with a constituent assembly elected through universal suffrage.[33]

It was within this fluid and shifting world of secret societies that Filippo Buonarroti, the most prominent Italian Jacobin and an admirer of Maximilien Robespierre at the time of his participation in the French Revolution, moved and acted. Buonarroti's idea of a secret society focused on a rigid pyramidal structure, partly derived from Freemasonry, with three degrees that represented different levels of knowledge of a revolutionary program and ideology; members at the highest of those levels were regarded as the vanguard of a revolutionary movement. After taking power through an insurrection, the revolutionary movement was to assume the dictatorship and implement a communist program focused on the abolition of private property. After 1815, Buonarroti became the *éminence grise* in the world of Italian secret societies, and between 1815 and 1820, he used the Carboneria's extensive network in northern Italy to build the preconditions for his revolutionary program. However, in 1818 the Austrian authorities discovered a network of *vendite* (Carbonari clubs) in the Kingdom of Lombardy-Venetia and arrested two major leaders, Silvio Pellico and Pietro Maroncelli. Then, in the Kingdom of Sardinia, the failure of the 1821 revolution led to a wave of repressions that left the Carboneria much weakened throughout the 1820s. Still, for young romantic spirits such as Mazzini, the Carboneria represented perhaps the only way to act, both covertly and effectively, against absolutist oppression and in the name of great ideals. Thus, as Franco Della Peruta has written, "it is significant that when the young Mazzini . . . decided to combine together literary commitment with political commitment, he decided to enter the ranks of the Carboneria in Genoa." Initiated by Antonio Doria in 1827, Mazzini distinguished himself immediately by his idealism and revolutionary thrust, and in 1829, after he was promoted to the second level, he revived the *vendite* not only in Liguria but also in Lombardy and Tuscany.[34]

However, just as he was nearing the highest point of his experience in the Carboneria, Mazzini was betrayed and arrested by the Sardinian police on 13 November 1830. They sent him to the prison of Savona, where he remained for three months—a period he spent meditating on his strategy and tactics and also on the aim of his revolutionary struggle. In prison, Mazzini became effectively a "grand master" of the Carboneria in Genoa, but his relationship with the secret society underwent a radical change after his term in prison. For Mazzini, as for Garrison at roughly the same age, the short experience in prison was a vector of change, to a certain extent, and led to a strengthening of resolve and commitment to fight for great ideals. In practice, Mazzini became critical of certain characteristics of the Carboneria that he thought flawed enough to prevent its success. He objected especially to the society's excessive secrecy, the complexity of its rituals, its elitist outlook, and the confusion in its objectives. Decades later, in his *Autobiographical Notes,* Mazzini wrote that he "did not admire much the complex symbolism, the hierarchical mysteries, and the faith—or rather the lack of faith—in the Carboneria." As a result of his meditations, he concluded that "the Carboneria had become a corpse and that, instead of wasting time and effort to revive it, it was better to look for life where it was and lay the foundations of a building with a new plan." Later, in 1831, that building eventually became the association Young Italy.[35]

In January 1831, the authorities released Mazzini after three months of detention, not finding strong evidence of his leadership in the local Carboneria, despite ongoing accusations by the Jesuits. In the end, Jesuit pressure prompted the Sardinian king, Carlo Felice, to issue a decree condemning Mazzini and forcing him to choose between confinement within the kingdom and exile. Opting for exile, Mazzini left for France, where the 1830 revolution had brought to the throne constitutional monarch Louis Philippe; the latter's liberal regime was particularly friendly to political exiles. In Lyons, and then Marseilles, France, Mazzini found many of the individuals he had seen leaving Genoa ten years earlier, and he found that they bore, he wrote, "the spark of a true life," since they were still ready to sacrifice their lives for the Italian cause. Among them was Carlo Bianco di Saint-Jorioz, a nobleman and former Piedmontese officer, who had written an enormously influential pamphlet, *Della guerra insurrezionale per bande applicata all'Italia* (On the guerrilla war of insurrection with squads applied to Italy, 1830), in which he theorized guerrilla warfare as the most effective method of liberation from foreign powers. Like many other Risorgimento revolutionaries, Mazzini found these ideas fascinating, and in addition to becoming a friend of Bianco's, he supported his secret society the Apofasimeni, whose mission was "to make Italy one, independent, and free." In France, Mazzini also met Buonarroti, but by then he had decided irrevocably that he cared little for either the Carboneria or Buonarroti's projects to reform it, especially since those projects focused on a French revolutionary initiative rather than an Italian one.[36]

Considering the significance of the formative period for both Garrison and Mazzini, it is fair to say that the origins of Garrison's sense of mission have much to do with his early years and the injustices he suffered as a child of a poor family, working in various apprenticeships in different places in Massachusetts. Yet that sense matured only later, in the period 1829–30, when he first worked on Benjamin Lundy's antislavery paper the *Genius of Universal Emancipation* and was able to see firsthand the horrors of slavery; by the time he was released from his jail sentence of forty-nine days for libeling a slave trader, Garrison had become the most outspoken advocate of immediate abolition of slavery in the United States. Conversely, Mazzini lived a happy childhood in Genoa, but he also had an early encounter with the injustices related to his future lifetime cause when he met, in his teens, an impoverished political refugee from Italy's 1820–21 revolution. As he came of age, Mazzini joined the famous secret society called Carboneria, which plotted the overthrow of Italy's reactionary governments, and was arrested for that association. It was during his stay of more than three months in jail, before being forced to expatriate, that Mazzini fully developed the conviction that his mission was to be the creation of a free Italian nation.

For both Garrison and Mazzini, an early experience of prison life had the effect of opening their eyes to a reality of which they were part, specifically, the associations to which they belonged, which they understood as fighting toward a goal they shared, but not fighting in the most effective way. The time they spent in contact with the ACS and the Carboneria proved to be invaluable for Garrison's and Mazzini's formation as a militant antislavery advocate in one case and a nationalist agitator in the other, but the critique they later mounted against the two associations also proved crucial in the parallel process of creating new movements—movements that would break completely with the past and prove to be immensely more effective in their purposes. Garrison's and Mazzini's quest for knowledge of world affairs and world history, the former as an apprentice journalist, and the latter as a university student, had already widened their gaze. Now, as they laid the groundwork for these momentous changes to happen, they entered a period when both their goals and their actions would transcend the specific local and national contexts, more clearly in Mazzini's case, given his early exile, and would eventually profoundly affect the entire Euro-American milieu to which they both belonged, through the creation of novel traditions of abolitionist and democratic nationalist activisms.

2

EXERCISES IN MEDIA PROSELYTISM

Journalism and Revolutionary Apostolate, 1831–1833

The Euro-American world was one marked by movement and flux in the early 1830s, when William Lloyd Garrison and Giuseppe Mazzini began their revolutions, the former with the publication of his radical abolitionist paper the *Liberator* and the latter with the foundation of his democratic nationalist association Young Italy. Each of the two at this point was operating with a focus on his own national context and on the consequences that his radical words and actions would have on it; but they were also both aware of an international dimension within which their struggles clearly fitted and which linked their ideas on radical abolitionism and democratic nationalism to similar and parallel movements outside the United States and Italy. In 1831, while Mazzini became aware of this international dimension as a result of his early exile, Garrison increased his already well-established awareness after his coeditorship of the *Genius of Universal Emancipation.* Still, for both Garrison and Mazzini, full realization of the significance of the wider milieus—transatlantic in one case, continental in the other—in which they were inserted and in which they operated did not come until a few years later; then, it assumed an increasingly important role in their lives and views. Therefore, it is appropriate to analyze briefly these early-1830s milieus.[1]

On one hand, the most progressive antislavery forces were creating a network of Atlantic abolitionism that spread throughout the English-speaking world to engage more effectively in the struggle to abolish slavery in the British Empire, a struggle that Garrison followed and supported. At the same time, the dislocated activists of the various nationalist movements that had been defeated in the 1820s and in 1830 were meeting, exchanging opinions, and plotting together in a larger and larger gathering of political exiles (including Mazzini) who were coming from all over Europe to live in liberal France.

In the late 1820s, the British abolitionist movement, headed by Thomas Fowell Buxton's Anti-Slavery Society (ASS), achieved some important results, forcing the British Parliament to pass measures that promoted the slaves' religious instruction, encouraged manumission, and banned the flogging of women. Although these achievements seemed limited, seen in an Atlantic dimension, the planters' resistance to moving toward emancipation in the British colonies led to a new wave of slave rebellions; the largest of these, the "Baptist War," occurred in Jamaica in 1831–32 and was almost concurrent with Nat Turner's revolt in Virginia in the summer of 1831. But by then, the abolitionist movements on both sides of the Atlantic, partly as a result of very active transatlantic contacts between radical black abolitionists, were moving in the same direction of transforming the struggle into an immediatist one, that is, one aiming at immediate emancipation as opposed to gradual abolition. This change influenced and radicalized the nascent network of Atlantic abolitionism.[2]

Within Atlantic abolitionism, it is possible to see a clear link between Garrison's beginning of the immediatist phase of the American abolitionist movement through publishing the *Liberator* in 1831, then founding the New England Anti-Slavery Society (NEASS) in 1832, and the 1830–31 founding of the radical Agency Committee by the London group of the ASS; the Agency Committee was based on the same principles of combining abolitionism and immediatism, principles likely inspired by Elizabeth Heyrick's influential pamphlet *Immediate, Not Gradual Abolition* (1824), which was certainly known to Garrison. Both Garrison's NEASS—and, later, the American Anti-Slavery Society—and the Agency Committee in Britain similarly engaged actively in the spread of abolitionist pamphlets and promoted the signing of petitions. Specifically, the British Agency Committee tried to persuade the British people to support plans and legal measures for the immediate and unconditional emancipation of all the slaves in the British Empire. Thus, the parallels, also chronological, between American abolitionism's immediatist change and the contemporary British abolitionists' support of immediatist views and strategies show us how Garrison's revolution is better understood when seen in a broader, Atlantic perspective and how it had an international dimension from the very beginning.[3]

A similar line of reasoning applies to the international ramifications of and contacts between the different varieties of nationalism and the activists that represented them in continental Europe in the early 1830s. A new wave of national revolutions shook Europe in 1830, less than ten years after the previous one had occurred in 1820–21. In France, as mentioned above, the 1830 revolution led to positive results with the overthrowing of the reactionary king Louis XVIII and the establishment of a constitutional monarchy under Philippe d'Orléans, while in Belgium it led to the independence of the country from Holland. But in Poland the national movement was crushed by Russia's reactionary forces. The Polish failure produced thousands more political exiles, adding to those already coming from other oppressed populations and converging mostly in France, where Philippe d'Orléans's liberal government allowed them to live and establish different communities in the major cities.[4]

This was the setting in which Mazzini found himself in exile in Marseilles, where he founded Young Italy, in 1831. There he became acquainted with the Italian community of political exiles and understood its significance, in relation not just to the Italian national struggle, but also to the struggles of other oppressed European nationalities. As the relevance of Garrison's immediatist abolitionism transcended the United States as a result of contemporary and parallel developments in the Atlantic world, the relevance of Mazzini's democratic nationalism transcended the confines of the struggle for a free and unified Italy as a result of its parallels with contemporary struggles for the creation of other European nations. Among those, Poland was particularly important because of the number and activity of its agitators. It was no coincidence that later on, when Mazzini started Young Europe, Polish nationalists were among the first to join his project; they founded their own Young Poland, modeled after Mazzini's Young Italy. At this time, the Atlantic abolitionist milieu of which Garrison was part and the continental European nationalist milieu to which Mazzini belonged were certainly aware of each other's struggles. They proceeded on mostly parallel tracks, but it was only a matter of time before exceptionally open-minded and morally committed individuals such as Garrison and Mazzini acted upon what both saw as a clear similarity in the ideals at the heart of the abolitionist and nationalist movements.[5]

The Manifestos of 1831–1832: The *Liberator* and *La Giovine Italia*

In 1831–32, William Lloyd Garrison and Giuseppe Mazzini launched their parallel revolutions in two different countries and in two different contexts, but with much in common. The striking fact that the chronologies coincide leads us to think that, by the beginning of the 1830s, Garrison and Mazzini were both mature enough, in age and experience, to take their first truly autonomous steps in terms of activism. But the parallels and the comparisons should also highlight the fact that they both chose the press to initiate and advertise their new ideas. This is hardly surprising, given that, though they were still in their midtwenties, both Garrison and Mazzini had already gained experience in editing and in holding positions of some responsibility in a few journals; they also had written for other publications. Their experiences as journalists were very different, however: Garrison had worked very early in newspapers to earn a living, and his formation was very much that of the journalist in the field; he was self-taught and, over time, had managed to reach a certain level of understanding of politics. Mazzini, a university student and then a graduate in law, had received a privileged and thorough education, particularly strong in history, literature, and philosophy; as a consequence, Mazzini's first steps in journalism were related to the world of literary critique—a far cry from Garrison's journalistic formation in the field.

The two different journalistic backgrounds shaped and profoundly influenced the revolutions that Garrison and Mazzini began in 1831–32. Garrison's *Liberator* aspired to be read by as many people as possible, some inevitably more educated than others, and thus its language was plain, clear, and accessible. It was, in many ways, the prototype of the modern militant journal that forms public opinion by taking issue on crucial debates in a democratic society, as the United States was in the 1830s, and on events in the rest of the world. Mazzini's *La Giovine Italia,* even though it also aimed at the widest possible readership so as to similarly influence the public opinion, was by its nature elitist; its comments, allusions, and interpretations related to important events and ideas in Italy and in Europe and assumed a high level of cultural knowledge and background. Its format was very much that of a literary review, a format that appealed to the educated classes accustomed to it but also served to disguise the incendiary content of the paper's essays in a society dominated by absolutism and censorship, as all the states that made up Italy in the 1830s were.[6]

Yet, if these are incontrovertible differences, the main parallel between Garrison's *Liberator* and Mazzini's *La Giovine Italia* is in the revolutions that began at roughly the same time with the publication of both papers, which were effectively "manifestos" of two different but comparable radical departures. In Garrison's case, the publication of the *Liberator* in 1831 began a new era in abolitionism, and from the first issue, it was clear that that era would focus on agitating for immediate abolition of slavery in the United States. In Mazzini's case, the publication of *La Giovine Italia* as the official organ of Young Italy in 1832 began a new era in the Italian national struggle, with the creation of the first public and publicized national program based on the achievement of Italian independence and national unity. In both cases, the publication of a paper constituted a point of no return in the history of radical ideas in the respective countries. In both cases, that publication prompted a radical change in the attitude of the public toward crucial issues—American slavery, Italian nationhood—as a result primarily of the exploitation of the enormous power of the press, a power that the nineteenth century was beginning to discover in its full extent. At the same time, both of these radical changes contained within themselves the first seeds of even deeper changes whose consequences would affect society as a whole in the two different contexts in which Garrison and Mazzini operated.[7]

The story of the beginning of the *Liberator* sheds much light both on Garrison's abolitionist network in 1831 and on the reasons for his new type of radical abolitionism—reasons that have a lot to do with his increasingly closer contacts with free African American activists. It is true that, from a purely practical point of view, Garrison's project for a new abolitionist paper would have not materialized without the substantial patronage and financial support of very wealthy individuals such as the Tappan brothers, Lucretia and James Mott, Samuel J. May, and Samuel Sewall. These were all confirmed evangelicals who welcomed the opportunity of doing good to humankind, and to the American people in particular, by attacking the great sin represented by slavery. Their support was crucial to Garrison's project. Garrison enlisted the additional help of Stephen Foster as printer and of his own childhood friend Isaac Knapp as publisher. Thus, listing himself as editor, Garrison was able to print and release the first four hundred copies of the *Liberator* on 1 January 1831.[8]

Still, the early fortunes of the paper were tightly linked with the support of free African Americans throughout the North, especially the black communities of Boston and Philadelphia, where wealthy African American businessman James Forten was eager to enlist all the help he could muster to support Garrison's abolitionist cause. Garrison and Forten also shared similar views of the relationship between the struggles for liberty against Europe's reactionary powers and the fight against slavery; galvanized by the 1830 European revolutions, both men thought, as Garrison wrote in May 1831, that in Europe "the revolution [was] marching onward with an earthquake step" and that soon the contagion of liberty would lead also to the abolition of slavery in the United States. The tie between the two men became particularly clear when, on 20 August 1831, Garrison published in the *Liberator* a letter by Forten that contained the controversial phrase, "Fight for liberty, or die in the attempt." Coming only two years after David Walker's *Appeal,* Forten's article seemed to anticipate the bloodshed that was to characterize Nat Turner's rebellion in Southampton County, Virginia, which occurred only the following day; the rebellion involved seventy African American slaves and led to the killing of sixty whites, and it helped to stigmatize both Forten and Garrison as inspirers of violent action against southern slaveholders.[9]

Yet, nothing could be further from the truth than this portrayal, as becomes clear by examining the context to which Forten's published letter belonged. From the very first issue of the *Liberator,* Garrison used a new harsh, direct language that aimed at shocking and shaking up the American people, and particularly the northerners, by showing them unapologetically the scandal represented by allowing slavery to exist in the United States. Garrison's language was violent because his was a revolution of words, an indispensable premise of what he hoped would become a revolution of consciences, leading to immediate emancipation of the slaves but never to a revolution of arms. In the famous editorial in the first issue of the *Liberator,* Garrison wrote an address "To the Public," in which he explained precisely this point, using the revolutionary power of words to an extent unknown to white America for the promotion of immediatism in the abolitionist cause: "I am aware that many object to the severity of my language, but is there not cause for severity? I *will* be as harsh as truth, and as uncompromising as justice. On this subject I do not wish to think, or speak, or write, with moderation. . . . I am in earnest—I will not equivocate—I will not excuse—I will not retreat a single inch—AND I WILL BE HEARD." Garrison's "severity" of language derived both from his consideration, following in Benjamin Lundy's footsteps, of the national shame represented by the existence of slavery and its international repercussions, and from his acknowledgment of the discrepancy between slavery and the ideals proclaimed by the American Revolution, as David Walker also argued.[10]

Already in the first issue of the *Liberator,* Garrison also gave no room for doubt as to his own and his abolitionist paper's position on what he saw as the closely related issues of slavery and freedom in the United States: "Asserting to the 'self-evident truth' maintained in the Declaration of Independence, 'that all men are created equal, and endowed by their Creator with certain inalienable rights—among which are life, liberty, and the pursuit of happiness,' I shall strenuously contend for the immediate enfranchisement of our slave population." In the following issues of the *Liberator,* Garrison returned again and again to these same points by showing through different rhetorical devices how the existence of slavery was a blatant mockery of the principles of the Declaration of Independence. For example, in the 8 January 1831 issue, Garrison wrote a list of twenty-four "truisms" in which he showed, point by point, how every single key tenet of the "proslavery argument"—the collective name for the rhetorical themes through which slaveholders justified slavery—was absurd and unreal; significantly, Garrison started his list with the words "all men are created equal . . . excepting Africans and their descendants." In the same issue of the *Liberator,* Garrison also published parts of Walker's *Appeal* with his own comments on it; since it was a free African American's message to his enslaved brethren to resist their oppressors, Walker's *Appeal* represented, for Garrison, exactly what he needed to drive his point home. By means of what William Cain has called a "punitive style," Garrison wanted to shake the white northerners' consciences, hoping that they would act upon slavery, especially if they felt the shame deriving from passively allowing slaveholders to oppress their slaves—effectively behaving in a way, Garrison argued, that was no different from the way the reactionary powers suppressing European liberty were behaving. Yet, Garrison could not prevent—as much as he wanted to, being a true pacifist—the possibility that the continuous oppression would lead to a general rebellion of enslaved southerners inspired by either David Walker's or James Forten's words. "*We* do not preach rebellion," Garrison wrote. "It is not we, but our guilty countrymen, who put arguments into the mouths, and swords into the hands of the slaves."[11]

Garrison's immediatist revolution led to his detachment from the colonization project and then his condemnation of it. His firm rejection of colonization shows perhaps better than any of his stated positions how close he was to the African American community. From the 1820s onward, through organizations such as the General Colored Association (GCA) in Boston (to which David Walker belonged) and the inexhaustible energies of prominent activists such as James Forten, African Americans denounced the ACS and its racist program of removal of the black population. Although Garrison's decision had matured as a result of personal experiences—both the coeditorship of the *Genius* with Benjamin Lundy and the spell in jail for libeling a slave trader—Garrison was very sensitive to the activities of black northerners, and his developing radical position found in them its best allies, as their enthusiastic support for the *Liberator* proved. Thus, already in 1831, in his editorial for the first issue of the *Liberator,* Garrison made clear that he had retreated from his former ambiguous attitude toward the colonization project's gradualist approach to emancipation: "In Park Street Church, on the Fourth of July, 1829," Garrison wrote, "in an address on slavery, I unreflectingly assented to the popular but pernicious doctrine of gradual abolition. I seize this opportunity to make a full and unequivocal recantation, and thus publicly ask pardon of my God, of my country, and of my brethren the poor slaves."[12]

By the following year, Garrison had decided to write a detailed pamphlet, for which he spent months accumulating all sorts of data and evidence, to show clearly the evil of colonization, focusing particularly on the policy of the ACS and the insidious and pernicious type of racism that underpinned the entire enterprise. Eventually, Garrison's pamphlet became a 238-page book called *Thoughts on African Colonization;* he published it on 2 June 1832. In it Garrison stated unequivocally, and from the very first pages, that "the colonization scheme [was] inadequate in its design, injurious in its operation, and contrary to sound principles." He also devoted ten different sections of the book to explaining in detail how, though pledging to act against slavery, the ACS was instead very much supporting the slave system and the slaveholders. Above all, Garrison showed how the ACS, by pursuing a racial policy of expulsion of free African Americans from the United States, denied any possibility for them to uplift their position within American society, deceiving the nation through the notion that gradual removal was preferable to immediate emancipation. Garrison supported his view not only with data and sound arguments, but also with the testimony of free African Americans who belonged to different organizations of black activists, including Boston's GCA. Thus, Garrison's *Thoughts* cemented his alliance with black northerners even more than the *Liberator* had done, and at the same time, the book confirmed Garrison's image as a radical who would not stop at anything to achieve his immediatist objective. However, while both of these outcomes ensured that his voice would remain confined within a minority of white activists, it is also true that, through *Thoughts,* Garrison managed to divert from colonization and convert to immediatism important personalities such as Theodore D. Weld, Nathaniel P. Rogers, and Amos A. Phelps.[13]

As the beginnings of Garrison's *Liberator* clearly reveal Garrison's radical type of abolitionism, the story of the beginnings of Mazzini's *La Giovine Italia,* the first paper Mazzini edited all on his own, indicates the novelty and sharp break that the latter represented in Italian democratic nationalism. In 1831–32, while he was in France, Mazzini reflected upon the political exiles he found there and began identifying the young exiles with the "children of a new world, sons of a new faith," or, in Maurizio Isabella's words, "apostles of the new religion of nationalism . . . the principal bearers of the national message." In giving so much importance to the youth and to the future, Mazzini doubtless was partly following the French philosopher Claude-Henri de Saint-Simon, as he did in other features of his thought. In fact, according to Arianna Arisi Rota, for Mazzini, "the past teaches and cautions, the present is contingency, but it is the future that substantiates the latter: it is Saint-Simon's 'political construction of the future' that Mazzini absorbs in the French emigré environment, and which he then applies to the objective of Italian unity." The fact that most of the exiles Mazzini encountered were young meant for Mazzini that they were ready for a new type of national movement, one that addressed specifically the young Italians and with language that spoke to them as the generation that bore the responsibility of freeing Italy from foreign oppression, achieving national unity, and establishing a democratic republic.[14]

This basic message, whose origins lay in Mazzini's meditations in prison in Savona, was at the heart of Young Italy, the new association Mazzini formed in Marseilles in 1831, and it was also the basic mission statement of *La Giovine Italia,* the paper that, from 1832, functioned as the actual organ of the association. Mazzini managed to publish only six issues of the paper, between 1832 and 1834, before he was forced to leave Marseilles, but in that short time he initiated a revolution no less significant and charged with consequences than the one Garrison started with the *Liberator* in those same years, a revolution in which, similarly, a new type of journalism, employing a new type of language, had an important place. Effectively, that journalism and that language represented at best the aspirations of a young generation that felt oppressed by the rigidity and lack of freedom of the Restoration regimes in Italy. According to Arianna Arisi Rota, the strength of Mazzini's message in 1831–32 was in his ability to transfer romantic images and ideals from literature into politics in such a way that he could appeal to the disaffected and idealistic Italian youth for his program of national liberation.[15]

Preceded by a distribution of manifestos that advertised its imminence in December 1831, the publication of the first two issues of *La Giovine Italia* on 18 March 1832 was possible thanks to the financial contribution of Mazzini's friends within the community of Italian political exiles in Marseilles. Also crucial was the help of Giuseppe Lamberti, Mazzini's secretary and close friend, and his old acquaintances the Ruffini brothers. *La Giovine Italia*'s subtitle was, significantly, *Serie di scritti intorno alla condizione politica, morale, e letteraria della Italia, tendenti alla sua rigenerazione* (A series of writings on the political, moral, and literary condition of Italy, arguing about her regeneration). Thus, even though the Sardinian police were very active in Marseilles, Mazzini made no secret of his nationalist program. The ten essays that formed the issue, mostly written by Mazzini himself, explained in detail what he meant by Italian regeneration: a program based on freedom of the homeland from foreign oppression and on the achievement of national unity. He also linked his program to a general European movement toward democratization through revolution, and he exhorted the young to take the lead in the regeneration, leaving behind the past failures. In particular, in the first essay, "Della *Giovine Italia*" (On the *Giovine Italia*), Mazzini explained why he chose that name: "With it, it would seem to us that, with a single word, we could show the Italian young the breadth of their duties, the solemnity of the mission they have been entrusted with, the reasons why the time has come to awaken to a full life of regeneration." The hopes Mazzini had in Italy's youth contrasted dramatically with the failures of "the men of the past," who were the expression of "a system [that had proven] powerless to regenerate a nation fallen to the bottom."[16]

In practice, Mazzini's writing "used the right pitch to stimulate the most ardent feelings of patriotism in a reader: whether the tone was angry, prophetic, or admonishing," according to Giuseppe Monsagrati. From that very first issue of *La Giovine Italia,* Mazzini's language and style were as direct as the circumstances of political exile and censorship allowed them to be, even though very much different from the language and style used by Garrison, who could express his opinions freely in a free and democratic country. Unlike the *Liberator,* which was openly distributed, *La Giovine Italia* was distributed with the complicity of sailors who smuggled it to Genoa, from where, as Mazzini intended, the paper would have reached the entire Italian peninsula as a clandestine publication amid the harsh censorship that characterized every Restoration state in Italy. In truth, both among the political exiles and in Italy itself, Mazzini's readership was a restricted elite made up primarily of young idealists, middle-class intellectuals, university students, and young public officers—in other words, the very categories that the absolutist governments already considered full of agitators. And yet, already in the third issue of *La Giovine Italia,* still in 1832, Mazzini clarified that Italy's regeneration was to occur through a people's revolution. In the second part of what became a famous essay, "D'alcune cause che impedirono finora lo sviluppo della libertà in Italia" (On some reasons that prevented the development of freedom in Italy), Mazzini wrote: "The revolutions must be made by the people and for the people," and "God and people: that is the program for the future."[17]

The novelty that *La Giovine Italia* represented was in the very fact that it showed clearly "Mazzini's understanding of the importance of the printed word," as Roland Sarti has remarked, and, even more, that it demonstrated the power of the printed word to shape public opinion, even in a situation of censorship. In this, Mazzini was as modern as Garrison in understanding the full implications of militant and radical journalism and the full impact it would have on both the public opinion and the society he lived in. In the last essay of *La Giovine Italia*'s first issue, entitled "Agli Italiani" (To Italians), Mazzini explained this concept clearly with the following words: "Today, the press is the arbiter of nations. Nations are thirsty for truth. Italy does not have a voice that would rise to proclaim it . . . and the troubles the governments go through to repress every freedom of writing teach us how much they fear the effect of these doctrines, because *the ink of the wise is worth as much as the sword of the strong.* . . . What is needed is that in every angle of their states, in the factories, in the theaters, in the universities, everywhere the *free word* face the oppressors." As Garrison famously stated "I WILL BE HEARD," Mazzini predicted that the spread of the "*free word*" through *La Giovine Italia*'s clandestine network would not pass unnoticed but would contribute in a major way to shaking an absolutist system of government that seemed as entrenched and impenetrable in Italy as the slave system was in the United States. Not accidentally, Mazzini began to use the analogy of masters and slaves to describe the oppression of Italians who were denied their freedom of nationality, in a way that Garrison would certainly have approved of. Thus, in an essay entitled "I collaboratori della *'Giovine Italia'* ai loro concittadini" (Young Italy's collaborators to their fellow citizens) and published in the fourth issue of *La Giovine Italia,* in 1833, Mazzini wrote, "Neither masters, nor slaves, we freely give our tribute to the holy cause [of Italy's freedom] . . . neither masters, nor slaves."[18]

Also, as Garrison rejected the doctrine of African colonization after he embraced immediatism through the *Liberator,* Mazzini rejected the Carboneria and the old secret societies' conspiratorial plans after he embraced an open program of Italian regeneration through *La Giovine Italia.* Mazzini utilized the latter as a true instrument of propaganda, and in the end, this was a determining factor in Young Italy's supplanting the Carboneria altogether; it was a result of the revolutionary novelty of the paper *La Giovine Italia* that in turn reflected the novelty of Mazzini's ideas and association. Unlike the Carboneria, with the publication and distribution of *La Giovine Italia,* Mazzini's Young Italy used a paper as its official organ to publicize its revolutionary program. Mazzini's break with the old tradition of secrecy, therefore, could not have been more definite. Above all else, Mazzini explained in his *Autobiographical Notes,* "the Carboneria called men to overthrow the system, it did not teach them how to raise a new building on the ruins of an old one." Instead, through the publication of *La Giovine Italia,* "Young Italy closed once and for all the period of the sects and began the period of the Educational Association," an association whose education focused on the understanding of and commitment to a public program of national regeneration.[19]

Even though they were different, the experiments begun with Garrison's *Liberator* and Mazzini's *La Giovine Italia* had some important elements in common. Within the two separate contexts, Garrison's paper was marked by a popular character, and Mazzini's was marked by an elitist character, but each of the two publications used a language and a style that were new to its nation's journalism. The new language and style were both direct and able to move readers to passion, so as to make them feel like participants in the struggles related to Garrison's and Mazzini's chosen causes: the abolition of American slavery and Italian national unity. The reason for this new direct and passionate style was not only the youth of the two editors but also the fact that both Garrison and Mazzini addressed primarily the young generations, those who, both believed, held the real power to change public opinion and common perceptions and, above all, the course of events in both societies. In this sense, the revolutions encapsulated in the first issues of the *Liberator* and *La Giovine Italia*—which were effectively, in this sense, two revolutionary manifestos, published in 1831–32—had far-reaching consequences, among them the formation of groups of agitators composed of young activists of the same age as Garrison and Mazzini. In this respect, and in comparable ways, Garrison and Mazzini made a major contribution in educating their own generation and in alerting it to the need of commitment in the form of active participation in new types of radical associations such as the New England Anti-Slavery Society in the United States and Young Italy in Italy.[20]

The New England Anti-Slavery Society and Young Italy

An evident difference between the two parallel revolutions begun in 1831–32 by Garrison and Mazzini is in their internal dynamic and chronology. Garrison published his paper, the *Liberator,* in 1831, and he used it as the primary vehicle for expression of his own radical ideas on abolitionism; even though soon afterward he contemplated an association with radical abolitionist aims, Garrison did not found the New England Anti-Slavery Society until 1832. Conversely, Mazzini first considered establishing a new type of association that would express his radical ideas on republicanism and democracy and begin a new course in Italian politics, as he eventually did with the foundation of Young Italy in 1831; not until the following year, 1832, did Mazzini decide to publicize the association's program and his own ideas by printing his paper, *La Giovine Italia.* The reasons for this difference have to do, most likely, with Garrison's and Mazzini's different backgrounds and contexts. From his early years, working as an apprentice in different newspapers, Garrison had understood much better than Mazzini the full impact of the power of the press and of the printed word—so much more evident in the American democratic republic than in Italy's repressive political system. Mazzini, as a result of his much more sheltered and elitist upbringing, which also affected his early journalistic experiences, and of the repressive society he lived in, did not discover the full significance and extent of the power of the press and of the printed word until later in life, when he became engaged in covert revolutionary activities in exile—and even then he was the first one in Restoration Italy to come to this understanding.

Moreover, American public opinion found the publication of a new radical abolitionist paper such as the *Liberator* a true novelty; in itself, such a novelty was bound to have an impact in preparing the background and offering the stimuli for the initially subordinate aim of forming a radical abolitionist society. In the world of suspicion and censorship that characterized both Italy and Mazzini's life as an Italian political exile—and countless other lives as well—the true novelty was the creation of a new radical nationalist association; in this sense, the rapidity with which the association's clandestine membership grew was the principal measure of its impact, while the creation of a radical nationalist paper was subordinate to the primary aim of increasing that membership. In both cases, though, the revolutions that Garrison and Mazzini either began or continued in journalistic form with the publication of the *Liberator* and of *La Giovine Italia* became cemented and stood on much firmer ground with the creation of associations—the NEASS and Young Italy—that gathered individuals wholly committed to the aims and strategies of the new radical types of thought expressed in the two papers. Garrison's foundation of the NEASS and Mazzini's foundation of Young Italy took, or had already taken, the revolution in words a step further, since the creation of these two associations represented effectively the formation of two revolutionary agencies that would work to implement Garrison's radical abolitionist and Mazzini's democratic nationalist programs.

After he began publishing the *Liberator,* Garrison felt that it was not enough simply to publish an abolitionist paper as the main vehicle for his immediatist ideas. To truly put in practice his program of shaking the consciences of his fellow citizens, he needed to establish an organization inspired by the same principles that guided the *Liberator,* an organization whose activity and influence would be felt throughout Boston and even beyond Massachusetts, where abolitionism was traditionally stronger than anywhere else in the United States. By November 1831, Garrison had already met with Isaac Knapp, Oliver Johnson, Samuel J. May, Samuel Sewall, and others to discuss the foundation of such an organization; however, because these individuals opposed Garrison's desire to state clearly in the foundational documents the main principles of immediate emancipation, civic equality, and opposition to colonization, the meeting led nowhere. But on 6 January 1832 Garrison and a few of his supporters met in the basement of the African Meeting House, a black church in Boston's Beacon Hill, and after further discussion and the final acceptance of Garrison's straightforward approach, they agreed to found a new local abolitionist organization, named the New England Anti-Slavery Society.[21]

At the 6 January meeting, Garrison stated: "We have met tonight in this obscure school-house; our numbers are few and our influence limited; but, mark my prediction, Faneuil Hall shall ere long echo with the principles we have set forth." Faneuil Hall was Boston's most renowned landmark, the "cradle of liberty," having been "the site of some of the American Revolution's greatest political theater," in Margot Minardi's words; fulfilling Garrison's prediction, in time Boston's abolitionists made the site the very symbol of their antislavery struggle. After the election of Arnold Buffum as president and Garrison and Joshua Coffin as secretaries, the NEASS immediately got to work, according to Roman Zorn, with "four standing committees . . . directed to aid and protect Boston's colored citizenry, and . . . reports on the slave trade, colonization, the status of American slavery, and the condition of the northern free Negro population." As these activities took place, Garrison did his own special research and prepared his crucial pamphlet *Thoughts on African Colonization;* he published it in June 1832 under the official sponsorship of the NEASS, which thus began a battle head-to-head with the ACS for popularity among abolitionist activists in the antislavery circles of Boston.[22]

In many ways, the NEASS was for Garrison the indispensable complement to the *Liberator* and the best conduit for him to engage in an organized way in abolitionist activities of the immediatist type in Boston and its surroundings. Thus, the NEASS philosophy, inspired by Garrison, was strongly influenced by the type of statements that Garrison had familiarized his readers and supporters with through his editorials and articles in the *Libera-*

tor. In fact, the preamble to the constitution of the NEASS stated, "Slavery is contrary to the precepts of Christianity, dangerous to the liberties of the country, and ought to be immediately abolished." At the same time, there was a clear and definite appeal to the citizens of Boston, of Massachusetts, and of other New England states, to act against slavery, as if they, among northerners, were the ones most likely to feel the moral shame associated with it and therefore best equipped to act: "We believe that the citizens of New England not only have the right to protest against it [slavery], but are under the highest obligation to seek its removal by a moral influence." This local focus stood in striking contrast with Garrison's belief in the universal principles of human freedom and dignity, but in the NEASS constitution there were more than a few elements of Garrison's unique brand of radicalism. Specifically, the constitution included some of his characteristically most radical aims in relation to white and black equality. In short, the NEASS strove to achieve "the abolition of slavery in the United States, to improve the character and condition of the free people of color, to inform and correct public opinion in relation to their situation and rights, and obtain for them equal civil and political rights and privileges with the whites."[23]

Thus, Richard Newman has correctly stated that, in more than one way, "when the *New England Anti-Slavery Society* formed in January 1832, it announced radical departures from the American abolitionist tradition." It was not just that the NEASS's basic tenets were identical to Garrison's revolutionary immediatist position regarding the abolition of slavery; the NEASS also waged, equally forcefully, a true battle against racial prejudice. It is no wonder that, just as blacks were prominent among the supporters of the *Liberator,* 25 percent of the signers of the original NEASS constitution were black activists. It was as radical a departure as it could be from previous, established practices in the American abolitionist movement. As Paul Goodman has remarked, "earlier white antislavery societies, formed in the post-Revolutionary era, had not included blacks, whereas the new immediatist movement was the result of black efforts to convert whites," with the help of radical white abolitionists such as Garrison. In this respect, the NEASS represented in 1832 "the latest fruit of white-black collaboration."[24]

In practice, the NEASS promoted numerous different activities to ensure collaboration between blacks and whites and fight racial prejudice. At the heart of these efforts was the struggle against colonization. According to James B. Stewart, "after the founding of the *New England Anti-Slavery Society* in 1832, abolitionist agents began anti-colonization rallies in Massachusetts, Connecticut, Vermont, and New Hampshire, and Garrison conducted a series of similar meetings with African American congregations in Massachusetts, Connecticut, and New York." After the publication of Garrison's *Thoughts,* it was open war with the ACS. Despite the double-pronged attack against the ACS that Garrison led through the NEASS and through his own editorials and published letters in the *Liberator,* the supporters of colonization and the ACS agents chose to ignore the immediatists' agitation, as if it were of minor importance. They even avoided reviewing Garrison's *Thoughts,* despite the response the pamphlet had received in papers and magazines. This tactic proved ineffective, so that Garrison could say, in a July 1832 letter to Henry Benson, "Conversions from colonization to abolition principles are rapidly multiplying in every quarter; and we have reason greatly to rejoice—for I look upon the overthrow of the Colonization Society as the overthrow of slavery itself—they both stand or fall together."[25]

But the NEASS did much more than simply winning the battle against the ACS and colonization. According to Merton Dillon, "it appointed standing committees charged with apprenticing black children to learn trades, ending school segregation, and improving the existing schools for black children." By engaging in these activities, the NEASS became what Richard Newman has called "the world's first integrated abolitionist society." Subsequently, to respond to the need of creating an NEASS official publication, one that would publicize all the antislavery and antiracist activities of the society, Garrison and his followers began issuing a new antislavery paper called the *Abolitionist;* in its first issue, the paper declared, "The object of the Abolitionist . . . is to promote the abolition of slavery, and also to improve the condition of the free people of color in the United States." Besides lecturing and promoting all types of interracial collaboration between blacks and whites, between 1832 and 1833, according to Roman Zorn, Garrison and the NEASS members "organized 12 local abolition societies, induced 124 clergymen to endorse immediate emancipation, and secured 2,500 signatures on petitions for the removal of slavery and the slave trade from the District of Columbia." Quite logically, as the NEASS program unfolded and its multiform activities took place, Garrison decided to utilize the examples of racial harmony that the NEASS actions had created to defend himself and his fellow immediatists—all firm supporters of nonresistance like himself—from the renewed accusation of fomenting slave revolts. In this connection, particularly revealing is a letter that Garrison wrote Samuel Whitcomb Jr., in February 1832, shortly after the foundation of the NEASS, when the memory of Nat Turner's August 1831 rebellion in Virginia was still fresh. Although the local authorities had succeeded in capturing most of the rebels, including Nat Turner, and had proceeded to a swift and harsh repression, the event had left white southerners still particularly prone to see in Garrison's language and actions an abolitionist conspiracy to foment slave revolts.[26]

In the letter to Whitcomb, Garrison responded to this charge by stating unequivocally, "The tragedy at Southampton fills me with as much horror as any individual in the country." He added, more generally, "I consider all wars, waged for whatever purpose, as abhorrent in the sight of God, and utterly inexcusable." Garrison also clarified, however, that his love of liberty was as strong as his pacifism; in addition, following a line of thought he had held since his early journalistic apprenticeships, he mentioned Europe's national struggles such as "the resistance of the Greeks to the Turks, or the Poles to the Russians" as if they were caused by a type of oppression no different from the one experienced by slaves in the United States; clearly referring to both cases, Garrison wrote, "I'd rather be a slave than fasten the chains of servitude upon a fellow creature." Thus, even maintaining firm his opposition to violence, Garrison thought that if the oppressors of European nations were as guilty of inexcusable crimes as American slaveholders were, the consequence was that "Nat Turner deserves as much applause as Markos Botzaris [one of the heroes of the Greek struggle for independence]"; even so, Garrison declared, "I class them both as murderers." In other words, Garrison wholeheartedly supported and justified all causes of opposition to oppression with an ultimate end of liberation—and in this he was similar to Mazzini—but not the violent means, because of his firm pacifist beliefs. As a reinforcement and clear indicator of Garrison's views, the official proceedings of the New England Anti-Slavery Convention often included the word *peace.* For example, the proceedings for May 1834 recited, "The words, Peace! Be still! when coming from the friends of freedom, are sufficient to assuage the wildest storm of revolutionary passion."[27]

While Garrison had thought about an abolitionist society since 1831 but not founded it until the following year, in 1831 Giuseppe Mazzini had already begun the activities of his own nationalist association Young Italy, whose official organ soon became *La Giovine Italia.* In his *Autobiographical Notes,*

Mazzini wrote that the idea for the association had come to him while he was in prison in Savona in 1830, pondering the failure of the Carbonari to spark the national revolution in Italy. And to be sure, Young Italy was in many ways a sharp break with the Carboneria, especially, as mentioned earlier, because of its publicized program with clear objectives, even though it initially continued to share at least some characteristics with secret societies. In fact, according to Roland Sarti, Young Italy's "members took secret oaths, shared secret passwords and symbols, vowed vengeance against tyrants and traitors, and conspired," because conspiracy was inevitable in a society devoid of freedom. In 1832, shortly after the publication of the first issue of *La Giovine Italia,* the French government ordered Mazzini's expulsion, and he was forced to hide. In 1833 Mazzini's friend Jacopo Ruffini was arrested for conspiratorial activities and committed suicide in prison; shortly afterward Mazzini himself was forced to leave France and go to Geneva. There is no doubt, though, that, however similar Young Italy might have been to older types of secret societies—and it was similar only in form, not in content—for the brief three years of its first period of activities, between 1831 and 1834, Young Italy represented a new model of revolutionary nationalist association.[28]

In practice, with Young Italy, Mazzini elaborated a coherent program for those nationalists who, like him, wished to establish a democratic republic—a program that he linked clearly to revolutionary struggles occurring in other parts of Europe—and thus he became the unchallenged head of democratic nationalism in Italy. In the 1831 "Istruzione generale per gli affratellati alla Giovine Italia" (General instructions to the members of Young Italy), Mazzini related the struggle to create an Italian nation to a more general idea of progress, and he provided a model for considering each national cause, as long as it was conducted with progressive aims, as part of humankind's advancement. Among Young Italy's five aims that Mazzini listed in the "Istruzione," particularly significant were these: "1st: the republic, one, indivisible, in all the Italian territory, independent, and free . . . 3rd: the abolition of every aristocracy and of every privilege . . . 5th: the most explicit declaration of the rights of man and citizen." As in the *Liberator,* no room was left for doubt as to where Young Italy stood in regard to the main issue, Italy's plight as a nation, although, in the great progressive struggle to which Italy's achievement of nationhood belonged, the language of sacred "mission," holiness, and martyrdom was ubiquitous.[29]

In fact, every member of Mazzini's Young Italy was to swear a rather revelatory oath, one in which some words clearly resonated with the principles of the American Declaration of Independence, so dear to Garrison: "I, Italian citizen . . . before God father of liberty, before all men, who were born to enjoy it . . . on the individual and social rights that form *man* . . . on the blood of the country's martyrs . . . swear to dedicate myself . . . to my country and its regeneration . . . to achieve Italy's union and liberty . . . to fight in every way inequalities among men of the same land." Even more explicit, in terms of making connections with America's struggle for freedom, were the words Mazzini used in the opening issue of *La Giovine Italia* in 1832 to describe the Italians' national oppression and the reason for the existence of Young Italy: "We are slaves. . . . Through which means can slaves acquire freedom? A stable freedom? An effective freedom? Which principles should support the efforts [to acquire it]?" It is important to notice that, even though in a different context, and in reference to American slaves, these were the same questions that, in those same years, Garrison asked himself and his readers in the *Liberator.*[30]

A strongly innovative feature of Mazzini's Young Italy, as in *La Giovine Italia,* was its attention and commitment to the young; as Mazzini wrote in an 1831 letter to Giuseppe Giglioli, Young Italy was "a brotherhood of young, who gather to work together with honesty, sincerity, and trust in one another." Through Young Italy, Mazzini made explicit his idea that the young generations were the ones who would be especially eager for a new nation, based on a republican government, with the goals of abolishing the hierarchies and privileges of church and aristocracy, providing education for all, and recognizing the rights of man and citizen—the great achievements of the French Revolution. Utilizing a concept taken from the New Testament, Mazzini thought about the young members of his association as if engaged in an apostolate, characterized by a strong moral commitment, similarly to how some American abolitionists also drew upon Christian terminology, calling one another "brother." Like apostles, Young Italy members were to spread republican ideas, educating the people and preparing them for the general insurrection that was to create the democratic Italian nation and, with the establishment of a constituent assembly, bring equality to all the citizens. It was no coincidence that Mazzini utilized a religious metaphor, since his nationalist ideas—strongly anticlerical and antipapacy—were already assuming traits of what some scholars have called a "religion of the nation," so that Mazzini thought that "God and the People" were working together toward the same aim of national regeneration. Especially in this respect, as we shall see later on, Mazzini had been inspired by the French thinker Claude-Henri de Saint-Simon, whose work had attempted to reconcile faith in God—in his case, but not so clearly in Mazzini's case, the Christian God—with social progress.[31]

Even though Mazzini subordinated politics to a firm moral commitment, Young Italy, whose complete name was, significantly, Federazione della Giovine Italia (Young Italy Federation), in its organization, in its structure, and in the publicity of its program, resembled a modern political association—so much so that scholars such as Franco Della Peruta have considered it the first real Italian political party. In fact, besides the requirement that Young Italy's members share a clear commitment to a definite political ideology, namely republicanism, the association itself functioned in ways comparable to those of a party, "not only," according to Giuseppe Monsagrati, "because it was equipped with very specific structures (an apparatus, a secretariat, a network, a press, financing channels, etc.), but also because a consistent and strongly motivated group of activists always operated to serve its cause." And thanks to its structure, organization, and network, in a relatively short time, Young Italy spread from Marseilles first to the universities and the cities of northern Italy, especially in Lombardy, and then to areas of the Center and the South, including Rome and Naples. By 1833 the members of Young Italy numbered between fifty thousand and sixty thousand; this number is all the more impressive because the association seemed to be confined to the cities, where there was a greater percentage of educated people, especially from the aristocracy and the bourgeoisie, and partly also from the working class; instead, most peasants in the countryside were illiterate and could not even understand Mazzini's oral propaganda—most likely they would denounce him to the authorities. As Mazzini wrote Niccolò Tommaseo in 1834, "the people cannot read, and do not know how to read; where oral apostolate meets the death penalty, I am not hoping to find apostles."[32]

Galvanized by Young Italy's success, Mazzini hoped and believed that the national revolution was around the corner. Consequently, in 1833, he organized a plan according to which Young Italy cells and agents, infiltrated into the Sardinian army and navy, would start a general insurrection in Piedmont and Liguria. But the discovery of the plot and the arrest and subsequent suicide of Jacopo Ruffini profoundly shook Mazzini, while the Sardinian king, Charles Albert—despite his fame as a liberal monarch—proceeded with a wave of harsh repression that disbanded Young Italy's organization in Piedmont and led to the execution of twelve conspirators and the exile of hundreds. A similar wave of repression, leading to arrests and trials, occurred in Lombardy, where the Austrian authorities discovered Young Italy's network in different areas of the kingdom. By the time Mazzini reached Geneva, he had been publicly branded an "enemy of the country" and condemned to death by Charles Albert. It was also during this period, 1833–34, that Mazzini arrived at a definite break with Filippo Buonarroti, as a result of the latter's attempt, since 1831, to take the initiative in the revolutionary movement by constituting an association called I Veri Italiani, parallel to Young Italy and with similar aims. As Giorgio Candeloro has written, "the contrast between Mazzini and Buonarroti contributed in no small part in worsening the consequences of the failure of Mazzini's insurrectional attempts and in leading to a crisis of the democratic national movement."[33]

Among the differences between Garrison's and Mazzini's revolutions, one of the most striking is how long they lasted, as a result of their different contexts and historical circumstances. In later times, long after the date of its foundation in 1832 and under a different name (the Massachusetts Anti-Slavery Society [MASS]), Garrison's NEASS continued to have an important role in shaping the democratic debate on American abolitionism and racial equality. Also, even though the NEASS was very much a regionally based association that expressed the particular antislavery character of its New England constituency, Garrison always regarded it as the first genuinely abolitionist, immediatist, and interracial association he established in the American nation as a whole. Conversely, Mazzini, hunted by the Restoration governments' police and forced to constantly change his location in exile, had no choice but to interrupt the Young Italy experiment in 1834, only three years after it began, largely as a result of the authorities' discovery of its wide network in large areas of the Italian peninsula. However, five years later, in London, as we shall see, Mazzini reconstituted Young Italy, and again the experiment was short-lived for reasons similar to the ones that ended the first version of the association. Nevertheless, like Garrison and his view of the NEASS, throughout his life Mazzini never ceased to think of Young Italy as the initiative that best represented his thought. He saw it as the first true expression of republican and democratic national politics on Italian soil, as it effectively was.

It is striking to notice the many parallels between the new, radical, uncompromising positions of Garrison and Mazzini in the early 1830s. It is even more striking to notice that in both cases, even though in very different contexts and under very different circumstances, the revolutions that they began were based on the power of the press and the printed word to spread radical ideas among the public, and also on the foundation of radical societies as means to implement their revolutionary projects. In this sense, it is not difficult to see which features made Garrison's *Liberator* and Mazzini's *La Giovine Italia* different from other papers. Both, quite simply, responded to their readerships' need to subscribe to publications that expressed their own very radical views on what they considered the most pressing problems, the abolition of American slavery, for the *Liberator*'s readers, and the creation of an Italian nation, for *La Giovine Italia*'s. There is no doubt that similar constituencies recognized themselves in the two radical papers and in the two societies that Garrison and Mazzini had founded in order to implement the radical programs that resonated with the content of their articles and essays.

It is also true that the two constituencies that subscribed to Garrison's radical abolitionist program and to Mazzini's democratic nationalist program were very different, and not merely because of the different contexts in which they lived. Many of those who read Garrison's *Liberator,* and even more of those who became members of the NEASS, certainly belonged to the middle class—even though, strikingly, they were both white and black—and their number was only a few thousands, whereas Young Italy had a much larger membership. However, among those few thousands, there were certainly also readers of the *Liberator* who came from the lower classes, especially if one recalls that the rate of literacy in the northeastern United States, and also the level of engagement in the crucial debates that shaped the life of the nation, was very high not just compared to America as a whole, but also by nineteenth-century standards—as we might expect from a democratic republic. Conversely, those who read Mazzini's *La Giovine Italia* and who became members of Young Italy, even though a respectable number by nineteenth-century European standards (but only if one does not take into account Daniel O'Connell's popular movement in Ireland, able to attract hundreds of thousands of people), were mostly a small elite of highly educated upper- and middle-class individuals. The reason for this was mainly the widespread illiteracy among the lower classes in all the regions of Italy, certainly among most of the urban working classes, but especially among the countryside peasants who made up the overwhelming majority of the Italian population.[34]

Equally important to notice is that, even though both Garrison and Mazzini linked their radical causes not only to their respective national contexts but also to the great universal principles of humanity and democracy, their struggles were of very different natures. The differences were not just the obvious ones related to their contents and contexts, but also others having to do with the ways Garrison and Mazzini related to the societies of which they were part. Garrison thought he had started a great moral revolution, whose objective was primarily ethical rather than political: he wished to shake the consciences of the citizens of the American democratic republic, but he had no explicit and direct political agenda for achieving the abolition of slavery. Mazzini, in contrast, thought he had begun an actual national revolution, whose objective was straightforwardly political but with a strong ethical component: in practice, Mazzini wished to create the conditions for the foundation of a morally superior Italian democratic republic that did not exist yet. Even though in both cases the moral dimension and the commitment to the chosen cause revealed a highly religious view of the world and played a large role in shaping thoughts and ideas, the difference in the actual nature of the two revolutions—a mostly ethical revolution with only indirect links to politics versus an outright political and ethical revolution—was a major divergence, and it was bound to increase in importance in the subsequent years of Garrison's and Mazzini's lives.

3

WORKING TOWARD GLOBAL MIDDLE-CLASS INCLUSIVENESS

The Fight for Freedom from Local to Federal, 1833–1837

In the mid-1830s, when William Lloyd Garrison and Giuseppe Mazzini decided to widen the scope of their revolutions with the foundation of the American Anti-Slavery Society and Young Europe, the Atlantic and Euro-American world underwent a profound change, mainly as a result of the 1833 Emancipation Act, which freed the slaves throughout the colonies of the British Empire. This act, as Garrison was one of the first to recognize, provided a large boost for the cause of freedom and for the struggle against any form of oppression generally. It also became a major symbolic and factual milestone on the road leading to a world of progressive ideas and actions that reformers and radicals living in Europe and the Americas hoped humankind was finally ready to take. However, the Emancipation Act had little direct or visible effect on the process of shaking up the international order of the Restoration or on the struggle against the oppression that its absolute regimes exercised over Europe's national movements. Nevertheless, most patriots and revolutionaries must have, like Mazzini, welcomed the Emancipation Act as an important proof that institutional democratization and recognition of human rights were the way to the future that the British Parliament—already at the vanguard of the antislavery struggle, after its abolition of the Atlantic slave trade in 1807—was then showing to the world.[1]

The actual causes of the passing of the 1833 Emancipation Act by the British Parliament were many. It occurred partly as a result of the continuous activity staged by the abolitionist and immediatist group of the Agency Committee, founded in 1830–31 and headed by Thomas Fowell Buxton; but the legislation also resulted from the West Indian planters' fear of a massive slave insurrection, such as the one that characterized the 1831–32 "Baptist War" in Jamaica. At the same time, there is little doubt that the increasingly popular argument for the moral and economic superiority of free labor over slavery played a significant role as well. In practice, the Emancipation Act freed almost eight hundred thousand slaves in all the British colonies by the time it became effective, on 1 August 1834. The act also gave compensation to slaveholders for their loss in the form of an unpaid "apprenticeship" period, originally of twelve, then six, and finally four years; thus, complete emancipation did not occur until 1838. Still, there is no doubt that many saw these measures as necessary compromises and that the majority, in Britain as well as in the United States, thought of the Emancipation Act as an immensely significant achievement and a milestone of progress. And yet, British abolitionists did not relinquish their struggle after Parliament passed the Emancipation Act. In 1837, the most radical among them in the Agency Committee founded the Central Negro Emancipation Committee, under the leadership of Joseph Sturge; this later committee's pressure on the British Parliament played a crucial role in prompting the measures that led first to the gradual reduction of the period of "apprenticeship" and then to its end altogether in 1838.[2]

In transatlantic perspective, British slave emancipation—which the legislators called "the mighty experiment"—gave a great boost to Atlantic abolitionism, strengthening the ties between the British and American radical movements that aimed at the obliteration of slavery from the Euro-American world. As Edward Rugemer has remarked, American abolitionist Lydia Maria Child's famous pamphlet *An Appeal in Favor of That Class of Americans Called Africans* "appeared in August 1833, the very month that the British Parliament passed the Emancipation Act. This could not have been mere coincidence." And in her pamphlet, Child took a true Atlantic perspective on the problem of abolition of slavery, stating quite clearly that the United States ought to join Britain on the path the latter had just opened. Not surprisingly, then, the echo of Britain's Emancipation Act was especially strong in the United States, where radical antislavery activists saw it as an example to imitate and follow. Foremost among them was William Lloyd

Garrison, who, in the 9 August 1834 issue of the *Liberator,* described the coming into effect of the Emancipation Act as "one of the most signal and glorious events in the history of the world." On that day, the Boston abolitionists began their annual celebrations of the Emancipation Act. According to Deborah Bingham Van Broekhoven, "the handful of American abolitionists . . . praised Britain and its reformers, and for decades they continued to compare their own struggle with the swift end of slavery in the West Indies." Thus, not only in Boston, but throughout the North, American abolitionists celebrated Britain's Emancipation Act's coming into effect with church services and ceremonial addresses; in the process, they also began a tradition of white and black antislavery activists remembering the crucial event together every year throughout the antebellum period, a tradition that was, in Caleb McDaniel's words, "a subversive alternative to the Fourth of July."[3]

At a different level, it is possible to connect the British abolition of slavery to a general policy of reform that the British government had inaugurated in the late 1820s. The policy's achievements had begun with the 1829 emancipation of Irish Catholics, who could now be elected members of Parliament without abjuring their own confession—largely thanks to the efforts of the great Irish reformer and "Liberator" Daniel O'Connell, who was also a convinced abolitionist. They continued with the 1832 parliamentary reform, the extension of suffrage to the middle class, the 1833 Emancipation Act, and finally the Poor Law of 1834. As C. A. Bayly has pointed out, these reforms prevented Britain from following the same course as the Restoration monarchies and states of continental Europe, all of which, in different ways and through different phases, went through a crisis of legitimacy, as a result of continuous radical challenges to their authority—challenges represented first and foremost by revolutionaries such as Giuseppe Mazzini. In this respect, we should recognize an important connection between the way Atlantic abolitionists such as Garrison, in both Britain and the Unites States, put pressure upon their respective governments through radical initiatives aiming at immediate slave emancipation and the way European revolutionaries such as Mazzini put pressure upon Restoration governments in Italy and in other countries of Europe for the implementation of radical reforms and, in the best-case scenario, the eventual establishment of republican nations. In both cases, the price the government would pay for moving toward a more incisive democratization of society might pave the way to a challenge to its legitimacy that could prove fatal to its very existence—what eventually happened in most of Italy's Restoration regimes.[4]

Garrison's Apotheosis and Mazzini's Crisis

In the mid-1830s, both Garrison and Mazzini could very well say that their revolutions had already managed to make a lasting impact on the course of radical reform in the United States and of radical politics in Italy. It is easier to see this outcome in Garrison's case, simply because neither the *Liberator,* nor the New England Anti-Slavery Society, nor, later on, the American Anti-Slavery Society ever experienced an interruption in the entire course of America's antebellum and Civil War periods; both the paper and the societies inspired by Garrison continued to play an important role, even though they represented a minority of the people, within the democratic debate on the abolition of slavery in the United States. Conversely, Mazzini's Young Italy and Mazzini's paper *La Giovine Italia* ended their first period of activity in 1834, having lasted only a few years, after the reactionary Sardinian authorities discovered the latest insurrection plotted by Mazzini and once again imposed mass imprisonment and exile on the Italian patriots; Young Italy resurrected some years later, but the continuity that characterized Garrison's publications and pursuits was absent at this time in Mazzini's case, as a result of his outlaw status of revolutionary agitator in Restoration Europe. This difference in contexts and events, in turn, led to very different attitudes on the part of Garrison and Mazzini toward their lives during this period. Garrison was engaged in a period of continuous activity, and his mostly unchallenged leadership of the radical abolitionist movement in the United States boosted his confidence. Mazzini experienced a difficult period of dislocation, not knowing where to go next but, at the same time, still plotting insurrections that might fail; he began to doubt himself and his aims.

Yet, even though the difference between their lives seems overwhelming at this time, in both Garrison's and Mazzini's cases the number and devotion of their followers—those who were fascinated by their ideas and by their suggestions on how to put them into practice—continued to grow, simply because the power and influence of the novelty of their radical convictions and attitudes was spreading wider and wider in the United States and in Italy. Besides the ideas themselves, though, and the message they carried with them—in both cases a message of deliverance from "servitude," whether American slavery or Italian national oppression—the charisma that Garrison and Mazzini exuded, and the strong moral aura that surrounded them, gave strength to their thought, already original. And to be sure, this strength was also a result of the unflinching devotion they both showed toward their causes, and of their readiness to sacrifice everything for those causes' sake, including their own safety and peace of mind. This is an important factor that reveals better than any other the legendary moral commitment that both Garrison and Mazzini had in such high measure that it impressed many of their contemporaries.

In the early 1830s, as he reached the height of his influence within the abolitionist movement in the United States, Garrison refined his thought and defined his position on several crucial issues that agitated American society at the time. On one hand, Garrison increased the radicalism of his nonviolent stance and applied it to different fields of action. On the other hand, he confirmed that, despite the success he had enjoyed in provoking a rupture and a new departure, not only within abolitionism but also within the American radical tradition at large, his true supporters and those who shared his same views—the so-called Garrisonians—were but a respectable minority vis-à-vis the public opinion of Boston and of New England in general, although they were a large group in abolitionist circles. Yet, Garrison succeeded in giving the Garrisonians what we can only describe as a true philosophy of life—one whose espousal implied, as was clear to all of them, an uncompromising, tireless, truly missionlike commitment to fighting not just for the abolition of slavery but for freedom and justice. While defining the parameters of his thought and how he saw the problem of slavery as interrelated with a much larger problem of freedom in a wider context and on more than one level, Garrison also thought increasingly that the issues he dealt with—especially slavery itself—were less local and more national, if not also universal; therefore, although his battle had started in New England, he wanted it to extend to the entire United States and, if possible, to the entire world. After all, on the masthead of the *Liberator,* Garrison had placed the phrase "Our Country is the World—Our Countrymen Are Mankind," adapted from Thomas Paine.[5]

What were the defining characteristics of Garrison's thought in the 1830s, at the peak of his influence over the abolitionist movement? The main feature, and the one that truly distinguished Garrisonians from other abolitionists, was an open attitude toward amelioration of society in as many fields as possible. "Those close to Garrison," Russell Nye has written, "understood his propensity for reform—any reform—and knew also that to him no worthy cause was minor. . . . Garrison could never see any logic in not fighting on several fronts at once." Having been strongly influenced by the doctrine of the perfectibility of the individual, and through him of society at large, spread by great evangelical preachers such as James G. Birney and Charles G. Finney, Garrison thought it was entirely possible to convince those who were doing wrong—either exploiting slaves, or allowing that exploitation to happen, or committing some other offense—to break with their habits, so that they would cease to be sinners. In the words of Ronald Walters, Garrison and his fellow abolitionists saw "reform as something akin to an act of repentance." Yet, Garrison and the Garrisonians believed that not only the slaveholders and their supporters could and should repent, but also all those who were involved in sinful activities. Earlier in his life, Garrison had edited a temperance paper; in the early 1830s, through the *Liberator* and the NEASS, he began fighting against colonization and racial prejudice; later on, he wholeheartedly supported Europe's democratic and national movements, from Ireland to Italy, as he had already started doing in his apprenticeship years; and he also famously joined the battle for women's rights.[6]

By the mid-1830s, at the heart of Garrison's attitude lay his enthusiastic support for "perfectionism," a tenet within antinomianism, which was a "heretical" Protestant movement based on the "belief that the workings of the indwelling spirit could place a Christian beyond the need for the moral law." During the religious revival of the 1820s and 1830s, the main proponent of perfectionism was Charles G. Finney, a convinced abolitionist and a favorite preacher of Garrison's. Finney spoke of sinners wholly cleansed by the action of the Holy Spirit and of a "universal emancipation from sin," because of which human institutions would become unnecessary because society would live in holiness. It was as a result of his own belief in this millennial vision, and therefore in the possibility of bringing about the perfect holy society, completely emancipated from sin and with no need of hierarchy, that Garrison engaged in every movement of moral reform and in every battle for justice, regardless of common sense and social conventions. Quite simply, Garrison's struggle was a struggle "to redeem the soul of America"—to use the words of the title of an important study of Martin Luther King Jr. And to be sure, despite the enormous differences between the two characters, Garrison, like King, wished to bring about change in the name of the Christian God he believed in, through nonresistance, that is, through strictly nonviolent means, and he did everything in his power to make it happen.[7]

In truth, Garrison's doctrine of nonresistance has received a great deal of attention from scholars, who have, indeed, drawn parallels not only between Garrison and Martin Luther King Jr., but also between Garrison and Leo Tolstoy and Garrison and Gandhi. However, among Garrison's contemporaries, the closest to his thought were John Humphrey Noyes, a utopian socialist famous for condemning civil government and marriage; abolitionist and women's right supporter Angelina Grimké, who held positions similar to Noyes's and also had a decisive influence on Garrison; and writer and philosopher Henry David Thoreau, who later elaborated his famous concept of "civil disobedience." Partially as a result of these influences, Garrison and the Garrisonians, according to Lewis Perry, "had come to believe that Biblical injunctions against violence meant that Christians had to renounce all manifestations of force, including human government; this is the belief we call non-resistance." Moreover, Perry's view is that, in their attempt to bring about the millennial Kingdom of God—the perfect holy society—rejecting through nonviolent means the authority of established, governmental, hierarchical human institutions, Garrison and the Garrisonians showed how much they belonged to a pacifist anarchist tradition, well represented in the projects and debates of the New England Non-Resistance Society, founded in 1838—a tradition that continued all the way to the later part of the nineteenth century and at that time reached Tolstoy.[8]

Nevertheless, as Henry Mayer has noted, Garrison soon discovered that, "as would later be true of Mahatma Gandhi and Martin Luther King, Jr. . . . non-resistance did not mean retreat, but conflict, for pacifist protest could draw out and expose the angry violence of a society and compel humanity to alleviate the suffering it caused." In fact, since he had started the *Liberator,* Garrison had had to confront anti-abolitionist mobs made of "gentlemen of property and standing," all strongly racist and thus supporters of the status quo. According to Herbert Aptheker, "much of their activity was collectively organized, deliberately financed, and maliciously conceived, and included palpably criminal behavior, sometimes even murder." In the 1830s alone, the authorities registered no fewer than 115 anti-abolitionist attacks, mostly in Boston and New York. On 21 October 1835, one such mob attacked and roughed up Garrison himself in Boston. Three days later, on 24 October, Garrison wrote Samuel Sewall, bravely dismissing his friends' urging that he move away from Boston: "It seems to me we ought to resolve that the Liberator, despite all opposition, shall continue to be printed—and printed, too, in Boston." A little earlier, Garrison had had reasons to express his concern over anti-abolitionist mob activity also in regard to George Thompson, a foremost British abolitionist and a close friend of his, whom Garrison had invited to lecture in the United States in 1834 and who had met with violent reaction more than once before returning to England a few months later. "How thankful I am," Garrison wrote in the same 1835 letter to Sewall, "that the mob seized me, and that he was safe with his family!"[9]

Anti-abolitionist activities reached their peak in 1836–37, a period that Garrison and his collaborators termed the "reign of terror," with an obvious reference to the bloodiest phase of the French Revolution. As Caleb McDaniel has pointed out, the "reign of terror" persuaded Garrison to follow even more closely in Noyes's footsteps, rejecting the sinful American nation that refused to listen to the abolitionists and even refusing patriotism altogether, so as to believe exclusively in the Kingdom of God, to which all nations were subordinated. However, there is no doubt that Garrison's faith and firm conviction that he should continue his nonviolent struggle for justice, even to the point of martyrdom, gave him the courage to state that it was "indeed a blessed privilege thus to suffer for Christ." But just as he was not prepared to relinquish his nonviolent means of fighting, no matter the cost, Garrison was also not prepared to condone those who were killed while violently defending the antislavery cause. When Reverend Elijah P. Lovejoy, an antislavery advocate and the editor of the reform paper the *Observer,* was murdered by a mob that also set a fire to his press at Alton, Illinois, in November 1837, even though other abolitionists rushed to proclaim him a true Christian martyr for their cause, Garrison and a few of his followers refused to consider him thus. In a pungent letter to Samuel J. May, Garrison commented significantly: "What was bro. Lovejoy's act? He died, not as an abolitionist, but as one of the police of Alton, regularly employed by the Mayor. . . . When he fell, and the murderers triumphed, government fell. . . . I wish all in our ranks could be led to see, that civil government—a government upheld by military power—is not justified *among Christians.*"

In truth, Garrison thought that Lovejoy had attracted violence by arming himself and setting up a militia with the authorities' permission, even if only out of self-defense. At the same time, the fact that Lovejoy had abandoned the first principle of nonresistance—that is, to consider all governmental authorities equally alien to Christian beliefs—had cast an inevitable dark shadow on him and his work, in Garrison's thought.[10]

In the central years of the 1830s, Garrison was experiencing his most influential period within the American abolitionist movement as the unchallenged leader of the radical Garrisonians. Mazzini, in contrast, went through a profound crisis in which he questioned himself, his beliefs, and his tactics. His crisis did not explode in its full power until 1837, after he was forced to leave Switzerland, but its seeds were sown in events of 1833–34. After the hard blow the Young Italy cells in Piedmont and Lombardy had received in the summer of 1833, Mazzini, in Geneva, Switzerland, where he was mostly based in 1834, still considered using what was left of the Young Italy network to plot a general insurrection focusing on nearby Savoy, then part of the Sardinian kingdom. In his plan, Mazzini thought of coordinating an attack on Savoy led by a few thousands of his Young Italy volunteers from Switzerland and France, while at the same time fomenting revolts in the Sardinian army and navy—and also hoping for the help of French republican forces. However, Mazzini had too much trust in an unreliable conspirator called Giuseppe Gallenga, and he also had exaggerated ideas of both the number of volunteers—who, by the time of the invasion, on 1 February 1834, turned out to be only a few hundreds—and the spontaneous mutinies that he expected to occur in the Sardinian military. Ultimately, these factors, combined with Mazzini's forced acceptance of the incompetent General Girolamo Ramorino as head of the already small invading force, and also with the Sardinian authorities' advance knowledge of the plot, led to a complete failure of the strategy and to a subsequent repression that caused many to go into exile. Among them was a young officer in the Sardinian navy and member of Young Italy named Giuseppe Garibaldi.[11]

The 1834 debacle in Savoy had a profound effect on Mazzini, even though he himself was only briefly arrested and then released, because his connection with the events could not be proved. Still, in the following years, despite the setbacks, the number of Mazzini's followers continued to increase and his radically new ideas had a profound impact on the minds of many young idealists and revolutionaries such as Garibaldi. It is therefore appropriate to pause at this point and analyze in detail the main tenets of Mazzini's thought, so as to understand not just the reasons for its popularity among radical activists but also the features that made his distinctive brand of democratic nationalism novel and unique, both in Italy and in Europe—similarly to how Garrison's radical views were novel within American abolitionism. In 1833, in the already cited essay "I collaboratori della *Giovine Italia* ai loro concittadini," Mazzini defended himself from criticisms and clarified further his views and programs. The central idea in his thought was the belief that republican government was the only form of government that would ensure the "true freedom of the people" of Italy. He also favored republican government because the republic would be the result of a popular revolution aimed at establishing the "nation," a community based on the principle of associationism, which Mazzini derived from the French philosopher Claude-Henri de Saint-Simon. As Salvo Mastellone has noted, for Mazzini, who was inspired by the French Republic's constitutions of 1791 and 1793, the people coincided with "the totality of the individuals who formed the nation"—by which he meant the republican nation—freely and spontaneously; the nation protected the people's basic rights, among them the right to vote through universal suffrage, by aiming at the "improvement and progressive development of the social forces and of their activities."[12]

As Lucy Riall has effectively remarked, "Mazzini's republican and democratic vision for Italy represented a fusion of romantic socialist and Jacobin ideas." Nevertheless, in order to represent in the most effective possible way what he considered as the absolute ideal of a free unified Italian republic and also the absolute commitment that this great cause required, Mazzini chose to use religious symbols, metaphors, and images, mostly taken from Christianity; no matter how socialist and Jacobin his views might have been, he even went so far as reconciling God with his republicanism. In part, Mazzini's highly religious, and highly anticlerical, view was a result of his Jansenist upbringing, but mostly it had to do with his "religion of the nation," which different scholars have variously related either to the "civil religion" of Rousseau's *Social Contract* (1762), to Saint-Simon's "civic faith," or to a twentieth-century type of "political religion" of nationalism—even though Mazzini utterly rejected both nationalism and patriotism as aggressive ideologies and practices. As Caleb McDaniel has pointed out, Mazzini's rejection of both was somewhat comparable to the way Christian perfectionism as practiced by Garrison, and even more by his close friend and collaborator Henry C. Wright, led to the rejection of all types of nationalist attachment, in the name of higher principles of humanity but ultimately in view of the coming of God's Kingdom. Interestingly, according to Maurizio Viroli, who calls Mazzini "the most influential apostle of the religion of the homeland [*patria*]," Mazzini's idea of religion, which he intended as a progressive principle, rather than a cult, was that of a "faith that gave the strength to put in practice the moral ideal, and as such regenerated the people."[13]

However, Mazzini went further than that, and in an 1835 essay on the concept of nationality, published in *La Jeune Suisse,* he wrote, "Nationality is the role that God assigned to a people. . . . It is their mission . . . the work that gives them their rights to citizenship within humanity." Thus, one of Mazzini's most famous mottos was "Dio e il popolo" (God and the people), which, for Simon Levi Sullam, meant that "the Mazzinian nation . . . was imagined as deriving *at the same time from below* (the people), *as well as from above* (God) . . . in an inner and permanent dialectic between authority . . . and freedom." In explaining the same Mazzinian motto, Franco Della Peruta and Tiziano Tussi have further clarified that God was "the divine spirit that ought to guide political and social actions, a spirit of absolute commitment to the cause, while the people were not just the poor, or proletarian, classes' undistinguished mass, but rather a brotherhood" of all the free citizens of a free nation—a concept of harmonious class relations that, as we shall see, was profoundly antithetical to Karl Marx's contemporary ideas on class struggle.[14]

To be sure, in referring to "people's mission" and "humanity" and also to the basic rights protected by the republican nation, Mazzini was speaking in terms of universal principles, such as, for example, the love of liberty—a language that Garrison would have understood well. And, as Nadia Urbinati has remarked, the very characteristics of Mazzini's ideal republican nation made it universal, since it was based on "equality and association . . . the two principles that made Mazzini's nation the agent of a new cosmopolitan order." In this new order, as in the Carbonari's intentions, and differently from the eighteenth-century doctrines of cosmopolitanism, according to Maurizio Isabella, the emancipation of nations would lead to the establishment of freedom and peace in the whole world. Still in Urbinati's words, Mazzini was "the political visionary who combined the Saint-Simonian religion of humanity and the Romantic ideal of nationality into a message that retained the universalistic temper of the Enlightenment"—a vision in which the legacy of Immanuel Kant's "cosmopolitanism of rights" was paramount. Based on these premises, Mazzini was never narrowly confined to the objective of creating an Italian republic; he was very instrumental in, and often an active force behind, the creation of many other movements of national emancipation. In fact, throughout his life, Mazzini did everything in his power to collaborate with activists and revolutionaries who sought to establish new nations with republican forms of government throughout Europe and beyond. In this universal view of his cause, he was comparable to Garrison, who did not hesitate to embrace the most diverse movements for reform far beyond the confines of American abolitionism.[15]

Where Garrison and Mazzini differed more profoundly in their thought was in their idea of violence, especially since for most of his life—though not all of it—Garrison was a convinced pacifist and supporter of nonresistance. Conversely, Mazzini did not hesitate to use or promote political violence to bring about change. Indeed, the very foundational act of Mazzini's ideal republican nation—whether it was in Italy or in another country—was expected to be a violent popular insurrection. But violence was also the result of a patriot's commitment to sacrifice his life for the sacred cause of the nation—an indispensable and totalizing commitment, in Mazzini's thought. In another 1835 article in *La Jeune Suisse,* Mazzini wrote, "Love the homeland; love it and strive to make it strong and sacred." As Alberto Banti has remarked, "the nation's 'resurrection' was supposed to occur through the 'sacrifice of its heroes, who were prepared to shed their own blood . . . experiencing a death which took on the religious character of a 'martyrdom.'" Yet, no matter how much Mazzini cast the patriots' deaths for the national cause in religious terms, their deaths were still very much political acts committed through violence and, as such, would have had no place in Garrison's mostly apolitical and nonviolent views.[16]

Among the general characteristics that Garrison's thought and Mazzini's thought had in common, perhaps the most important were their beliefs in the superiority of republican institutions as the only ones in which it was possible to exercise the right of engaging in true democratic debate and in the need for respect for and protection of the equality of all the citizens of the republican nation, regardless of class, gender, and race distinctions. In part, these convictions came from both Garrison's and Mazzini's continuous reliance on eighteenth-century Enlightenment and revolutionary universalist models, in which the figures of Thomas Paine and Immanuel Kant loomed much larger than that of Marx. From these assumptions and these legacies, then, derived the idea, in both Garrison's and Mazzini's cases, that the struggle for the amelioration of society was crucially important as a means to reach the goal of building a true and just democratic republic—a struggle that assumed in both cases highly religious tones.

However, when one moves from the general to the particular, it becomes clear that analogies between Garrison's thought and Mazzini's thought are increasingly difficult to find, and thus one should focus, instead, on comparing the many differences between the two views. Specifically, the two men differed strongly in their way of thinking about religion, if one excludes the fact that both were against the Catholic pope, and especially his temporal power. Garrison was a convinced Christian and an evangelical, like the overwhelming majority of those who engaged in all the great causes of radical reforms, including abolitionism, especially in 1830s Massachusetts and New England; Garrison's embrace of perfectionism, however, made him a minority radical also in the way he understood Christianity, even though it heightened his sense of absolute commitment to his cause and, in general, to the cause of freedom. Conversely, Mazzini, despite his Jansenist education—from which he mostly inherited his idea of a life's mission—had little time or sympathy for Christianity, even though he borrowed its powerfully suggestive images; yet, while he thought that "religion [was] subordinate to Progress, like everything else," he also believed in a higher God, who gave a purpose to the different struggles against oppression conducted around the world. Remarkably, though, Garrison's and Mazzini's moral commitment to their causes was absolute, whether it was derived from evangelicalism or from a progressive "civil religion" of a sort—and this might have been an important common element in the friendship that the two men established in later life.[17]

The American Anti-Slavery Society and Young Europe

During the biennium 1833–34, both Garrison and Mazzini transformed their regional struggles for the immediate abolition of slavery and for the creation of republican nations from local to continental affairs. With the creation of the NEASS and Young Italy, in fact, Garrison and Mazzini had succeeded in achieving a great impact with their revolutionary ideas, mostly at the local or regional level—in Garrison's case, mostly in the Atlantic Northeast within the nation-continent of the United States, and in Mazzini's case, mostly in the Italian peninsula and neighboring areas within the European continent. Both Garrison and Mazzini, though, had understood from the very beginning of their innovative paths—as early as 1831 in both cases—the wider implications of their struggles. They knew that to take full advantage of the impact of their novel ideas, they needed to widen their scope and move onto a higher level of radical activity. This was the sense and the main reason behind Garrison's foundation of the American Anti-Slavery Society (AASS) and Mazzini's foundation of Young Europe. Compared to the NEASS and Young Italy, in fact, the AASS and Young Europe—at least in Garrison's and Mazzini's plans—encompassed the whole of the United States and the whole of continental Europe, thus greatly broadening the impact of each man's revolutionary ideas and activities.

Both the AASS and Young Europe thus had a continental scope, even though in the case of the United States this scope identified with a single countrywide activity, given the continental dimension of the American nation, while in Europe it involved efforts to reach, in terms of activities and readership, several different countries at once. But there were also other affinities between Garrison's and Mazzini's continental projects. First of all, at the heart of both projects was the idea of widening the type of democratic debate—in one case the debate over the abolition of slavery and racial prejudice, and in the other case the debate over the features of democracy and of republican nations—that only republican institutions, whether already established or still to be established, could guarantee. Therefore, the projects of both Garrison and Mazzini had a strong element of expansion, and consequent radicalization, of different but related elements of the democratic discourse. Also, both projects, in their expansion of the democratic discourse, referred to a framework of federal republicanism, since the United States was already an established and flourishing federal republic and the Europe that Mazzini envisaged was based ultimately on a federation of the republican nations that would arise from the different democratic national movements. In this sense, we can say that the transformation that both Garrison and Mazzini put in motion in 1833–34 with the foundation of the AASS and of Young Europe was one in which their fight for freedom moved from the local level to the federal level.

By 1833 Garrison had become utterly convinced that to coordinate antislavery and antiracist action in a more effective way, he needed to make his struggle a national issue. Therefore he founded an organization that was not just local, or restricted to New England, but instead promoted activities throughout the federal republic of the United States. Such an organization was to be a particularly important new departure from previously established practices in American abolitionism, above all by being the first national abolitionist institution in America with immediatist aims; as such, it was to welcome among its members abolitionists with immediatist convictions from every state of the Union. As Garrison explained, "The guilt of slavery is national, its danger is national, and the obligation to remove it is national." In truth, the very first idea of a national abolitionist society had surfaced in discussions between Garrison, New York abolitionist Arthur Tappan, and others, among whom were some Philadelphia Quakers, at the First Annual Convention of the Free People of Color in Philadelphia, in June 1831, but nothing concrete had been decided. Then, for the following two years, while each main group of abolitionists worked in its own local setting—New England, New York, and Philadelphia—Garrison's conviction of the need for a national abolitionist society kept growing, but he had little success in convincing either New Yorkers or Philadelphians.[18]

In May 1833, Garrison left for his first trip to England, where, the *Liberator* explained, the NEASS sent him "for the purpose of procuring funds to aid in the establishment of the proposed MANUAL LABOR SCHOOL FOR COLORED YOUTH, and of disseminating in that country the truth in relation to American Slavery, and its ally, the American Colonization Society." Garrison's purpose, though, was also to establish a liaison with the British abolitionists, who were then at the height of their campaign for emancipation in the British Empire, so as to create a united radical antislavery front on the two sides of the Atlantic. In London, where "the *Thoughts on African Colonization* had earned Garrison a transatlantic reputation," he met with such renowned antislavery advocates as Thomas Clarkson and Thomas Fowell Buxton, the successor to William Wilberforce, whose funeral Garrison attended during this visit. He also succeeded in raising doubts about the ACS, while he even met the Irish "Liberator" Daniel O'Connell. Garrison remained impressed by the strength and organization of British abolitionism and by the major victory it was about to score in regard to emancipation. It was clear that the British Parliament was on its way to pass the bill that abolished slavery in the West Indian colonies. On account of this, when he returned from England in September 1833, Garrison felt motivated to push his fellow American abolitionists toward the creation of a national abolitionist society. It was helpful that the American public was favorable toward the British Emancipation Act when it passed in December 1833 (to become effective on 1 August 1834). Now the New York and Philadelphia groups finally yielded to Garrison's request to capitalize on the British success and convene a meeting to move forward with the establishment of an American abolitionist society.[19]

At the 4 December 1833 meeting in Philadelphia, sixty-two individuals—including Garrison's New Englanders, Philadelphia Quakers, New York associates of Arthur and Lewis Tappan, this latter by far the largest group, and three African Americans—signed the document founding the American Anti-Slavery Society, the first abolitionist organization in the United States with a national scope and immediatist aims. At this time, there were delegates only from the Northeast, but this situation changed within a year; already at the first anniversary meeting, in New York on 6–9 May 1834, delegates from the Midwest joined those from the Northeast. From then on, the AASS was no longer restricted to the Atlantic states; it was a truly national society in membership and representation. In practice, as Dwight L. Dumond has remarked, an important structural innovation in regard to the AASS was that "the principles of individual membership made this a national organization . . . whose delegates met at the annual conventions. Men in all parts of the free states were members of the *American Anti-Slavery Society*," while being, at the same time, also members of local abolitionist organizations.[20]

At the first meeting of the AASS, the delegates elected Garrison as the presiding officer, and he almost immediately set about drafting the "Declaration of Sentiments," together with New Englander Samuel J. May and Quaker John Greenleaf Whittier. In the "Declaration of Sentiments," which was largely inspired by his own thoughts, Garrison reiterated his main point that it was absolutely impossible for freedom and slavery to coexist in the United States. He referred to the Declaration of Independence and insisted that "the right to enjoy liberty is inalienable." More important still was how, in the "Declaration of Sentiments," Garrison related the cause of slave emancipation to much more general, universal principles, ideally joining American abolitionism with all the progressive struggles waged to ameliorate the quality of human life. Thus, abolitionism could be one with all the struggles for liberty in the Euro-American world and ultimately with the idea of a redemption that would follow from sacrifice and martyrdom—his thought was similar, in this sense, to Mazzini's thought—in the name of those great causes: "We will do all that in us lies . . . to overthrow the most execrable system of slavery . . . to secure to the colored population of the United States all the rights and privileges which belong to them as men and as Americans . . . whether we live to witness the triumph of JUSTICE, LIBERTY and HUMANITY, or perish untimely as martyrs in this great, benevolent and holy cause." Particularly significant, as this excerpt shows, was that in the "Declaration of Sentiments" Garrison maintained the struggle for black and white equality firmly at the heart of his message, together with the cause of slave emancipation. He saw such equality as just as important as emancipation, and he sought, ultimately, the recognition of full citizenship rights for African Americans.[21]

While the "Declaration of Sentiments" set forth the principles that inspired the AASS, the constitution of the organization declared as its primary objective "the entire abolition of slavery in the United States." As to how the AASS was to achieve this objective, the constitution stated that it would aim "to convince all our fellow citizens, by arguments addressed to their understandings and consciences, that slaveholding is a heinous crime in the sight of God" and "to influence Congress to put an end to the domestic slave trade, and to abolish slavery." Furthermore, the constitution also established as the AASS's aim "to elevate the character and condition of the people of color" and to "never, in any way, countenance the oppressed in vindicating their rights by resorting to physical force," thereby endorsing in full not just Garrison's principle of racial equality but also his condemnation of physical violence. Thus, it is fair to say that, at the moment of the AASS's creation, Garrison's and his followers' ideas on immediatism, interracial collaboration, and nonresistance constituted the dominant view and that, as a result, these ideas found perhaps their most complete expression in the two foundational documents of the AASS: the "Declaration of Sentiments" and the constitution.[22]

Spiritually headed by Garrison, while practically managed and mostly financed by Lewis Tappan, for the next four years the AASS saw its members dedicate themselves to converting to the abolitionist cause men of influence within northern public opinion—writers, editors, and clergymen—in addition to southern slaveholders. AASS members would engage in this effort at converting by employing moral suasion: they would show through various means the scandal and cruelty of allowing the existence of slavery on American soil, and they would then persuade sinners to repent. To Garrison and his followers, using the words of the "Declaration of Sentiments," the redeeming "power of love," together with the "potency of truth," were enough to generate "the spirit of repentance." With these premises, the AASS engaged in a gigantic campaign of moral reform, sending its members to speak against slavery and establish antislavery societies in towns and villages, while also publishing abolitionist pamphlets, tracts, and newspapers. Chief among the papers published by the AASS was the *Emancipator,* its official organ, established in 1833 and published by the Tappan brothers in New York under the editorship of Joshua Leavitt. It was soon joined by a growing number of other abolitionist publications, as the AASS's plans for moral suasion sharpened and unfolded.[23]

After two years of incessant publishing and speaking activity, in 1835 the AASS Executive Committee decided to engage in a Great Postal Campaign; the society would send four different monthly abolitionist journals, one for each week, to prominent northerners and southerners. The full pack included, according to Louis Filler, "a small folio paper called *Human Rights;* another, 'a small magazine with cuts,' the *Anti-Slavery Record;* still another, an enlarged sheet of *The Emancipator,* and a juvenile, the *Slave's Friend.*" Thus, northern businessmen and southern slaveholders alike were soon flooded with antislavery publications; by May 1836, the total number of antislavery publications issued reached 1 million. By then, the AASS massive postal campaign had prompted the legislatures of five southern states, Virginia, North Carolina, South Carolina, Alabama, and Georgia, to take antilibertarian action, supported by President Andrew Jackson, by censoring or suppressing abolitionist mail, and in the North, despite the enormous growth of antislavery societies, anti-abolitionist mobs were more active than ever. Still more was to come, though, as in May 1837 the AASS announced its forthcoming engagement in a National Petition Campaign. Long a favored standard tactic of abolitionist activists, both black and white, to protest against slavery through Congress, petitioning had already been used by AASS immediatists to request the abolition of slavery in the District of Columbia, where the U.S. capital Washington was located. A year after the beginning of the AASS petition campaign, petitions reached the number of 415,000, but with little consequence altogether, despite the monumental effort expended. In fact, already two years earlier, the House of Representatives had voted in favor of the "gag rule," according to which no parliamentary debate could be held on antislavery petitions.[24]

As Garrison understood the need to transform his radical abolitionist revolution into a nationwide enterprise in the United States, Mazzini also felt the need to widen the scope of his struggle; in his case it was by extending the fight for creation of an Italian republican nation to similar enterprises in the rest of Europe. It was Mazzini's experience of exile, and specifically his years in Switzerland (1833–37), that caused him to think of moving increasingly beyond the Italian national level. He eventually came to appreciate the continental dimension of the Italian struggle as akin to other fights conducted by other equally oppressed nationalities. Particularly important in this sense was Mazzini's contact with the Polish exiles, especially with Polish patriot and poet Adam Mickiewicz, who had been the heart and soul of the failed 1830 Polish revolution. From Mickiewicz, Mazzini borrowed one of the central concepts in the rhetoric of the Italian Risorgimento: the concept of the nation as a "martyr"—a martyr that one day would resurrect, as Christ did, to rejoice in final victory over its oppressors. As he reflected on his contacts with Polish and other political exiles from different parts of Europe, many of whom converged in Switzerland in the 1830s, Mazzini concluded that he ought to begin a new enterprise at the European level. But the seeds of Mazzini's new project had been sown with his famous 1829 essay on European literature, in which he had already advocated a common European culture that was to be the expression of the true needs of the European people as a whole. And to be sure, Mazzini had also thought about a Europe-wide revolutionary movement at the time he founded Young Italy; however, it was in Switzerland that finally, as Roland Sarti has remarked, Mazzini "extended the concept of cultural unity to the politics of revolution" at a European level.[25]

In fact, there is little doubt that, as Salvo Mastellone has argued, "to Mazzini, the Italian problem was connected to the cause of all the people of Europe." Therefore, the new European association through which Mazzini wanted to continue his revolutionary politics at the continental level was to be based on his principle of nation, or nationality, as he had applied it to the Italian case; moreover, the movement was to include primarily Germany, Poland, and Italy, the European peoples who had fought against Napoleon and had risen in revolt but had failed in 1830 partly because of the lack of help from France. These three peoples, as Mazzini wrote decades later, in 1863, "were not yet and aimed at being Nations," and therefore their struggles represented the quintessential types of oppressed national movements in Europe. Mazzini also considered them the guiding nationalities of Europe's "three families of peoples: the Germanic, the Slavic, and the Italic." In practice, Mazzini's idea was to create a politically revolutionary European federation called Young Europe, which included other national associations and movements akin to Young Italy. Initially, Young Italy–like associations were to spread mostly in Germany and Poland through the creation of a Young Poland (Mloda Polska) and a Young Germany (Junges Deutschland), to which Mazzini very soon added also a Young Switzerland (Jeune Suisse)—almost inevitably, given that Switzerland was the host country and that most of the political exiles who joined the three other associations gathered there. He did not anticipate creating similar associations in other countries, because at a later time, according to his vision, "Greece . . . Rumania, the Slavic countries of Southern Europe, Spain would have joined little by little gathering around the people closest to them among the three" original nationalities that had formed Young Europe.[26]

Based on those principles, on 11 and 15 April 1834, after Young Poland and Young Germany were formed, three groups of Italian, German, and Polish representatives—seven each for Italy and Poland, and five for Germany—founded Young Europe by signing an "Atto di Fratellanza" (act of brotherhood) and a "Statuto" (charter), both of them devised and written by Mazzini himself. In the "Statuto," Mazzini clarified the structure of Young Europe, which was to be directed by a central committee and was to welcome new member national associations into its federation. In the "Atto," Mazzini stated clearly the principles that had inspired him in his enterprise—principles that Young Europe's new members were to subscribe to—again using words reminiscent of the American Declaration of Independence that Garrison would have been comfortable with: "We . . . men of Progress and Liberty, believing in the Equality and Brotherhood of men, in the Equality and Brotherhood of People, believing that humankind is called to proceed on a *continuous progress* . . . and that it cannot do so if not with the *active participation of all* its members, *in free* association . . . have signed the following . . . the federation of Young Europe." As Franco Della Peruta has remarked, "Young Europe was presented as the anticipation of the future Europe, a federation of free people that combined together the two terms of country and humanity." In fact, of the two degrees of Young Europe's membership, the lower focused on love for one's country and the higher on love for all humanity.[27]

Subsequently, in an 1835 article entitled "Dell'iniziativa rivoluzionaria in Europa" (On the revolutionary initiative in Europe), Mazzini clarified further the reasons behind the European scope of his initiative and its revolutionary aims, using prophetic words: "It is the old Europe that is crumbling. . . . It is the young Europe that rises" in an "era of social obligation" whose program is "God and humanity." In this new era, the European youth's mission was "*to redeem the people, knowing about the special mission entrusted to each of them, and whose completion . . . must form their individual character and earn them a right of citizenship in the Young Europe of the next century.*" In practice, Young Europeans were the ones who, through revolution, would fulfill the mission of national emancipation that God had assigned to each European oppressed nationality. Although Mazzini did not state it in the article, what he had in mind was for Young Europe to be the actual agent of change on a continental level, by coordinating and promoting the different revolutions staged by national movements throughout Europe. In this respect, even though Mazzini thought of a brotherhood and an eventual federation of democratic European nations, in itself Young Europe could not be and was not, as Roland Sarti has noted, the precursor "of European unity as we understand it today."[28]

However, Mazzini soon decided that in order for the insurrections to occur according to the principles he had established, and on such a vast scale, Young Europe ought to first spread and promote its ideas as a background. Consequently, in writing Luigi Amedeo Melegari in 1835, Mazzini called Young Europe's mission one of "propaganda . . . of faith, of apostolate, of humanitarian religion," but not yet of revolutionary action or insurrection. Thus, by 1835, Young Europe had become an association that aimed at gathering those, within the intellectual elite of Europe, who were closest to Mazzini's democratic ideas and who would have been, therefore, ideal candidates for educating the masses in republican and democratic nationalism. Mazzini's project of assembling young associations to represent the countries he thought of as the historical nations of Europe—which, apparently, did not always correspond to today's nations—did not become a reality, despite his repeated attempts to promote particularly a Young Russia, a Young Austria, a Young Spain, a Young Greece, and a Young France. And within Young Europe itself, there were conflicts between Mazzini and Young Germany, while Young Poland, headed by the radical Joachim Lelewel, challenged Young Italy's primacy, which Mazzini had taken for granted. As a result, Mazzini resigned from Young Europe's central committee as early as June 1835; Young Europe itself ultimately failed as a project, mainly because non-Italian nationals feared, in Della Peruta's words, "that it was nothing but an instrument in Mazzini's hands, which he would have used exclusively for his Italian plans."[29]

In subsequent years, Mazzini's idea of a young national association with progressive ideas continued to generate imitators, though mostly with little resemblance to the original, in both Europe and the Americas, notably Young Ireland and, more importantly, Young America, whose impact on the Democratic Party in the 1840s and 1850s United States turned out to be strong. But the truth is that, already by the summer of 1835, as Mazzini began publishing his short-lived new paper *La Jeune Suisse,* the project of Young Europe was in crisis. At the same time, the widespread and mistaken belief that Mazzini was still very much active as the project's head, conspiring toward a great continent-wide revolution, led the Swiss authorities to expel him from Geneva. Initially, Mazzini remained in Switzerland and went first to Gretchen and then Langenau, in the Jura Mountains. There, in 1836, he wrote an essay called "Interessi e principii" (Interests and principles), in which he argued his position of defending principles over interests in Young Europe and in other enterprises, and another essay called "Fede e avvenire" (Faith and future). In the latter essay, he called republicanism a religious faith and reaffirmed in highly religious tones his beliefs in God, in humanity, in the principle of free association, and in what he called "the holy alliance of the people," which he contrasted with the "holy alliance of the monarchs"—the Holy Alliance set up by Europe's reactionary powers at the beginning of the Restoration. This last period Mazzini spent in Switzerland was, arguably, the darkest time in his life. He was about to be forced again into exile in yet another country, after both Young Italy's and Young Europe's failures; understandably, his spiritual crisis reached new depths.

In what he called "la tempesta del dubbio" (the storm of doubt), he came to doubt not only himself but also the righteousness of his revolutionary project and even his compatriots. Yet, he somehow managed to keep himself from sinking into desperation, and by the time he arrived in London with his longtime friends the Ruffini brothers in January 1837, Mazzini was on his way to feeling restored.[30]

While Garrison's foundation of the AASS and Mazzini's foundation of Young Europe have much in common, there are also important differences between them. Doubtless, the most striking similarities have to do with the attention given, in both cases, to the link between the foundation of the particular association and its universal principles, not just its wider historical and geographic contexts. We can clearly see the attention that Garrison and Mazzini paid to this link, especially in the AASS's "Declaration of Sentiments" and Young Europe's "Act of Brotherhood"; remarkably, but hardly surprisingly, in one case the universal principles invoked were justice, liberty, and humanity, while in the other case they were liberty, equality, and brotherhood. This parallel in itself should prompt us to think about how similar the languages of progressive thought were in the United States and Europe and how much the abolitionist struggle and the democratic nationalist struggle borrowed from similar readings and ideas, implicitly acknowledging the commonality embedded in two parallel radical fights for freedom. It was this commonality that inspired both Garrison and Mazzini to begin thinking much earlier about their two missions in transatlantic terms. Yet, notwithstanding a common language of universal human values, Garrison's main radical abolitionist activity wished to influence public opinion by remaining outside the American political arena, and this desire was even stronger when the movement widened its scope and became national. Conversely, Mazzini's move to a Europe-wide context meant for him a Europeanization of his national and also universal political principles. This was a major difference; together with the different national contexts in which Garrison and Mazzini lived, it determined the different courses that their lives took subsequently.

All in all, Garrison's thought and Mazzini's convictions were similar in their abstract form, mainly because the universal principles that inspired both men in their struggles for two different but related types of freedom were the same. They were the principles affirmed first in the Enlightenment and then in the great revolutions of the late eighteenth century, the American, Haitian, and French revolutions: liberty, equality, and human dignity. The long wave of that extraordinary revolutionary period had not completely subsided yet, and it had prompted the subsequent revolutionary waves of liberal and democratic agitations in the 1820s and 1830s Euro-American world, in addition to the radicalization of the Atlantic abolitionist movement and activities that became focused on immediatism. Both Garrison and Mazzini were very much part of this world of revolutions and radical reforms inspired by the great conquests of the late eighteenth century, which in turn had inspired the universal principles that they proclaimed in founding the AASS and Young Europe and in writing the "Declaration of Sentiments" and the "Act of Brotherhood," which were perhaps the most complete affirmations of those principles.

However, even though they were looking back at examples of radical thought produced in the eighteenth century, in many other respects Garrison and Mazzini proved very conscious of the novelty of the nineteenth-century world in which they lived. Aside from their awareness of the importance of the press in forming the public opinion—an importance they repeatedly acknowledged by continuously editing papers and writing articles and essays—it was the way they considered the great democratic struggles that they were engaged in, one for the abolition of slavery throughout the United States and ultimately in the entire Atlantic world and the other one for the creation of democratic and republican nations throughout Europe and ultimately in the entire Euro-American world, that showed they were truly men of their century. In fact, both Garrison and Mazzini thought of their chosen causes and missions as indispensable, and necessary, in order for humankind to enter the path that led toward progress. It was always in the framework of progress—the quintessential nineteenth-century idea—that both Garrison and Mazzini saw their thoughts and activities, and it was in order to link their struggles with other progressive struggles that they ultimately widened the scope of their parallel radical fights for freedom in their different contexts.

4

CONFRONTING IDEOLOGICAL INERTIAS

Garrisonians, Mazzinians, and Their Enemies, 1838–1846

In the early to mid 1840s, while in the United States and Italy William Lloyd Garrison and Giuseppe Mazzini were being challenged in their ideas and strategies for the fight for freedom by other groups of abolitionists and democrats, the Euro-American world of reform was undergoing a crucial phase of high activism and change. This activism led to an immensely significant result in the form of the World's Anti-Slavery Convention, held in London in 1840, which Garrison and his fellow abolitionists attended. It was the crowning achievement of years of background preparation by the network of Atlantic abolitionism. In addition, extremely important struggles against imperial powers for the freedom of national republics occurred in Brazil and Uruguay, with enormous resonance in the entire Euro-American world. Italy was especially affected, thanks to the prominent role played by Giuseppe Garibaldi, with whom Mazzini was in constant contact. Even though rarely connected by historians, these two developments were definitely seen by contemporaries as parts of the wider fight for freedom against the ongoing oppression of peoples and nationalities by reactionary forces. The Euro-American community of Atlantic progressives on both sides of the ocean—a "virtual" community that included both Garrison and Mazzini—perceived them as related events and comparable struggles for the common cause of progress and against reaction.

In London, in June 1840, for the first time, hundreds of delegates representing the abolitionist movements of various Atlantic countries gathered at the first World's Anti-Slavery Convention to discuss the prospects for the radical fight against slavery. Even though the representatives were mainly from English-speaking countries and there was a disproportionately large number of British and American delegates, it was the first large-scale Euro-American effort, and it showed the world how far the network of Atlantic abolitionism had progressed and how much influence it had gained in the course of its ongoing battle against slavery. With British slavery defeated by the British Parliament's passing of the 1833 Emancipation Act, British and American abolitionists, together with other representatives, especially from France, turned their attention to the next task: bringing about the abolition of slavery in the United States. In this respect, within the international effort represented by the World's Anti-Slavery Convention, the American abolitionist movement had pride of place. This was true regardless of the divisions between Garrison's followers and his opponents that were, at that same time, causing a parting of ways in the AASS.[1]

There were disappointments because of conflicts and divisions between abolitionist groups that were highlighted at the World's Anti-Slavery Convention, especially when set against the high expectations of the meeting as the "sign of a new era," in Unitarian minister William Ellery Channing's words; but even so, the final decisions made at the closing of the convention succeeded in tightening the links between the different abolitionist movements within the Atlantic network. In practice, for the first time, the World's Anti-Slavery Convention attempted an explicit experiment of international abolitionist cooperation through coordinated strategies of using regional and national churches, presenting petitions, and distributing pamphlets, with the declared aim of influencing public opinion and putting pressure on the governments of different countries. In this connection, it is remarkable that, little more than a year after the 1840 World's Antislavery Convention, in the December 1841 Convention of London, Britain headed a group of five powers, also including France, Austria, Prussia, and Russia, that signed a treaty revising international law with a view toward the final suppression of the Atlantic slave trade. Equally remarkable is that in 1843 Atlantic abolitionists managed to hold one more World's Anti-Slavery Convention, in London again, which built on the achievements of the 1840 convention, though with less success.[2]

In those same years, when the Atlantic abolitionist forces regrouped and, with the two London conventions, acquired clearer features of a true international and transatlantic network, other fights for freedom occurred on the western side of the Atlantic, specifically in South America. Here, since the central years of the 1830s, the two largest countries, Brazil and Argentina, one an empire and the other a dictatorship, were pursuing comparable policies of governmental consolidation through aggrandizement. In each case the policy aimed mainly at the incorporation of peripheral areas into a highly centralized administrative system; but there were other goals, specifically, the defeat of potentially centrifugal movements, such as secessionist initiatives, and of attempts by sovereign countries to maintain their independence. A centrifugal movement occurred in 1834, when the province of Rio Grande do Sul rebelled against Pedro II's Brazilian Empire, originating a secessionist initiative nicknamed *farroupilha* (from *farrapos,* or "ragamuffins," the derogatory nickname given to the rebels) and creating a republic with a provisional government headed by Bento Gonçalves. Between 1837 and 1841, in exile after his mutiny in the Sardinian navy and his subsequent death sentence, Giuseppe Garibaldi joined the revolt and fought, together with other Mazzinians, for the Republic of Rio Grande do Sul and in the name of those ideals of universal freedom and equality that he had learned from Mazzini and Young Italy, of which he was a member. Then Garibaldi moved to Montevideo, where, since 1838, the independent Republic of Uruguay had been kept under siege by Argentina's dictator Manuel de Rosas. There, between 1841 and 1846, Garibaldi continued to fight in the name of those same ideals. In order to also make a clear contribution to the cause of Italian freedom, he created a group of Italian volunteers called Legione Italica, with whom he achieved some of his most famous victories in the war to keep Uruguay independent from Argentina, all the while maintaining contact with Mazzini.[3]

The significance of these parallel and contemporaneous developments—the occurrence of the two World's Antislavery Conventions in London and Garibaldi's fight for freedom in South America—is multifaceted. First of all, their synchronic nature and the fact that they occurred on two opposite sides of the Atlantic world were important, especially since Garrison's and Mazzini's contemporaries considered these developments to be closely related, parts of an ongoing worldwide struggle for the universal causes of freedom and progress. At the same time, it is particularly noteworthy, within the context of the present study, that these parallel developments saw, in different ways and degrees, either the direct or the indirect participation of Garrison and Mazzini in events that went far beyond the regional, continental, or even federal horizons of their previous efforts. In this sense, the two developments testify of a clear move by both Garrison and Mazzini, during the course of the 1840s, toward increasingly strengthening the internationalization that already characterized their radical perspectives and actions.

Discourses of Equality and Utopian Visions

The 1830s had been a period of great activity for the American Anti-Slavery Society, under Garrison's leadership. It was engaged in the great project of moral suasion, through which abolitionists attempted to persuade Americans of the moral necessity of slave emancipation by flooding the United States with antislavery pamphlets and the U.S. Congress with antislavery petitions. By 1840, as the failure of these tactics became apparent, internal divisions within the abolitionist movement caused Garrison's opponents to leave the AASS, which Garrison and the Garrisonians continued to lead, though with diminished influence on public opinion. It is undeniable, however, that Garrison's indefatigable activity in support of the abolitionist cause and his inspired editorship of the *Liberator* contributed greatly toward keeping the American people's interest firmly focused on the problem of slavery. Garrison's own prestige continued to rise in parallel with the rise of sectional conflict between proslavery and antislavery forces in the United States. Yet, for Garrison, slavery was hardly an isolated issue in American politics and society. In his view, the fight against the greatest sin of all ought to be part of a much larger program of radical national regeneration; in fact, the fight against all wrongs, from slavery to alcohol consumption to women's lack of rights, was a necessary and much-needed step toward the true democratization of American society and, together with that, toward salvation. All of those injustices, in Garrison's evangelical-informed and highly utopian view, were sins that tainted America's soul. This exceptionally wide-ranging idea of reform and democratization was at the heart of the great difference between Garrisonian and non-Garrisonian abolitionists within the AASS and the ultimate reason for the great division of 1840 between the two currents.

In those same years, Mazzini was going through the early period of his exile in London. Here, in 1839, after he had been forced to cease Young Italy's activities in 1834 as a result of continuous persecution by the authorities, and only two years after reaching England, Mazzini managed to resume Young Italy once again. In London during the 1840s, Mazzini quickly became the most respected political exile in England. These years saw him plotting revolutionary actions in Italy and, at the same time, engaging in social activities for Italian workers and befriending prominent English intellectuals and politicians. However, Italy's democratic front—which, until then, Mazzini's mostly uncontested leadership had succeeded in uniting—began to show clear signs of internal divisions (something similar to what happened to the abolitionist front in the United States), as a result of increasingly strong opposition expressed by other democrats toward Mazzini's idea of revolution and his tactics and strategies for the creation of an Italian republican nation. Criticisms of Mazzini focused particularly on the manifestly scarce attention he paid to the enormous social problems caused by the existence of a large mass of illiterate peasants and on his preference for the North of Italy, rather the Italian South, or Mezzogiorno, as the place to start the national revolution. It is fair to say, however, that, even though these criticisms were real challenges to Mazzini's leadership, the radicalism of his ideas and actions was still, in the early 1840s, the most popular source of inspiration among Italian revolutionaries. In a comparable way, Garrison's radical ideas and actions continued to be a very popular source of inspiration among American abolitionists.

In the late 1830s, the differences between Garrison and the Garrisonians, on one hand, and their critics and opponents, on the other, reached a point of no return. The great project of moral suasion had failed amid the hostility of northern and southern public opinion and the passing of the "gag rule" in Congress. The project had been inspired by Garrison, and the project's objectives had much to do with Garrison's own vision of a universal type of moral reform and purge of American society as a whole, though one to be conducted individual by individual. The failure of moral suasion showed that Garrison's expectation that sinners would convert through their own conviction and rid themselves of sin was based on a highly utopian premise. The failure also revealed how much Garrison's idea of a universal moral reform for the American nation entailed at its core a truly radical view, according to which slavery was but the most important and urgent sin and social problem to deal with, among several problems. Garrison's view stood in plain disagreement with that of his opponents, all staunch supporters of evangelical orthodoxy and moderation, who had the much narrower view that slavery was the only real problem in American society. Moreover, to Garrison, the way forward in the achievement of the ultimate objective of total reform was, increasingly, an attitude of nonresistance to the measures and provisions of a human government that he deemed unjust, because it oppressed women and slaves alike. Thus, unlike their opponents, by maintaining their radical attitude of nonresistance, Garrison and the Garrisonians wished to engage in moral struggles on a variety of fronts, from slavery to gender; they actively sought to coordinate collaboration between the abolitionist movement—represented primarily by the AASS—and many other reform movements, the principal one being the women's rights movement, which they deemed equal in significance to abolitionism.[4]

An important achievement in modern scholarship on abolitionism has been to highlight the crucial role of women in abolitionist activities. In the words of Herbert Aptheker, abolitionism "was the first great social movement in U.S. history in which women fully participated in every capacity: as organizers, propagandists, petitioners, lecturers, authors, editors, executives, and especially rank-and-filers." Women had been present at the foundational meeting of the AASS in 1833, and in that same year Lydia Maria Child had published her famous *Appeal in Favor of That Class of Americans Called Africans.* In the 1830s, women's antislavery organizations proliferated both in the Northeast and the Midwest, and they were usually very interracial in character, gathering black and white members alike. Modern scholarship has also clarified the roots of women's rights activism in women's abolitionist activities, as well as the nature of the opposition to both by male supremacists. For his part, Garrison, since at least 1832, had clearly shown his sympathies toward women's involvement in abolitionist activities and beyond. That was when he expanded the original edition of the *Liberator* by adding a column of news from the female antislavery societies; at the same time he placed in the masthead the British icon of the pleading slave with the inscription "Am I Not a Woman and a Sister?" He soon became convinced that the antislavery struggle epitomized the denial of rights to women as much as the oppression of African Americans.[5]

In the January 12, 1838, issue of the *Liberator,* Garrison wrote a poignant article titled "Rights of Woman," in which he stated unequivocally that "both sexes are ultimately to stand upon the dead level of humanity, equal in rights, in dominion, in honor, in dignity, in renown. They are far from occupying this position now. . . . Women are almost regarded as household appendages.—Their rights and liberties are entrusted, to a fearful extent, to proud and tyrannical men." By then, also prompted and inspired by the influence of Sarah and Angelina Grimké, who were tireless antislavery and women's rights activists, Garrison and the Garrisonians—in plain contrast with the Tappan brothers and also with Ohio's prominent abolitionist Theodore Weld—had come "as close to being sexual egalitarian as was possible in antebellum America," according to Ronald Walters. In fact, still in Walters's words, "from 1837 onward, participation of women in all kinds of general antislavery work became a fixed principle" for the Garrisonians. It is worth quoting an 1839 letter from Rev. Horace Moulton, a revivalist clergyman and convinced anti-Garrisonian, to Amos Phelps in order to understand the prevalent mind-set on the "woman question" among Garrison's opponents: "I hope the next Annual meeting [the annual convention of the AASS] will be held at Worcester. . . . It sickens me to think the Massachusetts Board will send *females* as *delegates* . . . and I am *surprised* that any female can have affrontery [*sic*] enough to *go*." Significantly, Moulton stated, "I am for having women enjoy their rights, but also [do] not wish to have them claim the prerogatives of men." In the end, despite Moulton's fears, the 1839 AASS annual convention gave the same privileges to male and female members. Shortly afterward, at the May 1840 meeting in New York City, feminist Abby Kelley became the first woman elected to the AASS Executive Committee, an event that precipitated the schism between Garrisonians, who wholeheartedly supported her, and their opponents in the organization, who refused to recognize her.[6]

The gender issue was hardly the only matter of division between Garrisonians and their opponents, though. Equally important was the issue of direct participation in politics. In regard to this, perhaps, Garrison's utopian vision of how to reform American society revealed its full extent. As far as Garrison was concerned, true reform entailed a reform of consciences, a "universal emancipation" from sin, so as to bring about, through the perfectionist example of nonresistance to unjust human institutions, the Kingdom of God on earth. Also for this reason, while he denounced the exploitation of workers by the privileged rich, Garrison tended to stay away from all the activities staged by labor organizations such as the Workingmen's Party; to him, those were political rather than religious fights, and also they often led to deplorable acts of violence. As Garrison had written as early as 1831, "It is the highest degree criminal . . . to exasperate our mechanics to deeds of violence, or to array them under a party banner." We should notice, however, that Garrison and the Garrisonians, especially Wendell Phillips, later mostly supported the British workingmen's movement of Chartism. That movement arose in England from the 1838 publication of the *People's Charter,* which asked the British Parliament to implement six particularly radical reforms, among them universal adult male suffrage and abolition of property qualifications for members of Parliament. Yet, Garrisonians rejected the Chartists' arguments that white "wage slavery" was similar to black slavery and, effectively, that the exploited working poor and the slaves were similar. More importantly, the Garrisonians also refused to agree with the Chartists' principle of condoning physical violence in the achievement of their aims, all of which were clearly as much social as political. In fact, Garrison's utopian view of social reform could not and did not contemplate either the violence generated by class struggle—it looked instead for a harmony between employers and employees—or direct political involvement; neither of them, nor human government for that matter, had much to do with the inner change of the individual souls at the heart of the radical evangelical doctrine of perfectionism.[7]

If the anti-Garrisonians might still have agreed with Garrison's attitude toward labor, they certainly would not have agreed in regard to direct political involvement. Not only were AASS leaders such as the Tappan brothers, James G. Birney, Elizur Wright Jr., and Henry B. Stanton utterly convinced that the battle for reform had to focus exclusively on slavery; they also thought—especially given the failure of the project of moral suasion—that it was time to move to direct political action in order to more effectively support the abolition struggle. A letter sent by Reverend Orange Scott, a revivalist Methodist clergyman and an anti-Garrisonian, to James G. Birney in April 1839 illustrates the tensions, close to the breaking point by this time, over this issue: "There *must* be a new [abolitionist] organization in this state [New York] and I believe we are about ripe for it. . . . Garrison's peculiar notions are corrupting the cause. . . . The 'no human government theory' should be entirely separated from abolitionism." With this in mind, the anti-Garrisonians attempted a purge of the nonpolitical members and also of the women's rights supporters within the AASS, but with little success. Garrison's followers stood their ground, fending off any attempt to force them into direct political involvement. In a May 1839 letter to the editor of the *Emancipator,* Garrison wrote eloquently: "Abolitionists have but one work: it is *not to put any body into office,* but TO SET RIGHT THOSE WHO MAKE OFFICERS. . . . The great end at which we aim is to subvert the relation of master and slave—*not by machinery,* POLITICAL OR ECCLESIASTICAL, but by establishing in the hearts of men a deep and wide-spreading conviction of *the brotherhood of the human race.*" Thus, by 1840, Garrisonians were convinced more than ever that both slavery and human government were unjust institutions to be opposed with nonresistance activities, rather than by any type of outright participation in politics.[8]

In the end, however, it was the "woman issue"—with Abby Kelley's election to the AASS Executive Committee—that provided the pretext for a parting of ways between Garrisonians and anti-Garrisonians in 1840. The separation was as much about gender issues as about politics. After the 1840 division, Garrison remained the unchallenged leader of a smaller, apolitical, version of the AASS, one wholly devoted to gender equality. The Tappan brothers founded the American and Foreign Anti-Slavery Society (AFASS), a new abolitionist organization that was more male-dominated, while Theodore Weld refused to belong to either organization, considering them both corrupt to some extent, although he still continued his abolitionist activity. The more politically militant among the abolitionists went on to join the Liberty Party, an abolitionist political organization founded in November 1839 by former AASS members.[9]

Just as Garrison, in his leadership of the AASS, faced internal divisions within the American abolitionist movement, in the late 1830s and early 1840s Mazzini encountered serious challenges as leader of the democratic movement that aimed at establishing an Italian republic. Initially, the challenges to Mazzini came specifically from his followers and imitators in southern Italy. There, in the Bourbon Kingdom of the Two Sicilies based in Naples, ever since the 1833 wave of arrests by the Bourbon authorities, which had seriously damaged the activities of Young Italy, the association's local cells had acquired a large degree of autonomy from Mazzini under the leadership of Giuseppe Ricciardi. Ricciardi was eventually arrested in 1834, before his plan for a general insurrection in the South could take place, but the tradition of a Mazzinian movement somewhat autonomous from Mazzini lived on in the activity of Benedetto Musolino, a young Calabrian Jacobin who, in that same year, founded a secret society named I Figliuoli della Giovine Italia (Young Italy's sons). As the name implied, Mazzini's

Young Italy and Musolino's I Figliuoli had much in common: both societies sought to establish a republican Italian nation characterized by justice and equality. In addition, both men maintained an absolute moral commitment to the cause they had embraced. However, Musolino's Jacobin origins led him toward a much more radical critique of the disparities of wealth between the rich and the poor—so evident in the southern Italian countryside—than Mazzini's own, and toward a solution of the problem much closer to socialism than even Mazzini's most extreme revolutionary views, since Musolino emphasized the necessity of communal property.[10]

In its first four years, Musolino's I Figliuoli mainly worked in the background, waiting for the right time to strike; in 1836–37 his society was even forced temporarily to disband. However, in 1838, just a year after a large wave of popular unrest had hit the Bourbon Kingdom, Musolino began his association's activities again, extending them far beyond the original nucleus in Calabria, all the way to the Bourbon capital Naples. With his actions and his views, Musolino proposed a clear strategic alternative to Mazzini's northern-based plans, an alternative focused on an *iniziativa meridionale* (southern initiative). Musolino's plan was based on the suppositions that the large masses of oppressed southern Italian peasants were most likely to react to a revolutionary spark by joining in a general insurrection against the Bourbon monarchy and that they would also eventually support the creation of a republic. This strategy focused on the southern initiative, together with Musolino's socialist ideas, was a major challenge to Mazzini's plans and to his standing in the democratic movement. Moreover, Musolino was not the only democratic activist who supported the southern initiative. Since 1839, from his base in Malta, Nicola Fabrizi had been forming a special group of volunteers called Legione Italica (Italian legion), inspired by Carlo Bianco di Saint-Jorioz's 1830 pamphlet arguing that guerrilla warfare was the only type of warfare fit for a movement of national liberation. Like Musolino, Fabrizi was enthusiastic about the idea of the southern initiative, and he wrote in 1843, regarding the proposed national insurrection, "The Kingdom of Naples is the only possible basis, [while] Sicily is its rearguard and its depot." Because they were serious challenges, both Musolino's and Fabrizi's positions certainly had an impact on Mazzini, and they, along with the failures of his own initiatives, forced him to reconsider some of the premises of his own strategies in the early 1840s.[11]

In March 1838, a little more than a year into his exile in London, Mazzini had written a letter to his mother in which he confirmed, despite the setbacks and disappointments, his determination to continue to fight for his life cause, no matter the consequences. Significantly, in that same letter, Mazzini referred explicitly to the troubles of American abolitionists, whose cause of liberty was worth fighting for as much as the cause he himself felt compelled to put his heart and soul into: "The first men who preached against the enslavement of the poor negroes were derided and persecuted as they still are, shamefully, in some regions of republican America; yet, how many tears of poor negro mothers did those sermons dry in the end?" Mazzini expected that those who fought for the freedom of the Italian and European people would be persecuted as well, but in the meantime they could give a comparable hope to oppressed nationalities. Armed with a new resolve, after two years of virtual revolutionary inactivity, from his base in London Mazzini decided in 1839 to reorganize Young Italy; the society's second official foundation occurred on 30 April 1840.[12]

Even though the name was the same as the 1831 association, the new Young Italy was different from its earlier version in many respects. Mazzini still counted on some of the same collaborators, and he still addressed the young as the most significant sector of Young Italy's membership, calling them to exercise their "thought and action" as they joined him in his well-known "republican, popular, unitarian creed" for the establishment of an Italian nation, as he wrote in the *Circolare per la ricostituzione della Giovine Italia* (Document for the reconstitution of Young Italy). However, in response to criticisms of Mazzini's heavily centralized revolutionary activities, Young Italy's structure was now much less hierarchical, with a large degree of autonomy left to its local sections. Among those sections, together with the ones present in Italy and in the various European countries filled with Italian immigrants, sections that became particularly important were those in New York and in Montevideo, Uruguay; these two sections drew the bulk of the Italian exiles in North and South America. In particular, at the head of the Montevideo section in the early 1840s was the activist Giovan Battista Cuneo; among his tasks was to keep Mazzini well informed on Giuseppe Garibaldi's extraordinary military exploits in defense of the freedom of the Uruguayan Republic and on his attempt to promote the cause of Italian nationalism through his Italian Legion volunteers.[13]

The new Young Italy also had a focus on education and an emphasis on women and workers that the previous association had lacked. In regard to workers, this emphasis was partly a response to the criticism that Mazzini's strategy had seemed to be little concerned with the plight of the masses; now Mazzini placed their education at the very center of his plans. However, as Lucy Riall has noted, Mazzini's "new interest in working-class politics, expressed in the reorganization of Young Italy, clearly reflect[ed] the influence of Chartist associational life." Mazzini's early sojourn in London had coincided with the peak of activity of working-class radicalism in Britain and Chartism—a movement that, as we have seen, also had an influence on Garrison. Thus, it is not surprising that Mazzini created the Union of Italian Working Men and a new section of Young Italy and also started a new paper called *Apostolato Popolare* (People's apostolate), specifically targeting workers and promoting their education. In the paper, which ran for three years, Mazzini talked at length of an "ordinamento speciale per gli operai" (a specific constitution for workers); he justified it as part of the necessary preparatory work for a national revolution whose social aim was "moral and material improvement for everyone," not just the middle class, in that spirit of harmony among all the classes and cooperation between them that he thought a truly national movement needed in order to be successful. Mazzini's view, therefore, was profoundly opposed to the socialist idea of class struggle and was instead similar to Garrison's convictions. Mazzini's program of organization and education sought to make workers as autonomous as possible, so that they would be able to attend to their children's needs. One feature of his program was the creation in 1841 of a free Italian school in London for the children of workers. In a letter he wrote to Elia Benza in 1840, Mazzini expressed very meaningfully the break that this activity represented from his previous practices. He said, "We have, in the first period of our life, worked for the People, not with the People. We need to do it now."[14]

In practice, Mazzini's actions had limited effects beyond the lives of Italian immigrants in London, but his idea of a renewed democratic movement with a strong basis in the working class was immensely important, although it was little understood by other Italian democrats. Equally important was the new attention he showed toward the role of women in Italy's national revolution. Much like Garrison, Mazzini had always welcomed women and they were always among the supporters of his revolutionary efforts, particularly now in London, where upper-class English women showed eagerness to help the Italian cause. But in line with the most advanced ideas of his time, he thought women ought to find a way to become autonomous by participating in exclusively female associations. By doing this, Mazzini thought, women would emancipate themselves and achieve the long-sought equality with men, which he advocated as much as Garrison did; thus, women would be able to participate in their own right in Italy's national and republican revolution. To be sure, in Mazzini, this advanced thought coexisted with a somewhat contradictory tendency to see the woman relegated to her assigned gender role of "Angel of the Household," an idea that fit with the general culture of the family that characterized the Risorgimento image of the Italian nation. Yet, Maria Pia Roggero is correct in noting, "It is around Mazzini that for the first time in Italian history women of the most diverse social proveniences found themselves working together . . . for . . . the cause of the national redemption" and then, later on, "for woman's dignity and social role," which Mazzini continued to support even long after the creation of the Italian nation.[15]

Both Garrison's and Mazzini's radical views were wide-ranging visions of equality expressed through programs that were not just revolutionary but also, in many ways, ahead of their time and little understood by the men's contemporaries, even some of their fellow activists. Garrison envisioned an American democratic republic in which not only was slavery nonexistent, but also—equally important for him—both racial equality and gender equality were commonplace. Mazzini looked toward an Italian democratic republic in which members of all the classes had all they needed to live and act as full citizens (either they would able to produce what they needed or it would be given to them) and in which women were recognized as equal to men. It is striking to see how radical and advanced the two men's views of a progressive society were and how much in common they had in envisioning, truly ahead of their time, full gender and racial equality as a crucial component of a future democracy. The fact that the activities of radical female activists in America and Italy were drawn to Garrison and Mazzini was certainly a clear proof of that. At the same time, it is also important to notice that, partly because of the two activists' parallel radical support of gender equality, radical female activists from Harriet Martineau to Margaret Fuller—to cite just two prominent names—who participated in the transatlantic exchanges of a very flourishing, though only incipient, Atlantic women's rights network, were influential in maintaining contacts between the American and European milieus to which Garrison and Mazzini belonged, and in some cases, they maintained the actual contact between Garrison and Mazzini themselves. This was certainly the case of the daughters of their mutual friend William Henry Ashurst.[16]

Despite their radical character, though, it is undeniable that both Garrison's and Mazzini's visions contained highly utopian elements, above all in the way the two dealt with, but failed to address fully, the major social problems that agitated the nineteenth century. In particular, in both cases, despite the clear influence that the British radical workingmen's movement of Chartism had on both men, the sources of class struggle were mostly overlooked, and the revolutionary potential of working-class oppression—which the Socialists later exploited in full—was submerged within a call for, and an expectation of, harmony and cooperation across class divisions, no matter how sharp these were. This utopian feature, among others, certainly contributed decisively to ensuring that Garrison's and Mazzini's programs of redemption for the American and Italian nations, and the construction in both cases of a perfect society, remained difficult—if not outright impossible—to transform into realities. This same utopian feature was in large part responsible for the continuous challenges that Garrison and Mazzini met from other American abolitionists and Italian democrats whose projects tended to have a more realistic basis, either in terms of social strategy or of political action.

American Abolitionist and Italian Nationalist Cliques

In the central years of the 1840s, the challenges to Garrison's and Mazzini's ideas and strategies became more concrete and led, in both cases, to alternative views characterized by specific political programs. In Garrison's case, fellow abolitionists, but non-Garrisonians, convinced that Garrison's nonpolitical and wide-ranging project of reform could not result in any concrete achievement, gathered in a rival antislavery society or joined the Liberty Party, the first declaredly antislavery (and, in this case, abolitionist) party to enter the American political scene. In Mazzini's case, fellow democrats, convinced that his revolutionary plans that focused on the North and included little care for the masses had few hopes of success, turned to a strategy centered upon the southern initiative, while attempting to rouse the poorest and largest sector of the Italian peasantry in the South—as in the notorious case of the Bandiera brothers. Both Garrison and Mazzini responded to these challenges by taking into account some of the criticisms but ultimately by mostly standing their ground, so that by the mid-1840s the highest point in the crisis of each man's leadership had passed; by then they had managed to regain a great deal of their former positions of prominence and authority within large sections of the two movements.

In 1840, shortly after Garrisonians and non-Garrisonians parted ways in the AASS, William Lloyd Garrison traveled to England to participate in the World's Anti-Slavery Convention, due to commence in London on 12 June. Since Garrison's previous visit and the passing of the Emancipation Act in 1833, British abolitionists had continued to be active, protesting against "apprenticeship"—a forced-labor system that continued to bind former slaves to their former masters—and eventually obtaining its termination in 1838. The following year British abolitionists, led by Quaker Joseph Sturge, founded the British and Foreign Anti-Slavery Society (BFASS), with the purpose of eradicating slavery throughout the world. They enthusiastically accepted the proposal advanced by Joshua Leavitt, a collaborator of Garrison's in the AASS, of issuing a general call for delegates to a World's Anti-Slavery Convention, or World's Convention, to be held in London in 1840. The World's Convention was, according to Douglas Maynard, the first "attempt to strengthen and enlarge the crusade against slavery by drawing together into one combined effort the abolitionist forces of the mid-nineteenth century." Garrison was among the first to recognize this novel feature, and he manifested his expectations in a letter to Oliver Johnson: "The object of the Convention is not the gratification of an impious ambition, but the promotion of the cause of philanthropy and religion . . . to enforce the great, self-evident, pervading truth . . . that oppression and slavery, under all circumstances and modifications, in all climes and among all people, are in opposition to the will of God, and in opposition to the interests of our race." In the end, the World's Convention hardly represented the entire world, since the majority of the 409 delegates were from Britain and its territories, while only 40 were from the United States and fewer than 10 were from other countries, among which was France. Yet, even if the preponderance of Britons, as well as the BFASS's insistence that the official title of the meeting ought to be General Anti-Slavery Convention, led to disappointment among American abolitionists, the effort was clearly worthwhile.[17]

The discussions held during the thirteen days of the World's Convention focused on abolitionism in the United States and led to a better coordination of antislavery activities, mostly between Britain and America, through the use of the press, antislavery resolutions, and church networks. Yet, Garrison left the World's Convention with much disappointment, despite these important achievements and also the renewal of his contacts and his new acquaintance with important European progressives, especially Irish abolitionists Daniel O'Connell and Richard Davis Webb and British radical lawyer William Henry Ashurst. Because he needed to attend the May 1840 AASS meeting in New York City, Garrison arrived in London after the World's Convention had already started, and he discovered, to his chagrin, that the female delegates from Massachusetts and Pennsylvania had been excluded from the discussions. In fact, from the very first day, the issue of women's participation had been a focus of attention, especially because of the number of female delegates sent from the United States, among whom was Lucretia Mott; despite Wendell Phillips's efforts to the contrary, the BFASS London Committee had decreed that women were not allowed to take active part, only to assist from the balcony of the hall where the World's Convention took place. Both as a sign of protest and in support of women's rights, Garrison and the Garrisonians decided to join the women in the balcony, an act that earned him the admiration of female abolitionists and activists. Shortly after the end of the World's Convention, Garrison eloquently expressed his disappointment at the lack of democratic practice, writing, "On the score of respectability, talent and numbers, it [the World's Convention] deserves much consideration, but it was sadly deficient in freedom of thought, speech and action, having been under the exclusive management of the London Committee."[18]

According to James B. Stewart, the episode of the 1840 London World's Convention revealed that Garrison's "latest formulation of reform theology—perfectionism, non-resistance, and women's rights—did not compel the automatic assent that the slogans of immediatism once had, and neither did his claim as a prophetic leader of nonresistant perfectionism." In other words, the events at the World's Convention highlighted the fact that, with the creation in 1840 of two main abolitionist groups, the AASS, based in Boston, and the AFASS, based in New York, Garrison could no longer claim to represent all the American abolitionists; in fact, according to some scholars, including Gilbert Barnes, Garrison's Boston group might not even have been the more influential of the two. However, Garrison and his followers were still the most radical branch of American abolitionists, and he effectively headed the most radical association within the American abolitionist movement and the one that had more contacts with abolitionists abroad, though also fewer resources. Moreover, even though, after 1840, the AASS was forced to cease publication of the *Emancipator*—it was now the official organ of the AFASS—it produced an entirely new broadsheet, the *National Anti-Slavery Standard,* which quickly became very influential. And only a year later, Garrison could celebrate the tenth year of publication of the *Liberator,* still the most radical abolitionist paper in the United States.[19]

To be sure, Garrison's radical approach was clearly evident, not just through his extreme positions in regard to women's rights, as his attitude at the London World's Convention testified, but also—and equally so—in his approach to race, as his early acquaintance with Frederick Douglass indicates. The first meeting between Garrison and Douglass occurred in 1841, when Douglass, who had escaped from slavery in 1838 and since then had become a subscriber to the *Liberator,* gave a speech attended by Garrison at the Bristol Anti-Slavery Society in Massachusetts; they then traveled together to an antislavery meeting in Nantucket, where Douglass spoke in public for the first time. In the 1 July 1841 issue of the *Liberator,* Garrison described his meeting with Douglass, emphasizing the latter's powerful rhetorical abilities and, above all, his clear espousal of the cause of nonresistance and moral suasion, two pillars of Garrisonian thought. "His testimony," Garrison wrote, "was clear and empathic. The cause of non-resistance he declared to be divine, and essential to the overthrow of every form of oppression on earth." Based on this common ground, a collaboration between the two men arose and continued to thrive until the late 1840s. During that time, Garrison did everything in his power to promote Douglass as an abolitionist spokesman and a mainstream abolitionist writer. In fact, Douglass became a lecturer for the MASS, and in 1845 he published the first edition of his famous autobiography, *Narrative of the Life of Frederick Douglass,* which included a preface by Garrison.[20]

It was also at this time, in the early 1840s, that Garrison began to think of appealing to disunion as an antislavery tactic. As recent studies have shown, such as the ones by Caleb McDaniel and Angela Murphy, the inspiration came to Garrison from his transatlantic contacts with Irish activists, especially Daniel O'Connell. In 1841–42, O'Connell, who had just signed the Irish

Address, a document with sixty thousand Irishmen's signatures intended to appeal to Irish Americans to support abolitionism, was engaged heart and soul in his battle to obtain from the British Parliament the repeal of the 1801 Act of Union of England and Ireland. As Walter Merrill has noted, Garrison very likely thought something like this: "The Irish wished repeal of their union with England; Abolitionists should urge repeal of theirs with slavery." In fact, Garrison dedicated the editorial of the 6 May 1842 issue of the *Liberator* to the "Repeal of the Union"; it was in that same editorial that he first described the U.S. Constitution as a "covenant with death" and an "agreement with hell," because of its support of slavery—a statement that appeared in every issue of the *Liberator* and became the official position of the AASS from 1843 on. Thus, disunion became the most important tactical novelty in Garrisonian abolitionism in the 1840s. In a way, Garrison acknowledged that moral suasion was no longer enough as a tactic, but in another way, he also took to the extreme consequence his refusal of compromise over immediate emancipation that had characterized his ten-year-long abolitionist activity. Therefore, writing in language as urgent and as effective as the 1831 call to immediatism, in the 1840s Garrison launched his call for disunionism, with the 1844 motto "NO UNION WITH SLAVEHOLDERS!" appearing in issue after issue of the *Liberator.* By doing so, he appealed once more to the most radical abolitionist ethic, the one most opposed to organized politics, though not opposed to influencing politics from outside of it.[21]

In fact, Garrison's refusal of the Constitution was his ultimate refusal to engage directly in the political arena, since it meant that he recognized neither the government nor the parties as legitimate, simply because the whole system was founded on a document that supported slavery. However, while Garrison kept the Boston-based AASS well out of political action, the non-Garrisonians in the New York–based AFASS, which had separated from Garrison partly on the issue of direct political participation, did not waste time. Already at the time of the 1840 schism in the AASS, a group of non-Garrisonians that included, initially, Henry B. Stanton and James G. Birney had joined the Liberty Party, effectively the only political party with an abolitionist agenda, and Birney had been elected its president; a few years later, Arthur and Lewis Tappan also joined it. Despite rosy predictions that the Liberty Party would soon become a major political force, at the presidential election of 1840, Birney received only 7,069 votes, in a sense confirming Garrison's view that its importance was hardly what the New York–based abolitionists claimed it was. Yet, in the following years, while Garrison preached disunion and argued that "political action is not moral action any more than a box in the ear is an argument," Birney and the Tappan brothers saw the influence of the Liberty Party grow steadily in Ohio, Pennsylvania, and even Massachusetts. By the time of the next presidential election, in 1844, Birney gained 63,200 votes. This development reflected the growth of antislavery sentiment in the North, partly caused by widely followed cases such as the trial of the *Amistad*'s illegally enslaved Africans.[22]

But the truth was that the Liberty Party's platform in 1844 was broader than abolitionism. Liberty Party men stood for "Equal Rights" and "individual and social freedom," as Garrisonians did, implicitly rejecting the ideology of the Whig Party but also moving dangerously close to the Democratic Party, whose candidate James K. Polk, a Tennessee planter, the Liberty Party men, in the end, unwillingly helped to elect. Thus, on one hand, the Liberty Party's ideology—in its most idealistic aspects—was becoming closer to Garrisonianism. On the other hand, as Caleb McDaniel has shown, for all his antipolitical talk, Garrison was hardly apolitical; in fact, in Bruce Laurie's words, even "a close reading of *The Liberator,* and . . . his annual reports to the *Massachusetts Anti-Slavery Society* shows that he [Garrison] followed state and national politics ever more closely as the 1840s wore on."[23]

Even though Garrison did not meet Mazzini when he went to London to participate in the World's Convention, it is striking to think that they were both in London in 1840, although Garrison was there only for a few days, while Mazzini had lived there for the past three years. When he arrived with his friends the Ruffini brothers in 1837, Mazzini had not completely recovered from his self-doubting crisis, which worsened as a result of his beloved sister Cichina's death the following year. Also, even with the financial help that was guaranteed to him by the Rosselli and Nathan families, Mazzini initially found it difficult to earn a living in a way that allowed him to continue his fight for Italian freedom and cover the large expenses the cause required. Luckily, Mazzini soon began collaborating first with *Le Monde* and then with John Stuart Mill's *London and Westminster Review* and a few other journals, for which he wrote articles especially on contemporary literature, articles in which he tended to express his own patriotic ideas. Thanks to the contacts he acquired through this activity, Mazzini became acquainted with Thomas

Carlyle and his wife Jane, and despite the contrast between Carlyle's elitist views and Mazzini's radicalism, by 1840 Mazzini was a regular visitor at their house, where he met several important personalities of the time; he also attracted the sympathy of important women activists and, in turn, began to support the British women's rights' movement. In many ways, London was the perfect place for Mazzini to maintain an international network, to participate in democratic debates, and to make the cause of Italian freedom and republicanism known. In truth, it took him a relatively short time to begin taking advantage of the extraordinary possibilities offered to him by the city where he was going to spend most of the rest of his life.[24]

It was in 1841 that Mazzini began the activities of his free Italian School for workers' children at Hatton Garden, in London, after being asked to do so by a group of workers. As Mazzini wrote to his mother in September 1841, the classes, mostly taught by other Italian political exiles, occurred on weekday evenings and were based on "reading and writing . . . grammar . . . geography . . . arithmetic, elementary geometry, and mechanics"; other classes on Sunday afternoons were dedicated to readings in "Morality, National History, etc." An interesting feature was that a large meal celebrated the opening of the school every year, and, according to Roland Sarti, "Mazzini insisted so that the teachers, including himself, served the students and their families in a democratic inversion of roles"; equally interesting is that Mazzini considered his school a model of his projected cooperation between the middle class, represented by himself and the other teachers, and the working class, represented by the students. But even though similar schools opened later in France and in the United States, the school's model of interclass cooperation certainly did not become an example that was followed in Italian society at large. Because of Mazzini's reputation as a revolutionary, British conservatives considered the school to be a cover for conspiratorial activities, but even so, its classes continued with success for quite a few years—in its heyday it taught more than two hundred children—and at least until 1848, it was an important meeting point for the community of Italian immigrant workers in London.[25]

In 1841 Mazzini came in contact with an American evangelical group called Christian Alliance, a sort of missionary society headed by the charismatic preacher Lyman Beecher. Beecher was the president of Lane Seminary, a convinced abolitionist, and an important early influence on Garrison, despite having fallen out with him in 1836. Thanks to his Jansenist upbringing, Mazzini had always been close to Protestants and was even more so after he began living in Britain. Therefore, in 1842 he attempted a cooperation between Young Italy and the Christian Alliance, based on the common objective of overthrowing the pope. In practice, according to the plan, the Alliance would give Mazzini copies of the Protestant Bible to smuggle into Italy and sell in exchange for weapons. Despite the plan's minimal success, the cooperation was significant in several respects. It may very well be the case, as Eugenio Biagini has pointed out, that it constituted "a Transcendentalist moment in the Atlantic Republican tradition," since, through the Christian Alliance, Mazzini, with his republican convictions, came into contact with the transcendentalist circle headed by Ralph Waldo Emerson, whose writings Mazzini clearly knew. The circle also included Margaret Fuller, an important American feminist and activist who later married an Italian and became acquainted with all the major figures of the Risorgimento. It was Fuller who made Mazzini well known among the transcendentalists, and it is clear that she held him in particularly high esteem, describing him in her writings as "far above the stature of other men" and "with a mind far in advance on his times." In turn, Mazzini found he had a great deal of intellectual curiosity for the complex world of antebellum American philosophy and reform movements.[26]

By 1842 Mazzini was regaining much of his former authority as the inspiration and head of Italy's democratic movement, although his residence in England kept him removed from revolutionary activities in this period. This strengthening of his position was occurring partly because of his personal charisma and his popularity in London's liberal circles as the acknowledged head of the Italian national movement. It was also partly the result of the reconstitution of Young Italy, a legendary name by then, and partly a matter of his continuing successful rise in fame. His identification with what many in Britain and in the United States perceived as a just struggle for Italian freedom was linked to his careful publicity campaign focusing on Giuseppe Garibaldi. In the early 1840s, Mazzini succeeded in transforming Garibaldi into a legendary Risorgimento hero and a selfless fighter for freedom who put into action Mazzini's revolutionary ideas and strategies; at that moment, Garibaldi was doing so in South America, with his stunning military victories, but, as Mazzini wrote in 1845, Garibaldi was going, "one day or another, to try greater destinies than dying in London or Montevideo." It is also true, however, that Mazzini's reputation suffered a blow in that same period, as a result of the ill-fated expedition of the Bandiera brothers. In 1842 Attilio and Emilio Bandiera, Italian officers in the Austrian navy, informed Mazzini of their membership in the secret society Esperia, which was committed to the cause of Italian independence; two years later, the two brothers left with nineteen patriots for Calabria, in southern Italy, where false information maintained that a revolt against the Bourbon monarchy was about to happen. When the two brothers were captured and executed by the Bourbon army on 25 July 1844, Mazzini was flooded with accusations of his responsibility in the matter, even though all he had done had been to encourage the Bandieras in their enterprise.[27]

Nevertheless, in 1845 Mazzini published an article titled "The Martyrs for Italian Liberty: Attilio and Emilio Bandiera," in which he called the two brothers "Apostles" and contributed crucially to establishing them as sacrificial victims for the Italian cause. At the same time, Mazzini accused the British government of having transmitted sensitive information that alerted the Austrian authorities to the Bandieras' intentions, after opening his private correspondence. A scandal ensued, and Mazzini acquired new fame as public opinion mostly stood by him, considering him a victim of a despicable British scheme aiming to maintain diplomatic friendship with reactionary Austria; in the *Times* (London), Carlyle went so far as to call Mazzini "one of those rare men . . . who are worthy to be called martyr souls." By that time, however, different challenges were coming to Mazzini from outside the democratic movement, since by the mid-1840s differing views and plans for the creation of an Italian nation were competing against one another. Particularly popular were two views antithetical to Mazzini's radical idea of an Italian democratic republic and therefore appropriately termed "moderate." Vincenzo Gioberti, in his 1843 book *Il primato morale e civile degli Italiani* (On the moral and civic achievement of Italians), founded the "Neo-Guelf" movement, arguing that through cooperation with Austria, the pope could become head of a confederation of Italian states, thus promoting Italian unity. For his part, Cesare Balbo, in his 1844 book *Delle speranze d'Italia* (On the hopes of Italy) argued that the Piedmontese Kingdom of Sardinia, given its tradition and strength in both army and bureaucracy, should guide the movement for Italian unity with its present Savoy dynasty. Although Mazzini dismissed both of these views, they were becoming increasingly popular, and they offered for the first time dangerous alternative solutions for the "Italian question" that were both nonrevolutionary and nonrepublican.[28]

In 1846–47, Mazzini published the *Thoughts upon Democracy in Europe,* one of his most famous and influential pamphlets. Its premises came from his early idea of creating a Europe of free nations. That was his vision as early as 1834, when, still in Switzerland, he founded Young Europe together with other Italian, Polish, and German refugees. More than ten years later, in the *Thoughts upon Democracy,* he came to link in a lucid and compelling argument—as if they were two faces of the same coin—the national movements that were then springing up all over Europe and were about to cause a continent-wide revolution only a year or two later, with a more general movement toward democratization of society. More than this, Mazzini saw the movement toward the creation of free democratic nations in Europe as utterly unstoppable. Thus, he viewed it in much the same way as Garrison viewed the movement toward slave emancipation and a general democratization of society in the United States. In a particularly revealing section of the *Thoughts upon Democracy,* Mazzini wrote, "The democratic tendency of our times . . . is henceforth no Utopian dream. . . . It is a fact, a great European fact, which occupies every mind, influences the proceedings of governments, defies all opposition." However, the truth was that in the world of the 1840s the construction of a Europe of free nations, each of them embodying Mazzini's highly democratic ideals in both social and political terms, was still as far from happening as was the full democratization of the United States; Garrison knew this well.[29]

In retrospect, in both Garrison's and Mazzini's cases, the idea of national regeneration was paramount and was accompanied by a highly teleological view, which justified equally uncompromising positions in the face of criticism, in the name of the great causes of freedom and democracy that were destined to triumph. Yet, the fundamental differences in the two radicals' religious convictions, outlined in chapter 3, also had a clear influence on their attitudes toward their nations during the troubled and divisive years of the first half of the 1840s. Thus, Garrison, faithful to his perfectionist beliefs, ultimately went so far as advocating disunionism, or the dismemberment of the nation, as the ultimate moral means to reject slavery in the United States, while Mazzini maintained until the end that the achievement of God's plans for national unity was the tenet at the heart of his struggle for the creation of a unified Italian republic. Yet, as Caleb McDaniel has pointed out, in advocating disunionism and "denouncing the Union," Garrison "was really calling for a nation founded on a united belief in liberty, a concept of nationality similar to Mazzini's idea that a nation required a 'unity of belief.'"[30]

For both Garrison and Mazzini, the early to middle years of the 1840s were also years of increasing openness to the world, as both men had experiences that allowed them to understand even better than before the international dimensions of their parallel struggles for freedom in America and in Italy. And in both cases, what characterized the enhanced understanding was the ever-increasing awareness of being part of an Atlantic world of reform, one in which progressive activists of different countries agitated for causes that were not only parallel but were linked to one another. In this respect, it is worth noticing that London and Britain assumed a particularly important role for both Garrison and Mazzini, not just for maintaining their established international contacts, but also for broadening their perspectives even more through their acquaintance with radicals and agitators like themselves. Thus, in a comparable way, Garrison's and Mazzini's experiences of the Atlantic and Euro-American dimensions of their struggles occurred through that extraordinary international milieu that London represented in the nineteenth century.

In Garrison's case, his trip to London in 1840—even more than the previous trip in 1833—and his participation to the World's Convention led to a better appreciation of the worldwide antislavery struggle of which American abolitionism was a part and within which the latter was one of the leading movements. At the same time, during that trip Garrison tightened his links with English, Scottish, and Irish abolitionists, while also becoming acquainted with representatives of other non-English-speaking nations, such as France, where abolitionist movements were becoming active. Garrison thus became even more fully aware of the importance of maintaining links and exchanges with representatives of the network of Atlantic abolitionism as the true radical vanguard of a worldwide antislavery movement. Mazzini, even though he did not have an experience as meaningful as the London World's Convention in the same period, also broadened his horizons and began thinking increasingly in a transatlantic dimension in London, as a result of different events. For Mazzini it was the 1841 contact with the American evangelicals of the Christian Alliance that gave him the opportunity to understand that his struggle for the cause of Italian liberty was not just an active and fundamental part of a greater struggle for European freedom, as he came to argue with unparalleled clarity in his *Thoughts upon Democracy in Europe,* but it also had an important role in a much wider context, one in which both Europe and the United States featured prominently.

Thus, afterward, Mazzini continued to look at events in the United States and at the American struggle for the establishment of true freedom and democratic institutions as important developments that were parallel to his own struggles, within an increasingly transatlantic and Euro-American dimension of the context in which the movements for people's liberation occurred. For his part, Garrison was already accustomed to looking at events in Europe in a similar way. Therefore, Garrison's and Mazzini's international experiences in the early 1840s became an indispensable background for their 1846 personal encounter. In fact, it was the awareness of being part of the wider, Euro-American and Atlantic, contexts of progressive struggles for humankind's liberation from oppression that stimulated in both Garrison and Mazzini the wish to become acquainted, given the fame both had by then acquired as radicals utterly committed to their causes.

5

BAPTISMS OF FIRE FOR NEW SOCIAL IDEAS

Political Defeat, Radical Intransigence, and Internationalism, 1846–1853

In the late 1840s, the Euro-American world underwent a major, though brief, period of transformation that involved various countries and regions and even produced, in some cases, positive permanent results. In general, throughout the European continent, the biennium 1848–49 saw major revolutions oust established regimes and proclaim the rights of people and oppressed nationalities to govern themselves. This series of extraordinary events had a worldwide resonance that reached the Americas, where other, equally momentous, transformations occurred at roughly the same time; those changes had contradictory outcomes. As a direct consequence of the European events, another great colonial empire, the French, proceeded to abolish slavery. However, on the other side of the Atlantic, the end of the 1846–48 war between the United States and Mexico literally reshaped the geopolitics of the American continent and opened an enormous territory in western North America to the expansion of slavery. While William Lloyd Garrison was merely a witness and a harsh commentator on events such as the Mexican-American War and the subsequent conflict over slavery's expansion in the western territories, Giuseppe Mazzini was very much at the heart of the events of the revolutionary biennium in Europe, and specifically in Italy. At its end in 1849, he found himself at the head of the short-lived Roman Republic, one of the most radical governments newly established. In both cases, however, it is important to acknowledge the influence of the wider context by placing the transformations occurring at the regional level in contrast and comparison with one another and against a Euro-American and Atlantic background. Garrison and the Garrisonians did this themselves by making reference and drawing parallels between the U.S. and European situations.[1]

Chronologically, it was the Mexican-American War, fought over the annexation of Texas, that occurred first, in 1846. The involvement of two major countries in the American hemisphere gave the conflict a continental dimension. However, the crucial importance of the war on a world scale, besides reshaping the map of the Americas with a large increase in the size of the U.S. territory and a drastic reduction in Mexico's, was its direct link with the expansion of slavery. Plantation slavery, the type that was practiced in Texas, was associated with cotton agriculture in the antebellum American South, which was then the most profitable agricultural region among those associated with the "second slavery" and was still progressing toward its highest levels of production. With the 1848 end of the Mexican-American War, the slave system, which in the previous decade—with the emergence of the immediatist tradition of Atlantic abolitionism and with the 1833 British Emancipation Act—had seemed under threat, proved once again as powerful as ever. Slavery was bolstered also by the strong influence of American slaveholders on governmental institutions and politics. Thus, Garrison was hardly mistaken when he identified slavery as the major problem in the United States and the one that would lead sooner or later to an irreconcilable division within the country.[2]

In this sense, it is particularly significant that the last major victory scored as a result of the long wave of immediatism that had characterized Atlantic abolitionism was the 1848 abolition of slavery in the French colonies. The French law that abolished slavery came as a result of different and concomitant factors, but one of the most important was the recent immediatist turn taken by the most important French antislavery society, the Société Francaise pour l'Abolition de l'Esclavage (French society for the abolition of slavery), and by its activists, especially Victor Schoelcher. There is little doubt that French antislavery activists began thinking concretely in immediatist terms as a result of their participation in the 1840 London World's Convention and, more generally, as a result of their increasing contacts with British and American abolitionists. Equally important among the factors leading to French emancipation, though, was that, with the revolution that began in Paris in February 1848, the French people overthrew the constitutional monarchy of Philippe d'Orléans and established the Second French Republic. One of the first acts of the republic's constituent assembly, which included among its members French abolitionist Victor Schoelcher, was to enact the law that ended slavery throughout the French Empire. The assembly thus freed almost 250,000 slaves and practically reinstated legal measures dating to the revolutionary period, when, in 1793, the Jacobins had already abolished slavery once in the French colonies.[3]

The establishment of the French Republic and the latter's abolition of slavery in the French colonies show us, perhaps better than any other event, how tightly linked were the twin issues of demand for a national government that expressed the will of the people and freedom from oppressive institutions—among which slavery was but the most extreme—in 1848 Europe. Significantly, Garrisonians were among the first to recognize this link as the 1848 events in Europe unfolded, and it was not just as a result of the French Republic's abolition of slavery; Garrison, in particular, long a foe of Europe's reactionary powers, rejoiced when people throughout the European continent began a series of seemingly endless democratic revolutions against their oppressors. In spite of its brevity, the European revolutionary biennium 1848–49 provided models for what democratic nationalism could achieve in different countries when based on republican principles, and thus on principles that were in direct opposition to the reactionary ideas that characterized the absolutist regimes of the monarchies and empires of the Restoration. Therefore, at the heart of the European revolutions was the very idea of need for democratic forms of government that respected the basic human rights that Mazzini had advocated for the previous twenty years—an idea that had already inspired the previous revolutionary waves and that now stirred the entire European continent for two years.[4]

During that biennium, the revolutionary forces managed to establish provisional governments in several countries. In the Italian and German states, in the Habsburg lands, in Hungary, in Wallachia, and in Poland, revolutionary governments held on for several months against the forces of reaction of Austria, Prussia, and Russia, managing to construct not just the embryos of national experiments in many regions, but also attempting more profound social transformations, at least wherever the most radical forces had a real chance to do so, as in Mazzini's Roman Republic. However, in almost every single instance, the provisional governments fell after a while, for similar reasons: more moderate forces took control of the national revolutions, typically when the latter were becoming too radical in their political and social programs. By the end of 1849, all the regions of Europe that had experienced revolutions returned to normality after the suppression of national and democratic movements, while the agitators who had headed the revolutionary upheavals, including Mazzini and Garibaldi, were all forced into exile. Even in France, where the transformation had apparently been more profound and had caused permanent legacies such as the abolition of slavery, the republic suffered a backlash soon afterward, when Louis Napoleon became president of France in late 1848, and it eventually fell with his infamous 1851 coup, which proclaimed the Second Empire under himself as Napoleon III.[5]

By then, the brief revolutionary period in Europe could be said to be truly over, because of the success of the widespread counterrevolutionary measures taken by Europe's reactionary forces; and yet the period's brief duration was indirectly proportional to its enormous worldwide significance. Nevertheless, Europe's counterrevolutionary backlash seemed to mirror closely events in the United States, where the Compromise of 1850 on the vexing issue of the western territories acquired from Mexico opened two of them to slavery and led to the implementation of a new, harsher, fugitive slave law, now also encompassing the North. Not surprisingly, Garrison and the Garrisonians thought the fact that the "slave power" ruled the American republic was just another proof that the entire Euro-American world had fallen once again into the hands of reactionary regimes. This was a view Garrison shared with Mazzini, whom he had met for the first time in London in 1846 and with whom he then began establishing a lifelong friendship based on a commonality of sympathy for democratic causes of freedom—a friendship that led to Garrison's outright support for the 1849 Roman Republic and, especially in the 1850s, even to Mazzini's collaboration with the *Liberator* through its publication of some of his abolitionist pieces.[6]

Garrison, Mazzini, and the Midcentury's Political Crises

The late 1840s and the early 1850s were crucial periods for Garrison and Mazzini. The political crises that occurred in the mid-nineteenth century in both the United States and Italy were directly related to the issues for which the two activists had agitated since the early 1830s: the abolition of American slavery and Italian independence and unity. In different ways and degrees, both Garrison and Mazzini saw confirmations of their predictions in the momentous events of 1848–49, the end of the Mexican-American War in the United States and the end of the revolutionary biennium in Italy. The events shook the very foundations of the societies that Garrison and Mazzini related to, and they led to crucial transformations that affected deeply the nature of the struggles and the causes to which the two had dedicated their lives. Those struggles were transformed into matters of primary national importance and, from then on, were impossible to ignore in the United States and Italy. In the late 1840s and early 1850s, even though plagued by the setbacks and disappointments caused by the internal divisions within the American abolitionist movement, Garrison became even more radical and intransigent in his abolitionist positions, while he also became increasingly more convinced and adamant about his moral condemnation of American society. He was progressively involved in a wide range of reform activities, primarily the recently formed women's rights' movement. At the same time, even though firmly opposed to his own group of abolitionists' direct involvement in politics, Garrison held on to his belief in disunionism and thus to the idea that the American Union simply could not—and should not, in his view—live with slaveholders within it. He was thus clearly pointing his finger at what was quickly becoming the main cause of the impending American Civil War.

In the same period, Mazzini became more involved in revolutionary projects that focused not only on Italy but also often had a European dimension. It was at this time that Mazzini reached the height of his European popularity and enjoyed his one opportunity to put his radical ideas in practice as head of the 1849 Roman Republic's provisional government. At the same time, though, Mazzini came to realize even more clearly that increasingly stronger differences in people's views and opinions regarding the present and future of the Italian nation created a separation between him and other Italian democrats, whether they were more or less radical than he was. This experience of growing opposition to Mazzini's republicanism within the Italian democratic circles is comparable to the experience of growing opposition that Garrison faced within the American abolitionist circles. Comparison highlights the fact that, even before the late 1840s, the two radical traditions that Garrison and Mazzini had initiated were rapidly becoming more complex and diversified. As a consequence, Garrisonian abolitionism and Mazzinian republicanism were bound to face increasingly serious challenges in the United States and Italy in due course.

In the United States, the slaveholding republic of Texas entered the Union in 1845, becoming the state of Texas. A few months later, reacting to a series of skirmishes along the Mexican border, President James K. Polk, a Tennessee planter, began a war with Mexico, which lasted from 1846 to 1848 and resulted in a victory by the U.S. troops. Garrison had predicted since 1842 that "a war with Mexico will be waged on various pretexts," all related to the slaveholders' designs to acquire Texas for the Union. When his predictions became true, Garrison was horrified and wasted no opportunity to condemn the war as "the most atheistical and impious . . . ever recorded on the gory pages of history," while he openly wished that the U.S. troops—which he thought of as the strong arm of the slaveholders—would be defeated. Just as the war began, though, in July 1846, Garrison left for his third trip to England, aiming to strengthen the ties between radical abolitionists on the two sides of the Atlantic at a time when the slave power seemed to be growing stronger than ever. The trip was a success in this sense, since, with the help of George Thompson, Garrison succeeded in creating the "first formally organized Garrisonian antislavery society, the Anti-Slavery League," an abolitionist organization opposed as much to the U.S. Constitution as to political abolitionism. Garrison spent the following three months touring Britain with George Thompson and Frederick Douglass, hoping to find support for the isolation of the proslavery American churches by attending the preliminary meetings of the proposed Evangelical Alliance and of the World Temperance Convention in London.[7]

The 1846 trip did strengthen once more specifically the ties between Thompson and Garrison, and with them their renewed efforts to maintain their commitment to an immediatist program of action within the tradition of Atlantic abolitionism, which Garrison had been championing since the early 1830s. In a letter Thompson sent Garrison in October 1846, the Englishman acknowledged Garrison's role in highly laudatory terms: "You have been arising the lukewarm to exertion and encouraging those who were already in the field to go on and persevere in the good work, which you and me have so much at heart. I trust the friends of the Cause of Freedom, on both sides of the Atlantic, will be encouraged, and will not cease to use every effort . . . to have this abominable system of 'Slave Holding' and 'Slave *Living*' swept off from the face of the earth." Coming six years after the 1840 London World's Convention and three years after its 1843 less successful follow-up, Thompson's words were a powerful reminder to Garrison of the work that Atlantic abolitionists such as the two of them still needed to be engaged in.[8]

By the time Garrison was back in the United States, in November 1846, American politics were in turmoil. The war with Mexico had exacerbated sectional conflicts between the proslavery and antislavery forces within the two major parties, the Whigs and the Democrats, and the conflicts were quickly bringing the Liberty Party to an end as well. It was becoming clear that as soon as the war ended, the major issue would be the presence or absence of slavery in the newly conquered territories. Thus, antislavery Whigs—or "conscience Whigs"—and Liberty Party men were becoming more vocal, rallying in support of the Wilmot Proviso, a proposal introduced by antislavery Democrats to stop slavery's expansion in the West. The Proviso never became a law, but as the war drew to a close, the United States acquired five hundred thousand square miles from Mexico; then as the 1848 presidential election neared, many Liberty Party abolitionists found that, despite the conservative and racist tones of the two major parties' antislavery supporters, they had no choice but to join the latter in a large antislavery coalition to keep slavery away from the western territories. Thus, the Liberty Party experiment ended and the Free Soil Party was born upon a platform solely of restriction of slavery, with no hint of either abolition or racial equality. Even some Garrisonians (especially, as Bruce Laurie has noted, "African American leaders who were openly identified as friends of Garrison"), seeing the urgency of the situation, had rushed to join the Free Soil Party, but Garrison seemed to show mostly contempt for their compromising attitude; in July 1848 he declared sternly in the *Liberator,* "It is an absurdity in morals to talk about the boundaries of sin," and he reaffirmed once again his motto "NO UNION WITH SLAVEHOLDERS."[9]

A year earlier, in 1847, Frederick Douglass had returned to the United States from a very successful continuation of the English trip he had started with Garrison, after having spent time also in Ireland; however, even though he was supposed to promote the Anti-Slavery League, in the end, as Richard Blackett has remarked, "in Garrison's absence what Douglass did was he raised his own stock rather than the *League*'s." At that time Garrison was making plans to extend his influence in the midwestern United States through a series of lectures that would take him through western Pennsylvania and into Ohio, traditionally the stronghold of Theodore Weld's moderate abolitionist group. Garrison invited Douglass to come along; in the end, the trip was hardly a success, since Garrison became so ill that, upon his return, he had to put Edmund Quincy in charge of the *Liberator* for a while. During the trip, Douglass began thinking of starting his own newspaper; its title was the *North Star,* and its publication eventually began in December 1847. Quincy had wished Douglass well on his enterprise, and

Garrison, though somewhat resentful and weary of possible competition, did the same in the 28 January 1848 issue of the *Liberator.* Thereafter he asked for support for Douglass's paper and even reprinted extracts from it over the next three years.[10]

Then in July 1848, Lucretia Mott and Elizabeth Cady Stanton led the first Women's Rights Convention at Seneca Falls, New York, effectively beginning the modern women's rights' movement. Current analyses correctly see a link not only between the women's rights' movement and the radical stance of Garrisonian abolitionists toward gender equality, but also between the 1848 Seneca Falls convention and both the 1840 division within the AASS and the 1840 World's Convention in London. In both of the latter cases, in fact, the "woman issue" had been divisive, and Garrison, with his uncompromising position, had done much to make it even more so by drawing his supporters firmly to the female abolitionist side. Thus he made a crucial contribution to providing a future autonomous women's rights' movement with the recognition it needed. Having grown in experience within the ranks of Garrisonian abolitionists, several of the most famous women's rights' activists continued to share many of Garrison's own convictions, even his ideas of support for universal reform and worldwide struggle for progress and against oppression in any form. Thus, only a few months before the Seneca Falls convention, rejoicing at the proclamation of the French Republic in April 1848, renowned abolitionist and women's rights' activist Sarah Grimké could write, with words that Garrison would have entirely approved of, "France! France! . . . What a confirmation of the truth that the human race is progressive and that it is now progressing with a rapidity hitherto unexampled." In the end, Garrison did not participate at the 1848 Seneca Falls convention, but there is no doubt that his example as one who was in the vanguard in the fight for women's rights loomed large. The convention produced a "Declaration of Sentiments" very much in the spirit of the Garrisonian AASS document with the same name. The following year, from the pages of the *Liberator,* Garrison began to give immediate and wholehearted support for the first campaign waged for women's suffrage.[11]

At the presidential election of 1848, Free-Soil candidate Martin Van Buren received fewer than three hundred thousand votes—hardly a serious challenge to Whigs and Democrats—and did not help disentangle a situation in which sectional conflicts over the expansion of slavery were becoming increasingly unmanageable. Two years later, the major representatives of the proslavery and antislavery constituencies agreed on the Compromise of 1850, according to which the United States admitted California as a free state, two new territories were created in the West—New Mexico and Utah—open to slavery on the basis of popular sovereignty, and slave trade was prohibited in the District of Columbia. It is no wonder that the abolitionists cried against the victory of the slave power, also given the compromise's most outrageous provision: the new Fugitive Slave Law, which bound both federal authorities and northern citizens to collaborate in the capture of runaway slaves, with severe penalties for those who did not do so. Sadly, the public outcry by the abolitionists led to a recrudescence in mob actions, which went so far as disrupting the reception of English abolitionist George Thompson. In November 1850, Thompson came to visit Garrison and celebrate with him the twentieth anniversary of publication of the *Liberator,* scheduled for January 1851.[12]

In the speech he delivered on the occasion of the actual anniversary, 1 January 1851, Garrison commented somewhat bitterly on the continuous opposition he had faced specifically from his northern brethren ever since he had started his abolitionist crusade, although he was utterly convinced his cause would triumph in time. "The truth," Garrison wrote, "is they who start any reform which at last grows into one of surprising magnitude are always ill judged. . . . At the outset they are looked upon with utter contempt and are treated in the most opprobrious manner. . . . In due season the cause grows and expands and advances to its . . . triumph." Yet, more disappointment was in store for Garrison. Less than a year later, it was the turn of the great Hungarian nationalist Louis Kossuth to tour the United States; against all the abolitionists' expectations, Kossuth proclaimed that he would refrain from talking about American domestic affairs, including slavery. This prompted Garrison to write a long public letter to the Hungarian—first published in the *Liberator* and then as a pamphlet in 1852—protesting against the latter's behavior.[13]

As it happened, Louis Kossuth was not the only one with whom Garrison had broken his relationship on account of differences of opinion in that period. After the *North Star* changed its name to *Frederick Douglass' Paper,* in 1851, the relationship between Garrison and Douglass became increasingly difficult, because Douglass had elaborated an antislavery interpretation of the Constitution and had publicly repudiated Garrison's proslavery interpretation of it at the AASS annual meeting. In the first of a series of editorials in the *Liberator* in 1853, Garrison called Douglass "an altered man in his temper and spirit," one in whom the "curse of worldly ambition is the secret of his alienation." Their relationship went quickly downhill until, eventually, it was beyond repair—sadly, mainly because of Garrison's morose resentment at what he wrongly thought of as Douglass's disloyal conduct.[14]

By then, though, Garrison's attention was focused on what was, for the abolitionists, the most important literary event of the decade: Harriet Beecher Stowe's publication of *Uncle Tom's Cabin.* The novel had appeared first in serial form between 1851 and 1852 in the *National Era,* the official journal, at the time, of the anti-Garrisonian AFASS, dominated by Lewis Tappan and James Birney. As the novel's last chapters were being published, Garrison wrote a review of *Uncle Tom's Cabin,* which he published in the 26 March 1852 issue of the *Liberator.* Though impressed by Stowe's "descriptive powers," her "acquaintance with slavery," and her "uncommon philosophical acumen," Garrison also had criticisms to make, especially in regard to the portrayal of Uncle Tom himself. While Garrison acknowledged that Uncle Tom "triumphantly exemplifies the nature, tendency, and results of CHRISTIAN NON-RESISTANCE," he thought it strange that, in the novel, all the slaves were represented as passive and meek, and he asked himself very pointedly, "Is there one law of submission and non-resistance for the black man, and another law of rebellion and conflict for the white man?" In saying this, Garrison, always the radical supporter of racial equality, substantially accused Stowe of what George Fredrickson has termed "romantic racialism"—a somewhat crypto-racist victimization of black slaves by many abolitionists. For example, William Ellery Channing portrayed American slaves as "the mildest and gentlest of men, and therefore incapable of rising up in arms."[15]

While in the United States the late 1840s proved crucial in increasing the stakes in the conflict over slavery, as a result of the Mexican-American War and the acquisition of the western territories, in Italy the same period saw the brief, but momentous, peak of a high tide of democratic nationalism. Akin to what happened in most of continental Europe, the tide swept through the entire Italian peninsula, leading to revolutions that, in the course of 1848–49, succeeded in overthrowing several Restoration governments. It is fair to say that, for the past several years, no one had been better preparing than Mazzini for the momentous events of 1848–49; remarkably, at the end of 1847, according to Denis Mack Smith, Mazzini's "expectation was that the great European revolution might break out in three or four months' time." In fact, Mazzini's continuous attention to the European dimension of what he saw as a continent-wide struggle between the forces of progress, which Italy ought to lead, and the forces of reaction, unmistakably led by Metternich's Austria, shows clearly when one looks at the sheer number and diversity of Mazzini's activities in 1847; among these, together with the publication of the full text of *Thoughts upon Democracy,* the most important was the foundation of the People's International League in London. Recalling the earlier experiment of Young Europe, the People's International League was an attempt to gather all the progressive forces—liberal, radical, and republican—present in the British capital and represented by members of different European countries; effectively, the mission of the People's International League was to create awareness in the British public and "disseminate the principles of national freedom and progress" throughout Europe.[16]

As in earlier years, Mazzini managed to combine his European vision with a more specific concern for Italy, renewing his commitment to the national Italian cause through another crucial foundational act. At the beginning of March 1848, shortly before the 1848 French Revolution overthrew Philippe d'Orléans and established the French Republic, Mazzini, who was in Paris and had been in France twice in the past months to meet with Young Italy's secretary Giuseppe Lamberti, decided to dissolve Young Italy altogether and create, instead, the Associazione Nazionale Italiana (National Italian association). By then, unthinkable changes had already occurred in several Italian states—notably in the Papal State, where the recently elected Pope Pius IX had promoted mildly liberal reforms, prompting even Mazzini to write him a letter and ask him to guide the movement for Italian freedom. Also, in the Bourbon Kingdom of the Two Sicilies, in January 1848, the revolutions in Palermo and Naples had pressed King Ferdinand II into allowing the promulgation of a constitution; shortly afterward, Grand-Duke Leopold II of Tuscany; Charles Albert, King of Sardinia; and Pope Pius IX himself had followed suit. In the Associazione Nazionale's program, Mazzini took into account these extraordinary developments, and unlike what he did with Young Italy, he privileged "the idea of NATION" and the actual construction of "one nationality, free, independent" over the "pre-determined triumph of one or another form of government," thus effectively postponing until after Italian unification the crucial issue of what type of nation Italy would be, a democratic republic or a constitutional monarchy.[17]

In early April 1848, after learning that the population of Milan had risen up and forced the Austrian troops to leave the city and that Piedmontese king Charles Albert had declared war on Austria, Mazzini left London—where he had briefly returned—and traveled to Italy for the first time after seventeen years of exile. On his arrival in Milan, Mazzini was welcomed by a great deal of popular enthusiasm and was invited to take part in the Provisional Government established after the revolution. The most prominent republican members of the Provisional Government, which was dominated by moderate liberals, were two Milanese republicans, Carlo Cattaneo and Giuseppe Ferrari; although both were strongly democratic, they maintained substantially different views from Mazzini's on the Italian question. Both had trained as economists in Lombardy, then the most economically advanced part of Italy, and had a positivist view of history; thus, Cattaneo and Ferrari had little sympathy for Mazzini's distinctively religious ideas on the nation and the people. Of the two republicans, Cattaneo was the stronger supporter of federalism—in opposition to Mazzini's unitarian republicanism—in the construction of an Italian nation; he saw it as the only viable way to maintain Italy's regional identities. Ferrari also supported federalism but was much more radical than either Cattaneo or Mazzini, leaning, instead, toward socialism. Matters came to a head on the question of military help against Austria, for which Cattaneo and Ferrari looked to France, while Mazzini reluctantly looked to Piedmont, thinking of postponing—as he had proclaimed in the Associazione Nazionale's program—the issue of the form of government to the postwar period. What neither Cattaneo and Ferrari, nor Mazzini, were willing to accept was the annexation of Lombardy to Piedmont's Sardinian Kingdom; however, in May, the Provisional Government voted in favor of that action.[18]

The episode not only signaled the end of Mazzini's collaboration with the Milanese republicans but also led to his decision to oppose the dynastic war that Charles Albert had waged in order to form a northern Italian kingdom by means of a "people's war" conducted spontaneously by Lombardy's masses. To this end, on 13 May 1848, the day after the Provisional Government's decision, Mazzini founded a periodical called *Italia del Popolo* (People's Italy), which Franco Della Peruta has termed "the first daily paper of the Italian republican movement." From its pages, Mazzini opposed both the union of Lombardy with Piedmont and the federalist program and called the people to take the war of independence against Austria in their own hands and form their own government, since "only the constituent *assembly of the Italian people* can resolve our problem today." After the Piedmontese army signed an armistice with Austria in August 1848, at the end of a badly conducted military operation, and left Lombardy to its destiny, Mazzini hoped that his moment had come; thus, he wrote, "The king's war is over, the people's war starts." He joined Giuseppe Garibaldi—who had been given the command of the revolutionary forces after his return from South America—in the fight the general continued against the Austrians and attempted to rouse Lombardy's population. However, the war finished after a few weeks, and both Mazzini and Garibaldi were forced to take refuge in Switzerland.[19]

Toward the end of 1848, revolutionary governments with republican leaders still existed only in three cities in Italy: in Venice, under Daniele Manin; in Florence, under Giuseppe Montanelli; and in Rome, where Pope Pius IX had departed from the city under Bourbon king Ferdinand II's protection after the assassination of Papal State prime minister Pellegrino Rossi. As the pope fled, republicans seized the initiative and formed a constituent assembly that proclaimed the Roman Republic on 9 February 1849; a young Genovese poet named Goffredo Mameli telegraphed Mazzini with the words "Rome, Republic, Come." Thus, on 5 March, after stopping briefly in Tuscany, Mazzini arrived in Rome—a place that had a special meaning for him, since he believed that its historical mission was to give birth to a People's Rome, after the Emperors' Rome and the Popes' Rome. More than this, as Mazzini wrote in his *Autobiographical Memoirs,* "in Rome was the natural center of that [national] unity; and what was needed was to catalyze the Italians' attention and feelings toward that center." In truth, Mazzini hoped that the Roman Constituent Assembly would become the embryo of an Italian national parliament with representatives from all the regions; however, the representatives were mostly young patriots who wished to defend the freedom of the Roman people, fighting side by side with Garibaldi—now head of the Roman republican forces—against the French army that aimed at restoring the pope. Significantly recognized only by the United States, the Roman Republic held on remarkably until 4 July 1849; from the end of March on, Mazzini played a crucial part in it, having been elected head of the government's executive triumvirate, which included also Carlo Armellini and Aurelio Saffi.[20]

The text of the constitution of the Roman Republic approved by the assembly on 1 July 1849 and largely written or inspired by Mazzini testifies to the radical ideas that he did not hesitate to put into practice. The principles that had inspired the French Revolution, together with popular sovereignty, equality of all before the law, extinction of the temporal power and the privileges of the Catholic Church, and the state's guarantee to help the citizen "improve [his or her] moral and material conditions"—though not with measures leading to socialism—gave the Roman people their first democratic system of government in five hundred years. It is not surprising that both Mazzini and his contemporaries, including Garrison, always considered this experience Mazzini's finest hour, a brief but immensely significant period that ended in a glorious but tragic epilogue when the Roman Republic fell to the relentless French siege, despite a heroic and desperate defense by Garibaldi and his few thousand volunteers. After the Roman Republic's fall, Mazzini went to stay in Switzerland, and from there he attempted to reestablish a revolutionary network in Lombardy through the diffusion of the Associazione Nazionale and the distribution of his clandestine daily paper *L'Italia del Popolo*. However, while Mazzini's popularity had reached its peak during the 1848–49 revolutionary biennium, the national revolution's failure loomed large over him and forced him to come to terms with the strength of currents very different from his own within Italian democratic circles. Aside from Cattaneo and his federalist program, most critical of all were the republicans to the left of Mazzini, whose views were very close to socialist ideas. In particular, Neapolitan Carlo Pisacane, though recognizing Mazzini's leadership, wanted him to give more attention to the needs of the actual people, especially the peasants, while Milanese Giuseppe Ferrari looked to French socialism as the model to imitate; eventually, both Pisacane and Ferrari published pamphlets in which they described their ideas and looked back in that light at the events of 1848–49.[21]

Despite these criticisms, Mazzini continued to think concretely about enacting revolutionary change in both Italian and European terms, and in 1850 he created the European Central Democratic Committee in Paris, gathering French, German, and Polish republicans in the name of his old idea of the "Holy Alliance of the People"; later on, even famed Hungarian revolutionary Louis Kossuth, who had just fled from the Habsburg Empire, where he had led the 1848–49 Hungarian revolution, also joined the European Committee. At the same time, Mazzini also continued his work for Italy, creating in 1850 the Italian National Committee, which brought together British radicals and republicans who wished to contribute through a "National Loan" to the Italian cause. Then in 1851 he founded the Society for the Friends of Italy. In that same year, Mazzini published an important work titled *The Duty of Democracy,* in which he reinstated his faith in the republican and democratic principles that were the basis of a social program that answered the real needs of the people, and his opposition to socialism, especially that of French radicals such as Louis Blanc. In Mazzini's view, socialism was one of those "absolutist systems, which stepped at the same time on the individual's liberty, the country's sovereignty, and the continuity of progress." A year later, convinced that the revolutionary network in Lombardy was ready for action and that he was about to receive help from Kossuth and from the United States, Mazzini launched concrete plans for an insurrection, which was to occur in Milan on 6 February 1853. However, the Hungarians' help did not come—and as a result, like Garrison, Mazzini discovered he had little in common with Kossuth. In addition, an attempt to stir Milanese workers did not meet with success; it led instead to the Austrian government's harsh retaliation and to a subsequent decline in Mazzini's credibility within Italian democratic circles.[22]

Looking back at the late 1840s and early 1850s, it is undeniable that, for both Garrison and Mazzini, these were years of highly significant experiences and also of transformations and changes at different levels. As large-scale events such as the Mexican War and the 1848–49 revolutions occurred around them and they either witnessed them or became actively involved in them—continuing to maintain their consistent radical stances—Garrison and Mazzini saw their lives become even more closely linked to the causes of American slave emancipation and Italian republican unification that, by now, they represented in the eyes of world. Furthermore, as these events unfolded, both Garrison and Mazzini understood even more clearly—each in his own context and in different ways—how the progressive causes that they championed were part of a wider struggle for the deliverance of humankind that agitated the entire Euro-American world, from one side of the Atlantic Ocean to the other. In this respect, it is fair to say that the worldwide significance of the European 1848–49 revolutionary biennium was particularly clear to Garrison and Mazzini also because they were both part of a radical milieu of Euro-American and Atlantic progressives who were active in the global democratic struggle against the forces of reaction in many different countries.

In the late 1840s, this international radical milieu had had reasons to think that a new era of democracy was coming into being, with the 1848–49 European revolutions and with the abolition of French slavery decreed by another great European colonial power. Garrison applauded these developments; they confirmed his own prediction, ever since he was an apprentice at the *Newburyport Herald,* that the march of democracy and people's need for freedom—in America as in Europe—was unstoppable. Mazzini, who also saw his own long-term predictions on the inevitability of Europe-wide democratic national movements vindicated, rushed to join the revolutions as soon as he had a chance. By then, Garrison and Mazzini had met each other in person, and they followed the unfolding of the extraordinary events in Europe knowing that they shared a comparable view of the world and of the significance of supporting radical struggles for the ideals of freedom, republicanism, and democracy. Even though the subsequent reactionary backlash in Europe and the compromises over slavery in the United States in the early 1850s brought much disappointment to both, the connection between the two men continued, as neither of them ceased to think of himself as part of an ongoing international movement of support for the radical ideals they both believed in.[23]

Radical Internationalism and Transatlantic Exchange

In the summer of 1846, while he was in London, Garrison stopped by the residence of William Henry Ashurst. By then, Garrison had become well-known all over the world, thanks to his intransigent position on American slavery, his transatlantic abolitionist contacts in England, and his charismatic leadership of the AASS. The man Garrison went to visit, William Henry Ashurst, was a friend of his, a lawyer, a Christian thinker, and a politician. He was a man whose ideals knew no boundaries and who wholeheartedly embraced and supported different types of radical causes, including the struggle against slavery and the battle for women's rights. According to Henry Mayer, Garrison went to Ashurst's house in Muswell Hill in his June 1840 visit to London and there "met a number of liberal journalists . . . and interested the host—an admirer of Tom Paine and a friend of the socialist Robert Owen—in a subscription to *The Liberator.*" Thus, with a friendship established, Garrison was happy to pay a visit to Ashurst's house when he returned to London six years later. By then Garrison and Ashurst had also become engaged in a journalistic collaboration.[24]

Not surprisingly, at Ashurst's house Garrison met Mazzini, an activist no less famous for his intransigence and radicalism than Garrison himself, especially in Europe. At the time, Mazzini was in his ninth year of residence in London, having spent more than fifteen years in exile. In London, it was in the same liberal circles that supported Garrison's abolitionist struggle in the United States that Mazzini had become acquainted with many admirers of his commitment to the struggle for Italian liberty. Among those admirers, a particularly important one was Ashurst himself, a mutual acquaintance of Garrison and Mazzini, though at the time unbeknownst to them. According to Denis Mack Smith, it was only the previous year, in 1845, that Mazzini had "met the family of William Henry Ashurst, who became his closest friends in England." Thereafter, he spent most of his Sundays at the Ashurst residence in Muswell Hill. In short, during 1845–46, Mazzini had become a regular visitor at the Ashurst family house in London, where he had a particularly close relationship with Ashurst's daughters Emily and Caroline and where he had met politicians, agitators, exiles, and activists from different countries—a varied group of radicals that called itself the "Muswell Hill Brigade." It was thus particularly appropriate that the Ashurst residence was where the English lawyer's two distinguished American and Italian friends, Garrison and Mazzini, met for the first time in that summer of 1846, after hearing a great deal of talk about each other. We will never know for sure, but it is entirely possible that the meeting was not accidental, that Ashurst might have been eager to have the two great radical activists Garrison and Mazzini become acquainted with each other for the first time in his own house.[25]

As a matter of fact, Mazzini was already well known in American antislavery circles for being extremely sympathetic toward the abolitionist cause, since he had not kept secret his admiration for Garrison's uncompromising position on slavery, and he had not passed up any occasion to chastise the United States for allowing slavery to flourish upon its soil—a point that made him close to Garrisonian abolitionists, with their idea of slavery as a national shame. Mazzini became known among the abolitionists notably with his famous essay "Prayer for the Plantation Owners by an Exile"; the essay was published in the 1846 issue of an abolitionist gift book, *The Liberty Bell,* edited by Maria Weston Chapman, a close collaborator of Garrison's, and sold at the annual Boston abolitionist fair called the National

Anti-Slavery Bazaar, which was often, significantly, held at Faneuil Hall. In accepting the commission to write the essay, Mazzini claimed, "To write one or two pages on abolitionism is just the same to me as to have to prove that the Sun gives light and warmth, or to prove an axiom." And the "Prayer" was certainly a strong abolitionist piece; but in it, Mazzini did not forgo the chance to connect the American and the European struggles for liberty by writing about those "who endure and fight for the Good in Europe, and whose confidence is shaken by their [the planters'] stubborn crime." In other words, just as Garrison also thought, to Mazzini slavery was such a stain on American republicanism that the activists who fought for the creation of republics in Europe felt less strong in their convictions, as a result of it.[26]

To be sure, Mazzini was not the first Italian democrat to speak out against slavery. Cattaneo had already written publicly against it as early as 1833; yet he had favored a gradual, rather than an immediatist, approach to emancipation, and therefore he had alienated the abolitionists. Mazzini had always leaned toward the type of abolitionism favored by Garrison. For his part, Garrison knew about and sympathized with Mazzini's republican strand of nationalism, along with all the other democratic struggles against reactionary forces in Europe; he had also had occasion to see for himself, in his trips to England, that Mazzini enjoyed a high status among European radicals, such as the advocates of Chartism, the English workingmen's movement that both Garrison and Mazzini supported at different times. Significantly, Garrison always thought highly of Mazzini's republican nationalism, partly because of Mazzini's continuous support of abolitionist ideas and projects; in contrast, in 1851 Garrison broke with the other great European nationalist of the time, Hungarian Louis Kossuth, essentially because the latter failed to condemn slavery unequivocally for fear of alienating American support for the cause of Hungarian independence.[27]

In 1872, twenty-six years after their first meeting in London, Garrison remembered Mazzini with the following words: "He impressed me very favorably, not only by the brilliancy of his mind, but by the modesty of his deportment. . . . An exile from his native land, because of his lofty endeavors to rescue her from the degradation and misrule of ages, he strongly drew upon my sympathies. . . . There our personal friendship began, which revolving years served but to strengthen; *for, though our fields of labor were widely apart, and our modes of action in some respect diverse, we cherished the same hostility to every form of tyranny.*" The friendship between Garrison and Mazzini was going to last for many years. Even though the two did not actually meet again until 1867, more than two decades later, they continued to follow each other's activities and admire each other's commitment to their respective causes, and they even collaborated on a few occasions.[28]

Throughout those years, William Henry Ashurst and his daughters, being supporters of both Garrison and Mazzini, functioned as crucial links between the two activists. This was clear already in 1847, a year after Garrison's and Mazzini's first meeting in London, when Mazzini founded the People's International League, whose main aim was "to disseminate the principles of national freedom and progress." The president of the league was John Bowring, a prominent member of the British Parliament and a close friend of Mazzini's who was in correspondence with Garrison, whom he had met at the 1840 World's Convention in London. Among the leading members of the league was also Ashurst, who wrote Garrison how, with the league's foundation, "patriotism, elevated into love of the whole human race has now made its distinct and organized advent." Ashurst's article on the league's foundation appeared in the *Liberator,* confirming that Garrison wholeheartedly supported his friend Mazzini's initiative, particularly since he saw it as a further step in the cause of universal freedom.[29]

Afterward, collaboration between Garrison and Mazzini continued mostly through Ashurst's help and mediation; it led, first, to several endorsements of Mazzini and his republican politics and revolutionary deeds by Garrison and his collaborators in Garrison's own paper the *Liberator,* especially at the time of Mazzini's revolutionary government in the short-lived Roman Republic of 1849. During those crucial days, letters from Mazzini appeared regularly in the *Liberator.* In the 27 July 1849 issue of the paper, by way of introducing Mazzini to the American abolitionist public, Garrison placed before the first of Mazzini's letters published in the *Liberator* a short summary of the latter's life; there Garrison emphasized that Mazzini had "distinguished himself . . . by his writings, his general benevolence, and his love of liberty." Garrison thus explicitly linked Mazzini's struggle for a free Italian republic to the more general struggle for freedom, striking a particularly sensitive chord among American progressives.[30]

In the 1850s, numerous abolitionist pieces written by Mazzini were published by Garrison in the *Liberator.* Every time a piece by Mazzini appeared there, Garrison made sure readers knew who he was, by providing short introductions that always referred to the Italian revolutionary in extremely positive terms. Years later, in 1871, Garrison wrote a letter to New York philanthropist Theodore Roosevelt Sr., to hail "the completion of Italian Unity and the Emancipation of Rome," to the achievement of which Mazzini, whom Garrison called one of Italy's "profoundest of thinkers and noblest of advocates," had contributed a great deal. In the letter, Garrison spoke of "the long stride which the people of Italy have taken towards the assertion of civic and religious freedom," and he argued that "unification on this basis is an event to be hailed by all those who profess to worship at the shrine of liberty; and by none more enthusiastically than by the American people." In this way, Garrison clarified that the movement for Italian unification, by ending the temporal power of the pope, assumed a universal value of struggle for freedom, just as Mazzini thought, and that, even if for this reason alone, it had been worthwhile for him to support Mazzini's efforts in the previous decades. Significantly, Garrison closed the letter with words that Mazzini himself could certainly have written: "Yours, not only for Italian unity, but for the unity of all peoples in one sublime brotherhood of liberty, equality, fraternity."[31]

As a permanent testimony to the friendship between Garrison and Mazzini, soon after Mazzini's death in 1872, Garrison agreed to write the introduction to an influential collection of Mazzini's own autobiographical writings, *Joseph Mazzini: His Life, Writings, and Political Principles,* published by the New York publishing house Houghton & Hurd and edited by Emily Ashurst-Venturi, one of William Henry Ashurst's daughters, and aimed at an American readership. In that introduction, Garrison praised the Italian thinker and agitator, recalled his impressions of him, and explained what the two of them had in common in terms of thoughts and ideals. On the very first page of his twenty-five-page essay, Garrison recalled his first meeting with Mazzini and their subsequent lasting friendship. He also reproduced abolitionist letters by Mazzini that had been published in the *Liberator,* and he compared and contrasted the Italian nationalist with the Hungarian Louis Kossuth. Thus, Garrison's words are an invaluable and unusual window on Mazzini's "thought and action" in relation to his international antislavery activities. They are also the ideal starting point for an analysis of the reasons why Garrison, a prominent American abolitionist, found in Mazzini a natural ally in his attempts to involve prominent

European ideologues and activists in what he thought of as a transatlantic movement for freedom.[32]

At a very basic level of analysis, we could say that in virtue of their commitment to their respective causes—which, in both cases aimed at the emancipation of a subject population—Garrison and Mazzini epitomized the most immediately recognizable figures of freedom fighters for radicals all over the world. In this connection, it is important to notice that several of their contemporaries saw Garrison and Mazzini engaged in parallel radical struggles for freedom. Aside from Ashurst, among the most significant and prominent activists who were acquainted with both Garrison and Mazzini and sympathized with both of the causes they had embraced, we should include, first of all, transcendentalist and Unitarian minister Theodore Parker. A staunch supporter equally of Garrison's abolitionist efforts and of the 1848 European revolutions, Parker quoted Mazzini in his sermons and pamphlets so often that Joseph Rossi has said, "To Parker seems to belong the honor of having suggested the expression" "government of the people, by the people, for the people," which was first coined by Mazzini in 1832, to Abraham Lincoln, who had read some of Parker's sermons. More importantly, Henry C. Wright, a close collaborator of Garrison in the AASS and a regular contributor to the *Liberator,* met Mazzini in London in 1847 at Ashurst's house in Muswell Hill and reported that, in regard to Italy's national revolution, Mazzini "would make a stirring, active, and influential leader in such a revolution," much as Garrison was a leader in the abolitionists' moral revolution in America.[33]

The famous feminist intellectual and social scientist Harriet Martineau was also well acquainted with both Garrison and Mazzini and left interesting descriptions comparing the two. According to Henry Mayer, when Martineau first met Garrison in 1835, she thought he "ranked as the 'mastermind of the revolution' that would transform" the United States, since he had "molded the abolitionists into 'a body of persons who [were] living by faith'" and who were ready to be martyred for their cause. In her autobiography, Martineau described her impression of Mazzini, whom she first met in 1841, as parallel to the way she thought of Garrison in regard to his personal charisma and ability to attract followers as a result of his righteousness of character and moral commitment: "I entirely believe in all that his adorers say of the noble qualities of his heart and temper." Still, despite her admiration for both men for similar reasons, it is fair to say that, in practice, Martineau was very much more in favor of Garrison's nonresistant and pacifist tactics than of Mazzini's advocacy of revolutionary violence with its consequent loss of lives.[34]

Garrison and Mazzini themselves also recognized the parallels between their two radical causes. Thus, in his 1872 introduction to Mazzini's autobiographical writings, Garrison drew a parallel between all the democratic struggles for freedom, doubtless including implicitly the one for the abolition of slavery in America, when he wrote, "Within the last half century, Europe has produced some notable persons in connection with the cause of popular freedom; but at their head, above their utmost height, it seems to me, Mazzini is entitled to stand." For his part, Mazzini did everything in his power to create public awareness of the close link between the two issues of slave exploitation and national oppression, specifically by making analogies between the situation of his fellow Italians—as an example of an oppressed nationality—and that of the slaves.[35]

More directly, Mazzini wrote several letters to prominent antislavery personalities that were subsequently published in abolitionist periodicals in England and America. In them he clearly and repeatedly expressed his view of how closely related were the subjects of the liberation of the slaves and the liberation of oppressed nationalities. Mazzini's abolitionist writings increased in volume in the course of the 1850s, and this growing attention likely was partly a result of his continuous acquaintance with abolitionist circles and of the influence that Garrison himself had on him. In a letter he wrote in 1854 to Reverend Dr. Beard, chairman of the antislavery committee in England, Mazzini explained, "I have devoted my life to the emancipation of my own country. And I would feel . . . not an apostle of truth and justice, had I not felt from my earliest years that the right and duty of revolting against lies and tyranny were grounded on a far higher sphere than that of the welfare of one single nation; that they must start from belief in principle, which will have sooner or later to be universally applied. '*One God, one humanity, one law, one love from all for all.*'" The words in the last phrase, in particular, echo in an extraordinary parallel way Garrison's motto ("*Our country is the world—our countrymen are mankind*") for the *Liberator.* Significantly, William Cain has confirmed that the motto in the *Liberator*'s masthead was "a phrase adapted from Thomas Paine," long a favorite thinker of Garrison's and certainly one well known to Mazzini as well. It is worth noting, though, that Henry Mayer, instead of mentioning that connection, compares the *Liberator*'s motto with Garrison's "love to the whole world," which he wrote in an 1830 letter to Harriet Farnham Horton from the Baltimore Jail, where he served a forty-nine-day sentence for libeling a slave trader.[36]

Going back to Mazzini's 1854 letter, even more extraordinary and revealing is what he wrote next to Reverend Dr. Beard: "Blessed be your efforts if they start from this high ground of common faith; *if you do not forget, whilst at work for the emancipation of the black race, the millions of white slaves, suffering, struggling, expiring in Italy, in Poland, in Hungary throughout all Europe;* if you always remember that free men only can achieve the work of freedom, and that Europe's appeal for the abolition of slavery in other lands will not weigh all-powerful before God and men, whilst Europe herself shall be desecrated by arbitrary, tyrannical power, by czars, emperors, and popes." Significantly, in commenting on Mazzini's words, Garrison wrote, "These are sentiments to challenge the admiration of the wise and good throughout the world. They illustrate the all-embracing spirit of their author at all times and all circumstances." What Garrison meant was that the universality of the feelings at the heart of the two parallel struggles against slavery and against national oppression were self-evident. He himself proved this important point by publishing in the late 1840s and 1850s in the columns of the *Liberator* pieces by and about both Mazzini and Kossuth, the two greatest European nationalists at that time.[37]

We should also understand that, while Mazzini strengthened his abolitionist convictions through his acquaintance with Garrison and the Garrisonians and the influence they had on him, Garrison also felt the influence of Mazzini and his revolutionary group of democrats, though in a different and indirect way. It is very likely, as Mischa Honek has recently argued, that the reactions to the execution of Mazzinian activist Felice Orsini for his attempt to assassinate the French emperor Napoleon III in 1858, which led to impressive demonstrations of sympathy by American radicals, including abolitionists, for the Italian's "martyrdom," influenced Garrison and several Garrisonians in such a way that, a year before John Brown's execution, Garrison "slowly moved away from dogmatic non-resistance to embrace a more nuanced radicalism that also condoned revolutionary violence." This was first apparent when Garrison claimed, in an 1858 letter to Boston's Orsini sympathizers reprinted in the *Liberator,* that it was the "murderer Louis Napoleon who deserved to be beheaded, rather than Orsini." He then called for "Liberty for France, for Germany, for Italy, for all nations! Liberty for the slaves in America, for Russia, for all peoples who are held in thralldom!" It is not difficult to see here the similarity between Garrison's words and Mazzini's 1854 letter to Dr. Beard, published in the *Liberator* four years earlier.[38]

Throughout the 1850s, as Mazzini struggled to make his voice heard while Italian nationalism was taking an increasingly conservative turn, Garrison continued to publish pieces about him and letters written by him in the *Liberator,* focusing specifically on the connections between American abolitionism and European nationalism. A summary of Mazzini's thought on American slavery, which appeared in the *Liberator* in 1853, stated unequivocally, "The brave word spoken for Hungarian and Italian Liberty is a word, too, for American Liberty and against American Slavery." Another summary of the letter from Mazzini to Reverend Dr. Beard, which appeared in the *Liberator* the following year, highlighted Mazzini's comparison of America's "black slaves" with Europe's "white slaves" of national oppression and concluded, "It is a bastard philanthropy, which, in the United States, professes great zeal for freedom in Europe, while aiding to crush the southern slaves."[39]

Thus, echoing Garrison, who from the columns of the *Liberator* supported Europe's national revolutions as a crucial part of the great struggle for freedom, Mazzini wrote and spoke of how he considered the oppression of nationalities akin to slavery. In both Garrison's view and his own, patriots who suffered under foreign rule were the equivalent of white slaves denied their freedom. This was no mere rhetoric for Mazzini; he repeated the same comparison between black and white slaves in nearly every letter he sent to important figures involved in the abolitionist movement on both sides of the Atlantic. At the same time, it is very likely—and is supported by reading Garrison's writings—that this very same comparison must have been at the heart of the two activists' discussions about slavery and about the meaning of the struggle for liberty in different countries.[40]

Therefore, we should ask the following questions: Is there a deeper meaning behind Garrison's and Mazzini's idea of comparing and placing in similar categories those whom Mazzini called "black" and "white" slaves, that is, the type of exploitation suffered by African American slaves and the exploitation deriving from denial of civil rights and oppression of national feelings suffered by large numbers of Europeans? More importantly, what prompted both Garrison and Mazzini to believe that slavery and national oppression were so tightly linked? I believe the answer to these questions lies in the fact that, in the first half of the nineteenth century, the ideologies at the heart of antislavery—and particularly its radical variant, abolitionism—and of nationalism came to be tied together by a strong belief in progress. As numerous important studies have shown, especially those by David Brion Davis and Robin Blackburn, since the second half of the eighteenth century, slavery had become, in the minds of many intellectuals and in public opinion in general, a backward, barbaric institution; as a consequence, emancipation and abolition stood as the very symbols of progress. Significantly, around the same time, nationalism had started to be associated with the idea of progress, when the idea of the modern nation—and with it the modern notion of citizenship rights derived from the Enlightenment—had spread throughout Europe as a consequence of the French Revolution.[41]

Thus, nineteenth-century radical abolitionists and nineteenth-century democratic nationalists—Garrison and Mazzini at the forefront of them—believed that the twin fights against slavery and against national oppression led humankind onto an increasingly progressive path. For Mazzini, as well as for Garrison, national independence, political self-determination, and freedom from oppression were all linked together in a great struggle whose aim was the fulfillment of God's universal plan for the progression of humankind toward a new, improved era based on the principles of liberty and justice. There could be no real freedom without equality; until democratic republicanism was taken as a guiding principle for the formation of nations, humankind could not yet be said to be walking on a progressive path.[42]

The most eloquent proof of this is that Mazzini and Garrison agreed not only on the eradication of slavery and national oppression, but also on the fact that both were just the first necessary steps toward the full recognition of basic citizenship rights of those populations that had been deprived of them. From the time of the foundation of the AASS, in 1833, Garrison had continuously battled for the full recognition of equal rights for whites and blacks. He had taken every opportunity to explain clearly why African Americans should enjoy full citizenship just as whites did; for example, in an 1852 editorial in the *Liberator,* he stated: "Why, their country is ours. They were born here. They are bone of our bone, and blood of our blood." Mirroring Garrison's attitude, Mazzini wrote in *The Duties of Man* (1860) against "the owners of the Negroes in America [who] declare that race radically inferior and incapable of education and meanwhile persecute whoever attempts to educate them"; he considered those oppressors similar to Italy's reigning dynasties who "declare[d] . . . Italians badly fit for liberty," crushing their revolts "as if from tyranny could ever come education to liberty." Ultimately, even though he held deep reservations about Americans' obsession with individualism, Mazzini thought, much as Garrison did, that if the United States, the original republican nation, were to prove worthy to guide Italy and the other people of Europe along a progressive path, African Americans ought to be granted not just freedom but also the same citizenship rights as whites.[43]

In retrospect, the meeting between Garrison and Mazzini in 1846 was significant for several reasons. Each of the two men had spent his life up to that time building a radical tradition and espousing a cause with which he had become identified well beyond the borders of his own nation. For each one, by the time the meeting occurred, his cause had taken on a definitely international dimension, one clearly recognizable by people all over the world. In Garrison's case, the struggle for the abolition of slavery in the United States had become part of a wider network of Atlantic abolitionism, in which the underlying idea was that freedom from slavery had no real geographical limits and should extend to the rest of the world as well. In Mazzini's case, it was Europe that provided the wider network, with its displaced revolutionaries and conspirators who sought to oppose with a "Holy Alliance" of European oppressed nationalities the reactionary monarchies and empires that maintained absolutist regimes. At the same time, both activists and also several of their contemporaries saw clear parallels between their two radical causes. Then, even though already aware of each other's existence, with their meeting Garrison and Mazzini effectively established a crucial link between two radical movements that sought to ameliorate the Euro-American world by placing the principles of the American and the French revolutions—set in the 1776 Declaration of Independence and in the 1789 Declaration of the Rights of Man—back on the center stage of two continents that had fallen into the hands of reactionary forces and needed to be stirred back onto the path of progress.

Timing was particularly crucial, because the 1846 meeting occurred on the eve of momentous transformations in both the United States and Europe. Within the wider international context, the fact that Garrison and

Mazzini first met on the eve of Europe's continental revolutions is significant in that the first test of their collaboration came with Garrison's support of Mazzini's 1849 Roman Republic. As a consequence of that first test, collaboration between the two continued in the 1850s, amid disappointments over the reactionary backlash felt in both Europe and America. In America, after 1846, slavery became central in political discussion and in public debate, as a prelude to the following exacerbation of sectional conflicts and eventually the Civil War, which, with many contradictions and failed promises, resulted in the abolition of the slave system. In Italy, after 1846 the attempt and failure to create the conditions for an Italian national revolution that was as much social as political weighed heavily on the future course of the making of Italy and helped to accelerate the monarchical—rather than republican—unification of the country. Seen from this perspective, the meeting between Garrison and Mazzini could not have occurred at a better time, since it allowed each of them to better understand and take part in events that, in completely different ways and with utterly different results, led to the transformation of their life causes—the struggle over slavery in America and the struggle for national liberation in Italy—into matters of primary importance and urgency at a national level.

6

ENDORSEMENT AND REFUSAL OF MAINSTREAM RADICALISM

Garrison's and Mazzini's Times for Action, 1854–1861

The late 1850s and early 1860s saw William Lloyd Garrison and Giuseppe Mazzini confronting the monumental changes brought by the beginning of the American Civil War and the unification of Italy. To understand the significance of these changes, we need to place them in the context of the mid-nineteenth-century world, to which the two phenomena belong—both being at the same time military and nation-building operations, though on very different scales. The American Civil War was an event that marked a real watershed on a global scale, for a variety of different reasons, as much recent scholarship has shown. Its resonance and influence went far beyond the confines of the United States, or even the Americas, to reach Europe and eventually affect the entire Atlantic world. For this reason, several scholars have analyzed different aspects of the Civil War from a comparative perspective, making reference to contemporary events in Europe, including those occurring in Risorgimento Italy. As early as 1968, David Potter argued that the American Civil War "forged a bond between nationalism and liberalism when it appeared that the two might draw apart and move in opposite directions" after the defeat of the European 1848–49 revolutions; in the same article, Potter also implied that a particularly fitting case study to compare to the American Civil War would be Italy's movement for national unification, precisely because its success was the most celebrated example of a victory of a liberal nationalist movement in nineteenth-century Europe.[1]

Stimulated by Potter's observations and by subsequent historiographic developments, some American and European scholars, including transnational U.S. historians Thomas Bender, Ian Tyrrell, and Carl Guarneri, have hinted, at one time or another, at possible comparisons between the American Civil War and Europe's nineteenth-century nationalist movements. These scholars have shown the way toward a comparative reconsideration of the changes brought by the American Civil War and Europe's nationalist movements in a perspective at once transnational and transcontinental. Thus, if we were to take a transcontinental dimension as the focus of a comparative study, following some of the above suggestions, we could very well say that 1848 simply preannounced the subsequent, much larger, continental upheavals in both North America and Europe. The American Civil War was certainly a phenomenon that changed the geopolitics of the American hemisphere on a continental scale. In the first half of the 1860s, the conflict at the heart of the Civil War was between two large nations extended over wide areas of North America. The conflict also affected neighboring countries, particularly Mexico. There, Emperor Maximilian of Habsburg, supported by French emperor Napoleon III, and Mexican revolutionary Benito Juarez—Maximilian helped by southern U.S. Confederates and Juarez helped by northern U.S. Unionists—fought their own "civil war" for the control of the Mexican government roughly in the same years of the American conflict (1862–67). Comparable changes on a continental scale occurred in Europe in those years. Particularly, the final victory of the movement for national unification in Italy in 1861 and, later on, the unification of Germany in 1870, after a series of wars fought also in 1859 and 1866, permanently changed the arrangement of the European continent with the creation of two new and large countries that had not existed previously.[2]

Yet, if we were to write a comparative history of North America and Europe in the 1860s, we should also see the two continents very much in direct connection with each other, in clear transnational fashion, given that large contingents of volunteers came from various European countries to fight in the American Civil War. Virtually all the European nations whose rights to self-determination and independence, based on liberal principles, had undergone suppression in the wake of the reactionary wave following the failure of the 1848–49 revolutions—and also Italy, which by 1861 had become a nation in its own right—supplied groups of volunteers; although many of them joined the Confederate army, the majority fought in the battalions of the northern-based, antislavery Union government headed by Lincoln. In making this choice, the aspiring citizens of these suppressed

European nationalities hoped to advance the cause of freedom for their own nations by joining a struggle that they saw as closely linked to the victory of the universal principles of freedom and human dignity as delineated in the Declaration of Independence and to the defeat of slavery and human degradation—even though initially the Civil War was not about slave emancipation. Thus, for example, the Thirty-Ninth New York Volunteers was known in the Union Army as the "Garibaldi Guard," in honor of the legendary Italian general and freedom fighter; It included three companies of Hungarians and three of Germans, as well as one each of Italians, Swiss, French, and a combination of Portuguese and Spanish. Also, the Fifty-Eighth New York Infantry was known as the "Polish Legion" because of the many Polish immigrants in it and also the nationality of its commander, exiled Polish grand duke Wlodzimierz Krzyzanowski.[3]

It is particularly important to see the American Civil War in its truly world historical dimension, as C.A. Bayly does when he claims that it was "a global event in the same sense as the Taiping Rebellion or the 1848 revolutions, because direct connections of trade, government and ideology spread its effects across the globe." More than this, the global dimension of the American Civil War is particularly evident in that, as a phenomenon that led to the reunification of a country—as recent studies such as Thomas Bender's *Nation among Nations* have pointed out—it was clearly akin to other phenomena of either creation or restructuring of nations that characterized especially the central decades of the nineteenth-century Euro-American world. Therefore, following the early suggestions by David Potter and other scholars, not only is a comparison between the American Civil War and the movement for Italian national unification appropriate; it also forms an ideal context through which to understand Garrison's and Mazzini's actions in the late 1850s and early 1860s in comparative perspective. By maintaining a context formed by a comparison between the coming of the American Civil War and the coming of Italian unification, it is possible to see how and why Garrison and Mazzini responded as they did—that is, by holding on, in different ways, to their commitments to radical solutions to the American and Italian "national questions"—to comparable challenges presented to them by the sudden and somewhat unexpected unfolding of events and developments that were partly or mostly beyond their control. It is also important to recognize that both Garrison and Mazzini acknowledged the Euro-American and global dimension of the significance of the American

Civil War, which they both saw as a great struggle as much for the definition of freedom and democracy in the modern world as for the suppression of slavery.[4]

Militant Abolitionism and Democratic Nationalism

In the mid to late 1850s, both Garrison and Mazzini and their radical messages faced increasing isolation, for various reasons. In all likelihood, a major factor was their continued attempts to present themselves as the ultimate moral authorities and as the only individuals able to guide their movements onto virtuous paths. It is true that, as a result of these comparable attitudes, highly committed radical individuals continued to feel attracted to Garrison and Mazzini. However, these same attitudes also alienated large groups of potential supporters, who were more willing to make compromises in order to achieve the two ultimate objectives of the liberation of American slaves and of Italian unification. Moreover, Garrison's and Mazzini's somewhat utopian ideas on the best ways to reach these two objectives caused them to be increasingly detached both from more practical solutions and from crucial concrete issues. Thus, in the second half of the 1850s, Garrison was forced to confront the increasing influence of a new type of militant abolitionism, one that sought to practically provoke, with violence, an armed slave insurrection in the United States. Mazzini was forced to confront the increasing influence of democratic programs and strategies different from his own—particularly from the federalist and socialist camps—programs that sought to address ab initio the problem of the actual form of government of the future Italian nation and the concrete needs of the majority of its people.

Ultimately, though, the major challenges that Garrison and Mazzini confronted were of very different types, and consequently their responses were very different. In the United States, the challenge that militant abolitionism represented was internal within the American abolitionist movement. Initially, Garrison handled this challenge by simply holding on to his views of peaceful nonresistance. Later on, however, partly influenced by Mazzinians at the time of Orsini's 1858 attempt on Napoleon III's life, as we have seen, Garrison allowed himself enough leeway to be able to support slave revolts and the violent attempts made to provoke them—as when he ultimately praised John Brown's actions at Harpers Ferry in 1859. In Italy, the major challenge that Mazzini faced came from outside the democratic movement, even though it affected its members deeply: it was the formation of the National Society, a moderate political organization committed to the unification of Italy through collaboration with the Piedmontese Kingdom of Sardinia. It soon became far more difficult for Mazzini to watch the departure of Italian democrats who left to join the National Society than it was for Garrison to accept the existence of a more violent type of militant abolitionism in the United States. Therefore, in contrast to Garrison, who accommodated the challenge represented by the growth of abolitionist violence within his own radical beliefs, Mazzini ultimately reacted against the powerful challenge to his radical politics, never ceasing to condemn its cause, the National Society, and continuing to organize plots to spark a revolution—most famously in 1857 at Sapri, where, like John Brown with the American slaves, Carlo Pisacane lost his life attempting to start an insurrection among the southern Italian peasantry.[5]

Two almost simultaneous events in 1854 confirmed once and for all William Lloyd Garrison's deepest fear—that the "slave power" controlled the federal government—and led him to perform his most radical act. The first event was the 22 May 1854 passing of the Kansas-Nebraska Act, despite the opposition of the Free Soil Party; masterminded by Democrat Stephen Douglas, the Kansas-Nebraska Act invalidated the previous dispositions of the 1821 Missouri Compromise, which kept slavery below the 36°30' line, and effectively opened the northern Territories of Kansas and Nebraska to slavery on the basis of popular sovereignty. In the *Liberator,* Garrison wrote that the Kansas-Nebraska Act was passed "against the laws of God and the rights of universal man." Then, only two days later, a fugitive slave named Anthony Burns was captured in Boston, and after a failed attempt by the mob to free him, he was taken back to slavery by the federal authorities, in accordance with the 1850 Fugitive Slave Act, amid enormous popular resentment. For many New Englanders—among them transcendentalist intellectual Ralph Waldo Emerson—this was the shocking proof that slaveholders could now extend their power to the once safe and free North. To Garrison, it was the ultimate affront to freedom and proved that the Union made a mockery of the principles of the Declaration of Independence.[6]

On 4 July 1854, Independence Day, at the MASS outdoor meeting in Framingham, Massachusetts, on a platform draped in black and surmounted by the American flag turned upside down and by the state seal with the words "Redeem Massachusetts," Garrison did the unthinkable. After reading from the Bible, he proceeded to burn first a copy of the Fugitive Slave Act and then a copy of the U.S. Constitution itself, calling it once again "a covenant with death, an agreement with hell" and ending with the words "So perish all compromises with tyranny," followed by "Amen." After that, the events that exacerbated sectional conflicts over slavery followed in unbroken succession. First, a miniature civil war broke out in Kansas between proslavery and antislavery forces that tried to force the issue of the territory's popular sovereignty one way or the other; in the conflict, militant abolitionist John Brown played a key role, burning and looting proslavery bases and even killing five proslavery leaders in the 25 May 1856 Pottawatomie massacre. Then in 1857, Chief Justice Roger Taney ruled that a Missouri slave named Dred Scott, despite his residence for several years in free territories in the North, remained a slave; Taney also stated that slaves were not citizens and that Congress could not prohibit slavery anywhere on U.S. soil. Garrison's response was to write a fierce protest "against the alarming aggressions of the Slave Power upon the people of the North" and to advocate, louder than ever, "disunion with liberty and good conscience, rather than Union with slavery and moral degradation."[7]

One momentous consequence of the crisis of the 1850s was that a new type of militant abolitionism came into being. Best exemplified by John Brown, it was radical in a sense opposite to Garrison's nonresistant radicalism, since Brown did not refrain from violence. Militant abolitionists built stronger alliances with free African American activists, and together they quickly became the most active force in promoting a general armed revolt of southern slaves; the second half of the 1850s saw a crescendo of their attempts at provoking such a revolt. This was in part a reaction to what some abolitionists perceived as the failure of both Garrisonians and anti-Garrisonians to change the turn of events in a peaceful way. In addition, it was a combination of frustration at what seemed to the militant group a string of victories by the "slave power" and of response to the increasingly violent atmosphere of sectional conflicts in the 1850s that prompted some abolitionists to redefine both their means and their aims. Jane and William Pease have argued that the failure of the antislavery politics of the Free-Soil Party and the passing of the Fugitive Slave Act of 1850 had forced the new generation of abolitionists—among whom, however, was also Frederick Douglass—to change strategy and move toward direct, violent, action against the slave system. According to James B. Stewart, "Abolitionists who endorsed non-violence for practical reasons would obviously feel free to discard the tactic whenever desperate circumstances seemed to justify so. For some Abolitionists, the pro-slavery triumphs of the early 1850s were such a compelling reason."[8]

What about Garrison? Despite his radical commitment to nonresistance and peace against all violent action, Garrison had already questioned more than once, as in his 1852 review of *Uncle Tom's Cabin,* the fact that for some abolitionists, whites seemed to hold a monopoly on active resistance. The rise of militant abolitionism and the worsening of sectional conflicts prompted him to reconsider at least some of his positions, if it is true that, as Merton Dillon has remarked, Garrison "wavered in his commitments to non-resistance and . . . declared his belief in the justice of slave rebellion." However, it is also true that, for himself and for his fellow abolitionists in the AASS, Garrison continued to contemplate nothing short of outright pacifism. Still in 1855, in response to preacher Henry Ward Beecher, who condoned the use of weapons in the fight against proslavery forces in Kansas, Garrison did not hesitate to condemn violence, even though he clearly stated that he sided with those who fought the slave power; and he engaged once again in a passionate defense of peaceful nonresistance as "the reform of reforms" and the only way to free humankind from "the sanguinary code" that ruled over the world. Yet, there is no doubt that, as the sectional conflicts of the 1850s precipitated toward civil war, Garrison's position was increasingly uncomfortable and difficult to maintain. If already in 1858, Garrison showed his support, like most other Garrisonians, for Felice Orsini's failed assassination of Napoleon III, calling Orsini "a brave man, true to his convictions of duty," then effectively, as Walter Merrill phrased it, "for Garrison the supreme test of non-resistance principles came following [John] Brown's raid at Harper's Ferry in October 1859."[9]

Before Brown organized his raid, other militant abolitionists had also advocated slave insurrection and had engaged in a battle as much of words as of actions against the slave system. Among the most active was James Redpath, a leading propagandist of slave insurrection from the early 1850s up to the Civil War. Maintaining contact with other militant abolitionists, including John Brown, Redpath undertook several trips to the South to see for himself the conditions of the slaves and the possibilities of slave insurrection. Despite this fundamental difference of opinion with Garrison—who, even though growing increasingly militant, still continued to hold on to his support of peaceful nonresistance—Redpath had initially collaborated with the *Liberator,* which in turn had published his letters on southern slavery. And like most abolitionists, Redpath considered Garrison a model of a radical activist, one who had engaged in abolitionist activities ahead of his time and against all conveniences. In an 1854 letter to Garrison, Redpath stated precisely these points by calling Garrison "a journalist who opposed slavery when opposition to it was a question of life or death" and contrasting him with "those who did not discuss the topic until it had become simply a matter of profit and loss." Significantly, in the same letter, Redpath defined himself as "an 'ultra' Abolitionist," claiming, therefore, that he was taking Garrison's revolution a step further with his plans for slave insurrection. Eventually, Redpath's views found their most complete expression in his book *The Roving Editor* (1859), in which he collected all his articles on slavery. "Let the Abolitionists of the North not be deceived," Redpath wrote; "the South will never liberate their slaves unless compelled to do so." To compel them to do so, Redpath did "not hesitate to urge the friend of the slave to incite insurrection"—a position that only a few years earlier would have been antithetical to Garrison's but in line with the one held from the start by militant abolitionists such as John Brown.[10]

Among the militant abolitionists willing to use violence to achieve their aim, John Brown, whom Garrison had known since 1857, was certainly the most famous. In the words of Herbert Aptheker, "he was the apotheosis of revolutionary commitment" of the last generation of abolitionists. Together with a fanatical religious belief, Brown held the view that "physical resistance by or on behalf of the slaves was not only just, but necessary." In his view, slave emancipation could occur only after a general slave insurrection had been sparked through acts of guerrilla warfare directed at the very heart of the slave system. These acts, he believed, would achieve the double aim of prompting a general revolt of the slaves and shaking public opinion in the North. At the time of the miniature civil war in Kansas, Brown had already shown that he was prepared to use violence whenever necessary to achieve his aim of exterminating the slave power. It was this conviction that prompted him to organize the tragic raid at Harpers Ferry on 16 October 1859. That raid ended with his capture and then his hanging in December. Effectively, John Brown's death made him a martyr and also a powerful symbol for the abolitionist struggle on the eve of the Civil War.[11]

Initially, Garrison's reaction to the raid at Harpers Ferry was repulsion at the appalling act of violence and at the loss of human life. At the same time, though, despite holding on as much as he could to his radical pacifist beliefs, in an article entitled "The Tragedy at Harper's Ferry" in the *Liberator,* Garrison also recognized John Brown's bravery and the valor of his actions and aims, however misguided. "Captain Brown was a hero," Garrison wrote, "struggling . . . to redeem others . . . to be justified in all that he aimed to achieve, however lacking in sound discretion." But in the following months, as John Brown's plight transformed gradually into a martyrdom for the abolitionist cause, Garrison, perhaps also thinking back to the Orsini case, began questioning deeply his view of the events and the significance of his uncompromising pacifist stance. By the time of Brown's execution, Garrison had reached a conclusion that he himself would have considered unthinkable only a couple of years earlier. Thus, in December 1859, Garrison wrote in the *Liberator:* "I am a non-resistant . . . yet, as a peace man—an 'ultra' peace man—I am prepared to say: 'Success to every slave insurrection at the South, and in every slave country.'" Even more significant was another comment of his, whose origins can be traced to his reactions to Orsini's action: "Resistance to tyrants is obedience to God," a God who, according to Garrison, now had shown himself through the generous attempt made by John Brown.[12]

As Garrison struggled to maintain his radical principle of nonresistance in the mid to late 1850s, amid the rapid rise of militant abolitionism, and ran the risk of becoming increasingly isolated in his position, Mazzini, after the failed Milan insurrection of February 1853, saw his status as acknowledged leader of the Italian democrats increasingly subject to scrutiny and criticism. Even more than before, criticism focused on Mazzini's single-minded radical objective to build a specifically republican Italian nation, with no room for either federalist or socialist alternatives, and on his insistence on plotting insurrections from afar through a network of sects and conspiracies. In March 1853, with the essay "Agli Italiani" (To Italians), Mazzini responded to these criticisms by rejecting federalism as a viable alternative, by clarifying that his failure was due to internal divisions and quarrels between the Italian democrats, and by pointing the way forward with the foundation of a new organization, the Party of Action. He explained, "[It is a] party of men who intend to *attain* freedom in the name and with the forces of the nation . . . who have faith in the *people* . . . a party of initiators who feel that the time [for revolution] has come." Thus, taking issue with those who still thought—despite Louis Napoleon's 1851 coup and his proclamation as emperor Napoleon III—that it was possible to receive help from the French republicans, Mazzini stated clearly that it was up to the Italian people to create the necessary conditions for their own national revolution.[13]

Once again, Mazzini called on the young—but only those who had no hesitation. They were the ones he invited to form the Party of Action. Later, in 1855, Mazzini wrote, "The Party of Action must be considered the militant church of the great National Party." Thus, Mazzini was asking the young to light a spark through an insurrection wherever they were, since Italy was ready and the fire of the revolution would then inevitably extend to the entire peninsula. In practice, Mazzini was changing his tactics. Rather than fomenting insurrections in the large cities and seats of government, he now contemplated moving the revolution from the centers to the peripheries through guerrilla actions conducted by fighting bands in different areas. It was with this conviction that, between 1853 and 1854, together with Felice Orsini, Mazzini embarked on the attempt to spark the revolution in two relatively isolated areas of northern Italy, Lunigiana and Valtellina. The eventual failure of this latest attempt showed that Mazzini was not fully aware of the complexity of the situation and of the changes occurring in Italy in those years. It also initiated a period of profound crisis for the movement headed by Mazzini, whose strategy seemed increasingly ill suited for the achievement of Italian independence and unity.[14]

The main beneficiary of the crisis of the Mazzinian movement was Count Camillo Cavour. A Piedmontese nobleman and an agrarian entrepreneur, Cavour since 1852 had been the prime minister who headed the government and the parliament of the Kingdom of Sardinia, the only constitutional monarchy left in Italy after 1849. A shrewd politician, Cavour had as his primary objective the strengthening of Piedmont through the creation of a large northern Italian kingdom headed by the Savoy dynasty of Victor Emmanuel II, who had succeeded Charles Albert after the latter's abdication and through the expulsion of the Austrians from the peninsula; Cavour loathed Mazzini's radicalism and his republican ideas, but he was prepared to fight side-by-side with the democrats to reach his objective. Against Mazzini's utopian revolutionary and radical republican program, Cavour presented an alternative with Piedmont's constitutional monarchy as a legitimate political subject in the international arena heading the movement for Italian independence and unity. Thus, as Roberto Romani has recently remarked, "in the 1850s, the Piedmontese moderate liberals [headed by Cavour] created a peculiar political culture, suited to the twofold task of strengthening representative institutions at home and justifying Piedmont's Italian mission." Then Cavour's diplomatic skills scored a major success when, through Piedmont's participation in the 1855–56 Crimean War, he obtained a seat on the winning side of the peace table together with Great Britain and France and was able to present the Italian situation as one in which Austria acted as a major factor of instability in Europe. Unable to think about the entire operation as anything more than another dynastic war conducted by the Savoy dynasty, Mazzini made a major mistake in calling on Piedmontese soldiers to desert the Sardinian army in Crimea. By doing so, he further alienated those whose prime goal was to reach a resolution to Italy's national question, whether by diplomacy or by other means, together with some sectors of British supporters.[15]

Interestingly, as these events were unfolding during the difficult period of the first half of the 1850s, Mazzini seemed to find support from unexpected quarters in the United States. Specifically, he received an offer of help from the Young America movement, whose roots went as far back as the 1840s. Since 1852 this movement had been a wing of the Democratic Party—the party of the president, Franklin Pierce—committed, as much as Pierce himself, equally to the expansion of American republicanism and to the support of Europe's national movements. To be sure, aside from the name and a commitment to republicanism, Young America had little in common with Mazzini, especially given its support for nationalist expansion leading to the projected annexation of Cuba and even its proslavery politics—both harshly criticized by Garrisonian abolitionists—but Mazzini badly needed help at the time, and so he accepted, through the mediation of Kossuth, Young America's promises of concrete support in his plans for Italy's national revolution. As Mazzini wrote in an August 1853 letter to Ambrogio Ronchi, because of the support promised by Young America's leaders George Sanders, U.S. consul in London, and Pierre Soulé, U.S. ambassador in Madrid, "If a revolutionary republican government is established anywhere in Italy, it will be immediately recognized" by the United States, and then "the individual Americans will have a right to help it." Through Sanders's influence, Mazzini obtained American passports for himself and his friend Aurelio Saffi, and he even participated in a party Sanders gave in London in 1854, to which all the European republicans were invited, to discuss his future aid to them. Mazzini subsequently fell out with Sanders and Soulé over his own uncompromising opposition to slavery, while Young America's promised funds and weapons never materialized. And after 1855, with the election of James Buchanan as U.S. president, Young America's influence on American national politics became negligible.[16]

In 1856 a major blow came to Mazzini: Venetian Daniele Manin, one of the most prestigious Italian democrats and the former head of the 1848–49 Venetian Republic, met with Cavour and agreed on a common program focused on what Manin's collaborator Giorgio Pallavicino called "national unification." It was to be a gradual process open to different possibilities and thus contrasted with Mazzini's strictly republican national unity. In May 1856, in an article in the *Times* of London, Manin attacked Mazzini's conspiratorial and violent tactics, while he vigorously proposed joining Cavour's Piedmont in the struggle for Italian independence. As a matter of fact, an increasing number of democrats had come to agree with Manin, abandoning their former radical positions and uniting with Cavour's moderate liberals and their program. Faced with a real scattering from the republican ranks, Mazzini responded by calling for a "neutral banner." His formula was "With the nation, for the nation," by which he meant that both democrats and moderate liberals should participate in the national revolution and then decide later about the form of government. Mazzini wrote Nicola Fabrizi in July 1856, saying, "First, war in everybody's name, with everybody's help; then, the nation will do what she wants, what the facts will decree." It was an attempt to regain the initiative for the democrats using the moderate liberals' superior resources, but it came too late. In that same summer of 1856, Manin founded the Italian National Society, which gathered republican and moderate representatives around the program "Italy and Victor Emmanuel"; the National Society was willing to recognize the leadership of Piedmont's constitutional monarchy as long as Cavour and the Savoy king committed themselves to Italy's unification. Manin died only a year later, but Sicilian Giuseppe La Farina, the National Society's secretary, kept in constant contact with Cavour. Shortly afterward even Giuseppe Garibaldi, the most prestigious republican leader, joined the National Society; by then, Mazzini's isolation had become almost complete.[17]

To move out of his isolation, Mazzini met in London with fellow democrat Carlo Pisacane. The two had irreconcilable differences: Mazzini's spiritual views and his emphasis on interclass cooperation were the opposites of Pisacane's materialism and socialism. But they agreed to devise another plan for insurrection to return to the democrats the radical initiative in the process of Italian unification. The plan had its basis in the coordination of simultaneous actions in Genoa and Livorno, with Mazzini fomenting revolts among the city workers and around Naples, where Pisacane, landing with a party of volunteers, would rouse the peasants to revolt against Bourbon King Ferdinand II and march on the southern capital. Unfortunately, when they attempted to carry out the plot in 1857, the planned revolts did not occur, and Pisacane and his volunteers, hunted down by the Bourbon army at Sapri, eventually were killed. That failure weighed very heavily on Mazzini, who received his second death sentence from the Piedmontese government, confirming not only the crisis of the democratic movement but also his own rigidity in strategy and tactics in the attempts to achieve the radical, but increasingly utopian, objective of a united Italian republic. In response to criticisms of his tactics, Mazzini published a long essay, "La situazione" (The situation), in which he described Italy's situation as if a people's revolution was around the corner, given the right circumstances: "The popular element—yearns undoubtedly for action; we need to either lead it or fight alongside it, or else we need to leave room for it. . . . The people in the cities [are] capable and longing to rise, fight, and win. . . . [They are] lacking leaders and expecting them from the middle class. . . . [They are] imbued with the national idea and ready to sacrifice everything for it." Mazzini was accusing particularly the middle class sympathetic to the national movement of preventing the Party of Action from leading the people into revolution by being inert and infecting the people with their inertia.[18]

After returning to London, in 1858, Mazzini founded a periodical with the specific purpose of stimulating debate over these issues and showing the way forward in the Italian situation; the name of the periodical was, significantly, *Pensiero e Azione* (Thought and action), by which Mazzini meant that the theoretical and the practical sides of the revolution ought to be linked together in a program that emphasized both equally. It was also during this period that Mazzini completed his theory of social reform. At its heart were the initial creation of workers' associations and the ultimate goal of a society in which all individuals, no longer divided between bosses and workers, participated in the process of production and were paid accordingly. As Franco Della Peruta has noticed, Mazzini had proposed, as early as 1857, a radical program of "constitution of a 'National Fund' to be formed with the expropriation of the riches of different Rulers, with the appropriation of the properties of the high clergy, and of all those who had fought or conspired against the nation." In theory, the program was geared toward funding both workers' and peasants' associations; however, there is no doubt that Mazzini continued to privilege the workers in the cities as the leading element of the future revolution, while his understanding of the countryside and of the peasants' needs continued to be fairly vague and not focused on their actual need for a redistribution of lands.[19]

The challenges faced by Garrison and Mazzini in the mid to late 1850s were serious enough for each of them to reflect carefully upon the validity of both his strategies and his tactics. Even though, initially, both Garrison and Mazzini continued to similarly hold on to their own established radical beliefs, not just in regard to the righteousness of their chosen causes, but also in the correctness of their chosen ways to achieve their aims, the truth was that the challenges they faced had arisen as a result of their failures to achieve those aims—leaving aside all external factors. More than this, those challenges indicated clearly the existence of attempts by other groups of American abolitionists and of Italian democrats to resolve the issues of slave emancipation and Italian independence and unity by means other than the ones devised by Garrisonian and Mazzinian radicalisms, means that implied more violence or more compromising tactics.

Among those who contributed decisively to forcing the issues of slave emancipation and Italian independence and unity in a particularly violent and direct way—by sparking a slave insurrection in the United States and a peasant insurrection in Italy—were the two individuals who came to be remembered as true martyrs for the two causes to which Garrison and Mazzini had dedicated their lives: John Brown and Carlo Pisacane. Even though Brown had not collaborated with Garrison, while Pisacane did collaborate with Mazzini, Brown's and Pisacane's deeds—bold, desperate attempts in both cases—at Harpers Ferry in 1859 and at Sapri in 1857 had incalculable consequences in precipitating the slavery issue in the United States and the independence-unification issue in Italy, in comparable terms. Therefore, it is no accident that historians from Raimondo Luraghi to Giulio Schenone and Timothy Roberts not only have seen some interesting parallels but have also discovered connections between Brown, Pisacane, and Mazzini, not just in their absolute commitments to the necessity of using any means to achieve their aims, but also in the existence of a clearly shared culture of guerrilla warfare against reactionary forces. The main written statement of that culture was, significantly, Carlo Bianco di Saint Jorioz's famous 1830 book on guerrilla tactics and national insurrection. This small comparative point is a particularly good example of how we need to keep in mind the significance of connections and comparisons within the wider Atlantic and Euro-American milieu of which Garrison and Mazzini were both very much part, in order to understand better the significance of the challenges met by the two during this period and the different responses they gave to these challenges—Garrison effectively embracing some premises of militant abolitionism by the time of the death of John Brown, and Mazzini giving more importance to the social factor as a result of his contact with Carlo Pisacane.[20]

Lincoln, Cavour, and Garibaldi

In the late 1850s in the United States, the Republican Party with its moderate program succeeded in gathering antislavery forces with a wide spectrum of specific agendas into a major political coalition, whose main objective was to keep the influence of the slave power at bay. In the same period in Italy, the National Society succeeded in gathering both democrats and liberals in support of a moderate program whose objective was the gradual creation of an Italian nation. In both cases, it was the rise of a charismatic and innovative statesman—Lincoln in the United States and Cavour in Italy—that led to an acceleration of events that eventually transformed the initial moderate objective into a more radical one. Thus, as Lincoln's rise in the United States led eventually to the American Civil War, Cavour's rise in Italy accelerated the process of national unification. In the course of a few years, Lincoln's increasingly confrontational antislavery attitude, even though a far cry from Garrison's abolitionism, exacerbated sectional conflicts and led to the 1861 beginning of a long and costly war between the antislavery North and the proslavery South. In Italy, Cavour's increasingly bold diplomacy of provocation and rupture of the international order and his growing support for programs with a wider scope of national unification, though completely opposite to Mazzini's idea of a unitary Italian republic, led directly to a war with Austria and were also instrumental in the sudden and unexpected way in which, also in 1861, Italy was unified. As a result of these developments between the late 1850s and the early 1860s, Garrison and Mazzini found themselves forced to confront a series of major issues in rapid succession.[21]

First, the Republican Party and the National Society continued to increase in power and importance as hegemonic forces in the American antislavery and Italian nationalist camps; then, Lincoln and Cavour continued their rise in prestige and influence as the quintessential moderate politicians; finally, in both cases, wars began whose declared objectives hardly coincided with the radical ideas Garrison and Mazzini held about the future of their nations. Both Garrison and Mazzini reacted showing little sympathy for the moderate programs and for the wars they generated. Both, however, also recognized the opportunities that the new situations entailed for the progress of their causes. Thus, Garrison came to acknowledge the importance of the Republican Party as a major antislavery force, even though not an abolitionist one, while Mazzini acknowledged the importance of the National Society's resources to achieve the primary objective of Italian unification.

It is also true, though, that as wars broke out, while both Garrison and Mazzini saw their enormous potential for radical change, they also relentlessly voiced their criticisms regarding the narrow scopes of the wars. To Garrison, the American Civil War, in addition to bringing the disunion that he had so long advocated, should have naturally led to the emancipation of the slaves; however, this was not in Lincoln's initial plans. To Mazzini, the war of 1859, and even more Garibaldi's 1860 expedition to the South, should have been an opportunity for the Italian people to take the revolution into their own hands; this even though both of these wars were conducted in the name of King Victor Emmanuel II. Understandably, by the end of 1861 Garrison and Mazzini found themselves equally disappointed at the course of events: the American Civil War was continuing with no end to slavery in sight, while Italy had achieved its unification as a monarchy ruled by the Savoy dynasty from Piedmont.

Amid the exacerbation of sectional conflicts, which, as a result of the divergence of opinions over the 1850 compromise and the Fugitive Slave Act, led to the transformation of the Free Soil Party into the Free Democrats—with half the constituency and also half the 1848 votes in the presidential election of 1852—the real novelty in American politics in the 1850s was the formation of the Republican Party. That party essentially formed in February 1854 in opposition to the Kansas-Nebraska Act and the spurious doctrine of popular sovereignty that underpinned it, and it gathered the broadest coalition ever seen of antislavery forces across the U.S. political spectrum. Many members of the Republican Party were former members of the Free Soil Party, but equally important were the antislavery Whigs—who, by their defection, became a major cause of the collapse of the Whig Party—and the antislavery Democrats. Two years later, in 1856, the Republican Party held its first national convention, electing John Frémont as a nominee for the coming presidential election and outlining its platform in the following terms: slavery was "a relic of barbarism," and the federal government had the duty to secure the rights to life, liberty, and the pursuit of happiness "to all persons under its exclusive jurisdiction" and to "prohibit [slavery] in the territories." Eventually, these ideas found their clearest and most concise expression in the famous motto "Free Soil, Free Labor, Free Men." Despite the election of James Buchanan, a proslavery southerner, in 1856, as Bruce Levine has remarked, "Frémont received a full third of the nation's popular vote and 45 percent of all ballots cast in the free states . . . eleven states out of sixteen free states." The Republican Party was clearly a political force to be reckoned with.[22]

On the eve of the 1856 election, Garrison wrote a letter to James McKim, in which he recognized several merits of the Republican Party, such as its clear antislavery character and the historical significance of its character as a major antislavery force. "Unquestionably," Garrison wrote, "it embodies the whole *political* antislavery strength of the country—the legitimate product of the *moral* agitation on the subject of slavery for the last quarter of the century." Garrison also recognized the novelty of the Republican Party's exclusively northern constituency and the importance of its focus on restricting slavery from expanding further in the West. Nevertheless, Garrison did not feel any more compelled to join politics than he had before, and he continued to hold firmly to his view of the Constitution and to advocate "no Union with slaveholders." Still, in a later, unfinished letter written to Parker Pillsbury in 1859, Garrison showed that he had become more positive toward the possibilities that the Republican Party offered the antislavery cause as a whole. "My hope is in the Republican Party," he said, but he clarified, "not the Republican Party where it now stands, or as to its non-extension policy, but as to its MATERIALS—embodying as it does the intelligence, virtue, moral sentiment, and political A.S. [antislavery] feeling in the North." At times Garrison also criticized the Republicans' discrimination against African Americans, calling the party "a complexional party, exclusively for white men, not for all men," but he was particularly perplexed by the Republicans' moderate stance. As Richard Sewell has noticed, Garrison "continued to view the Republican Party . . . as an imperfect accomplice in the destruction of slavery."[23]

By 1859, however, the rise of Abraham Lincoln within the ranks of the Republican Party had contributed in a major way to sharpening the focus of its mission and, in a way, to throwing the full force of the moderate antislavery coalition behind a project that, at the time, had little in common with Garrison's own. A firm believer as much in the principles of the Declaration of Independence as in the crucial importance of the Constitution, Lincoln, who was a Whig early in his life, had joined the Republican Party only in 1856, when he saw the growing importance of the issue of slavery, but he had made his clear public stand against the "peculiar institution"—or rather, his stand in principle against it and in practice against its expansion—as early as 1854, in his "Peoria Address." In 1858, during the famous debates in the contest with Democrat Stephen Douglas for the Illinois seat in the Senate, Lincoln showed the Republican Party a new way to the future, by affirming in the "House Divided" speech his absolute belief in the indissolubility of the Union as his highest priority. In that speech, Lincoln stated eloquently, "I do not expect the Union to be *dissolved*—I do not expect the house to *fall*—but I *do* expect it will cease to be divided. It will become *all* one thing [slave], or *all* the other [free]."[24]

How, then, did Garrison react to Lincoln's rise within the Republican Party and to his uncompromising belief in the perpetuity of the Union—a belief as uncompromising as Garrison's own on slave emancipation? It is important to notice, as Henry Mayer has, that Garrison had also "in his arguments . . . often invoked [as Lincoln had done in his famous speech] Christ's precept 'a house divided against itself cannot stand,' [but] as an imperative for achieving the moral clarity of a nation purged of slavery," not as a warning against the "nationalization" of slavery by the slave power. Thus, Lincoln's ideas on the Union represented the opposite of Garrison's "no Union with slaveholders!"—a motto that promoted disunionism as the only viable solution to the moral, more than the sectional, crisis. Garrison was especially dismayed by Lincoln's unwillingness to engage in radical action against slavery; the latter's behavior during the 1860 presidential campaign did much to convince Garrison that Lincoln would, "do nothing to offend the South." Meanwhile, Garrison maintained his transatlantic contacts with European supporters of abolitionism, receiving confirmation from them of the continuous importance of the radical crusade for slave emancipation that he had begun almost thirty years earlier with the *Liberator.* Thus, in a letter Garrison received in August 1860, William Henry Ashurst—the son of Garrison's and Mazzini's friend of the same name, who had died five years earlier—described Garrisonian abolitionism as "one of the most important movements now taking place for the progress of man." However, as the 1860 presidential election neared, Garrison recognized in the *Liberator* that "the pending Presidential election witnesses a marked division between the political forces of the North and of the South; and though it relates, ostensibly, solely to the question of the further extension of slavery, it really signifies a much deeper sentiment in the breasts of the people of the North, which, in the process of time, must ripen unto more decisive action." In other words, Garrison saw the full potential of a possible Republican victory for the radical abolitionist project—after all, the Republican Party was the first and only major political force with an official antislavery platform.[25]

It is fair to say that Garrison had hardly been favorable to Lincoln's nomination as the presidential candidate for the Republican Party, given Lincoln's very mild antislavery stance. Garrison had gone so far as to declare, on 4 July 1860, "Such a man shall never have my vote, either to occupy the Presidential chair, or any other station." However, upon Lincoln's election as president in November 1860, Garrison joined the infectious enthusiasm that seemed to have seized his fellow abolitionists, noticing also the disproportionate effect that the election had on the slave states. Thus, Garrison wrote in the *Liberator,* "The election of the Republican candidate, Abraham Lincoln, to the Presidency of the United States has operated upon the whole slaveholding South in a manner indicative of the torments of the damned," adding then a quote from the New Testament book of Revelation, "Babylon is fallen."[26]

When only a few weeks later, in December 1860, South Carolina seceded from the Union, fearing Lincoln's "abolitionist" measures, Garrison saw his long-term calls for disunionism vindicated, even though disunion was becoming a reality on the side of the slave states, rather than on that of the free states. In January 1861 Garrison wrote, somewhat optimistically, but also prophetically: "All Union-saving efforts are idiotic. At last, 'the covenant with death' is annulled. . . . Hail the approaching jubilee, ye millions who are wearing the galling chains of slavery; for, assuredly, the day of your redemption draws nigh, bringing liberty to you, and salvation to the whole land!" Only a month after Garrison published these words, Jefferson Davis became president of the Confederate States of America, which, between February and June 1861, assembled the eleven southern states that seceded from the Union before and after the Confederate seizure of the Union garrison at Fort Sumter, near Charleston, South Carolina. As these events unfolded, Lincoln's inauguration took place, on 4 March 1861, and Garrison was impressed enough by his speech to reprint it in the *Liberator,* noticing how Lincoln's moderation stood in marked contrast with the warmonger southern secessionists.[27]

Then, when the American Civil War broke out, in July 1861, Garrisonian abolitionists effectively saw in it what Wendell Phillips called "the great struggle between the disguised aristocracy and the democracy of America," a struggle that resembled and was closely connected to a similar one that had been happening in Europe from the time of the French Revolution. For his part, Garrison showed a strong will to modify his radical pacifist and nonresistance principles in order to support the cause of the Union. As Walter Merrill has remarked, Garrison wrote "his friends and associates . . . saying that they must not criticize Lincoln and the Republican Party, for they are fighting the forces of evil." However, from the beginning of the war, Garrison also had made clear that his opinion was very different from that of Lincoln, who declared that he had undertaken the war solely for the restoration of the Union; for Garrison, the true issue at stake, as always, was slavery. In May 1861, as preparations for the war were under way, Garrison had written unequivocally in the *Liberator:* "What shall be said, then, of those who insist upon ignoring the question of slavery as not involved in this deadly feud and maintain that the only issue is the support of the government and the preservation of the Union? Surely, they are 'fools and blind'; for it is slaveholders alone who have conspired to seize one, and overturn the other." Then, in the early stages of the conflict, as the months passed and Lincoln seemed to show no intention of acting against slavery, Garrison grew increasingly weary. A tug of war began between the president and the abolitionists, with the latter—first and foremost Garrison—pressing Lincoln on the subject of immediate emancipation, and Lincoln cautiously maintaining a certain distance from them and waiting for the right moment to strike directly at slavery. After some wrong starts and turns, that moment finally came a little more than a year after the start of the war.[28]

As in the United States the Republican Party was the hegemonic political force within the antislavery camp, in Italy in the late 1850s the National Society was the hegemonic force, among a whole spectrum of supporters of Italy's national unification who held different beliefs but shared the same primary objective. By 1859, thanks to a very well orchestrated propaganda campaign, including the distribution of a host of pamphlets and other publications, the National Society had successfully drawn away from the democratic camp and toward the pro-Piedmontese side most of the high-profile exponents of the republican programs for Italy's national unification. The National Society had become effectively a serious moderate-liberal alternative to Mazzini's revolutionary Party of Action. The National Society was an alternative that most members of the middle class with nationalist tendencies definitely found much more appealing. Thus, as Lucy Riall has noted, "the presence of the National Society served to emphasize the legitimacy of Piedmontese leadership over the nationalist struggle." No one knew this better than Cavour, who established increasingly stronger ties with the National Society through its secretary La Farina and eventually managed to draw the society toward his own political and diplomatic objectives; as a result, Cavour could successfully present himself as the actual credible leader of a moderate and liberal—and thus nonradical and nonrevolutionary—party and program for Italy's national unification.[29]

The test of the alliance between Cavour and the National Society came with the 1859 war, which saw Piedmont and France fighting against Austria. The war's origins had much to do with the failed assassination of Napoleon III in 1858 by Orsini, who had declared he had merely acted in the interest of Italy; with another diplomatic master stroke, Cavour had taken the opportunity to press the French emperor into an alliance with Piedmont in a war to end Austria's domination of northern Italy and thus halt a destabilizing situation that was likely to provoke more actions such as the one by Orsini. After Cavour and Napoleon III agreed on the war's gains and strategy at a secret meeting in Plombiéres, it was only a matter of time before hostilities broke out. Meanwhile, the National Society was very active in advertising the imminent conflict as a war for Italian independence under the leadership of Sardinian King Victor Emmanuel II and in mobilizing volunteers from all over northern Italy, many of them in the Cacciatori delle Alpi unit, under the leadership of Garibaldi. For his part, even though fearing that the war might be nothing more than a plan for Sardinian and Napoleonic dynastic expansions, Mazzini also saw that it could be an opportunity to start a popular insurrection. Finally, war broke out between Piedmont and Austria, and then France and Austria, in April 1859; although casualties were very high, it lasted only a short time. Inexplicably, and in blatant violation of the Plombiéres agreements, in July 1859, after drawing the Austrians away from Lombardy, Napoleon III decided to sign the Armistice of Villafranca, leaving Piedmont in control of only Lombardy, which made up about half of the Austrian territory in northern Italy. Although Mazzini saw then the opportunity to start a people's war, since the dynastic war was over, as he had seen in 1849, the popular insurrection did not occur.[30]

Still, Mazzini adapted rapidly by changing his strategy and adhering even more clearly to the principles he had expressed in an article called "La Guerra" (The war), published in *Pensiero e Azione* in May 1859. In that article, Mazzini had called on Italians to stage a general insurrection: " It is necessary that Italy rises, from one end to the other, and thus constitutes its own army. . . . The insurrection should occur everywhere: in the North in order to *gain,* not receive, liberty, in the South to form a reserve of the national army." What Mazzini was beginning to understand was that the decisive events for Italy's unification would take place in southern Italy, that the democrats might still have a chance to lead the national revolution by moving from central Italy to the South. Thus, by late 1859, Mazzini's motto became "Al centro, al centro, mirando al Sud" (To the center, to the center, aiming at the South). In August 1859, he went to Tuscany, where the people of Florence in an insurrection had ousted the Habsburg grand duke Leopold II and proclaimed a provisional democratic government headed by Baron Bettino Ricasoli. Ricasoli was in favor of an Italian monarchy, rather than an Italian republic, but he and Mazzini agreed on the need for Italy's unification; by then Mazzini was so eager for national unification that he even wrote King Victor Emmanuel II, urging him to lead the Italian people. In truth, Mazzini hoped to be able to both help and control Garibaldi, who was preparing, under the aegis of the National Society, an expedition to the South. To this end, Mazzini attempted to gather a group of volunteers among the Tuscan democrats. However, shortly after Mazzini's arrival,

Ricasoli managed to clear the way for Tuscany's annexation to Piedmont, and Mazzini, who had suddenly become persona non grata, had to leave for London.[31]

While Mazzini was in London, in January 1860, Cavour, who had resigned after the Armistice of Villafranca, again became prime minister of Piedmont. His immediate preoccupation was to negotiate another agreement with Napoleon III; in its final form, the agreement called for France to recognize Piedmont's annexation of Tuscany and Emilia Romagna—which occurred through plebiscites in March 1860—and for the eventual formation of a kingdom of Italy headed by Piedmont's Savoy dynasty, in exchange for Piedmont's relinquishing of Nice and the Savoy region. Cavour also attempted, with little success, an agreement with Naples's Bourbon king Francis II to achieve an equal division of the Italian peninsula between a northern kingdom and a southern kingdom. Meanwhile, with important help from Mazzini, who organized volunteers and fomented revolts, Garibaldi's plan for an expedition to the South was become increasingly a reality that focused on Sicily. Garibaldi and his Thousand Red Shirts left for Sicily on 4 May 1860 on behalf of the National Society and in the name of "Italy and Victor Emmanuel," but Mazzini was still convinced that the general's action could be that "splendid, daring deed" that could return to the democrats the radical initiative in Italy's unification. On his side, Mazzini had among Garibaldi's volunteers two important activists, Francesco Crispi and Agostino Bertani, both of absolutely republican faith and both convinced of the necessity of starting a radical revolution. Although he could not join Garibaldi, partly because he was ill, Mazzini followed the general's extraordinary military exploits step by step, while he carefully prepared his alternative plan for Italy's unification.[32]

With the help of Crispi and Bertani, Mazzini, arriving in Italy shortly after Garibaldi's departure, gathered volunteers in both Genoa and Tuscany; the plan was for them to move to the Papal State, take Rome, and then meet Garibaldi, who was moving up the peninsula from Sicily, so as to unify the entire country under the republican movement. However, Cavour ordered Mazzini's volunteers to be relocated in Sicily, and the plan did not materialize. On 7 September 1860, after an impressive string of victories that occurred as much because of the corruption of Bourbon high officials as because of Garibaldi's brilliant strategies, Garibaldi arrived in Naples, having effectively conquered southern Italy. Ten days later, Mazzini also arrived; despite being ignored by the provisional government, receiving death threats from the moderate liberals, and only barely managing to speak with Garibaldi, Mazzini did his best to create the basis for strong republican public opinion in Naples. In October 1860, he founded the radical paper *Il Popolo d'Italia* (The Italian people). In his article "Programma del Popolo d'Italia" (The Italian people's program), Mazzini said Italian unification was "timely, inevitable, [and] wanted by providence"; he urged the people to support Garibaldi's program of creating a free Italian nation with its center in Rome, as against Cavour's program of leaving Rome to the pope; and he stated that the paper was the official organ of the Associazione unitaria italiana (Italian unitary association), devoted to the same purpose. However, after defeating the Bourbon army at Volturno, Garibaldi met with Victor Emmanuel II, who had fought his way from the North, invading the Papal State to meet with Garibaldi's army, and Garibaldi quite simply handed him southern Italy, partly to avoid an otherwise inevitable civil war between democratic and moderate forces. Soon afterward, on 21 October 1860, plebiscites sanctioned the annexation of southern Italy to Piedmont. Garibaldi and his volunteers were soon cast aside, while Piedmontese soldiers and bureaucrats took control of the situation. Italy was unified, but Cavour had won against both Mazzini and Garibaldi.[33]

The relationship between Mazzini and Garibaldi, uneasy as it was, improved for a time, as both recognized their defeat and plotted revenge. Thus, on 5 November 1860, they met and discussed how to move "for Venice and Rome with or without Louis Napoleon, and to attempt to overthrow Cavour during the winter," while also plotting an insurrection in the South; with Garibaldi in command, Mazzini was going to gather funds, as long as no decision was made yet over the ultimate form of government in liberated Italy. By the end of November, Garibaldi was back on his beloved Caprera island, while Mazzini was once again in London, from where he was to witness, powerless and profoundly disillusioned, the proclamation of the Kingdom of Italy on 17 March 1861. During this period, even though he rescinded his ties with the Workers' School, Mazzini paid increasing attention to social issues; in 1860 he published his reflections and writings over a twenty-year period in the pamphlet *Doveri dell'uomo* (Duties of man). Later reprinted in more than a million copies, *Doveri dell'uomo* was a work that, in line with Mazzini's thought, rejected both capitalism and Marxism in favor of what Mazzini called "the language of love" and cooperation both between capital and labor and among workers. The pamphlet acknowledged workers' rights but began with Mazzini telling workers, "I come to talk to you about your duties"—duties as citizens and members of a democratic society, a society in which education had a central role. In Mazzini's view, workers, like nations, had a mission given to them by God. Also, and more important to Mazzini, the workers' fight against oppression was akin to the fight conducted by other oppressed groups, from women, to serfs, to slaves—a crucial point that shows how, in 1860, Mazzini clearly had in mind the connections between his view of the world and the much wider framework he was part of at a time when slavery had become the dominant issue in Garrison's Civil War America.[34]

In late 1861, both Garrison and Mazzini stood at crossroads in their lives. Their continuously uncompromising radical stances over the strategies through which to achieve the abolition of American slavery and the creation of an Italian republic, and the meaning that these ultimate objectives represented, had led to increasing isolation for the two men within the abolitionist and democratic circles. Though still acknowledged as bellwethers and authorities by many abolitionists and democrats, both Garrison and Mazzini were less able than in the past to understand correctly the rapid changes that the United States and Italy were going through, while new ideas and new ways of fighting advanced to the fore and took center stage in the struggles to which they had dedicated their lives. To a certain degree, both Garrison and Mazzini faced the dilemma of either adapting somehow to the changes of the times or perhaps hoping that new occasions might arise for them to turn their initial radical programs into reality.

Thus, confronted by the rise of militant abolitionism and by the increasingly violent atmosphere of sectional conflicts, despite initially holding firm to his radical attitude of pacifist nonresistance, Garrison ultimately found himself praising abolitionists who fomented violent slave insurrections. At the same time, despite his dislike for Lincoln's and the Republican Party's moderate antislavery program, Garrison also found virtues in the party's rise and in Lincoln's election, while still keeping a detached attitude toward both until the beginning of the Civil War; at that point he abandoned both his caution and his pacifism and rallied to support the Union in its war effort, also recognizing the wider significance of its ideological position. Mazzini, confronted by a host of criticisms from within democratic circles over his strategies and programs, and despite the profound crisis his movement was going through, intensified his calls for revolution and held firm to his radical republican beliefs. But he also changed strategy several times to avoid completely losing his supporters. In particular, a major threat came to Mazzini both from the National Society and from Cavour's posing as a viable moderate liberal alternative for Italy's national unification; although he profoundly disliked Cavour, Mazzini went so far as rallying the democratic forces under a "neutral banner" in order to reach his primary objective of a free Italian nation.

But by late 1861, neither of the changes in strategy employed by Garrison and Mazzini had led to any tangible result; for the most part, they had led to deep disappointments. Despite Garrison's continuous protests, the American Civil War continued relentlessly with neither a near end of slavery in sight, nor any sign from the Union government that slave emancipation was a central issue. Across the Atlantic, despite Mazzini's best efforts, Italy had finally achieved unification—though without Rome and Venice—but Cavour and Victor Emmanuel II had managed to create a liberal monarchy, casting aside Garibaldi and his Red Shirts. However, even though both Garrison and Mazzini had their reasons to be disappointed, their situations in late 1861 were profoundly different: in the United States, the Union government could still decide to implement slave emancipation, but in Italy, the possibility to transform the monarchy into a republic through a revolution seemed, by then, very remote. Nevertheless, it was not just that the two situations were different; there was also a difference in the character of the two men: they effectively reacted in opposite ways to the latest challenges they faced. Garrison ultimately proved more willing to compromise over the events, as long as his final objective was reached one way or another, while Mazzini continued to be as uncompromising as ever, perhaps even more so, as his final objective seemed to move increasingly out of his grasp.

7

POLITICAL STALEMATE BETWEEN OPPOSITE EXTREMISMS

Garrison's Compromise and Mazzini's Defeat, 1862–1870

In the 1860s, an age of emancipation, the radical seeds that William Lloyd Garrison and Giuseppe Mazzini, together with countless others, had sown yielded substantial fruit in terms of developments and measures geared toward release of people and nations from oppression across the Euro-American world. Although 1863, when Abraham Lincoln issued his Emancipation Proclamation and abolished American slavery, was the high point of the movement for people's freedom in the American hemisphere, we cannot forget that 1861, when Russian serfdom was abolished and Italy was unified as a free Italian nation, held a comparable meaning for the European continent. In 1864 Romania also emancipated its serf population. Then in 1867, the old reactionary power of the Habsburg Empire, with liberals firmly in power, yielded partially to its nationalities' demands for autonomy by allowing the creation of a double-centered Austro-Hungarian monarchy; across the Atlantic, the Spanish Empire, in the midst of the Ten Years' War (1868–78), took the first step toward abolition of slavery in Cuba with the 1870 Moret Law. In transnational and transatlantic perspective, we can very well say that it seemed to many American and European reformers that the Euro-American world was truly beginning to embark on a path leading toward a progressive future in which respect for humankind's fundamental rights and freedoms would be commonplace—and this despite the inevitable compromises and shortcomings that accompanied each of these momentous developments.[1]

In hemispheric perspective, Lincoln's 1863 Emancipation Proclamation appears to have been part of a long-term and much wider set of reforms and measures, starting with the 1850 abolition of the Brazilian slave trade, that together would have brought to an end the "second slavery" in the entire American continent; these reforms continued until the end of the 1880s, with the final abolition of slavery first in Cuba and then in Brazil. From the point of view of Atlantic abolitionists such as Garrison, these developments were a sort of vindication of the enormous efforts made in the 1830s and early 1840s, culminating in the two World's Anti-Slavery conventions in London, to build a truly transatlantic movement committed to the complete eradication of the slave systems. To be sure, since then, the efforts had become far more sporadic and not nearly as incisive as at earlier times, so that it is fair to say, with Richard Blackett, that "Lincoln's Emancipation Proclamation went a long way to seal the fissures that had appeared in the transatlantic Garrisonian movement." In this sense, given that the "second slavery" not only had survived all sorts of attacks, not only from Atlantic abolitionism, but had proved extraordinarily resilient and profitable at the same time, the wave of antislavery measures, when it began, certainly took Atlantic abolitionists by surprise. Also, only in the United States, in contrast with the mostly peaceful transition in the other slave societies in the New World, was the actual abolition of slavery an immensely traumatic experience, in that it constituted the end result of a civil war that left more than six hundred thousand dead.[2]

Compared especially with the freeing of Russian serfs, the abolition of American slavery was a much more violent and costly affair in terms of human lives—even though ten times more serfs were emancipated in Russia after 1861 than slaves in the United States after 1863. In Russia, opposition to serfdom had built up gradually at least since the 1825 Decembrist revolt, supported by the educated upper classes—among whose most important representatives was Mazzini's longtime London acquaintance Alexander Herzen—as a necessary requirement for the modernization of the country. Other factors, similar to the ones that had prompted the English upper classes to pass the 1833 Emancipation Act—such as the constant fear of agrarian revolts—contributed in no small part to the outcome. After Czar Alexander II announced his intention to emancipate Russian serfs with the Nazimov Rescript in 1857, an editing committee prepared a draft of the Emancipation Law, which finally went into effect on 19 February 1861, freeing 47 million individuals and thus theoretically releasing from their ties to the land the single largest agricultural workforce in the entire Euro-American world. As early as 18 April 1861, Garrison announced Russian emancipation in the *Liberator,* publishing in full Czar Alexander II's decree. In reality, even more than it happened in the British case, emancipation proved not to be as complete and transforming as the czarist propaganda depicted it, because serfs were forced to work for their former masters for an additional period before being free. Significantly, commenting on the situation of the Russian peasantry in September 1861, Mazzini stated with true prescience, "The elements of a great revolution exist already in Russia."[3]

Legal Emancipation and Monarchical Unification

Until the summer of 1862, both Garrison and Mazzini thought the radical causes to which they had dedicated their lives were not going to end successfully. Despite supporting the Union and Abraham Lincoln, Garrison did not see the abolition of slavery as a priority for either the president or Congress. Consequently, he renewed his efforts to prompt the Union government to take decisive action toward emancipation, especially through very pointed editorials in the *Liberator.* Mazzini, having witnessed the formation of an Italian kingdom that shattered his hopes of unifying Italy through a republican government, had already had his share of disappointments. Never one to admit final defeat, though, Mazzini, like Garrison, renewed his efforts, and he continued to denounce the farce of an Italian unification that had been carried out as little more than a dynastic project by the Piedmontese House of Savoy. However, the truth was that, while in 1862 Garrison could and did still hope for a change in a situation that was very much in flux in the middle of the American Civil War, Mazzini could only harbor a slim hope to alter the outcome of events that seemed by then more or less fixed. In other words, at this time in their lives, Garrison and Mazzini were still very much on parallel paths, since they were agitating in opposition to the status quo—as they had done throughout their lives—but before long their paths were going to diverge.

From a wider perspective, parallels and connections between the American and Italian situations within a common milieu of radical struggle for freedom and democracy continued to exist and were further reinforced by the Civil War struggle, which pitted the antislavery Union against the proslavery Confederacy, symbolizing nothing short of the central confrontation for the future of freedom in the Euro-American world. This was certainly the interpretation that both Garrison and the Garrisonians, and also Mazzini, gave to the Civil War. In particular, Mazzini sent a letter to his close friend and collaborator Jessie White Mario in September 1861, in response to persistent rumors that Garibaldi might join the Union Army, in which he clarified the specific connection between the two different struggles for freedom that were conducted in Civil War America and Risorgimento Italy. He wrote: "We [Italians] have Venice and Rome to emancipate; and by doing so, we would build up a free anti-slavery Nation, and would be enabled to give far more powerful help to the abolitionists of America than by going and fighting their actual battles." Then in another letter, published in the Milan periodical *Unità Italiana* (Italian unity) on 6 December 1862, regarding the sufferings of the Lancashire workers as a result of the interruption of the supply of American cotton to the English factories, caused by the Civil War, Mazzini described the Civil War and its global significance in terms comparable to Wendell Phillips's words, as "the great contest the world fights in the name of Liberty against the Evil Spirit whose names are Inequality and Slavery."[4]

By then, though, matters had suddenly moved forward in regard to the antislavery cause in the Civil War, since, for many different reasons, Lincoln had taken decisive steps that eventually led to his issuing the Emancipation Proclamation, which was effective 1 January 1863. As a result, in Europe, as Caleb McDaniel has remarked, prominent "liberals in Britain and France swelled the ranks of the Union's transatlantic allies." A year later, Mazzini, together with many of those liberals, joined the London Emancipation Society, a strong antislavery and pro-Union institution, which had been founded in 1859 by Frederick William Chesson, son-in-law of George Thompson, Garrison's longtime friend, and Thompson himself. Given these momentous developments, it seemed to Garrison—and also to many of the abolitionists turned radical Republicans—that the seeds sown with the hard struggle for the abolition of American slavery, which had begun thirty-two years earlier on the same day of the year as the Emancipation Proclamation, with the publication of the first issue of the *Liberator*, had finally yielded their fruits. From then on, despite the many problems related to emancipation and its aftermath, Garrison embarked on a path that, by the time of Lincoln's re-election in 1864, left him with no reservations about the president; and he was now an even more ardent supporter of the Union, since the Union's cause was now nothing less than freedom itself.[5]

From then on, Garrison's and Mazzini's paths, which had followed a somewhat parallel course, began to diverge significantly. Only an event in Mazzini's life of importance comparable to that of slave emancipation in Garrison's life—specifically, the creation of an Italian republic—could have prevented this divergence. Such an event would have fulfilled expectations that had been brewed through a struggle as relentless as Garrison's and as long-lasting. Instead, even though events such as Garibaldi's 1862 expedition to Aspromonte and the "civil war" that ravaged the Mezzogiorno effectively created the preconditions for a revolutionary upheaval, Italy continued to be a monarchy—and one in which, despite its constitutional structure and liberal ideology, authoritarian government left little room for ideals or causes. The fact that the emancipation of American slaves, the radical event Garrison had longed for, actually occurred, while the creation of an Italian republic, the radical event Mazzini had longed for, did not occur is what ultimately explains why the later lives of the two men ceased to run on a parallel course and began to turn in fundamentally different directions.

By mid-1862, William Lloyd Garrison was convinced that Lincoln and the Union government had no intention to act on emancipation while fighting the American Civil War. On 4 July 1861, Garrison had publicly prompted the masses to press the Union government to abolish slavery, and on 13 December 1861 he had changed the masthead of the *Liberator* so that, instead of "The United States Constitution Is a Covenant with Death and an Agreement with Hell," it read "Proclaim Liberty to all the Land, to all the Inhabitants Thereof." To be sure, the Union government's record in regard to emancipation was rather poor up until late 1862. In August 1861, in Missouri, General John Frémont had issued a martial law that declared free all the slaves of rebellious individuals; Garrison published the law's text in the *Liberator,* commenting, "Laus Deo!—The Beginning of the End." However, Lincoln revoked the measure, and Garrison accused the president of a "serious dereliction of duty in not making it applicable to all other slave states in revolt." Congress then passed the First Confiscation Act, according to which all the slaves used in Confederate military services should not be returned to their owners; a year later, in July 1862, Congress passed the Second Confiscation Act, according to which slaves could be legally confiscated from Confederate masters and declared free. Neither measure impressed Garrison, though, partly because, in the meantime, Lincoln had revoked once again a much more radical measure decreed by General David Hunter, who had proclaimed all the slaves in South Carolina, Georgia, and Florida free. As a result of Lincoln's actions—it seemed to Garrison—immediate, unconditional emancipation was hardly around the corner.[6]

Yet, the truth was that Lincoln was biding his time, waiting for the right moment, in both political and military terms, to act against slavery. As the radical members of the Republican Party—many of whom were abolitionists—grew in strength in Congress, while the war continued seemingly without an end, Lincoln saw his opportunity and his justification for striking directly at the slave system. Accordingly, in July 1862, he drafted the first text of the Emancipation Proclamation, and in September 1862, after the Union Army won a major battle at Antietam, he presented the Preliminary Emancipation Proclamation in Congress, informing congressmen that it would become effective on 1 January 1863. Justified by Lincoln as a necessary military measure needed to crush Confederate resistance, the Emancipation Proclamation of 1 January 1863 was, as Brooks D. Simpson has remarked, "a revolutionary document cloaked in conservative terms." While the Preliminary Emancipation Proclamation still talked about compensation for slaveholders and African colonization following the abolition of slavery, the final version of the Emancipation Proclamation made no mention of those measures. However, Lincoln did not abandon completely his conviction that both would be necessary; in fact, as Eric Foner has remarked, "Lincoln still retained an interest in colonization. But he would never again publicly advocate this policy." More importantly, the proclamation declared unequivocally, "On the first day of January, in the year of our Lord one thousand eight hundred and sixty-three, all persons held as slaves within any state, or designated part of a state, the people whereof shall then be in rebellion against the United States, shall be then, thenceforward and forever free." Thus, immediate, uncompensated, and perpetual emancipation—the very radical cause to which Garrison had dedicated his life—was finally going to take effect. But it is also true—and Garrison took notice of this—that the Emancipation Proclamation affected only the slaves still living in the Confederate territories.[7]

When Garrison heard about the September 1862 Preliminary Emancipation Proclamation, he recognized its importance, but he was also disappointed at the mention of African colonization and at the postponement of emancipation for three months. Hence his still harsh judgment on Lincoln as a "president who can do nothing for freedom in a direct manner, but only by circumlocution and delay," as he wrote in a letter to his daughter Fanny. However, when 1 January 1863 came, and the final version of the Emancipation Proclamation became effective, Garrison changed his attitude and did not pass up any occasion to mark the event as a true historic moment. He even went so far as postponing publication of the *Liberator* to 2 January 1863, so that he could print the full text of the Emancipation Proclamation in his paper. In the *Liberator,* Garrison commented on the Emancipation Proclamation with the following words: "It is a great historic event, sublime in its magnitude, momentous and beneficient in its far-reaching consequences, and eminently just and right alike to the oppressor and the oppressed, as well as imperatively called for by the fearfully imperiled state of the country. THE PEOPLE will sustain it—the army will receive fresh inspiration—and all Rebeldom be filled with consternation in view of their inevitable doom." As Russell Nye has noted, "the Emancipation Proclamation fixed William Lloyd Garrison's place in history"; quite simply, it seemed like the final vindication of Garrison's more than thirty years of radical abolitionist activity. A few weeks after the proclamation's release, Garrison clarified this point at a meeting of the MASS, when he stated, "Thirty years ago it was midnight with the anti-slavery cause; now it is bright noon of day with the sun shining in his meridian splendor."[8]

There is no doubt that the Emancipation Proclamation did a great deal to persuade Garrison of Lincoln's soundness and that as a result, from then on, Garrison became a "tenacious Unionist," as he called himself in the *Liberator.* There is also no doubt, though, that, initially, Garrison continued to maintain a somewhat critical stance on the Union government's actions. He pointed out that the Emancipation Proclamation was hardly "universal," since it freed only the slaves in Confederate territories. Moreover, in an editorial in the *Liberator* at the end of January 1863, Garrison went so far as attributing the main reason for the protracted length of the Civil War to the Union government's missed occasion to emancipate the slaves from the beginning of the conflict: "During all that time [the time elapsed from the first Civil War battle to 1 January 1863], why were not the rebels conquered . . . if the aid of the Negroes was not needed?" Yet, Garrison's observations were a far cry from the much more incisive and critical attitude of those radical abolitionists—especially Wendell Phillips—who had become radical Republicans. Both Wendell Phillips and Frederick Douglass, in particular, accused Lincoln of having achieved a hollow objective by not securing emancipation with additional measures, such as the redistribution of confiscated Confederate land, designed to help the freed people achieve economic independence and arrive at a full meaning of citizenship that would end racial discrimination. In other words, radical Republicans thought there was an impelling need, in James B. Stewart's words, for "all true Abolitionists to redeem their original commitment to racial equality by obtaining for freed people access to land, to education, and above all, to political power through ballot."[9]

In 1864 Garrison and Phillips confronted each other in a series of debates during Lincoln's campaign for his second presidential term. First, in January 1864, at the annual meeting of the MASS, while Phillips accused Lincoln of racism, given his shortcomings, Garrison responded that "the re-election of Lincoln would be the safest, wisest course," a position Garrison sustained wholeheartedly from the pages of the *Liberator.* A second confrontation occurred in May 1864, at the annual meeting of the AASS in New York. There Phillips said, partly because Lincoln opposed extending suffrage to African Americans, that the Union government intended to leave relations between blacks and whites after the war as they had been before the war. To these criticisms, Garrison first responded that black enfranchisement was not an actual part of the AASS mission statement in the "Declaration of Sentiments," and then he defended Lincoln by citing his accomplishments—above all else, the fact that "Lincoln . . . struck the chains from the limbs of more than three million slaves." A month later, Garrison finally met Lincoln in Washington, after the Republican convention in Baltimore renominated him as the party's presidential candidate. Commenting in the *Liberator* on the unanimity of Lincoln's nomination, Garrison called the Republican Party's 1864 platform "the first NATIONAL VERDICT ever recorded, in form and fact, in letter and spirit, against slavery, as a system 'incompatible with the principles of republican government.'" Given that, thirty-four years earlier, Garrison had spent time in jail for libeling a slave trader in the same city where the Republican convention took place, this represented no small victory for him.[10]

Shortly afterward, Garrison went to Washington to meet Lincoln, and the president invited Garrison to join him in a private conversation at the White House. After their talk, which occurred on 10 June 1864, both men clearly came away satisfied. There is no doubt that Lincoln held a certain admiration for Garrison's unquestionable moral authority, which he expressed by stating, in regard to emancipation, that "the logic and moral power of Garrison and the antislavery people of the country and the army have done it all." For his part, Garrison came away from the meeting with Lincoln impressed by the honesty and moral stature of the president and, above all, reinforced in his commitment to Lincoln's administration. As he wrote his wife Helen on 11 June 1864, Garrison sincerely believed Lincoln's resolve to "do all that he can see it right and possible for him to do to uproot slavery," especially by proposing an amendment to the Constitution. But there was more than that. More than a year later, in November 1865, months after Lincoln's death, Garrison gave a speech in the Illinois House of Representatives in which he expressed his opinion on Lincoln's achievements—an opinion that, in all likelihood Garrison had held at least from 1864, if not earlier. In his speech, Garrison echoed the president's own words by stating that, in acting on emancipation, Lincoln was "animated by the conviction that he was an instrument in the hands of God to bring about great and glorious ends—to feel strong in his purpose to make no compromise with the dark spirit of slavery."[11]

Thus it appears that, partially as a result of his convictions of Lincoln's absolute, divinely inspired, righteousness and the righteousness of his program, by 1864 Garrison—once the most radical abolitionist voice—had begun taking a strictly reductionist position on the problem of African American freedom. In practice, Garrison had come to believe that, even though it provided freedom to the slaves only in strictly legal terms, the Emancipation Proclamation in itself had done most of what was needed in order to secure a true end to slavery and the beginning of a more racially equal world. There is little doubt that Garrison thought he was acting consistently with the views he had held from the 1830s onward, since his objective had always been, first and foremost, emancipation. However, it is difficult not to see Garrison's move away from more radical positions—which once included visions of true racial equality—as a compromise he made with his own principles, perhaps because he was tired and ailing at this time, or perhaps because, as Russell Nye has suggested, "after thirty years as a dissenter, Garrison found it pleasant to be on the winning side."

Certainly, this somewhat "new" attitude brought Garrison the benefits of a popularity he had never experienced before, but it also blinded him to the existence of crucial problems experienced by African Americans from the end of the Civil War to Reconstruction.[12]

In mid-1862, while in the United States Garrison was divided between his support for the Union in its war against slaveholders and his disappointment in Lincoln's policy for its lack of abolitionist focus, in London Mazzini was attempting to overcome his disappointment at the unification of Italy under the Savoy dynasty, by once again plotting insurrections that he hoped would lead to the establishment of an Italian republic. Only a few months later, Lincoln signed the Emancipation Proclamation, prompting Garrison to abandon, in time, his most radical positions and to support the Union wholeheartedly. In contrast, Mazzini's staunch refusal to compromise on his republican principles caused him to remain "the monarchy's outlaw," an expression he coined for himself after refusing an offer of pardon from Victor Emmanuel II, now the Italian king. Thus, unlike Garrison, Mazzini preserved his radicalism, paying a very high price for it. Mazzini continued to be an exile in a foreign country, and in the same years during which he published *Duties of Man,* while he called for universal suffrage and agitated for women's rights (as Garrison also had done), Mazzini gave increasing attention to the workers' associations, inciting them to become the backbone of Italy's democratic movement. In truth, not all the odds were against a successful democratic uprising in Italy. Under the guidance of unprepared and mediocre right-wing statesmen, Italy's monarchical system had barely managed to survive the untimely death of Cavour in 1861, and half of the newly formed Italian army was actually engaged in a "civil war" in the South, where thousands of peasants—derogatorily called "brigands" by the authorities—had rebelled against the new Italian state and the draft and the harsher taxes that had resulted. If only this large-scale revolt could find a leader among the democrats, the chances of a large-scale insurrection against the Italian monarchy would increase.[13]

Back in 1861, Mazzini had agreed with Garibaldi that they would join forces to help the democratic movement regain the initiative through the recruitment of volunteers and the conquest of Venice and Rome, which were still under the control of Austria and the pope. To this end, in March 1862, Mazzini and Garibaldi founded the Associazione Emancipatrice Italiana (Society for Italy's emancipation), whose aim was to foment a people's war for the completion of Italy's unification. From the start, though, there was disagreement between Garibaldi and Mazzini; while Garibaldi wished to liberate Rome first, Mazzini argued, instead, that conquering Venice would weaken Austria and eventually lead to the end of the post-1815 system of alliances between Europe's reactionary regimes. In the end, against the opinion of most democrats in addition to Mazzini, Garibaldi gathered volunteers in Sicily and, in August 1862, attempted for the second time to move up the Italian peninsula from the South with Rome as his primary objective; however, the Italian Army blocked Garibaldi's advance, and in the battle that ensued at Aspromonte, in Calabria, the general received a wound in his leg. Despite his disapproval of Garibaldi's initiative, Mazzini was genuinely shocked at the news, which he received while he was in Lugano, Switzerland. He could not believe that the Italian Army had fired against Italy's true hero, and he thought the people's outrage would have provoked a radical insurrection, but his idea proved wrong. The following month, from Lugano, Mazzini published a short pamphlet entitled *Agli Italiani!* (To Italians!) in which he wrote, significantly, that "the bullet, shot from a royal rifle, which wounded Garibaldi, has torn apart the last line of the agreement . . . between the Republicans and the monarchy. . . . We go back, free from all conditions apart from the sacred cause of the homeland, to our old [republican] flag."[14]

In practice, according to Mazzini, if any democrat still thought that the alliance that had originated in the collaboration between the National Society and the Savoy dynasty in the 1850s had any reason to exist—even only for the sake of completing Italy's unification—the events in Aspromonte should have convinced them that that was no longer the case. Mazzini continued: "The monarchy cannot make Italy. . . . Today, after only two years of Italy's early life, the monarchy rules . . . through the state of siege, with the systematic violation of individual liberty, with the suppression of freedom of the press and duty of association, with the cavalry charges. . . . In France, in Spain, in Belgium, in Germany, in Greece . . . constitutional monarchies have proven incompatible with the people's progress." While Italy's monarchy seemed to be unable to rule without causing bloodshed—as the army was clearly proving through its brutal suppression of the peasants' rebellion in the South, to which the "state of siege" referred—Mazzini once again saw Italy's problem in its wider context, as part of a long series of failures by constitutional monarchical systems throughout Europe to provide the conditions for a type of progress that led to the democratization of society and politics; this was a point he had been making for the past thirty years. Interestingly, as if to prove Mazzini right, insurrections and revolutions had sprung up all over eastern Europe. Stimulated partly by these developments, soon after Aspromonte, Mazzini created a secret organ called Falange Sacra (Sacred phalanx), which was to work as a liaison between the Society for Italian Emancipation and the peasants in the rural areas; few democrats expressed interest in Mazzini's organization, though, and his own inexplicable decision to focus on the Veneto region, rather than the South—where the peasants' revolts had created a potentially revolutionary situation—doomed the initiative from the start.[15]

In 1863, Mazzini, a fervent admirer of Lincoln, rejoiced at the Emancipation Proclamation. Shortly afterward, Mazzini wrote an open letter to the editors of the periodical *Dovere,* in which he asked for his name to be added to an address written by Garibaldi, "To Abraham Lincoln, Emancipator of the Slaves in the American Republic." Mazzini praised—in terms with which Garrison would certainly have agreed—the principle at the heart of Lincoln's decision to emancipate the slaves. It was "the principle of Humanity . . . the principle that states: God created not kings, masters and servants, but man." He went on: "The White freedom, for which I have fought and I still fight as much as my weak health allows, does not have either reason to exist or certainty of victory if it does not obey the same *principle* that commands Black freedom." To Mazzini, both Lincoln and Garibaldi had become the very symbols of that universal freedom to which he had dedicated his life, through their work of liberating people from the regimes that oppressed them in one form or another. Consequently, despite the disagreements that had often characterized his relationship with Garibaldi, when he finally managed to persuade the Italian hero to come to London, Mazzini was full of expectations for the possible effects of Garibaldi's immense popularity and how this could both help raise money for the cause of a republican Italy and rouse republican sentiment among the English workers. However, as soon as he arrived, Garibaldi was drawn into a continuous series of celebratory events that did not allow him any spare time. He did meet with Mazzini three times, though, and on one occasion, at a dinner at Alexander Herzen's house, Garibaldi even drank a toast to Mazzini with the words "I drink to him, to my friend, to my teacher." Even so, all together, Garibaldi's visit to London turned out to be a big disappointment for Mazzini.[16]

A few months after Garibaldi's departure, in September 1864, London witnessed the momentous formation of the International Workers' Association, or First International, which was to become the European working classes' premier revolutionary organ. As a long-term exiled radical and acknowledged international revolutionary who had continually attempted to organize workers in associations that defended their rights, Mazzini should have been at the forefront of the First International. Unfortunately, his poor health kept him away from these meetings. Furthermore, from the start, Karl Marx dominated the meetings and succeeded in steering the First International toward an openly declared socialist agenda. Mazzini had long been a critic of socialism, and as Salvo Mastellone has shown, he had engaged in debate with both Karl Marx and Friedrich Engels from as early as the 1840s and the 1850s, when they all had written, for a time, in the Chartist periodical *Northern Star,* directed by Feargus O'Connor and Julian Hearney and based in London. Like Marx, Mazzini was then "considered as the theoretician of 'liberation' from political despotism, reactionary oppression, social exploitation," according to Mastellone. However, since that time, Mazzini had become convinced that the prominence of rigidly deterministic economics in Marx's thought and the latter's vision of history as class struggle removed that type of socialism as far as possible from his own commitment to democratic republicanism and class cooperation. For his part, Marx scorned above all Mazzini's "bourgeois patriotism," while he utterly despised his religious view of history and of the people's role in it. By 1864 the conflict between the two revolutionaries had reached a point of no return; as a result, the following year, with the help of Mikhail Bakunin, Marx was instrumental in expelling Mazzinian delegates from the First International, which, by then, had become an exclusively socialist domain.[17]

To be sure, Bakunin was not nearly as hostile as Marx toward Mazzini. Bakunin and Mazzini had known each other since 1862, and initially Bakunin admired Mazzini, whom he saw as the only truly selfless radical and single-mindedly committed revolutionary in all of Europe. Afterward, Bakunin came to share Marx's criticisms of Mazzini, but he never lost his respect for him. This is particularly important when we think that Bakunin was at that time enormously influential in Italian democratic circles; he was effectively replacing Mazzini in popularity among the radical Italian youth. That more than a few former followers of Mazzini's republicanism defected to join Bakunin's socialism—and, later on, his eventual move to anarchism—should alert us to the fact that by the early to mid 1860s, Mazzini was losing his grip on the Italian revolutionary movement and, above all, on the means and ends of the revolution itself. Many in Italian democratic circles, though venerating Mazzini as an initiator of the idea and struggle for Italian national unity, thought his conspiratorial activities were ineffectual and old-fashioned and his commitment to a republican form of government either too idealistic or little focused on the people's conditions.[18]

In the long run, the events of 1862–63 had a lasting impact on the later lives of Garrison and Mazzini, an impact that determined how different their trajectories became—even though this difference never affected their long and very strong friendship. In practice, the Emancipation Proclamation and the eventual abolition of slavery transformed Garrison's role: instead of an agitator embodying the moral conscience of the United States and the quintessential radical voice, mostly in opposition to any American government in power, he became a wholehearted supporter of the new American nation, with its newly found freedom, that Lincoln and his government envisioned. Conversely, the existence of a unified Italian nation posed more than one problem for Mazzini, since the great struggle for Italy's freedom and unification, in which he had engaged heart and soul and in which he had played such a crucial role, had ended. Mazzini felt no sympathy for Italy's new regime and, as a result, unlike Garrison, he continued to be very much a radical voice on the side of the opposition—"the monarchy's outlaw," in his own words—even though his influence was clearly declining. Ultimately, this fundamental difference affected and shaped in very profound ways the subsequent courses of the lives of the two men.

Garrison's Triumph and Mazzini's Exile

The difference that the abolition of slavery in the United States and monarchical unification in Italy made in the lives of Garrison and Mazzini was bound to create an increasing divergence between them over time. Even though the two not only continued to be friends and to hold each other in high esteem, but also occasionally collaborated—as in Mazzini's creation of the Universal Republican Alliance—the truth was that, from 1863 onward, Garrison and Mazzini could not have been further apart in commitment to their causes, their radical activism, their undisputed roles as moral consciences of their own nations, and, more generally, the way they felt about themselves and their achievements as parts of wider schemes of progressive action and reform. Whereas for more than thirty years, these features had been constant priorities leading to comparable trajectories in Garrison's and Mazzini's lives, now that parallelism seemed to be irretrievably lost. The reason for the loss, however, was not just the different turn of events in the United States and Italy and the effect those events had on the lives of the two men; it was also very much related to the different attitudes that characterized Garrison and Mazzini in the later periods of their lives.

Garrison's decision to close down the *Liberator* in 1865 and his retreat from antislavery activities—even though partly justified by the sense that he had completed the task of achieving slave emancipation—seem inexplicable in view of his tireless efforts to promote all sorts of radical causes geared toward the complete moral reform of humankind. Only Garrison's continuous commitment to the cause of women's rights seems to have been an exception to an otherwise never-ending series of engagements in celebratory events praising his greatness as an initiator of emancipation. In these actions, which are emblematic of his post-1863 attitude, lay the seeds of Garrison's compromise over what freedom actually meant beyond the legal abolition of slavery and his eventual acceptance of the status quo, despite his life-long radicalism, at a time, after the Civil War, when the need for fighting radical battles for African American civil rights was stronger than ever. Conversely, certainly partly as a result of different historical circumstances, Mazzini remained very consistent with his earlier radical persona, not just in supporting women's rights—where a point of convergence with what was left of Garrison's former radicalism still existed—but also in continuing to fight for causes such as African American civil rights, simply because he knew the struggle for freedom was not yet complete.

Thus, in 1865, when Moncure Conway, a friend of Mazzini's and a leading abolitionist in the United States, asked his opinion on the crucial issue of black suffrage, Mazzini responded with a letter in which, while he praised the United States for abolishing slavery, he warned the American people—with an argument that Wendell Phillips would have supported, as Caleb McDaniel has noted—that their task of building a truly free republic was not finished until they gave full citizenship to African Americans. Mazzini compared the United States to an Old World monarchy—hardly masking his disappointment over Italy's unification under the Savoy kings—since, by keeping civil rights restricted to the white population, it was as if Americans were building an aristocracy of a sort. Said Mazzini: "You have abolished slavery[;] you have decreed that whoever breathes air within the Republic must be free . . . [but] can you mutilate this great principle? . . . reduce it to the proportions of the half liberty enjoyed within monarchies? . . . Would you want to transform your democracy into an incipient aristocracy?" It was to prevent this from happening, Mazzini reasoned, that African Americans—whom he called, significantly, "the armed apostles of national union"—had to be granted the same citizenship rights as whites.[19]

As he criticized what happened in the United States, in his own country Mazzini also did not allow himself to willingly compromise any of his principles simply for the sake of supporting an Italian nation in whatever form it had come into being. In fact, it appears that for Mazzini, the most urgent problem continued to be the political and governmental form of the new Italian nation and how democratic that form turned out to be. In this attitude of opposition toward the Italian monarchical government as the source of betrayal of his and the democrats' expectations lay the reason why Mazzini continued on an increasingly bitter and difficult radical path—in many ways an opposite path to Garrison's, and one that, in the midst of a partly self-imposed exile on a matter of principles, led to Mazzini's increasing isolation and to his repeated defeat and even imprisonment for a few months.

In the United States, after Lincoln's re-election Garrison demanded the immediate passage of an amendment to the Constitution that would sanction the final abolition of slavery. To be sure, in the following, hectic months, Lincoln himself asked his party to support the amendment. And on 31 January 1865 Congress finally passed the Thirteenth Amendment to the Constitution, which abolished slavery throughout the United States. In the *Liberator,* Garrison described the amendment as "the most important . . . in the history of congressional legislation," and on 4 February he addressed a large crowd at a Grand Jubilee Meeting at Music Hall in Boston, recounting all the years of abolitionist struggle and proclaiming their final reward. Significantly, Garrison ended the meeting with the words: "In view of the dominant Anti-Slavery sentiment of the land, it may now be comprehensively declared, 'We are all abolitionists, we are all loyalists, to the backbone.'" By then, the American Civil War was truly nearing its end, as the Confederacy rapidly lost ground against the larger Union forces and their better equipment. The end of the war came eventually on 9 April 1865, when Robert E. Lee surrendered to Ulysses S. Grant at Appomattox Court House. Shortly afterward, on 14 April 1865, Lincoln was assassinated, to Garrison's dismay; the 21 April issue of the *Liberator* bore thick black marks as a sign of mourning. Acknowledging Lincoln's greatness with words Mazzini would have agreed with, Garrison said in his eulogy, reprinted in the 7 July 1865 issue of the *Liberator,* that "no man ever did so large a business on so small a capital in the service of freedom and humanity."[20]

In May 1865, convinced that its purpose had been successfully fulfilled with the passing of the Thirteenth Amendment, Garrison thought of ending the AASS, but opposition from Wendell Phillips and Frederick Douglass prevented him from doing so. In the end, Garrison resigned from his post as AASS president, but the AASS lived on until 1870, still fighting crucial battles for racial equality and for the civil rights of African Americans. For reasons similar to the ones that had prompted him to attempt to end the AASS, Garrison decided to close down the *Liberator.* On 29 December 1865 he published the last issue of the paper, in which he reprinted the 1 January 1831 statement of intentions and wrote a "Valedictory" recounting his career and explaining his decision to discontinue the paper's publication: "The object for which *The Liberator* was commenced—the extermination of chattel slavery—having been gloriously consummated, it seems to me specially appropriate to let its existence cover the historic period of the great struggle." In May 1866, Garrison also withdrew from the MASS. It would seem that he made all these decisions at a time when the struggle over African American civil rights was reaching its peak with the tug-of-war between the radical Republicans in Congress and the conservative and obstructionist new president, Andrew Johnson.[21]

In practice, at a time when American public opinion needed more than ever the radical voice of an individual with indisputable moral authority to press home the issue of racial equality, Garrison seemed to be acting as if he had fulfilled once and for all his mission in public life. In truth, Garrison's relationship with the big issues that agitated the Reconstruction period after the Civil War was a complex one. Back in 1864, when Lincoln had proposed his plan for postwar Reconstruction, Garrison had defended it, despite both Lincoln's hostility to full racial equality and the plan's focus on the establishment of a system of wage labor, rather than on the full recognition of citizenship rights to the freed people. In Garrison's view, freed people needed to be taught Christian principles and a labor ethic in "preparation for assuming such rights" as citizenship. Thus, sounding now as conservative as he had sounded radical only a decade earlier, Garrison had asked "when was it ever known that liberation from bondage was accompanied by a recognition of political equality?"[22]

However, when Johnson attempted to enforce presidential Reconstruction, leaving much of a status quo in the South, with Confederate officers back in power in local governments and racist laws, the infamous "black codes," enforced by them, Garrison rushed to call him—in an April 1866 letter to his son Wendell—"a perfidious successor" of Lincoln and to support the radical Republicans in their attempt to impeach the president. Then in January 1867, Garrison went so far as claiming, in a letter to his son Francis, "Without the President being impeached I do not see how any plan of Reconstruction by Congress can be made available." Finally, when Congress passed the Reconstruction Acts over Johnson's veto, Garrison gave an eloquent and critical speech called "Our National Situation" in which he clarified his reasons for supporting radical Reconstruction. In a further letter to his son Francis, in March 1867, referring to the speech he had given, Garrison explained: "I went for the removal of the President by impeachment. I trust it will be effected, for I see no way of protecting freedom, or freedmen, or Unionists at the South, so long as he sits in the Presidential chair. . . . The Reconstruction Bill passed over the President's veto is very stringent, and places the whole South under military jurisdiction. . . . It is a courageous measure. The South will probably reject it, and be the loser." Even so, by then Garrison was hardly—and hardly wished to be—the same incisive force in the American public opinion that he had been in earlier times.[23]

Despite his support for Johnson's impeachment and in general for the congressional measures proposed by radical Republicans, Garrison "remained largely aloof from the struggles of Radical Reconstruction that preoccupied the nation throughout the later 1860s," in James B. Stewart's words. In fact, in the midst of the most difficult and crucial times during the Reconstruction period, in May 1867, Garrison left for England, where he met old friends. In June, he attended a public breakfast given in his honor at St. James Hall in London, where he met, among others, John Stuart Mill. Still in London in August, Garrison dined with Mazzini for the second time at the Ashursts' house. Then Garrison went to France to attend the Paris Anti-Slavery Convention; he returned to the United States at the beginning of November 1867.[24]

In the following years, Garrison was involved in a host of different activities, even though he did not play a truly major role in any of them. He contributed articles to the *New York Independent* for seven years, between 1868 and 1875, and he was an active supporter of many radical causes that expanded the meaning of freedom—chief among them women's suffrage, for which he continued to be in contact with Elizabeth Cady Stanton, Susan B. Anthony, and other famous feminist activists. Many advocates of women's rights correctly considered Garrison an initiator of the battles over gender equality that increased in intensity in the 1870s. Among those advocates was transatlantic reformer William Henry Ashurst Jr., the son of Garrison's former friend, who had died in 1855. In April 1877, two years before Garrison himself died, Ashurst wrote Garrison very significant words in regard to his role in the abolitionist and women's rights struggles: "I know you deeply sympathize with the enfranchisement of women. The first great Abolitionist . . . for an anti-slavery struggle it is, until women have equal rights with men in the meaning of the laws." In other words, according to Ashurst—and many others—Garrison had understood before anyone else did the link between slavery and women's subjection and had been prepared to fight against both at the same time; in this, more than anything else, Garrison was consistent throughout his life.[25]

In 1870 Garrison became a nominal associate editor of the *Woman's Journal* and contributed articles to the paper for a while. In general, he also spent most of the 1870s appalled at how the United States was drifting into a web of corruption during Ulysses S. Grant's two consecutive presidential terms. But most of all, as William Cain has remarked, "Garrison's main activity in the postwar years was performing the role of the abolitionist hero, the person who had initiated the struggle when doing so was most lonely and arduous." In this guise, Garrison was honored and revered as an initiator of emancipation, and important public figures rushed to show their admiration for him. They even established a special fund for Garrison to support his retirement—it was supposed to be a fitting conclusion to his glorious career as America's acknowledged prophet of freedom.[26]

In London, Mazzini rejoiced as Garrison had done when the end of the American Civil War signaled the victory of the Union over the Confederacy and of freedom over slavery. However, Mazzini's joy was brief, because only a few days later Lincoln—perhaps the man Mazzini admired most after Garrison in the United States—was assassinated. In a letter to Clementia Taylor dated 1 May 1865, Mazzini expressed his feeling of utter sadness over the terrible event: "Yes, I mourned for Lincoln and much more for his wife and all those who loved him. As for him, he died with the consciousness that the cause to which he had devoted himself was triumphant; and the thought must have soothed his last hours. Those are to be pitied who die doubting." Clearly, in writing these words, Mazzini also thought of himself; it is clear from the same words that Mazzini admired in Lincoln, as in Garrison, the absolute commitment to causes to which they, like Mazzini himself, had dedicated their lives, even to the point of being prepared to die for them.[27]

Given Mazzini's affinity for Lincoln, it is certainly not surprising that the latter's legacy, together with the victory of the Union and of the republican ideal of freedom over slavery in America, had a profound impact on the Italian revolutionary. As a consequence, in 1866 Mazzini drew up plans to create the Universal Republican Alliance (URA) between the United States and Europe. The United States had long been a strong inspiration for his own republicanism, despite his reservations about the Americans' exaggerated emphasis on individualism. Although it might have been in part a project to counter Marx's socialist First International, in practice, the URA was supposed to be instrumental in helping to overthrow czars, kings, and emperors in the Old World. The first statement in the Oath of the URA read: "I believe in the *REPUBLIC—the organization of a free people on the ground of equal political and social rights*—as the only means through which a nation may be enabled to will and act, as one man, for the fulfillment of its own destiny and the accomplishment of its duty to Humanity." Thus, in its principles, the URA would have been, perhaps, the most eloquent proof that liberty was a universal concept that rested on the idea of equality—the exact opposite of oppression, regardless of its form: slavery or denial of national self-determination.[28]

In Mazzini's thought, having resolved the crucial problem of slavery, the American government was now free to support antimonarchical, republican, and libertarian movements in the European continent, and it should have done so precisely through the URA. Unfortunately, despite Garrison's enthusiastic approval, the project fell through in less than two years, mainly because of the very little support Mazzini managed to garner in both the United States and Europe. Nevertheless, the URA remains as an important statement of Mazzini's tireless attempts to draw together the progressive forces not just of Europe, but of the entire Euro-American world, into a movement that upheld universal and radical ideals of freedom and democracy.[29]

In the same year, 1866, Mazzini also launched an Italian version of the URA, the Italian Republican Alliance. The reason for the latter had a lot to do with the conflict that was about to begin between Count Otto Von Bismarck's Prussia and the Austro-Hungarian Empire; because it was an ally of Prussia, the Italian kingdom hoped to gain the annexation of Venice in the likely event of Prussia's victory. Although many Italian democrats were suspicious of supporting a war headed by King Victor Emmanuel II, to Mazzini, as in 1849 and in 1859, the imminent war appeared once again to be a chance to transform the kings' and emperors' war into a people's war, one that would lead to an insurgence of all the nationalities oppressed by the Habsburgs—especially in the Balkans, where Young Serbia and the Balkan Emancipation Society were very active—and to the creation of republics in their place. The Italian Republican Alliance was to advertise the cause, recruit volunteers for the people's war, and organize them, much as previous revolutionary organizations devised by Mazzini had done. In practice, however, the war ended shortly after its beginning for the Italian army, which was soundly defeated at Custoza by the Austrians. Despite heroics by Garibaldi and his volunteers and also the fact that, in the end, Italy gained Venice exclusively by means of diplomacy, the result of the war, once again, signaled a complete failure of Mazzini's plans.[30]

Mazzini might have felt disillusioned, but he was not utterly defeated. In September 1867, when the Peace Congress met in Geneva to promote disarmament, Mazzini wrote its members an address stating that peace was not possible as long as tyrannical governments continued to oppress people and nationalities, denying their freedom. In the address, Mazzini mentioned Garrison, by far the most prestigious American representative of the URA, whom he had met with the previous August and who was due to attend the Peace Congress, as (in Mazzini's words) "a man whose friendship honors me" and as an activist who deserved nothing but admiration. Mazzini also noticed, though, that "the crowning of his [Garrison's] apostolate and the immense conquest of freedom for our Black brethren [were] the result of four years of gigantic struggle." In other words, even though he wholeheartedly admired Garrison's absolute commitment and dedication to the cause of slave emancipation, Mazzini also thought the latter could hardly have occurred without the American Civil War. It appeared to Mazzini that as admirable as Garrisonian pacifism and nonresistance were, they could not help the cause of the European people, since it was action that was very much needed. With this in mind, Mazzini turned his thoughts back to southern Italy, where only a year before, in Sicily, a large separatist revolt had threatened the Italian government's rule of the island, and to Rome, where he hoped to coordinate action with Garibaldi to lift the city from papal power and make it the capital of a future Italian republic. The plan was for Mazzini to foment a revolt within Rome while Garibaldi's volunteers attacked the city from the outside; however, French troops defeated Garibaldi at Mentana in November 1867, and this led to an exacerbation of the rift between Mazzini and the general.[31]

Nevertheless, throughout 1868 and 1869, Mazzini renewed his conspiratorial activities against the Italian government, waiting for the right occasion to strike with a major revolutionary upheaval. In truth, in 1869 the entire Mezzogiorno was in tumult, as peasants in every province gathered in mass to protest against the latest of a series of taxes that weighed heavily upon them. Predictably, the Italian government declared martial law in numerous places, leading to protests and demonstrations held against the Savoy monarchy and in the name of Mazzini and his idea of an Italian republic. Accused of having fomented the protests, Mazzini was expelled from Switzerland, where he had recently moved; he then attempted to reach Sicily, from which he hoped to coordinate a large republican insurrection and the eventual conquest of Rome. However, as soon as Mazzini arrived in Palermo, on 14 August 1870, the authorities arrested him and took him to the prison-fortress of Gaeta; there he remained until after the Italian kingdom's troops finally conquered Rome, which had been left unguarded by the French as a result of Napoleon III's defeat by Bismarck in the 1870 Franco-

Prussian War. Thus was defeated once and for all Mazzini's radical objective of building a republican nation. Released on 13 October 1870, Mazzini resented the king's general amnesty that had given him back his freedom; he continued to think of himself as "the monarchy's outlaw." But by then he was paying a heavy toll for his unwavering radicalism with increasingly ill health, which added to his bitterness and delusion at seeing Rome become the capital of a monarchy, rather than a republic: "The . . . dream of my life has vanished," he wrote. Even though he was acknowledged as the prophet of Italian national unity, Mazzini felt as if all his efforts to create an Italian nation of morally responsible citizens, dedicated to the highest republican and democratic ideals, had resulted in defeat. As Giuseppe Monsagrati has written, Mazzini had suddenly realized that "with 1870 the Risorgimento had truly concluded . . . as a result of the end of the importance of ethics, which were now being constrained by the narrow views of a political class devoid of ideals." As a consequence, Mazzini continued until the end to be an "outsider" in the very nation—though not its form of government—he had greatly contributed to creating.[32]

By 1870, the difference that slave emancipation in the United States and monarchical unification in Italy had created between Garrison's and Mazzini's lives could not have been more striking, especially in comparison to the clear parallels that had characterized them in earlier times. By 1870, Garrison, convinced that he had achieved his primary objective, was completely enveloped in a self-celebratory mood. It is true that in principle he still supported radical causes, but not with nearly the same strength and conviction as before—even though the momentous and dramatic events of Reconstruction were unfolding before his very eyes. Conversely, with the 1870 Italian conquest of Rome, Mazzini found himself forced to witness the last in a series of defeats of all his attempts to reverse the course of events that had led to the formation of an Italian monarchy. With little luck or success, until then he had been remarkably resilient in continually devising new ways to bring about a people's revolution that would eventually lead to the creation of an Italian republic, but to no avail. Nevertheless, despite the fundamental difference that now existed between them—Garrison "the abolitionist hero" and Mazzini "the monarchy's outlaw"—in matters of principle, at least, the two men continued to be very close. The high esteem they continued to hold for each other testifies to that fact beyond doubt, as does the very similar way in which Garrison and Mazzini reacted to and mourned over Lincoln's untimely death.

To be sure, much like Garrison and also Lincoln, Mazzini considered republicanism to be the true indicator of national freedom; this was the very reason why he had sympathized with and admired both the American people and their Republican president. But this was also the reason why Garrison and Mazzini had agreed in chastising the American people for their betrayal of republican principles through the existence of slavery and, worse, their protection of the "peculiar institution." Now that the problem of slavery was removed, and the acknowledgment of African American civil rights was hopefully on its way, Garrison thought, to a certain extent at least, that the United States had finally begun its path toward becoming a true republic living in harmony with God. Mazzini's thought took a different direction: even keeping his reservations, he felt that the time had come to consider the United States the natural ally in the creation of republican forms of government in Europe. Not for the first time, Mazzini's idea showed well how the twin radical issues of American freedom and European national self-determination were tightly linked, and not only for him. More than this, that idea was very much the result of profound reflections on the belief in a universal and progressive type of liberty and equality that Garrison and Mazzini clearly shared, a belief that elevated their "missions" far above the narrow confines of American abolitionism and Italian democratic nationalism.

It was, after all, this belief that allowed Garrison and Mazzini to see each other as natural allies in parallel struggles, against slavery and against national oppression, struggles that they conducted on different sides of the Euro-American world but in both cases in the name of what they thought of as "the sacred principle of liberty"—a universal principle but also one at the heart of a very wide (and not yet fully studied or comprehended) transatlantic movement for the achievement of freedom in all its forms. In this sense, Garrison's introduction to Mazzini's autobiographical writings is, arguably, particularly illuminating, besides being the best exposition of Garrison's ideas on this particular point. In practice, we can certainly say, with Henry Mayer, that at least until their paths began to diverge in 1863, in the Old World "Mazzini and his European counterparts contended with monarchical tyranny, while Garrison fought against what he regarded as a moral despotism equally harsh in its suppression of freedom" in the United States. Afterward, even though no longer following parallel courses, the lives of Garrison and Mazzini continued to be seen and considered as equally emblematic of the two related progressive and radical struggles, which they had sustained with such a strong commitment for longer than three decades.[33]

CONCLUSION

Different Ends and Parallel Fame of Two Iconic Radicals

In the later years of their lives, Garrison and Mazzini seemed to diverge from their parallel paths as a result of very different historical circumstances. After the 1865 passing of the Thirteenth Amendment to the U.S. Constitution—which abolished slavery—Garrison abandoned several of his radical activities and, most of all, his primary role as a voice in opposition to the American government. In contrast, Mazzini, after the creation of the Kingdom of Italy in 1861 and the consequent shattering of his hope to form an Italian republic, was more than ever the voice of opposition to the Italian government headed by the House of Savoy, and he renewed his efforts to provoke a revolution. Thus it is not surprising to see that the two men died in very different circumstances and with very different states of mind: Garrison comforted by his family and convinced of his success, Mazzini hunted by the police and consumed by his failure. Yet we need to recognize that the difference that characterized the later parts of Garrison's and Mazzini's lives, and even their deaths, pales in comparison to the much longer and more significant parallel paths they had walked for well over thirty years.

From the time they began publishing the *Liberator* and *La Giovine Italia* in 1831–32, to the time they founded the American Anti-Slavery Society and Young Europe in 1833–34, through the time of divisions in the American abolitionist and the Italian democratic movements and then of national crises in the 1840s and 1850s, and even at the beginning of the American Civil War and at the birth of the Kingdom of Italy in 1861, Garrison and Mazzini had shared visions of radical thought and action that were consistently in opposition to those of the governments in power in their countries and that were part of an activist milieu of radical ideas of freedom and equality spread across the Euro-American world. The reason for their opposition was that their visions were egalitarian in a way that transcended boundaries considered immutable—boundaries imposed by slavery and racial prejudice and by national oppression and monarchical authority. This was perhaps the deepest sense of Garrison's explanation of his friendship with Mazzini: "We shared the same hostility to every form of tyranny." Even though unaware of this deep connection between the two men, the immense crowds that spontaneously gathered for Garrison's and Mazzini's funerals in the United States and Italy ultimately showed the true valor and significance of the two long, parallel, and radical struggles for freedom that Garrison and Mazzini had engaged in for most of their lives.[1]

In his late years, Garrison conveyed the impression that he felt fulfilled, that he had successfully concluded his life with the permanent ending of slavery in the United States. Even Wendell Phillips, despite his alienation from Garrison as a result of his opposite views, could not help but notice, "He seems wholly at rest." In time, Phillips and Garrison became close again, first supporting together the 1875 Civil Rights Act and then, tragically, as a result of the death of Garrison's wife Helen in 1876. Remarkably, in 1877 Garrison managed to take one last trip to England, where he bade farewell to what was left of the old Atlantic abolitionist clique, and especially to George Thompson. In a moving recollection of the meeting between the two men—both once capable of influencing their countries' public opinions with their radical abolitionist activities and now weak and at the end of their lives—Garrison's son Francis noticed how Thompson "embraced Father in silence, the tears coming into his eyes." Thompson was certainly moved by seeing his old friend, but he also grieved with him about the fact that the great, heroic times of Atlantic abolitionism were well and truly finished. Garrison might also have felt that his sense of fulfillment came with an acute nostalgia. It was not only a result of the death of so many who were dear to him. This was clearly revealed by his particularly nostalgic travel back to the headquarters of the *Newburyport Herald* in October 1878, to mark the sixtieth anniversary of the beginning of his apprenticeship there.[2]

Afterward, finally having relented to his daughter Fanny's pleas that he come live with her in New York, Garrison had barely arrived in the city when he fell ill, and less than a month later, on 24 May 1879, he died at age seventy-three. Four days later, an immense crowd of men and women, white and black, witnessed Garrison's funeral service in Boston, one in which abolitionists, women's rights activists, advocates of racial equality, and reformers in general gathered for one last time to honor the man who had succeeded in drawing them all together by his radical example. Among those who spoke were famous abolitionists and friends of Garrison, such as Wendell Phillips and Theodore Weld, who recalled the achievements of a remarkably full life. Both of them quoted from the already-famous words of the first issue of the *Liberator.* However, it was women's rights' advocate Lucy Stone who gave the most interesting speech. Recalling Garrison's remarkable contribution to her cause, she focused on the 1840 World's Convention in London. She described Garrison's stubborn refusal to move from the gallery, where abolitionist women from various countries had been confined by the meeting's organizers, and stated emphatically, "Nothing could induce him [Garrison] to place himself with those who did not recognize the equal rights of all, whether black or white, men or women"; thus she characterized, in unequivocal terms, Garrison's life role as that of a true Atlantic and Euro-American progressive with radical ideas that knew no boundaries.[3]

In complete contrast with Garrison's late years and his sense of fulfillment and consequent serenity, Mazzini's late life seems to have been no different from the life he had conducted since his youth. Frustrated by the completion of Italian unification under the Savoy monarchy, instead of the republic he had spent his life trying to create, Mazzini could only—understandably—feel that he had failed somehow in achieving his life's aim. At the same time, his enemies and opponents did not pass up any occasion to attack his ideas and strategies. After greeting his friends in London for the last time, in the early months of 1871, Mazzini embarked on a series of travels, first in Switzerland and then in Italy, under the pseudonym George Brown, partly because he was effectively hunted by the Italian police, but also partly because he wanted to make a political statement by being forced to assume a fake identity in his own country. Yet, despite this, and even despite the death of Giuditta Sidoli—the woman he had loved since his time in Marseilles, forty years earlier—Mazzini continued his radical activity, writing and producing article after article in the periodical *Roma del popolo* (Rome of the people), among whose collaborators he welcomed particularly Italian women's rights activist Anna Maria Mazzoni. As perhaps was expected, Mazzini fought his last battle against Marx when he opposed the Paris Commune as the transformation into reality of what he thought of as the pernicious ideas of class struggle spread by the socialists. Thus he alienated, as leading Italian socialist Andrea Costa noted, "the warmest and most generous part of the youth" in Italy. By then, in fact, under the combined attack of both Marx and Engels and Italian socialism, even control of the Italian workers' association was rapidly falling out of the hands of Mazzini's followers.[4]

In early 1872, ill and still traveling incognito, Mazzini went to Pisa to visit Jane Nathan Rosselli, the daughter of longtime friends. Once he arrived there, his health rapidly deteriorated, and on 10 March 1872, Mazzini died at age sixty-six. A week later, on 17 March 1872, the city of Genoa saw thousands of men and women—activists, patriots, reformers, and revolutionaries—gather at Mazzini's funeral; whatever the Italian monarchy and Italian socialists thought and said about him, clearly the people knew the man and his radical life and ideas better, and they showed it. Only Federico Campanella, Mazzini's friend and collaborator since his university years, spoke at the tribute. Sara Nathan, Jane Nathan Rosselli's mother, would have spoken also, but her tears prevented her from giving a speech that, in all likelihood, would have praised Mazzini's absolute and unique commitment to the cause of women's rights. In the end, very appropriately, it was William Lloyd Garrison who, though not participating at the funeral, left the most significant judgment of Mazzini's achievements in this sense. In the introduction to *Joseph Mazzini,* the selection of Mazzini's autobiographical writings that Emily Ashurst Venturi edited and published on 1 May 1872, a few months after Mazzini's death, Garrison wrote that "Mazzini's concern for the rights of man was never, on any pretext, in a purely masculine sense. Years ago he inculcated the equality of the sexes in regard to all civil and political immunities." In writing this, a tribute similar to Lucy Stone's at his own funeral, Garrison honored the universal characteristics of Mazzini's progressive thought, which, as radical as his own, did not know boundaries of sex, race, or country.[5]

Having lived most of their lives on parallel paths, Garrison and Mazzini went through comparable stages both in posthumous fame—starting with the similar, overwhelming tributes that the American and Italian people gave them at their funerals—and in the scholarly interpretations of their ideas and achievements. Not surprisingly, the changing cultural and political climates in the United States and Italy produced alternating periods of positive and negative evaluation. First there would be works and publications that praised the two men, and then there would be works that denigrated them, in a recurring pattern. In this sense, the parallel stories of Garrison's and Mazzini's posthumous popularity and interpretations reveal a great deal about their legacies in the history of the American and Italian societies; in fact, even though in different circumstances and at different times, in both countries it was often the prevalence of more conservative or more radical elements within public opinion that determined the popularity of similar ideas and views of two individuals equally famous for their absolute moral standing and their commitment to the causes to which they dedicated their lives. In this respect, the fact that the parallels between Garrison and Mazzini mostly ended toward the later parts of their lives, as a result of different historical circumstances, subtracts nothing from the comparability between the overall judgments of them expressed by posterity. In both cases, those judgments focused mostly on the influence of their ideas and on the significance of their achievements—at times in positive, at times in negative terms—among their contemporaries and also, in the long term, within the histories of their respective countries.

In the United States, shortly after his death, Garrison was lauded as a selfless abolitionist hero, especially in the biographies published by Oliver Johnson in 1879 and by Garrison's children in 1889. Then, after a long period during which he was mostly ignored and sometime criticized, Garrison's radicalism received full scholarly attention that coincided with the rise of the civil rights movement in the 1950s and 1960s and the "neoabolitionist" scholarship, which produced classic biographies of him. More recently, again after a few decades of silence, scholars have gone back to study Garrison, casting a somewhat more critical eye though not overlooking his undeniable achievements. In contrast, Mazzini received from the very beginning a great deal of attention from foreign scholars; an English school of historiography stretched from Emily Ashurst Venturi in 1872 and 1875 to Bolton King in 1902. In Mazzini's case it was easier for scholars of different beliefs to interpret his complex and eclectic thought, emphasizing one or another of its many radical features. Thus, the scholars of liberal and fascist Italy extolled his nationalism, while antifascist scholars praised his struggles for freedom. Studies on Mazzini understandably flourished during the early life of the new Italian Republic in the 1950s and 1960s—akin to the modern studies on Garrison in the United States. In fact, we could very well talk as much of a "neorepublican" historiography for Mazzini as of a "neoabolitionist" historiography for Garrison. Then, studies about Mazzini also went through a period of silence, to resurface only recently, with a comparable critical vein that also did not deny the latter's many achievements.[6]

This short glance at the trends in attention to Garrison's and Mazzini's thoughts after their deaths shows that, even though very few scholars have put the two men in relation with one another in their studies, the truth is that the seasons of interpretation of their ideas and actions—much like the course of their lives—have followed parallel and comparable paths. Specifically, it is striking to notice how, in both cases, it was the resurgence of a struggle for freedom—the civil rights movement in the United States and the creation of a republican government in Italy—that led to the rise of modern historiography, with studies truly capable, for the first time, of understanding the most radical aspects of the two men's ideas. In fact, whatever shortcomings Garrison and Mazzini might have had in their characters, in the ways they thought about themselves, in their modes of implementing their "thought and action," and in their "strategy and tactics," it is undeniable that, from a comparative perspective, they both appear to have been ahead of their times in their attempts to build truly democratic republics in the United States and Italy and in their support for a universal type of freedom that annulled race and gender differences at the same time and gave equal dignity to all social classes. The fact that modern scholarship on Garrison and Mazzini began, comparably, when the ideas of racial equality in the United States and republican government in Italy—which they had sustained for most of their lives—finally came to fruition is a powerful testimony to the parallel relevance and significance of their radical lives and legacies in the histories of their respective countries.

And yet, besides being parallel and comparable, in their own time Garrison's and Mazzini's radical lives were also somehow connected both between themselves, as demonstrated by their friendship and collaborations, and, in true transnational and transatlantic fashion, as parts of a wider Euro-American milieu, within which they felt they operated from the time of their very early journalistic experiences. This was something that several of their contemporaries and also those who began the task of preserving the two men's radical legacies noticed early on. An interesting hint at how

Garrison's and Mazzini's contemporaries saw their radical lives and legacies as both parallel and connected comes from a letter that Garrison's son Francis wrote to George Thompson's son-in-law Frederick William Chesson in June 1884, while he was preparing with his brother Wendell the famous biographical volume on their father. In the letter, Francis Jackson Garrison left no doubt that Mazzini had to figure in the volume by stating, "Mazzini will of course appear more than once in our work, as Father met him in 1846 at Muswell Hill, and again in 1867 at the Ashurst's." With that simple phrase, Francis Jackson Garrison highlighted for a close relative of a famous British abolitionist the relationship between the most prominent American abolitionist, the most prominent Italian (and European) democratic nationalist, and a radical English reformer. It symbolizes how the nineteenth-century Atlantic and Euro-American worlds of progressive reform and radicalism within which William Lloyd Garrison and Giuseppe Mazzini lived and operated were connected in transnational ways that we have just begun to really understand.[7]

NOTES

ABBREVIATIONS

BPL Boston Public Library, Anti-Slavery Collection, Rare Book and Manuscript Division.

EN *Edizione Nazionale: Scritti editi ed inediti di Giuseppe Mazzini.* Vols. 1–106. Edited by Mario Menghini. Imola: Galeati, 1906–43.

GMD *Scrittori politici dell'Ottocento.* Vol. 1, *Giuseppe Mazzini e i Democratici.* Edited by Franco Della Peruta. Milan: Feltrinelli, 1966.

HL Houghton Library, Harvard University.

GI *La Giovine Italia.* Vols. 1–6. Edited by Mario Menghini. Rome: Società editrice Dante Alighieri, 1902–25.

LWLG *The Letters of William Lloyd Garrison.* Vols. 1–6. Edited by Walter M. Merrill and Louis Ruchames. Cambridge, MA: Harvard University Press, 1971–81.

MHS Massachusetts Historical Society, Boston.

SEI *Scritti editi ed inediti di Giuseppe Mazzini.* Vols. 1–18. Edited by Giuseppe Mazzini and Aurelio Saffi. Bologna-Milan: G. Daelli, 1861–91.

WLGFS *William Lloyd Garrison and the Fight against Slavery: Selections from "The Liberator."* Edited by William E. Cain. New York: Bedford/St. Martin's, 1995.

PREFACE

1. On these issues, see Don H. Doyle, *Nations Divided: America, Italy, and the Southern Question* (Athens: University of Georgia Press, 2003); Bruce Levine, *Half Slave and Half Free: The Roots of Civil War,* 2nd ed. (New York: Hill & Wang, 2005); and Derek Beales and Eugenio F. Biagini, *The Risorgimento and the Unification of Italy* (London: Longman, 2002).

2. William Lloyd Garrison, introduction to *Joseph Mazzini: His Life, Writings, and Political Principles,* ed. Emily Ashurst Venturi (New York: Hurd & Houghton, 1872), vii.

3. On Garrison's espousal of evangelical Christianity and abolitionism, see particularly

James B. Stewart, *William Lloyd Garrison and the Challenge of Emancipation* (Arlington Heights, IL: Harlan Davidson, 1992), 33–37. On the "religious" dimension of Mazzini's nationalism, see especially Simon Levi Sullam, "Dio e il popolo: La rivoluzione religiosa di Giuseppe Mazzini," in *Storia d'Italia,* annali 22, *Il Risorgimento,* ed. Alberto M. Banti and Paul Ginsborg (Turin: Einaudi, 2007), 401–422.

4. See William E. Cain, "Introduction: William Lloyd Garrison and the Fight against Slavery," in *WLGFS,* 4–12; and Salvo Mastellone, *Il progetto politico di Mazzini (Italia-Europa)* (Florence: Olschki, 1994), 41–54.

5. On the meeting between Garrison and Mazzini, see chapter 5.

6. Aida Audeh and Nick Havely, *Dante in the Long Nineteenth Century: Nationality, Identity, and Appropriation* (New York: Oxford University Press, 1994), 290; Garrison, introduction to *Mazzini: His Life,* vii. According to Caleb McDaniel, "In that single, telling line [We cherished the same hostility to every form of tyranny], Garrison opened a revealing window onto the world he had known for fifty years: a world in which American abolitionists were connected to a transatlantic host of reformers as diverse as Thompson, Follen, Chesson, Mazzini, and Mill." W. Caleb McDaniel, *The Problem of Democracy in the Age of Slavery: Garrisonian Abolitionists and Transatlantic Reform* (Baton Rouge: Louisiana State University Press, 2013), 3.

7. John Stauffer, *Giants: The Parallel Lives of Frederick Douglass and Abraham Lincoln* (New York: Twelve, 2008), xii. For another seminal parallel biography with the same subjects, see James Oakes, *The Radical and the Republican: Frederick Douglass, Abraham Lincoln, and the Triumph of Antislavery Politics* (New York: Norton, 2007).

8. For the wider context, see especially C. A. Bayly, *The Birth of the Modern World, 1780–1914: Global Connections and Comparisons* (Oxford: Blackwell, 2004); and Enrico Dal Lago, *American Slavery, Atlantic Slavery, and Beyond: The U.S. "Peculiar Institution" in International Perspective* (Boulder, CO: Paradigm, 2012).

INTRODUCTION: GARRISONIAN ABOLITIONISM, MAZZINIAN DEMOCRATIC NATIONALISM, AND TRANSNATIONAL COMPARISONS

1. See, above all, Caleb McDaniel's recent seminal study *Problem of Democracy.*

2. Dale Tomich and Michael Zeuske, "Introduction: The Second Slavery: Mass Slavery, World-Economy, and Comparative Microhistories," *Review* 31, no. 2 (2008): 91–92. See also Dale Tomich, *Through the Prism of Slavery: Labor, Capital, and the World Economy* (Lanham, MD: Rowman & Littlefield, 2003), 56–71; and Seymour Drescher, *Abolition: A History of Slavery and Antislavery* (New York: Cambridge University Press, 2009).

3. Stefan Berger, "Germany: Ethnic Nationalism par Excellence?" in *What Is a Nation? Europe, 1789–1914,* ed. Timothy Bancroft and Mark Hewitson (Oxford: Oxford University Press, 2006), 43. See also Robin Blackburn, *The American Crucible: Slavery, Emancipation, and Human Rights* (London: Verso, 2011); and Stefan Berger, "National Movements," in *A Companion to Nineteenth-Century Europe, 1789–1914,* ed. Stefan Berger (Oxford: Blackwell, 2009), 178–192.

4. On general parallels and connection between nineteenth-century U.S. abolitionism and Italian democratic nationalism, see Enrico Dal Lago, "Radicalism and Nationalism: Northern 'Liberators' and Southern Laborers in the USA and Italy, 1830–1860," in *The American South and*

the Italian "Mezzogiorno": Essays in Comparative History, ed. Enrico Dal Lago and Rick Halpern (New York: Palgrave, 2002), 197–214; and Roland Sarti, "La democrazia radicale: Uno sguardo reciproco tra Stati Uniti e Italia," in *La democrazia radicale nell'Ottocento europeo: Forme della politica, modelli culturali, riforme sociali,* ed. Maurizio Ridolfi (Milan: Feltrinelli, 2005), 133–158.

5. For a review of the literature on American abolitionism as a radical movement, see W. Caleb McDaniel, "What Counts as Radical Abolitionism? A Reconsideration of Recent Scholarship," paper presented at the annual meeting of the Organization of American Historians, Seattle, 27 March 2009. See also Gilbert H. Barnes, *The Antislavery Impulse, 1830–1844* (New York: Classic Textbooks, 1933); Dwight L. Dumond, *Antislavery: The Crusade for Freedom in America* (New York: Norton Library, 1961); James McPherson, *The Struggle for Equality: Abolitionists and the Negro in the Civil War and Reconstruction* (Princeton, N.J.: Princeton University Press, 1964); Aileen S. Kraditor, *Means and Ends in American Abolitionism: Garrison and His Critics on Strategy and Tactics, 1834–1850* (Chicago: University of Chicago Press, 1969); Lewis Perry, *Radical Abolitionism: Anarchy and the Government of God in Antislavery Thought* (Ithaca, NY: Cornell University Press, 1971); Ronald G. Walters, *The Antislavery Appeal: American Abolitionism after 1830* (New York: Norton, 1978); and James B. Stewart, *Holy Warriors: The Abolitionists and American Slavery* (New York: Hill & Wang, 1996; 1st ed. published in 1976). On Garrison specifically, see Russell B. Nye, *William Lloyd Garrison and the Humanitarian Reformers* (Boston: Little, Brown, 1955); John L. Thomas, *The Liberator: William Lloyd Garrison: A Biography* (Boston: Little, Brown, 1963); and Walter M. Merrill, *Against Wind and Tide: A Biography of William Lloyd Garrison* (Cambridge, MA: Harvard University Press, 1963).

6. See Benjamin Quarles, *Black Abolitionists* (New York: Oxford University Press, 1969); Jane H. Pease and William H. Pease, *They Who Would Be Free: Blacks' Search for Freedom, 1830–1861* (Urbana: University of Illinois Press, 1974); Richard J. Blackett, *Building an Antislavery Wall: Black Americans in the Atlantic Abolitionist Movement, 1830–1860* (Baton Rouge: Louisiana State University Press, 1983); Julie Roy Jeffrey, *The Great Silent Army of Abolitionism: Ordinary Women in the Antislavery Movement* (Chapel Hill: University of North Carolina Press, 1998); Richard S. Newman, *The Transformation of American Abolitionism: Fighting Slavery in the Early Republic* (Chapel Hill: University of North Carolina Press, 2002); John Stauffer, *The Black Hearts of Men: Radical Abolitionists and the Transformation of Race* (Cambridge, MA: Harvard University Press, 2002); Bruce Laurie, *Beyond Garrison: Antislavery and Social Reform* (New York: Cambridge University Press, 2005); Patrick McCarthy and John Stauffer, eds., *Prophets of Protest: Reconsidering the History of American Abolitionism* (New York: New Press, 2006); and Stacey Robertson, *Hearts Beating for Liberty: Women Abolitionists in the Old Northwest* (Chapel Hill: University of North Carolina Press, 2010).

7. McDaniel, "What Counts as Radical Abolitionism?" 10; and James B. Stewart, "Humanitarian Reform and Antislavery," in *A Companion to Civil War and Reconstruction,* ed. Lacy K. Ford (Oxford: Blackwell, 2005), 101. See also Barnes, *Antislavery Impulse;* Roger H. Abzug, *Cosmos Crumbling: American Reform and the Religious Imagination* (New York: Oxford University Press, 1994); Thomas Bender, ed., *The Antislavery Debate: Capitalism and Abolitionism as a Problem of Historical Interpretation* (Berkeley: University of California Press, 1992); Paul Goodman, *Of One Blood: Abolitionism and the Origins of Racial Equality* (Berkeley: University of California Press, 1998); Kathryn Kish Sklar, ed., *Women's Rights Emerges within the Antislavery Movement,*

1830–1870 (New York: Bedford/St. Martin's, 2000); McDaniel, *Problem of Democracy,* 11–12, 105–136; and James B. Stewart, *Abolitionist Politics and the Coming of the Civil War* (Amherst: University of Massachusetts Press, 2008).

8. See David Brion Davis, *The Problem of Slavery in the Age of Revolution, 1770–1823* (Ithaca, NY: Cornell University Press, 1975); and Davis, *Slavery and Human Progress* (New York: Oxford University Press, 1985); Betty Fladeland, *Men and Brothers: Anglo-American Antislavery Cooperation* (Urbana: University of Illinois Press, 1972); Robin Blackburn, *The Overthrow of Colonial Slavery, 1776–1848* (London: Verso, 1988); Thomas Bender, *A Nation among Nations: America's Place in World History* (New York: Hill & Wang, 2006), 122–129; Ian Tyrrell, *Transnational Nation: United States History in Global Perspective since 1789* (New York: Palgrave, 2007), 39–51; Carl Guarneri, *America in the World: United States History in Global Context* (New York: McGraw-Hill, 2007), 153–155; Richard J. M. Blackett, "'And There Shall Be No More Sea': William Lloyd Garrison and the Transatlantic Abolitionist Movement," in *William Lloyd Garrison at Two Hundred,* ed. James B. Stewart (New Haven, CT: Yale University Press, 2008), 13–40; Edward B. Rugemer, *The Problem of Emancipation: The Caribbean Roots of the American Civil War* (Baton Rouge: Louisiana State University Press, 2008); and McDaniel, *Problem of Democracy.*

9. See McDaniel, *Problem of Democracy;* Henry Mayer, *All on Fire: William Lloyd Garrison and the Abolition of Slavery* (New York: St. Martin's Press, 1998); and Stewart, *Garrison at Two Hundred.* See also Stewart, *Garrison and the Challenge.* For further literature on the transnational approach to American abolitionism, see especially Clare Taylor, ed., *British and American Abolitionists: An Episode in Transatlantic Understanding* (Edinburgh: Edinburgh University Press, 1974); Bonnie S. Anderson, *Joyous Greetings: The First International Women's Movement, 1830–1860* (New York: Oxford University Press, 2000); Maurice Jackson, "The Rise of Abolition," in *The Atlantic World, 1450–2000,* ed. Toyin Fayola and Kevin Roberts (Bloomington: Indiana University Press, 2005), 211–248; Kathryn Kish Sklar and James B. Stewart, eds., *Women's Rights and Transatlantic Slavery in the Age of Emancipation* (New Haven, CT: Yale University Press, 2007); Timothy M. Roberts, *Distant Revolutions: 1848 and the Challenge to American Exceptionalism* (Charlottesville: University of Virginia Press, 2009); Angela F. Murphy, *American Slavery, Irish Freedom: Abolition, Immigrant Citizenship, and the Transatlantic Movement for Irish Repeal* (Baton Rouge: Louisiana State University Press, 2010); and Mischa Honeck, *We Are the Revolutionists: German-Speaking Immigrants and American Abolitionists after 1848* (Athens: University of Georgia Press, 2010).

10. See Giovanni Gentile, *I profeti del Risorgimento italiano* (Florence: Vallecchi, 1923); Arturo Codignola, *Mazzini* (Turin: UTET, 1946); Antonio Gramsci, *Il Risorgimento* (Turin: Einaudi, 1966; written in the 1930s), 103–104, 115–119; Piero Gobetti, *Risorgimento senza eroi* (Turin: Edizioni del Baretti, 1926); Nello Rosselli, *Mazzini e Bakunin: Dodici anni di movimento operaio in Italia, 1860–1872* (Turin: Fratelli Bocca, 1927); Giuseppe Berti, *I democratici e l'iniziativa meridionale nel Risorgimento* (Milan: Feltrinelli, 1962); Alfonso Scirocco, *I democratici italiani da Sapri a Porta Pia* (Naples: Edizioni Scientifiche Italiane, 1969); Giuseppe Galasso, *Da Mazzini a Salvemini: Il pensiero democratico dell'Italia moderna* (Florence: Le Monnier, 1974); Franco Della Peruta, *Mazzini e i rivoluzionari italiani: Il Partito d'Azione, 1830–1845* (Milan: Feltrinelli, 1974); Emilia Morelli, *Giuseppe Mazzini: Saggi e ricerche* (Rome: Edizioni dell'Ateneo, 1950); and Salvo Mastellone, *Mazzini e la "Giovine Italia," 1831–1834,* 2 vols. (Pisa: Domus Mazziniana, 1960).

11. See Clara M. Lovett, *The Democratic Movement in Italy, 1830–1876* (Cambridge, MA:

Harvard University Press, 1982); Benedetto Croce, *Storia d'Italia dal 1871 al 1915* (Bari-Rome: Laterza, 1928); and Rosario Romeo, *Risorgimento e capitalismo* (Rome-Bari: Laterza, 1959). The "revisionist" approach is best shown in the essays in Giovanni Sabbatucci and Vittorio Vidotto, eds., *Storia d'Italia,* vol. 1, *Le premesse dell'Unità* (Rome-Bari: Laterza, 1994). See also Denis Mack Smith, *Mazzini* (New Haven, CT: Yale University Press, 1994); and Roland Sarti, *Mazzini: A Life for the Religion of Politics* (Westport, CT: Prager, 1997).

12. Lucy Riall, *Risorgimento: The History of Italy from Napoleon to Nation State* (New York: Palgrave, 2009), 142. See also Albert Russell Ascoli and Krystyna Von Henneberg, "Introduction: Nationalism and the Uses of Risorgimento Culture," in *Making and Remaking Italy: The Cultivation of National Identity around the Risorgimento,* ed. Albert Russell Ascoli and Krystyna Von Henneberg (Oxford: Berg, 2001), 1–26; Alberto M. Banti, *La nazione del Risorgimento: Parentela, santità e onore alle origini dell'Italia unita* (Turin: Einaudi, 2000); Silvana Patriarca, "Indolence and Regeneration: Tropes and Tensions of Risorgimento Patriotism," *American Historical Review* 110, no. 2 (2005): 380–408; Lucy Riall, *Garibaldi: Invention of a Hero* (New Haven, CT: Yale University Press, 2007); and Paul Ginsborg, "Romanticismo e Risorgimento: L'io, l'amore e la nazione," in Banti and Ginsborg, *Il Risorgimento,* 5–68.

13. Alberto M. Banti and Paul Ginsborg, "Per una nuova storia del Risorgimento," in Banti and Ginsborg, *Il Risorgimento,* xxiii; Silvana Patriarca and Lucy Riall, "Introduction: Revisiting the Risorgimento," in *The Risorgimento Revisited: Nationalism and Culture in Nineteenth-Century Italy,* ed. Silvana Patriarca and Lucy Riall (New York: Palgrave, 2012), 5. See also Giovanni Belardelli, *Mazzini* (Bologna: Il Mulino, 2010); Roberto Balzani, "Il problema Mazzini," *Ricerche di storia politica* 8, no. 2 (2005): 159–182; Arianna Arisi Rota, *I piccoli cospiratori: Politica ed emozioni nei primi mazziniani* (Bologna: Il Mulino, 2010); Axel Korner and Lucy Riall, "Introduction: The New History of Risorgimento Nationalism," *Nations and Nationalism* 15, no. 3 (2009): 396–401; Alberto M. Banti et al., "Presentazione," in *Atlante culturale del Risorgimento: Lessico del linguaggio politico dal Settecento all'Unità,* ed. Alberto M. Banti et al. (Rome-Bari: Laterza, 2011), v–xv; and Laura Fournier-Finocchiaro, "Le paradoxe Mazzini: Ennemi et pére de l'Italie du Risorgimento," *Italies* 15 (2011): 357–379.

14. C. A. Bayly and Eugenio Biagini, eds., *Giuseppe Mazzini and the Globalization of Democratic Nationalism, 1820–1870* (Oxford: Oxford University Press, 2008); Sarti, "La democrazia radicale," 133–158; Mastellone, *Il progetto politico di Mazzini;* Mastellone, *Mazzini scrittore politico in inglese: Democracy in Europe (1840–1855)* (Florence: Olschki, 2004); Maurizio Isabella, *Risorgimento in Exile: Italian Emigrés and the Liberal International in the Post-Napoleonic Era* (Oxford: Oxford University Press, 2009); Isabella, "Nationality before Liberty? *Risorgimento* Political Thought in Transnational Context," *Journal of Modern Italian Studies* 17:5 (2012): 507–515; Isabella, "Rethinking Italy's Nation-Building 150 Years Afterwards: The New *Risorgimento* Historiography," *Past and Present* (2012): 247–268; and Roberts, *Distant Revolutions.* For study of Mazzini's negative legacy, instead, see Simon Levi Sullam, *L'apostolo a brandelli: L'eredità di Mazzini tra Risorgimento e Fascismo* (Rome-Bari: Laterza, 2010).

15. On "Atlantic Abolitionism," see especially Drescher, *Abolition,* 267–293; and Dal Lago, *American Slavery,* 125–133. On European nationalism, see particularly Eric J. Hobsbawm, *Nations and Nationalism since 1780* (Cambridge: Cambridge University Press, 1983); and Lloyd Kramer, *Nationalism in Europe and America: Politics, Cultures, and Identities since 1776* (Chapel Hill: University of North Carolina Press, 2011). On the recent scholarship on the nineteenth-century

Atlantic world, see Donna Gabaccia, "A Long Atlantic in a Wider World," *Atlantic Studies* 1 (2004): 1–27; Aaron Spencer Fogelman, "The Transformation of the Atlantic World, 1776–1867," *Atlantic Studies* 6 (2009): 5–28; and José C. Moya, "Modernization, Modernity, and the Transformation of the Atlantic World in the Nineteenth Century," in *The Atlantic in Global History, 1500–2000,* ed. Jorge Cañizares-Esguerra and Erik Seeman (Upper Saddle River, NJ: Pearson, 2007), 176–198. On the new transnational history of the Civil War era, see Eugenio Biagini et al., "Interchange: Nationalism and Internationalism in the Era of the Civil War," *Journal of American History* 98, no. 2 (2011): 455–489; Douglas R. Egerton, "Rethinking Atlantic Historiography in a Postcolonial Era: The Civil War in a Global Perspective," *Journal of the Civil War Era* 1 (2011): 79–95; W. Caleb McDaniel and Bethany L. Johnson, "New Approaches to Internationalizing the History of the Civil War Era," *Journal of the Civil War Era* 2 (2012): 145–150; and André Fleche, *The Revolution of 1861: The American Civil War in the Age of Nationalist Conflict* (Chapel Hill: University of North Carolina Press, 2012).

16. See Tyrrell, *Transnational Nation,* 1–9; and Daniel T. Rodgers, "Worlds of Reform," in *America on the World Stage: A Global Approach to U.S. History,* ed. Gary W. Reichard and Ted Dickson (Urbana: University of Illinois Press, 2008), 147–157. See also Guarneri, *America in the World,* 153–155; and Bender, *Nation among Nations,* 122–129. A study that provides a model of focus on transatlantic connections between ideas and ideologies for a later period is Daniel T. Rodgers, *Atlantic Crossings: Social Politics in a Progressive Age* (Cambridge, MA: Harvard University Press, 1998).

17. George Fredrickson, "From Exceptionalism to Variability: Recent Developments in Cross-National Comparative History," *Journal of American History* 82, no. 2 (1995): 587; Bayly, *Birth of the Modern World,* 1; Paola Gemme, *Domesticating Foreign Struggles: The Italian Risorgimento and Antebellum American Identity* (Athens: University of Georgia Press, 2005), 116. See also Deborah Cohen and Maura O'Connor, "Introduction: Comparative History, Cross-National history, Transnational History—Definitions," in *Comparison and History: Europe in Cross-National Perspective,* ed. Deborah Cohen and Maura O'Connor (London: Routledge, 2004), ix–xxx; and Eric J. Hobsbawm, *The Age of Revolutions, 1789–1848* (London: Abacus, 1962); Hobsbawm, *The Age of Capital, 1848–1875* (London: Abacus, 1975); Hobsbawm, *The Age of Empire, 1875–1914* (London: Abacus, 1983); and Blackburn, *American Crucible.*

18. See McDaniel, *Problem of Democracy.*

19. See Dal Lago, "Radicalism and Nationalism," 197–214. On Garrison, Bolivar, and O'Connell, see McDaniel, *Problem of Democracy,* 43. See also Mayer, *All on Fire,* 97–168; and Joseph Rossi, *The Image of America in Mazzini's Writings* (Madison: University of Wisconsin Press, 1954).

1. EARLY ATTEMPTS AT DEMOCRATIZATION: THE MAKING OF TWO RADICAL LEADERS, 1805–1830

1. See Robert R. Palmer, *The Age of Democratic Revolution: A Political History of Europe and America, 1760–1800,* 2 vols. (Princeton, NJ: Princeton University Press, 1959, 1964). See also Hobsbawm, *Age of Revolutions;* Wim Klooster, *Revolutions in the Atlantic World: A Comparative History* (New York: New York University Press, 2009); and David Armitage and Sanjay Subrahmanyam, eds., *The Age of Revolutions in Global Context, c. 1760–1840* (New York: Palgrave, 2010).

2. For the global context, see David Armitage and Sanjay Subrahmanyam, "Introduction: The Age of Revolutions, c. 1760–1840: Global Causation, Connection, and Comparison," in Armitage and Subrahmanyam, *Age of Revolutions,* xii–xxxii; and Bayly, *Birth of the Modern World.*

3. See C. A. Bayly, "The Age of Revolutions in Global Context: An Afterword," in Armitage and Subrahmanyam, *Age of Revolutions,* 209–217; Blackburn, *American Crucible;* and Anthony E. Kaye, "The Second Slavery: Modernity in the Nineteenth-Century South and the Atlantic World," *Journal of Southern History* 75, no. 2 (2009): 627–650.

4. See David Brion Davis, *Inhuman Bondage: The Rise and Fall of Slavery in the New World* (New York: Oxford University Press, 2006), 236–237; and Franco Venturi, "L'Italia fuori d'Italia," in *Storia d'Italia,* vol. 3, *Dal Primo Settecento all'Unità,* ed. Ruggero Romano and Corrado Vivanti (Turin: Einaudi, 1973), 1223–1236.

5. Simon Bolivar is quoted in Lester Langley, *The Americas in the Age of Revolutions, 1750–1850* (New Haven, CT: Yale University Press, 1990), 195. See also David Brewer, *The Greek War of Independence: The Struggle for Freedom from Ottoman Oppression and the Birth of the Modern Greek Nation* (London: Overlook Press, 2003); John Lynch, *Simon Bolivar: A Life* (New Haven, CT: Yale University Press, 2006); and David Brion Davis, *Revolutions: Reflections on American Equality and Foreign Liberations* (Cambridge, MA: Harvard University Press, 1990).

6. On this period as a whole, see Charles Sellers, *The Market Revolution: Jacksonian America, 1815–1848* (New York: Oxford University Press, 1990); and Sean Wilentz, *The Rise of American Democracy: From Jefferson to Lincoln* (New York: Norton, 2006). On the importance of religion, see Abzug, *Cosmos Crumbling;* and Richard Carwardine, *Transatlantic Revivalism: Popular Evangelicalism in Britain and America, 1790–1865* (Westport, CT: Greenwood Press, 1978).

7. See Abzug, *Cosmos Crumbling.* See also Dumond, *Antislavery,* 156–157; Barnes, *Antislavery Impulse,* 3–16; and Ronald Walters, *American Reformers, 1815–1860* (New York: Hill & Wang, 1996).

8. See Daniel Walker Howe, *"What Hath God Wrought": The Transformation of America, 1815–1848* (New York: Oxford University Press, 2008), 164–202; T. G. Garvey, *Creating the Culture of Reform in Antebellum America* (Athens: University of Georgia Press, 2006); David Turley, "Religion and Approaches to Reform: Boston Unitarians versus Evangelicals in the Context of the 1820s and 1830s," *American Nineteenth Century History* 10, no. 2 (2009): 187–209; A. C. Loveland, "Evangelicalism and 'Immediate Emancipation' in American Antislavery Thought," *Journal of Southern History* 32 (1966): 172–188; and Dumond, *Antislavery,* 158–165.

9. Stewart, *Garrison and the Challenge,* 2. See also Mayer, *All On Fire,* 10–14. On the concepts of sin, redemption, and salvation among early-nineteenth-century evangelicals, see also Walters, *Antislavery Appeal,* 37–53; and Loveland, "Evangelicalism and 'Immediate Emancipation,'" 172–188.

10. See Stewart, *Garrison and the Challenge,* 3–11. See also Thomas, *Liberator,* 13–25. Years later, Garrison recalled his childhood in somewhat idealistic terms in a letter to his nine-year-old son, Francis Jackson; see William Lloyd Garrison to Francis Jackson Garrison, 17 August 1857, William Lloyd Garrison Papers, MHS. See also Harriet Hyman Alonso, *Growing Up Abolitionist: The Story of the Garrison Children* (Amherst: University of Massachusetts Press, 2002), 9–23, 78–108.

11. Matthew Mason, "Federalists, Abolitionists, and the Problem of Influence," *American Nineteenth Century History* 10, no. 1 (2009): 7. See also Mark M. Arkin, "The Federalist Trope:

Power and Passion in Abolitionist Rhetoric," *Journal of American History* 88 (2001): 75–98; and Sean Wilentz's opposite argument about the paramount influence of antislavery Jeffersonians on abolitionism in "Jeffersonian Democracy and the Origins of Political Antislavery in the United States: The Missouri Crisis Revisited," *Journal of the Historical Society* 4 (2004): 375–401.

12. McDaniel, *Problem of Democracy,* 24; [William Lloyd Garrison], "A Glance at Europe," *Newburyport Herald,* 16 May 1823, quoted in McDaniel, *Problem of Democracy,* 25.

13. William Lloyd Garrison to Frances Maria Lloyd Garrison, 26 May 1823, in *LWLG,* 1:11; William Lloyd Garrison to the editor of the *Salem Gazette,* 6 August 1824, in *LWLG,* 1:27. See also Stewart, *Garrison and the Challenge,* 20–25; and Thomas, *Liberator,* 28–53. On the importance of moral issues—and especially temperance—to early-nineteenth-century American reformers, see Walters, *American Reformers,* 125–147. On Jacksonian and anti-Jacksonian politics in the 1820s, see especially Harry L. Watson, *Liberty and Power: The Politics of Jacksonian America* (New York: Hill & Wang, 1990).

14. See Christopher Duggan, *The Force of Destiny: A History of Italy since 1796* (London: Penguin, 2008), 30–68; Carlo Capra, *L'età giacobina e napoleonica in Italia, 1796–1815* (Turin: UTET, 1978); Giorgio Candeloro, *Storia dell'Italia moderna,* vol. 1, *Le origini del Risorgimento (1700–1815)* (Milan: Feltrinelli, 1958); and Alberto M. Banti, *Il Risorgimento italiano* (Rome-Bari: Laterza, 2004), 17–37.

15. See especially Marco Meriggi, *Breve storia dell'Italia settentrionale dall'Ottocento a oggi* (Rome: Donzelli, 1996), 18–24; Marco Meriggi, *Gli stati italiani prima dell'unità* (Bologna: Il Mulino, 1997); Guido Pescosolido, "L'economia e la vita materiale," in Sabbatucci and Vidotto, *Le premesse dell'Unità,* 5–118; Luciano Cafagna, *Dualismo e sviluppo nella storia d'Italia* (Venice: Marsilio, 1989); and Riall, *Risorgimento,* 104–108.

16. Harry Hearder, *Italy in the Age of the Risorgimento, 1790–1870* (London: Longman, 1983), 50. See also Anna Maria Rao, "Republicanism in Italy from the Eighteenth Century to the Early Risorgimento," *Journal of Modern Italian Studies* 17, no. 2 (2012): 140–167; Carlo Zaghi, *L'Italia di Napoleone dalla Cisalpina al Regno* (Turin: UTET., 1986); Stuart J. Woolf, *A History of Italy, 1700–1860: The Social Constraints of Political Change* (London: Routledge, 1979); and Banti, *Il Risorgimento italiano,* 3–14.

17. Eugenio Biagini, "Mazzini and Anticlericalism: The English Exile," in Bayly and Biagini, *Mazzini and the Globalization,* 149. See also Giorgio Spini, *Risorgimento e protestanti* (Milan: Il Saggiatore, 1989).

18. Ros Pesman, "Mazzini and/in Love," in Patriarca and Riall, *Risorgimento Revisited,* 99. See also Sarti, *Mazzini,* 15–17; Gaetano Salvemini, "La giovinezza di Giuseppe Mazzini (1911)," in Salvemini, *Scritti sul Risorgimento* (Milan: Feltrinelli, 1963), 285–307; Telesforo Nanni, "Mazzini nel giudizio di Gaetano Salvemini," in Vincenzo Pirro, *Mazzini nella cultura italiana* (Terni: Associazione mazziniana italiana, 2008), 39–54; and Arturo Codignola, *La giovinezza di G. Mazzini* (Florence: Vallecchi, 1926).

19. Francesco Landogna, *Giuseppe Mazzini e il pensiero giansenistico* (Bologna: Zanichelli, 1921), 3. See also Codignola, *La giovinezza di G. Mazzini,* 7–40; Oreste Sagramola, *Giuseppe Mazzini nel Risorgimento italiano: Pensiero, azione, educazione politica* (Viterbo: Sette Città, 2007), 61–78. On Mazzini's mother, see especially Marina D'Amelia, "Between Two Eras: Challenges Facing Women in the Risorgimento," in Patriarca and Riall, *Risorgimento Revisited,* 117–122; and Bruno Montale, *Maria Drago Mazzini* (Genova: Comune di Genova, 1955).

20. Franco Della Peruta and Tiziano Tussi, *Mazzini* (Varese: Arterigere, 2007), 30. See also Codignola, *La giovinezza di G. Mazzini,* 41–90; and, on the Ruffini brothers, Carlo Cagnacci, ed., *Giuseppe Mazzini e i fratelli Ruffini: Lettere Raccolte e annotate* (Porto Maurizio: Tipografia Berio, 1893).

21. Giuseppe Mazzini's quote in Ashurst Venturi, *Mazzini: His Life,* 2. See also Della Peruta and Tussi, *Mazzini,* 27–32.

22. See Howe, *"What Hath God Wrought,"* 125–163; and Woolf, *History of Italy,* 229–274.

23. See David Brion Davis, *Challenging the Boundaries of Slavery* (Cambridge, MA: Harvard University Press, 2003), 62–73; and Beales and Biagini, *Risorgimento and the Unification,* 28–40.

24. Stewart, *Holy Warriors,* 42. See also Margot Minardi, *Making Slavery History: Abolitionism and the Politics of Memory in Massachusetts* (New York: Oxford University Press, 2010), 43–69; Newman, *Transformation of American Abolitionism,* 1–15; and Alice Dana Adams, *The Neglected Period of Antislavery in America (1808–1831)* (Boston, 1908).

25. Richard Newman, "'A Chosen Generation': Black Founders and Early America," in McCarthy and Stauffer, *Prophets of Protest,* 70. See also Mitch Kachun, "'Our Platform Is as Broad as Humanity': Transatlantic Freedom Movements and the Idea of Progress in Nineteenth-Century African American Thought and Activism," *Slavery and Abolition* 24, no. 3 (2003): 7–9; and Newman, *Transformation of American Abolitionism,* 86–106.

26. See Mayer, *All on Fire,* 74–75. On the Missouri crisis, see especially Robert Pierce Forbes, *The Missouri Compromise and Its Aftermath: Slavery and the Meaning of America* (Chapel Hill: University of North Carolina Press, 2009). For the general context, see Randall Richardson Butler, "New England Journalism and the Question of Slavery, the South, and Abolitionism" (PhD diss., Brigham Young University, 1980).

27. Merton L. Dillon, *The Abolitionists: The Growth of a Dissenting Minority* (New York: Norton, 1974), 35. See also McDaniel, *Problem of Democracy, 31–37;* and Merton L. Dillon, *Benjamin Lundy and the Struggle for Negro Freedom* (Urbana: University of Illinois Press, 1966). See also Dumond, *Antislavery,* 136–138; and Louis Filler, *Crusade against Slavery: Friends, Foes, and Reform, 1820–1860* (New York: Harper & Row, 1960), 43–45.

28. William Lloyd Garrison to Francis Todd, 13 May 1830, in *LWLG,* 1:93–94. See [William Lloyd Garrison], *A Brief Sketch of the Trial of William Lloyd Garrison for an Alleged Libel on Francis Todd of Newburyport, Mass.* (Boston: Garrison and Knapp, 1834); Amy Reynolds, "William Lloyd Garrison, Benjamin Lundy, and Criminal Libel: The Abolitionists' Plea for Press Freedom," *Communication Law and Policy* 6 (2001): 577–607; and Mayer, *All on Fire,* 71–96.

29. On the ACS, see Eric Burin, *Slavery and the Peculiar Solution: A History of the African Colonization Society* (Gainesville: University Press of Florida, 2005); Douglas R. Egerton, "Its Origin Is Not a Little Curious: A New Look at the American Colonization Society," *Journal of the Early Republic* 5 (1985): 463–480; and P. J. Staudenraus, *The African Colonization Movement, 1816–1865* (New York: Columbia University Press, 1961).

30. Mayer, *All on Fire,* 62; William Lloyd Garrison, "Address to the American Colonization Society, July 4, 1829," in *WLGFS,* 69. See also George Fredrickson, *The Black Image in the White Mind: The Debate on Afro-American Character and Destiny, 1817–1914* (New York: Ardent Media, 1971), 1–42; and Allan Yarema, *The American Colonization Society: An Avenue for Freedom?* (Lanham, MD: University Press of America, 2006), 54–55.

31. See Giovanni Assereto, "Genova e la Liguria nella prima metà dell'Ottocento," in *Pen-*

siero e Azione: Mazzini nel movimento democratico italiano e internazionale, ed. Stefania Bonanni (Rome: Istituto per la Storia del Risorgimento italiano, 2006), 11–28; Alfredo De Paz, *Europa romantica: Fondamenti e paradigmi della sensibilità moderna* (Naples: Liguori, 1994), 170–187; Silvia Tatti, "Ugo Foscolo," in *Vite per l'unità. Autori e scrittori del Risorgimento civile,* ed. Beatrice Alfonzetti and Silvia Tatti (Rome: Donzelli, 2011), 3–18; Codignola, *La giovinezza di G. Mazzini,* 91–148; and Woolf, *History of Italy,* 327–329.

32. Giuseppe Mazzini, "D'una letteratura europea (1829)," in *GMD,* 272; Steven A. Epstein, *Speaking of Slavery: Color, Ethnicity, and Human Bondage in Italy* (Ithaca, NY: Cornell University Press, 2001), 55.

33. See Gian Mario Cazzaniga, "Nascita del Grande Oriente d'Italia," in *Storia d'Italia,* annali 21, *La Massoneria,* ed. Gian Mario Cazzaniga (Turin: Einaudi, 2006), 545–558; Carolina Castellano, "Segreto e società segrete," in Banti et al., *Atlante culturale del Risorgimento,* 176–186; Carlo Francovich, *Albori socialisti del Risorgimento: Contributo allo studio delle società segrete, 1776–1835* (Florence: Le Monnier, 1962), 1–39; R. John Rath, "The *Carbonari:* Their Origins, Initiation Rites, and Aims," *American Historical Review* 69, no. 2 (1964): 353–370; and Gian Mario Cazzaniga, "Origine ed evoluzione dei rituali carbonari italiani," in Cazzaniga, *La Massoneria,* 559–578.

34. Franco Della Peruta, "Il mondo latomistico della Restaurazione," in *La nascita della nazione: La Carboneria: Intrecci veneti, nazionali, internazionali,* ed. Giampiero Berti and Franco Della Peruta (Rovigo: Minelliana, 2003), 19. See also Sarti, *Mazzini,* 47–55; Alessandro Galante Garrone, *Filippo Buonarroti e i rivoluzionari dell'Ottocento (1828–1837)* (Turin: Einaudi, 1951); and Alessandro Luzio, *Giuseppe Mazzini carbonaro: Nuovi documenti dagli archivi di Milano e Torino* (Turin: Bocca, 1920). On the 1821 Revolution, see especially Banti, *Il Risorgimento,* 38–52.

35. *SEI,* 1:21, 34. See also Codignola, *La giovinezza di G. Mazzini,* 149–162; Sarti, *Mazzini,* 51–53; Pietro Galletto, *Mazzini nella vita e nella storia: Nel secondo centenario della nascita (1805–2005)* (Padova: G. Battaglin, 2005), 1:145–164; and Edward E. Y. Hayes, *Mazzini and the Secret Societies: The Making of a Myth* (New York: P.J. Kenedy, 1956).

36. *SEI,* 1:40; Carlo Bianco di Saint-Jorioz, *Della Guerra d'insurrezione per bande applicata all'Italia* (Malta, 1830), 167. On the significance of the experience of exile abroad for the Italian patriots' construction of an Italian nation, including Mazzini, see Maurizio Isabella, "Esilio," in Banti et al., *Atlante culturale del Risorgimento,* 65–74; and Isabella, *Risorgimento in Exile.* See also Della Peruta, "Il mondo latomistico della restaurazione," 20–21; Vittorio Parmentola, "Carlo Bianco, Giuseppe Mazzini e la teoria dell'insurrezione," *Bollettino della Domus Mazziniana* 5 (1959): 5–40; and Alessandro Galante Garrone, *L'albero della libertà: Dai giacobini a Garibaldi* (Florence: Le Monnier, 1987), 59–97.

2. EXERCISES IN MEDIA PROSELYTISM: JOURNALISM AND REVOLUTIONARY APOSTOLATE, 1831–1833

1. On Garrison, see McDaniel, *Problem of Democracy;* on Mazzini, see Rossi, *Image of America.*

2. See Rugemer, *Problem of Emancipation,* 96–143; and Fladeland, *Men and Brothers.*

3. See Elizabeth Heyrick, *Immediate, Not Gradual, Abolition; or, An Inquiry into the Shortest, Safest, and Most Effectual Means of Getting Rid of West Indian Slavery* (London: Hatchard, 1824). See also David Brion Davis, "The Emergence of Immediatism in British and American

Antislavery Thought," *Mississippi Valley Historical Review* 49, no. 2 (1962): 209–230; and Cecelia Catherine Walsh-Russo, "'The World Is My Country and My Countrymen Are All Mankind': Transnational Diffusion of Anglo-American Abolitionism, 1824–1839" (Ph.D. diss., Columbia University, 2008), 107–123.

4. See especially Franco Della Peruta, *Storia dell'Ottocento: Dalla Restaurazione alla "belle epoque"* (Florence: Le Monnier, 1992), 135–156; and Hobsbawm, *Age of Revolutions.*

5. On Italian Risorgimento exiles in international and European context, see specifically Isabella, *Risorgimento in Exile.*

6. On the importance of the press for Garrison's abolitionism, see Robert Fanuzzi, *Abolition's Public Sphere* (Minneapolis: University of Minnesota Press, 2003), xi–xl; on Mazzini and the power of the press, see Riall, *Risorgimento,* 134–137.

7. Throughout the present work, I will distinguish between Young Italy, the association founded by Mazzini in 1831, and *La Giovine Italia,* the paper that, from 1832, was the official organ of the association; both ended their first period of activities in 1834.

8. See Mayer, *All on Fire,* 97–126; Newman, *Transformation of American Abolitionism,* 80–107; and Fanuzzi, *Abolition's Public Sphere,* 51–52.

9. William Lloyd Garrison, "Prospectus of the Liberator," *Liberator,* 28 May 1831; James Forten, "Men Must Be Free," *Liberator,* 20 August 1831, quoted in Julie Winch, "Onward, Onward Is Indeed the Watchword: James Forten's Reflections on Revolution and Liberty," in McCarthy and Stauffer, *Prophets of Protest,* 87. See also Julie Winch, *A Gentleman of Color: The Life of James Forten* (New York: Oxford University Press, 2002), 244–245; and McDaniel, *Problem of Democracy,* 38–40. On Nat Turner's rebellion, see especially Scot A. French, *Nat Turner in History and Memory: The Rebellious Slave in the American South* (New York: Houghton Mifflin, 2004); and Kenneth S. Greenberg, ed., *Nat Turner: A Slave Rebellion in History and Memory* (New York: Oxford University Press, 2003).

10. William Lloyd Garrison, "To the Public," *Liberator,* 1 January 1831. See also Thomas, *Liberator,* 114–128; Merrill, *Against Wind and Tide,* 40–55; McDaniel, *Problem of Democracy,* 36–42; and Augusta Rohrbach, "'Truth Stronger and Stranger than Fiction': Reexamining William Lloyd Garrison's *The Liberator,*" *American Literature* 73, no. 4 (2001): 727–755.

11. William Lloyd Garrison, "Truisms"; and "Walker's Appeal," both in *Liberator,* 8 January 1831; see also Cain, "Introduction," 37–44; Denis P. Brennan, "The Printer's Stand: William Lloyd Garrison and *The Liberator*" (PhD diss., State University of New York, 2003), 187–225; and Peter P. Hinks, *To Awaken My Afflicted Brethren: David Walker and the Problem of Antebellum Slave Resistance* (University Park: Pennsylvania State University Press, 1997).

12. Garrison, "To the Public." See also Newman, *Transformation of American Abolitionism,* 100–106; Timothy P. McCarthy, "To Plead Our Own Cause: Black Print Culture and the Origins of American Abolitionism," in McCarthy and Stauffer, *Prophets of Protest,* 114–146; Blackett, *Building an Antislavery Wall,* 42–78; and Burin, *Slavery and the Peculiar Solution,* 6–33.

13. William Lloyd Garrison, *Thoughts on African Colonization; or, An Impartial Exhibition of the Doctrine, Principles, and Purposes of the American Colonization Society, together with the Resolutions, Addresses, and Remonstrances of the Free People of Color* (Boston: Garrison and Knapp, 1832), 2. See also Mayer, *All on Fire,* 134–144; Merrill, *Against Wind and Tide,* 60–67; Bruce Rosen, "Abolition and Colonization, the Years of Conflict: 1829–1834," *Phylon* 33, no. 2 (1972): 177–192; Burin, *Slavery and the Peculiar Solution,* 21–22; and Yarema, *American Colonization Society,* 53–55.

14. Giuseppe Mazzini, "Ils sont partis" (1834), in *EN,* 4:97; Maurizio Isabella, "Exile and Nationalism: The Case of the *Risorgimento,*" *European History Quarterly* 36 (2006): 503; Arisi Rota, *I piccoli cospiratori,* 18. See also Galante Garrone, *L'albero della libertà,* 59–97.

15. Arisi Rota, *I piccoli cospiratori,* 105. See also Luca Mannori, "Alla periferia dell'Impero: Egemonia austriaca e immagini dello spazio nazionale nell'Italia del primo Risorgimento (1814–1835)," in *Gli imperi dopo l'Impero nell'Europa del XIX secolo,* ed. Marco Bellabarba et al. (Bologna: Il Mulino, 2008); and Belardelli, *Mazzini,* 39–42.

16. Giuseppe Mazzini, "Della *Giovine Italia,*" in *LGI,* 34; Mazzini's quote in Franco Della Peruta, "Giuseppe Mazzini dalla *Giovine Italia* alla *Giovine Europa,*" in *Potere e circolazione delle idee: Stampa, accademie e censura nel Risorgimento italiano,* ed. Domenico Maria Bruni (Milan: FrancoAngeli, 2007), 33. See also Alessandro Galante Garrone, "I giornali della restaurazione, 1815–1847," in *La stampa italiana del Risorgimento,* by Alessandro Galante Garrone and Franco Della Peruta (Rome-Bari: Laterza, 1979), 140–150; and Paolo Murialdi, *Storia del giornalismo italiano: Dalle gazzette a Internet* (Bologna: Il Mulino, 2006).

17. Giuseppe Monsagrati, *Giuseppe Mazzini* (Florence: Giunti, 1994), 42; Giuseppe Mazzini, "D'alcune cause che impedirono finora lo sviluppo della libertà in Italia," quoted in Leone Ravenna, *Il giornalismo mazziniano: Note ed appunti* (Florence: Le Monnier, 1967), 35. See also Roberto Balzani, "Mazzini e la stampa democratica," in Bruni, *Potere e circolazione delle idée,* 74–75; and Galletto, *Mazzini nella vita,* 1:235–261.

18. Roland Sarti, "Giuseppe Mazzini and His Opponents," in *Italy in the Nineteenth Century,* ed. John Davis (Oxford: Oxford University Press, 2000), 82; Giuseppe Mazzini, "Agli Italiani," in *LGI,* 1:129–130; Giuseppe Mazzini, "I collaboratori della 'Giovine Italia' ai loro concittadini," in *EN,* 3:28, 56. See also Mastellone, *Il progetto politico di Mazzini,* 55–78; Lucy Riall, "The Politics of Italian Romanticism: Mazzini and the Making of a Nationalist Culture," in Bayly and Biagini, *Mazzini and the Globalization,* 172–173; Riall, *Risorgimento,* 134–135; and Giuseppe Tramarollo, "Il giornalismo di Mazzini," *Il Risorgimento* 29, no. 3 (1977): 113–126.

19. *SEI,* 1:85; 120. See also Maurizio Isabella, "Mazzini's Internationalism in Context: From the Cosmopolitan Patriotism of the Italian Carbonari to Mazzini's Europe of the Nations," in Bayly and Biagini, *Mazzini and the Globalization,* 37–39; Codignola, *La giovinezza di G. Mazzini,* 149–188; and Hayes, *Mazzini and the Secret Societies.*

20. On the importance of public opinion for abolitionism in the antebellum United States, see especially Fanuzzi, *Abolition's Public Sphere.* On public opinion in *Risorgimento* Italy, see Maurizio Isabella, "Freedom of the Press, Public Opinion, and Liberalism in the *Risorgimento,*" *Journal of Modern Italian Studies* 17:5 (2012): 551–567.

21. See Mayer, *All on Fire,* 127–132. See also Joanne Pope Melish, *Disowning Slavery: Gradual Emancipation and Race in New England, 1780–1860* (Ithaca, NY: Cornell University Press, 2000), 200–202; and, on the New England Abolitionists' "Boston Clique" and the NEASS, Lawrence J. Friedman, *Gregarious Saints: Self and Community in American Abolitionism, 1830–1870* (New York: Cambridge University Press, 1982), 45–47.

22. Garrison's quote in Oliver Johnson, *William Lloyd Garrison and His Times; or, Sketches of the Anti-Slavery Movement in America and of the Man Who Was Its Founder and Moral Leader* (Boston: B.B. Russell, 1879), 88; Minardi, *Making Slavery History,* 80; Roman J. Zorn, "The *New England Anti-Slavery Society:* Pioneer Abolition Organization," *Journal of Negro History* 42, no. 3

(1957): 160. On the importance of Faneuil Hall for Boston's Abolitionists, see Fanuzzi, *Abolition's Public Sphere,* 129–166.

23. [William Lloyd Garrison], "Constitution of the *New England Anti-Slavery Society* (1832)," in New England Anti-Slavery Society, *First Annual Report of the Board of Managers of the New England Anti-Slavery Society* (Boston, 1833), 49. See also Mayer, *All on Fire,* 138–141; Merrill, *Against Wind and Tide,* 157–160; and Dillon, *Abolitionists,* 49–54.

24. Newman, *Transformation of American Abolitionism,* 107; Goodman, *Of One Blood,* 35. See also Stewart, *Holy Warriors,* 56–57; and Filler, *Crusade against Slavery,* 81–83.

25. Stewart, *Holy Warriors,* 57; William Lloyd Garrison to Henry E. Benson, 21 July 1832, in *LWLG,* 1:158. See also Zorn, "*New England Anti-Slavery Society,*" 162–166; and Kraditor, *Means and Ends,* 3–5.

26. Dillon, *Abolitionists,* 69; Newman, *Transformation of American Abolitionism,* 120; *Abolitionist,* 1 January 1833, Samuel J. May Anti-Slavery Collection, Cornell University; Zorn, "*New England Anti-Slavery Society,*" 171. On the impact of Nat Turner's rebellion in the South, see Kenneth Greenberg, introduction to *The Confessions of Nat Turner and Related Documents,* ed. Kenneth Greenberg (New York: Bedford/St. Martin's, 1996), 1–34.

27. William Lloyd Garrison to Samuel Whitcomb Jr., 20 February 1832, Whitcomb Family Papers, MHS; *Proceedings of the New England Anti-Slavery Convention Held in Boston on the 27th, 28th, and 29th of May, 1834,* quoted in Robert H. Abzug, "The Influence of Garrisonian Abolitionists' Fear of Slave Violence on the Antislavery Argument, 1829–1840," *Journal of Negro History* 55, no. 1 (1970): 23. See also Jonathan H. Earle, *Jacksonian Antislavery and the Politics of Free Soil, 1824–1854* (Chapel Hill: University of North Carolina Press, 2004), 30–33.

28. Sarti, "Mazzini and His Opponents," 82. See also Mastellone, *Il Progetto politico di Mazzini,* 41–54; Sarti, *Mazzini,* 74–85; Mack Smith, *Mazzini,* 5–7; Antonino De Francesco, "Ideologie e movimenti politici," in Sabbatucci and Vidotto, *Le premesse dell'unità,* 284–293; and Franco Della Peruta, *Politica e società nell'Italia dell'Ottocento: Problemi, vicende e personaggi* (Milan: FrancoAngeli, 1999), 201–240.

29. Giuseppe Mazzini, "Istruzione generale per gli affratellati alla Giovine Italia," in *GMD,* 325–326. See also Alberto Mario Banti, "Sacrality and the Aesthetics of Politics: Mazzini's Concept of the Nation," in Bayly and Biagini, *Mazzini and the Globalization,* 59–74.

30. Mazzini, "Istruzione generale," 325–326; Mazzini, "Della Giovine Italia," in *LGI,* 1:33. See also Della Peruta, *Mazzini e i rivoluzionari italiani,* 69–160.

31. Giuseppe Mazzini to Giuseppe Giglioli, 21 July 1831, in *EN,* 5:33. See also Mastellone, *Mazzini e la "Giovine Italia,"* 1:133–172. On Young Italy's appeal to the Italian youth, see Arisi Rota, *I piccoli cospiratori.* On Mazzini's "religion of the nation," see Simon Levi Sullam, "The Moses of Italian Unity: Mazzini and Nationalism as Political Religion," in Bayly and Biagini, *Mazzini and the Globalization,* 107–124; Sullam, "'Dio e il popolo,'" 401–422; and Banti, *La nazione del Risorgimento,* 58–59. For an example of American abolitionists calling each other "brother," see William Lloyd Garrison to "My dear brother" [Amos] Phelps, 16 December 1835, BPL. See also, for further comparison, John L. Myers, "Organization of 'The Seventy': To Arouse the North against Slavery," *Mid-America* 48 (1966): 29–46.

32. Monsagrati, *Giuseppe Mazzini,* 41; Giuseppe Mazzini to Niccolò Tommaseo, 1834, quoted in Banti, *Il Risorgimento italiano,* 66. See also Arisi Rota, *I piccoli cospiratori;* Franco Della Peruta,

"La Giovine Italia in Lombardia," in *Mazzini e la Lombardia: Lo sviluppo dell'ideale unitario: Aspetti editi ed inediti,* ed. Gianfranco De Paoli (Pavia: Cardano, 1997), 21–30; Della Peruta, *Mazzini e i rivoluzionari italiani;* and Lovett, *Democratic Movement in Italy,* 92–93.

33. Giorgio Candeloro, *Storia dell'Italia moderna,* vol. 2, *Dalla Restaurazione alla rivoluzione nazionale (1815–1846)* (Milan: Feltrinelli, 1962), 228. See also Arianna Arisi Rota, *Il processo alla Giovine Italia in Lombardia (1833–1835)* (Milan: FrancoAngeli, 2003); and Salvo Mastellone, *Mazzini e la "Giovine Italia,"* vol. 2.

34. On O'Connell, see especially Gearoid O'Tuathaigh, "Daniel O'Connell," in *Dictionary of Irish Biography Online,* ed. James McGuire and James Quinn (Cambridge: Cambridge University Press, 2009), available at http://dib.cambridge.org.

3. WORKING TOWARD GLOBAL MIDDLE-CLASS INCLUSIVENESS: THE FIGHT FOR FREEDOM FROM LOCAL TO FEDERAL, 1833–1837

1. See especially Drescher, *Abolition;* and Blackburn, *American Crucible,* 277–389.

2. See Davis, *Inhuman Bondage,* 231–249; Howard Temperley, *British Antislavery, 1833–1870* (London: Longman, 1972); and Seymour Drescher, *The Mighty Experiment: Free Labor versus Slavery in British Emancipation* (New York: Cambridge University Press, 2002).

3. Rugemer, *Problem of Emancipation,* 134; William Lloyd Garrison, *Liberator,* 9 August 1834; Deborah Bingham Van Broekhoven, "Perspectives on Slavery: Opposition to Slavery," in *Macmillan Encyclopedia of World Slavery,* ed. Paul Finkelman and Joseph Miller (New York: Macmillan, 1997), 691; McDaniel, *Problem of Democracy,* 49. See also Jeffrey R. Kerr-Ritchie, *Rites of August First: Emancipation Day in the Black Atlantic World* (Baton Rouge: Louisiana State University Press, 2007).

4. See Bayly, *Birth of the Modern World,* 139–142. On O'Connell, see especially Oliver McDonagh, *O'Connell: The Life of Daniel O'Connell, 1775–1847* (Dublin: Four Courts Press, 1991); and Cristine Kinealy, *Daniel O'Connell and the Anti-Slavery Movement: The Saddest People the Sun Sees* (London: Pickering & Chatto, 2010).

5. See Cain, "Introduction," 4–5. See also McDaniel, *Problem of Democracy,* 13–14.

6. Nye, *Garrison and the Humanitarian Reformers,* 105; Walters, *American Reformers,* 80. See also William L. Van Deburg, "William Lloyd Garrison and the 'Pro-Slavery Priesthood': The Changing Beliefs of an Evangelical Reformer, 1830–1840," *Journal of the American Academy of Religion* 43 (1975): 224–237; and Loveland, "Evangelicalism and Immediate Emancipation," 172–188.

7. Mayer, *All on Fire,* 224. See also Abzug, *Cosmos Crumbling,* 219–221; and Stewart, *Garrison and the Challenge,* 94–95. On Martin Luther King Jr., see especially Adam G. Fairclough, *To Redeem the Soul of America: The Southern Christian Leadership Conference and Martin Luther King, Jr.* (Athens: University of Georgia Press, 2001).

8. Lewis Perry, *Radical Abolitionism: Anarchy and the Government of God in Antislavery Thought* (Ithaca, NY: Cornell University Press, 1971), 57. See also Garrison's daughter Fanny's pamphlet: Fanny (Garrison) Villard, ed., *William Lloyd Garrison on Non-Resistance, Together with a Personal Sketch by His Daughter, Fanny Garrison Villard, and a Tribute to Leo Tolstoy* (New York: Haskell House, 1924); Stewart, *Holy Warriors,* 89–90; Richard O. Curry, "Romantic Radicalism in Antebellum America," *Reviews in American History* 1, no. 4 (1973): 524–530; and David A. J.

Richards, *Disarming Manhood: Roots of Ethical Resistance* (Athens: Ohio University Press, 2005), 8–37, 131–180.

9. Mayer, *All on Fire,* 251; Herbert Aptheker, *Abolitionism: A Revolutionary Movement* (New York: Twayne, 1989), 46; William Lloyd Garrison to Samuel E. Sewall, 24 October 1835, William Lloyd Garrison Papers, MHS. See also Leonard Richards, *Gentlemen of Property and Standing: Anti-Abolitionist Mobs in Jacksonian America* (New York: Oxford University Press, 1970); Dillon, *Abolitionists,* 93–97; and Stewart, *Garrison and the Challenge,* 83–84. On Garrison's and Thompson's friendship, see McDaniel, *Problem of Democracy,* 51–53.

10. The first Garrison quote is in Cain, "Introduction," 2; William Lloyd Garrison to Samuel J. May, 30 December 1837, in *LWLG,* 2:332. See also McDaniel, *Problem of Democracy,* 53–56 ; and Rachel Hope Cleves, *The Reign of Terror: Visions of Violence from Anti-Jacobinism to Antislavery* (New York: Cambridge University Press, 2010).

11. See Sarti, *Mazzini,* 87–96; Candeloro, *Dalla restaurazione,* 238–240; and Alfonso Scirocco, *Garibaldi: Battaglie, amori, ideali di un cittadino del mondo* (Bari-Rome: Laterza, 2001), 19–27.

12. *EN,* 3:45; Mazzini's quotes in Mastellone, *Il progetto politico di Mazzini,* 119. See also Stefano Recchia and Nadia Urbinati, "Introduction: Giuseppe Mazzini's International Political Thought," in *A Cosmopolitanism of Nations: Giuseppe Mazzini's Writings on Democracy, Nation-Building, and International Relations,* ed. Stefano Recchia and Nadia Urbinati (Princeton, NJ: Princeton University Press, 2009), 1–30; Salvo Mastellone, *La democrazia etica di Mazzini (1837–1847)* (Pisa: Archivio Guido Izzi, 2000); Paolo Bagnoli, *L'idea dell'Italia, 1815–1861* (Reggio Emilia: Diabasis, 2007), 208–243; and Nadia Urbinati, "'A Common Law of Nations': Giuseppe Mazzini's Democratic Nationality," *Journal of Modern Italian Studies* 1, no. 2 (1996): 197–222.

13. Riall, *Garibaldi,* 20; Maurizio Viroli, *Come se Dio ci fosse. Religione e libertà nella storia d'Italia* (Turin: Einaudi, 2009), 194. See also Simon Levi Sullam, "'Fate della nazione una religione': Aspetti del nazionalismo mazziniano come religione politica," *Società e Storia* 106 (2004): 705–730; Emilio Gentile, *Politics as Religion* (Princeton, NJ: Princeton University Press, 2006); and McDaniel, *Problem of Democracy,* 131–134.

14. Giuseppe Mazzini, "Nationalité: Quelques idées sur une constitution nationale," *La Jeune Suisse* 19 (1835), in *SEI,* 6:125; Sullam, "Moses of Italian Unity," 113, 116; Della Peruta and Tussi, *Mazzini,* 41. See also Sullam, "'Dio e il popolo,'" 401–422.

15. Nadia Urbinati, "The Legacy of Kant: Giuseppe Mazzini's Cosmopolitanism of Nations," in Bayly and Biagini, *Mazzini and the Globalization,* 23, 11–12. See also Isabella, "Mazzini's Internationalism in Context," 37–58; and Martin Thom, "Europa, libertà e nazioni: Mazzini e Cattaneo nel Risorgimento," in Banti and Ginsborg, *Il Risorgimento,* 331–378.

16. Mazzini's and Banti's quotes in Banti, "Sacrality and the Aesthetics of Politics," 62–63. See also Isabella, "Exile and Nationalism," 493–520.

17. Mazzini's quote in Viroli, *Come se Dio ci fosse,* 193. On Garrison's and Mazzini's friendship, see chapter 5 in the present book.

18. Garrison's quote in Dillon, *Abolitionists,* 52. See also Merrill, *Against Wind and Tide,* 76–77; and Thomas, *Liberator,* 155–176.

19. *Liberator,* 9 March 1833; McDaniel, *Problem of Democracy,* 46. See also Nye, *Garrison and the Humanitarian Reformers,* 65–86; and Mayer, *All on Fire,* 151–165; Blackett, "'There Shall Be No More Sea,'" 17–19; and Rugemer, *Problem of Emancipation,* 132–139.

20. Dumond, *Antislavery,* 177. See also Filler, *Crusade against Slavery,* 86–87.

21. William Lloyd Garrison, "The American Anti-Slavery Society's Declaration of Sentiments (1833)," in *Slavery and Emancipation,* ed. Rick Halpern and Enrico Dal Lago (Oxford: Blackwell, 2002), 300; William Lloyd Garrison, "Declaration of the National Anti-Slavery Convention, December 14, 1833," in *WLGFS,* 94. See also Stewart, *Holy Warriors,* 51–54; Dillon, *Abolitionists,* 55–56; and Newman, *Transformation of American Abolitionism,* 124–125.

22. The quotes from the constitution of the American Anti-Slavery Society are in Dumond, *Antislavery,* 178. See also, on the AASS's aims, David Blight, "William Lloyd Garrison at Two Hundred: His Radicalism and His Legacy for Our Time," in Stewart, *Garrison at Two Hundred,* 6–7.

23. Garrison, "Declaration of the National Anti-Slavery Convention," 91. See also Stewart, *Garrison and the Challenge,* 70–74; Walters, *American Reformers,* 80–81; and Stewart, *Holy Warriors,* 55–57.

24. Filler, *Crusade against Slavery,* 123. See also James Brewer Stewart, "Peaceful Hopes and Violent Experiences: The Evolution of Reforming and Radical Abolitionism, 1831–1837," *Civil War History* 17, no. 4 (1971): 293–309. On the postal campaign, see also Dillon, *Abolitionists,* 89–92. On the petition campaign, see Barnes, *Antislavery Impulse,* 121–145; and Aptheker, *Abolitionism,* 91–92.

25. Sarti, "Mazzini and His Opponents," 86. See also Mazzini, "D'una letteratura europea," 271–306; Simon Levi Sullam, "Costruire un nazionalismo e un 'gran convegno de' popoli: Giuseppe Mazzini tra Europa e Polonia," in *L'eredità di Giuseppe Mazzini: La democrazia tra coscienza nazionale e coscienza europea,* ed. Giampietro Berti (Padova: Il Poligrafo, 2006), 49–64; Banti, *La nazione del Risorgimento;* and Duggan, *Force of Destiny,* 130–131.

26. Mastellone, *Il progetto politico di Mazzini,* 130; *SEI,* 5:20–21. See also Mack Smith, *Mazzini,* 11–12; Franco Della Peruta, "Giuseppe Mazzini dalla *Giovine Italia* alla *Giovine Europa,*" in Bonanni, *Pensiero e Azione,* 29–46; and Venturi, "L'Italia fuori d'Italia," 1258–1263.

27. Giuseppe Mazzini, "Atto di Fratellanza della Giovine Europa," in *La Giovine Italia e la Giovine Europa dal Carteggio unedito di Giuseppe Mazzini a Luigi Amedeo Melegari,* ed. Dora Melegari (Milan: Fratelli Treves, 1906), 265–266; Franco Della Peruta, "Mazzini e la Giovine Europa," *Annali dell'Istituto Gian Giacomo Feltrinelli* 5 (1962): 18. See also Roland Sarti, "Giuseppe Mazzini and Young Europe," in Bayly and Biagini, *Mazzini and the Globalization,* 275–291; Belardelli, *Mazzini,* 65–74; and Della Peruta and Tussi, *Mazzini,* 42–48.

28. Giuseppe Mazzini, "Dell'iniziativa rivoluzionaria in Europa," in *GMD,* 450, 455, 464; Sarti, "Mazzini and His Opponents," 86. See also Mastellone, *Il progetto politico di Mazzini,* 183–203; and Karma Nabulsi, "Patriotism ad Nationalism in the 'Oath of Allegiance' to Young Europe," *European Journal of Political Theory* 5, no. 1 (2006): 61–70.

29. Giuseppe Mazzini to Luigi Amedeo Melegari, 26 August 1835, in *SEI,* 9:63; Della Peruta, "Mazzini e la Giovine Europa," 39. See also Della Peruta, *Mazzini e i rivoluzionari italiani,* 169–219; Zefiro Ciuffoletti, "Mazzini e la *Giovine Europa,*" in *Giuseppe Mazzini dalla Giovine Europa alla Lega Internazionale dei popoli,* ed. Cosimo Ceccuti (Florence: Polistampa, 2008), 27–34; and Venturi, "L'Italia fuori dall'Italia," 1262–1264.

30. See Sarti, *Mazzini,* 110–114. See also Sarti, "Giuseppe Mazzini and Young Europe," 291–295; Galletto, *Mazzini nella vita,* 1:348–376; Duggan, *Force of Destiny,* 133–134. On Young Ireland and Young America, see Richard P. Davis, *The Young Ireland Movement* (London: Gill and MacMillan, 1988); and Yonatan Eyal, *The Young America Movement and the Transformation of the Democratic Party, 1828–1861* (New York: Oxford University Press, 2007).

4. CONFRONTING IDEOLOGICAL INERTIAS: GARRISONIANS, MAZZINIANS, AND THEIR ENEMIES, 1838–1846

1. See especially Drescher, *Abolition,* 267–283; McDaniel, *Problem of Democracy,* 66–85; and Dal Lago, *American Slavery,* 123–144.

2. William Ellery Channing to James G. Birney, 14 April 1840, quoted in McDaniel, *Problem of Democracy,* 69. See also Fladeland, *Men and Brothers,* 259–273; and Steven Heath Mitton, "The Free World Confronted: The Problem of Slavery and Progress in American Foreign Relations, 1833–1844" (PhD diss., Louisiana State University, 2005), 55–86.

3. See Scirocco, *Garibaldi,* 40–137; and Riall, *Garibaldi,* 36–47.

4. See Stewart, *Holy Warriors,* 65–96; Walters, *Antislavery Appeal,* 3–18; Dillon, *Abolitionists,* 113–140; and Stewart, *Abolitionist Politics.*

5. Aptheker, *Abolitionism,* 77. See also Mayer, *All on Fire,* 132–133; Friedman, *Gregarious Saints,* 129–159; Robertson, *Hearts Beating for Liberty,* 11–36; Jean Fagan Yellin, *Women and Sisters: The Antislavery Feminists in American Culture* (New Haven, CT: Yale University Press, 1989); Jeffrey, *Great Silent Army;* and Anne M. Boylan, *The Origins of Women's Activism: New York and Boston, 1797–1840* (Chapel Hill: University of North Carolina Press, 2002).

6. William Lloyd Garrison, "Rights of Woman," *Liberator,* 12 January 1838; Walters, *Antislavery Appeal,* 11; Rev. Horace Moulton to Amos Phelps, 8 May 1839, BPL. See also Kraditor, *Means and Ends,* 39–78; Stewart, *Garrison and the Challenge,* 107–113; and Dillon, *Abolitionists,* 116–119.

7. William Lloyd Garrison, "Working Men," *Liberator,* 1 January 1831. See also Mayer, *All on Fire,* 117–118; Kraditor, *Means and Ends,* 244–255; and Goodman, *Of One Blood,* 153–155. On Garrison and the Garrisonians and Chartism, see McDaniel, *Problem of Democracy,* 143–152. On Chartism, see especially Malcolm Chase, *Chartism: A New History* (Manchester: Manchester University Press, 2007); and Dorothy Thompson, *The Chartists: Popular Politics in the Industrial Revolution* (New York: Pantheon, 1984).

8. Rev. Orange Scott to James G. Birney, 12 April 1839, BPL; William Lloyd Garrison to the editor of the *Emancipator,* 31 May 1839, in *LWLG,* 2:473–474. See also Mayer, *All on Fire,* 280–284; Stewart, *Holy Warriors,* 93–95; and Dillon, *Abolitionists,* 113–140.

9. See Filler, *Crusade against Slavery,* 135–171; Walters, *American Reformers,* 87–94; Francesca Gamber, "The Public Sphere and the End of American Abolitionism, 1833–1870," *Slavery and Abolition* 28, no. 3 (2007): 351–368; and Reinhard O. Johnson, *The Liberty Party, 1840–1848: Antislavery Third Party Politics in the United States* (Baton Rouge: Louisiana State University Press, 2009).

10. See Della Peruta, *Mazzini e i rivoluzionari italiani,* 258–263; Berti, *I democratici e l'iniziativa meridionale,* 196–199; Lovett, *Democratic Movement in Italy,* 92–97; and Enrico Dal Lago, *Agrarian Elites: American Slaveholders and Southern Italian Landowners, 1815–1861* (Baton Rouge: Louisiana State University Press, 2005), 225–230.

11. Nicola Fabrizi's quote in Della Peruta, *Mazzini e i rivoluzionari italiani,* 283. See also Candeloro, *Dalla restaurazione,* 377–380; Franco Della Peruta, "Mazzinianesimo e democrazia nel Mezzogiorno (1831–1847)," in A.A.V.V., *Democrazia e mazzinianesimo nel Mezzogiorno d'Italia, 1831–1872* (Geneva: Librairie Droz, 1975), 6–27; and Franco Della Peruta, "Le teorie militari della democrazia risorgimentale," in *Garibaldi condottiero: Storia, teoria, prassi,* ed. Filippo Mazzonis (Milan: FrancoAngeli, 1984), 66–69.

12. Giuseppe Mazzini to Maria Drago, 9 March 1838, in *EN,* 14:291. See also Sarti, *Mazzini,* 130–131; and Belardelli, *Mazzini,* 104–115.

13. Giuseppe Mazzini, "Circolare per la ricostituzione della Giovine Italia (1840)," in *EN,* 22:408. Candeloro, *Dalla restaurazione,* 373–377; Riall, *Garibaldi,* 36–47; Silvano Candido, "La 'Giovine Italia' a Montevideo (1836–1842): Contributo alla storia mazziniana nelle Americhe," *Bollettino della Domus Mazziniana* 21, no. 1 (1975): 53–76; and Jorge Myers, "Giuseppe Mazzini and the Emergence of Liberal Nationalism in the River Plate and Chile, 1835–1860"; and Peter Burke, "Mazzini and Brazil," both in Bayly and Biagini, *Mazzini and the Globalization,* 323–346 and 347–354.

14. Riall, *Garibaldi,* 35; Mazzini's first quote is in Candeloro, *Dalla restaurazione,* 374; Giuseppe Mazzini to Elia Benza, 10 May 1840, in *EN,* 19:118. See also Della Peruta, *Mazzini e i rivoluzionari italiani,* 315–368; Massimo Scioscioli, *Giuseppe Mazzini: I principi e la politica* (Naples: Guida Editori, 1995), 239–279; and Enrico Verdecchia, *Londra dei cospiratori: L'esilio londinese dei padri del Risorgimento* (Milan: Tropea, 2010), 218–247. On Mazzini and Chartism, see Mastellone, *Mazzini scrittore politico in inglese,* 73–74.

15. Maria Pia Roggero, "L'emancipazione della donna nel pensiero italiano dai lumi a Mazzini," *Il Risorgimento* 35, no. 2 (1983): 154. See also Sarti, *Mazzini,* 132–133; Pesman, "Mazzini and/in Love," 97–117; Banti, "Sacrality and the Aesthetics of Politics," 59–74; and Marta Bonsanti, "Amore familiare, amore romantico e amor di patria," in Banti and Ginsborg, *Il Risorgimento,* 127–152.

16. See especially McDaniel, *Problem of Democracy,* 76–78, 186–187; David Brion Davis, "Declaring Equality: Sisterhood and Slavery"; and Deborah A. Logan, "The Redemption of a Heretic: Harriet Martineau and Anglo-American Abolitionism," both in Kish Sklar and Stewart, *Women's Rights and Transatlantic Antislavery,* 3–18 and 242–265; and Eve Kornfeld, "Minerva and the Muse," in *Margaret Fuller: A Brief Biography with Documents,* ed. Kornfeld (New York: Bedford/St. Martin's, 1997), 1–76.

17. Douglas H. Maynard, "The World's Anti-Slavery Convention of 1840," *Mississippi Valley Historical Review* 47 (1960): 452; William Lloyd Garrison to Oliver Johnson, 22 May 1840, in *LWLG,* 2:625–626. On Garrisonians and the different names given to the meeting, see McDaniel, *Problem of Democracy,* 67–74. See also Blackett, "'There Shall Be No More Sea,'" 21–28.

18. William Lloyd Garrison to Helen E. Garrison, 29 June 1840, in *LWLG,* 2:654. See also Donald R. Kennon, "An Apple of Discord: The Woman Question at the World's Anti-Slavery Convention," *Slavery and Abolition* 5 (1984): 244–266; Lisa Shawn Hogan, "A Time for Silence: William Lloyd Garrison and the 'Woman Question' at the 1840 World Anti-Slavery Convention," *Gender Issues* 25 (2008): 63–79; and Kathryn Kish Sklar, "Women Who Speak for an Entire Nation: American and British Women at the World Anti-Slavery Convention, London, 1840," in *The Abolitionist Sisterhood: Women's Political Culture in Antebellum America,* ed. Jean Fagan Yellin and John C. Van Horne (Ithaca, NY: Cornell University Press, 1994), 301–311.

19. Stewart, *Garrison and the Challenge,* 121. See also James B. Stewart, "The Aims and Impact of Garrisonian Abolitionism, 1840–1860," *Civil War History* 15, no. 3 (1969): 197–209; and Daniel John McInerney, *The Fortunate Heirs of Freedom: Abolition and Republican Thought* (Lincoln: University of Nebraska Press, 1994), 79–106.

20. William Lloyd Garrison, "On Frederick Douglass," *Liberator,* 1 July 1841. See also Oakes,

Radical and the Republican, 8–14; and William McFeely, *Frederick Douglass* (New York: Norton, 1991), 150–160.

21. Walter H. Merrill, "Organization and Appeal: 1841–1842," in *LWLG,* 3:3; William Lloyd Garrison, "Repeal of the Union," *Liberator,* 6 May 1842. See also W. Caleb McDaniel, "Repealing Unions: American Abolitionists, Irish Repeal, and the Origins of Garrisonian Disunionism," *Journal of the Early Republic* 28, no. 2 (2008): 243–269; Murphy, *American Slavery, Irish Freedom;* Mayer, *All on Fire,* 330–332; Stewart, *Garrison and the Challenge,* 120–145; and Ronald Osborn, "William Lloyd Garrison and the United States Constitution: The Political Evolution of an American Radical," *Journal of Law and Religion* 24 (2008–9): 65–88.

22. Garrison's quote in Stewart, *Garrison and the Challenge,* 126. See also Kraditor, *Means and Ends,* 141–176; Richard R. Sewell, *Ballots for Freedom: Antislavery Politics in the United States, 1837–1860* (New York: Norton, 1976), 43–130; and Laurie, *Beyond Garrison,* 49–83. On the *Amistad* case, see Davis, *Inhuman Bondage,* 12–26.

23. The Liberty Party's 1844 platform is quoted in Walters, *Antislavery Appeal,* 16; Bruce Laurie, "Putting Politics Back In: Rethinking the Problem of Political Abolitionism," in Stewart, *Garrison at Two Hundred,* 79. See also McDaniel, *Problem of Democracy,* 66–75; Dillon, *Abolitionists,* 141–148; Stewart, *Holy Warriors,* 95–110; Johnson, *Liberty Party;* and Mark Voss Hubbard, "Slavery, Capitalism, and the Middling Sort: The Rank and File of Political Abolitionism," *American Nineteenth-Century History* 4, no. 2 (2003): 53–76.

24. See Christopher Duggan, "Giuseppe Mazzini in Britain and Italy: Divergent Legacies, 1837–1915," in Bayly and Biagini, *Mazzini and the Globalization,* 187–190; Verdecchia, *Londra dei cospiratori;* Emilia Morelli, *L'Inghilterra di Mazzini* (Rome: Istituto per la Storia del Risorgimento italiano, 1965); Maurizio Isabella, "Italian Exiles and British Politics before and after 1848," in *Exiles from European Revolutions: Refugees in Mid-Victorian England,* ed. Susan Freitag (Oxford: Oxford University Press, 2003), 59–87; Maura O'Connor, *The Romance of Italy and English Political Imagination* (New York: Palgrave, 1998), 65–67; and Marco Barducci, "Giuseppe Mazzini e Thomas Carlyle," in *Mazzini e gli scrittori politici europei, 1837–1857,* ed. Salvo Mastellone (Florence: Centro Editoriale Toscano, 2005), 2:29–42.

25. Giuseppe Mazzini to Maria Drago, 3 September 1841, in *EN,* 20:303; Sarti, *Mazzini,* 141. See also Mack Smith, *Mazzini,* 38–39; Michele Finelli, "Il prezioso elemento": Giuseppe Mazzini e gli emigrati italiani nell'esperienza della Scuola Italiana a Londra (Verrucchio: P.G. Pazzini, 1999); and Emilia Morelli, *Mazzini: Quasi una biografia* (Rome: Edizioni dell'Ateneo, 1984), 189–200.

26. Biagini, "Mazzini and Anticlericalism," 156; Margaret Fuller's quote in Mack Smith, *Mazzini,* 53. See also Rossi, *Image of America;* Sarti, "La democrazia radicale," 141–144; and, on Margaret Fuller, especially Gemme, *Domesticating Foreign Struggles,* 89–106; Charles Capper, *Margaret Fuller: An American Romantic Life,* 2 vols. (New York: Oxford University Press, 1994, 2010); and Gigliola Sacerdoti Mariani, "Fuller e Mazzini: Tra fede e fato," in Mastellone, *Mazzini e gli scrittori politici europei,* 95–116.

27. Mazzini's quote in Scirocco, *Garibaldi,* 129. See also Riall, *Garibaldi,* 46–56; Della Peruta, *Mazzini e i rivoluzionari italiani,* 369–440; Candeloro, *Dalla restaurazione,* 380–383; and Alfonso Scirocco, *L'Italia del Risorgimento* (Bologna: Il Mulino, 1990), 191–193.

28. Giuseppe Mazzini, "The Martyrs for Italian Liberty: Attilio and Emilio Bandiera," in

EN, 34:29; Thomas Carlyle's quote in Mack Smith, *Mazzini,* 43. See also Riall, "Politics of Italian Romanticism," 167–186; Banti, *Il Risorgimento italiano,* 67–71; and De Francesco, "Ideologie e movimenti politici," 295–305.

29. Giuseppe Mazzini, "Pensieri sulla democrazia in Europa," in *EN,* 34:92. See also Mastellone, *Il progetto politico di Mazzini,* 204–222; Mastellone, *Mazzini scrittore politico in inglese,* 119–130; Scioscioli, *Giuseppe Mazzini,* 209–238; Salvo Mastellone, "L'europeismo democratico di Mazzini," in Bonanni, *Pensiero e Azione,* 85–114; and Leonardo La Puma, *Giuseppe Mazzini democratico e riformista europeo* (Florence: Olschki, 2008), 56–74.

30. W. Caleb McDaniel, "Our Country Is the World: Radical American Abolitionists Abroad" (PhD diss., Johns Hopkins University, 2006), 366. See also Iain McMenamin, "'Self-Choosing' and 'Right-Acting' in the Nationalism of Giuseppe Mazzini," *History of European Ideas* 23, nos. 5–6 (1997): 221–234.

5. BAPTISMS OF FIRE FOR NEW SOCIAL IDEAS: POLITICAL DEFEAT, RADICAL INTRANSIGENCE, AND INTERNATIONALISM, 1846–1853

1. On American reactions to the European 1848, see Roberts, *Distant Revolutions;* specifically on the Garrisonians, see McDaniel, *Problem of Democracy,* 185–193.

2. On the expansion of southern slavery, see especially Brian Schoen, *The Fragile Fabric of Union: Cotton, Federal Politics, and the Global Origins of the Civil War* (Baltimore: Johns Hopkins University Press, 2009).

3. See Drescher, *Abolition,* 282–283; and Blackburn, *American Crucible,* 348–349.

4. See Bayly, *Birth of the Modern World,* 155–161; McDaniel, *Problem of Democracy,* 185–193; and Dal Lago, *American Slavery,* 142–144.

5. See the essays in Axel Korner, ed., *1848—A European Revolution? International Ideas and National Memories of 1848* (New York: Palgrave, 2000).

6. See both Roberts, *Distant Revolutions;* and McDaniel, *Problem of Democracy,* 193–198.

7. *Liberator,* 25 March 1842; 25 December 1846; Stewart, *Garrison and the Challenge,* 152. See also Merrill, *Against Wind and Tide,* 209–214; and Blackett, "'There Shall Be No More Sea,'" 28–31.

8. George Thompson to William Lloyd Garrison, 2 October 1846, BPL.

9. Laurie, *Beyond Garrison,* 159; *Liberator,* 14 July 1848. See also Stewart, *Holy Warriors,* 116–120; Sewell, *Ballots for Freedom,* 170–201. For a reappraisal, see Stewart, "Aims and Impact," 202–203.

10. Blackett, "'There Shall Be No More Sea,'" 30. See also Blackett, *Building an Antislavery Wall,* 79–117; and Merrill, *Against Wind and Tide,* 227–251.

11. Sarah Grimké to Elizabeth Pease, 18 April 1848, MS Am 1906 (574), Garrison Family Papers, HL. See also Davis, "Declaring Equality," 3–18; Filler, *Crusade against Slavery,* 178–179; and Mayer, *All on Fire,* 390–391.

12. See Sewell, *Ballots for Freedom,* 162–168; Levine, *Half Slave and Half Free,* 188–189; Stewart, *Holy Warriors,* 123–125; and Filler, *Crusade against Slavery,* 231–260.

13. William Lloyd Garrison's handwritten note on the speech for the twentieth anniversary of the *Liberator,* 1 January 1851, BPL; [William Lloyd Garrison], *Letter to Louis Kossuth concerning Freedom and Slavery in the United States on Behalf of the American Anti-Slavery Society* (Boston: R. F. Walcutt, 1852). See also Mayer, *All on Fire,* 394–401, 416–417.

14. William Lloyd Garrison, "Frederick Douglass and His Paper," *Liberator,* 23 September 1853. See also McFeely, *Frederick Douglass,* 168–169; Cain, "Introduction," 48–52; and Patrick T. J. Browne, "'To Defend Mr. Garrison': William Cooper Nell and the Personal Politics of Antislavery," *New England Quarterly* 70, no. 3 (1997): 415–442.

15. William Lloyd Garrison, "Review of Harriet Beecher Stowe's Novel *Uncle Tom's Cabin,*" *Liberator,* 26 March 1852; William Ellery Channing's quote in Fredrickson, *Black Image,* 106. See also Filler, *Crusade against Slavery,* 250–254; Mayer, *All on Fire,* 417–424; Merrill, *Against Wind and Tide,* 265–266; and Stewart, *Garrison and the Challenge,* 161.

16. Mack Smith, *Mazzini,* 55; Giuseppe Mazzini, in *EN,* 28:264. See also Mastellone, *Mazzini scrittore politico in inglese,* 131–138.

17. Giuseppe Mazzini, "Programma dell'Associazione Nazionale Italiana" (1848), in *GMD,* 570–571. See also Monsagrati, *Giuseppe Mazzini,* 63–66; De Francesco, "Ideologie e movimenti politici," 306–320; and Banti, *Il Risorgimento italiano,* 74–77.

18. See Giorgio Candeloro, *Storia dell'Italia moderna,* vol. 3, *La rivoluzione nazionale (1846–1849)* (Milan: Feltrinelli, 1970), 153–201; Lovett, *Democratic Movement in Italy,* 52–53; Nicola Badaloni, "La cultura," in Romano and Vivanti, *Dal primo Settecento all'Unità,* 948–961; and Thom, "Europa, libertà e nazioni," 331–378.

19. Franco Della Peruta, "Giuseppe Mazzini: Nota introduttiva," in *GMD,* 241; Giuseppe Mazzini, "Programma dell'Italia del Popolo" (1848), in *GMD,* 575; Giuseppe Mazzini, "Agli Italiani," in *GMD,* 582. See also Sarti, *Mazzini,* 158–169; Mack Smith, *Mazzini,* 56–64; and Franco Della Peruta, *Il giornalismo italiano del Risorgimento: Dal 1847 all'Unità* (Milan: FrancoAngeli, 2011), 100–103.

20. Goffredo Mameli's quote in Sarti, "Mazzini and His Opponents," 94; *SEI,* 7:192. See also Sarti, *Mazzini,* 169–180; Belardelli, *Mazzini,* 145–157; Antonio Ghisalberti, *Momenti e figure del Risorgimento romano* (Milan: Giuffrè, 1965); and Candeloro, *La rivoluzione nazionale,* 425–452. On the United States and the Roman Republic, see Daniele Fiorentino, "Il governo degli Stati Uniti e la Repubblica romana del 1849," in *Gli Americani e la Repubblica romana del 1849,* ed. Sara Antonelli, Daniele Fiorentino, and Giuseppe Monsagrati (Rome: Gangemi Editore, 2000), 89–139.

21. The Roman Republic's constitution is quoted in Giuseppe Monsagrati, "La Repubblica romana del 1849," in *Gli Italiani in Guerra. Conflitti, identità, memorie dal Risorgimento ai giorni nostri,* vol. 1, *Fare l'Italia: Unità e disunità nel Risorgimento,* ed. Mario Isnenghi and Eva Cecchinato (Turin: UTET, 2008), 146–147. See also Domenico Demarco, *Una rivoluzione sociale: La Repubblica romana del 1849 (16 Novembre 1848–3 Luglio 1849)* (Naples: M. Fiorentino, 1944); Riall, *Garibaldi,* 73–81; and Franco Della Peruta, *I Democratici e la rivoluzione italiana: Dibattiti ideali e contrasti politici all'indomani del 1848* (Milan: Feltrinelli, 1958), 67–108. On Pisacane, see especially L. Russi, *Carlo Pisacane: Vita e pensiero di un rivoluzionario senza rivoluzione* (Naples: ESI, 2007).

22. Giuseppe Mazzini, "La Santa Alleanza dei Popoli," in *EN,* 39:203–221; Giuseppe Mazzini, *The Duty of Democracy,* in *EN,* 46:208–209; and Mario Menghini, "Luigi Kossuth nel suo carteggio con Giuseppe Mazzini," *Rassegna Storica del Risorgimento* 8, nos. 1–2 (1921). See also Mastellone, *Mazzini scrittore politico in inglese,* 277–294; Galletto, *Mazzini nella vita,* 2:814–849; and Giorgio Candeloro, *Storia dell'Italia moderna,* vol. 4, *Dalla rivoluzione nazionale all'unità (1849–1860)* (Milan: Feltrinelli, 1964), 88–104.

23. See both McDaniel, *Problem of Democracy, 122–127;* and Sarti, "La democrazia radicale."

24. Mayer, *All on Fire,* 292. On William Henry Ashurst, see McDaniel, *Problem of Democracy;* and Matthew Lee, “Ashurst, William Henry,” in *Oxford Dictionary of National Biography* (Oxford: Oxford University Press, 2004), available at www.oxforddnb.com.

25. See Sarti, “Mazzini and His Opponents,” 88–89; Mack Smith, *Mazzini,* 45; and Verdecchia, *Londra dei cospiratori,* 270–272. On the meeting, see also Edyth Hinkley, *Mazzini: The Story of a Great Italian* (London: Ayer, 1924), 80–81.

26. Mazzini’s quote in Rossi, *Image of America,* 123; Giuseppe Mazzini, “Preghiera a Dio per i piantatori scritta da un esule,” in *GMD,* 290. See also McDaniel, *Problem of Democracy,* 84.

27. See Eugenio Biagini, “The Principle of Humanity: Lincoln in Germany and Italy, 1859–1865,” in *The Global Lincoln,* ed. Richard Carwardine and Jay Sexton (New York: Oxford University Press, 2011), 77–78; and Mayer, *All on Fire,* 416–417.

28. Garrison, introduction to *Mazzini: His Life,* vii (italics mine).

29. Mazzini’s quote in Mack Smith, *Mazzini,* 52; Ashurst’s quote in McDaniel, “Our Country Is the World,” 365.

30. [William Lloyd Garrison], “Joseph Mazzini,” *Liberator,* 27 July 1849.

31. William Lloyd Garrison to Theodore Roosevelt Sr., 10 January, 1871, in *LWLG,* 6:185–186. Aida Audeh and Nick Havely have commented on the content of the letter, saying that Garrison held “the Pope responsible for having enslaved Italy” and that this was “a position with which Mazzini expressed sympathy guardedly at various points in his life, although he could never say it quite as openly as his Protestant friend from Boston.” Audeh and Havely, *Dante in the Long Nineteenth Century,* 291.

32. See Garrison, introduction to *Mazzini: His Life,* i–xxv.

33. Rossi, *Image of America,* 134; McDaniel, “Our Country Is the World,” 337.

34. Mayer, *All on Fire,* 209; Harriet Martineau, *Harriet Martineau’s Autobiography* (New York: Cambridge University Press, 2010, orig. pub. in 1877), 378. See also Ginevra Conti Odorisio, *Harriet Martineau e Tocqueville: Due diverse letture della democrazia americana* (Soveria Mannelli: Rubettino, 2003), 259–290.

35. Garrison, introduction to *Mazzini: His Life,* xii. See also Thomas, *Liberator,* 352–353; and McDaniel, *Problem of Democracy,* 2–3.

36. Mazzini’s letter is quoted in Garrison, introduction to *Mazzini: His Life,* xv–xvi; Cain, “Introduction,” 5; Mayer, *All on Fire,* 379. On the universality of Mazzini’s thought, see particularly Urbinati, “‘Common Law of Nations,’” 197–222; and Recchia and Urbinati, “Introduction,” 1–30.

37. Mazzini’s quote in Garrison, introduction to *Mazzini: His Life,* xvi (italics mine); Garrison’s comment is on xviii. On these points, see Epstein, *Speaking of Slavery,* 54–57. See also, for example, “Mazzini and Kossuth,” *Liberator,* 30 July 1852; and “Mazzini, Kossuth, and Mr. Sanders,” *Liberator,* 11 August 1854.

38. Mischa Honeck, “Freemen of All Nations: Bestir Yourselves! Felice Orsini Transnational Afterlife and the Radicalization of America,” *Journal of the Early Republic* 30 (2010): 610; “Orsini and Pierri Meeting,” *Liberator,* 7 May 1858.

39. “Mazzini on American Slavery,” *Liberator,* 2 September 1853, 135; “Letter of Mazzini,” *Liberator,* 21 July 1854.

40. See especially Rossi, *Image of America,* 123–136.

41. See Davis, *Slavery and Human Progress,* xvi–xvii; Davis, *Revolutions,* 74–75; Blackburn, *Overthrow of Colonial Slavery;* and Blackburn, *American Crucible.* See also, for the larger con-

text, Bayly, *Birth of the Modern World,* 125–170; Dal Lago, *American Slavery;* and Bender, *Nation among Nations,* 116–181. I should point out that Mazzini's notion of "white slaves" as members of nations that were denied self-determination had very little to do with the more common notion of "white slavery" in the antebellum United States. The latter essentially derived from the fact that, in the words of Jeremy Krikler, "the labor movement in the United States . . . offered its critique of a nascent capitalism by assimilating the dangers of the new system to slavery," and yet "the dynamic of this incessant comparison was . . . not one which led white workers to identify with the plight of slaves"; see Jeremy Krikler, "Lessons from America: The Writings of David Roediger," *Journal of Southern African Studies* 20, no. 4 (1994): 666. Indeed, as David Roediger has clarified, in the common comparisons, "white slavery," intended as "wage slavery," or the exploitative system of wage labor, routinely came second after black slavery in terms of degree of exploitation; see David Roediger, *The Wages of Whiteness: Race and the American Working Class* (London: Verso, 1991), 64–67.

42. On these points, see Dal Lago, "Radicalism and Nationalism," 197–214; and Sarti, "La democrazia radicale," 133–158.

43. *Liberator,* 20 February 1852; Giuseppe Mazzini, "Doveri dell'uomo," in *EN,* 18:70. In relation to his rejection of American individualism, Mazzini observed, with distress, that in the United States "the individual is sovereign . . . and the rights of the individual person are everything"—a concept opposite to his own ideas of the importance of individual and collective duties; see Mazzini's quote in Sarti, "La democrazia radicale," 147.

6. ENDORSEMENT AND REFUSAL OF MAINSTREAM RADICALISM: GARRISON'S AND MAZZINI'S TIMES FOR ACTION, 1854–1861

1. David Potter, "Civil War," in *The Comparative Approach to American History,* ed. C. Van Woodward (New York: Oxford University Press, 1968), 143. See also Biagini et al., "Interchange"; McDaniel and Johnson, "New Approaches," 145–150; Fléche, *Revolution of 1861;* and Dal Lago, *American Slavery,* 145–172.

2. See Bender, *Nation among Nations,* 116–181; Tyrrell, *Transnational Nation,* 84–93; Guarneri, *America in the World,* 148–165; Raimondo Luraghi, *Storia della Guerra Civile americana* (Milan: Rizzoli, 1966); and Raimondo Luraghi, "The Civil War and the Modernization of American Society: Social Structure and Industrial Revolution in the Old South before and during the War," *Civil War History* 18 (1972): 230–250; Carl N. Degler, *One among Many: The Civil War in Comparative Perspective* (Gettysburg, PA: Gettysburg College, 1990); Michael Geyer and Charles Bright, "Global Violence and Nationalizing Wars in Eurasia and America: The Geopolitics of War in the Mid-Nineteenth Century," *Comparative Studies in Society and History* 38, no. 4 (1996): 619–657; Stig Förster and Jörg Nagler, eds., *On the Road to Total War: The American Civil War and the German Wars of Unification, 1861–1871* (New York: Oxford University Press, 1997); Peter Kolchin, *A Sphinx on the American Land: The Nineteenth-Century South in Comparative Perspective* (Baton Rouge: Louisiana State University Press, 2003); Tiziano Bonazzi, "Postfazione: La guerra civile Americana e la 'nazione universale,'" in *La Guerra Civile Americana vista dall'Europa,* ed. Tiziano Bonazzi and Carlo Galli (Bologna: Il Mulino, 2004), 463–502; and Gemme, *Domesticating Foreign Struggles.*

3. See Dean B. Mahin, *The Blessed Place of Freedom: Europeans in Civil War America* (Wash-

ington, DC: Potomac Books, 2003); Martin Ofele, *True Sons of the Republic: European Immigrants in the Union Army* (Westport, CT: Praeger, 2008); and Michael Bacarella, *Lincoln's Foreign Legion: The 39th New York Infantry, the Garibaldi Guard* (New York: White Mane, 1997).

4. Bayly, *Birth of the Modern World,* 162. See also Bender, *Nation among Nations,* 116–181; McDaniel, *Problem of Democracy,* 210–231; and Edward L. Ayers, "The American Civil War, Emancipation, and Reconstruction on the World Stage," in Reichard and Dickson, *America on the World Stage,* 125–137.

5. See Luraghi, *Storia della Guerra Civile americana;* and Dal Lago, "Radicalism and Nationalism," 197–214.

6. Garrison's quote in Thomas, *Liberator,* 382. See also Levine, *Half Slave and Half Free,* 192–198; Albert J. Von Frank, *The Trials of Anthony Burns: Freedom and Slavery in Emerson's Boston* (Cambridge, MA: Harvard University Press, 1998); and Philip F. Gura, *American Transcendentalism: A History* (New York: Norton, 2007), 248–256.

7. Garrison's speech during the burning of the Constitution is quoted in Cain, "Introduction," 36; William Lloyd Garrison, "Dred Scott and Disunion," *Liberator,* 12 March 1858. See also Elizabeth Varon, *Disunion! The Coming of the Civil War, 1789–1859* (Chapel Hill: University of North Carolina Press, 2008), 235–272; and Kenneth M. Stampp, *America in 1857: A Nation on the Brink* (New York: Oxford University Press, 1992), 68–143.

8. Stewart, *Holy Warriors,* 155. See also Jane H. Pease and William H. Pease, "Confrontation and Abolition in the 1850s," *Journal of American History* 58, no. 4 (1972); James Brewer Stewart, "From Moral Suasion to Political Confrontation: American Abolitionists and the Problem of Resistance," in *Passages to Freedom: The Underground Railroad in History and Memory,* ed. David Blight (Washington, DC: HarperCollins, 2004), 67–92; Dillon, *Abolitionists,* 219–34; Friedman, *Gregarious Saints,* 196–224; and Stauffer, *Black Hearts of Men.*

9. Dillon, *Abolitionists,* 236; Garrison's quote in Mayer, *All on Fire,* 449; [William Lloyd Garrison], "Orsini and Pierri Meeting," *Liberator,* 7 May 1858; Merrill, *Against Wind and Tide,* 271. See also Stewart, *Garrison and the Challenge,* 165–168; and Honeck, "Freemen of All Nations."

10. James Redpath to William Lloyd Garrison, 26 July 1854, BPL; James Redpath, *The Roving Editor; or, Talks with Slaves in the Southern States* (New York: A.B. Burdick, 1859). See also James R. McKivigan, *Forgotten Firebrand James Redpath and the Making of Nineteenth-Century America* (Ithaca, NY: Cornell University Press, 2008); and Albert J. Von Frank, "John Brown, James Redpath, and the Idea of Revolution," *Civil War History* 52, no. 2 (2006): 142–150.

11. Aptheker, *Abolitionism,* 123–124, 131. See also Stauffer, *Black Hearts of Men,* 236–261; David S. Reynolds, *John Brown, Abolitionist: The Man who Killed Slavery, Sparked the Civil War, and Seeded Civil Rights* (New York: Knopf, 2006), 309–333; and Evan Carton, *Patriotic Treason: John Brown and the Soul of America* (New York: Simon & Schuster, 2009), 320–344.

12. William Lloyd Garrison, "The Tragedy at Harper's Ferry," *Liberator,* 28 October 1859; William Lloyd Garrison, "John Brown and the Principle of Disunionism," in *WLGFS,* 136–137. See also Perry, *Radical Abolitionism,* 231–267; and Reynolds, *John Brown, Abolitionist,* 50–55. Interestingly, Caleb McDaniel has noted that Garrisonian "non-resistants often compared the martyr of Harper's Ferry to European revolutionaries like Garibaldi, whom [William C.] Wright called both 'the Italian John Brown' and 'the Italian Nat Turner.'" McDaniel, *Problem of Democracy,* 25.

13. Giuseppe Mazzini, "Agli Italiani," in *GMD,* 698. See also Della Peruta, *I Democratici e la*

rivoluzione italiana, 364–365; Alessandro Galante Garrone, *I radicali in Italia (1849–1925)* (Milan: Garzanti, 1973), 28–35; and Sergio La Salvia, "Mazzini, il partito e la rivoluzione," in Bonanni, *Pensiero e Azione,* 115–306.

14. Giuseppe Mazzini, "Indirizzo del Comitato d'Azione italiano" (1855), in *SEI,* 55:115. See also Della Peruta, *I Democratici e la rivoluzione italiana,* 366–367; Mack Smith, *Mazzini,* 104–105; and Belardelli, *Mazzini,* 173–185.

15. Roberto Romani, "Reluctant Revolutionaries: Moderate Liberalism in the Kingdom of Sardinia, 1849–1859," *Historical Journal* 55, no. 1 (2012): 45. See also Banti, *Il Risorgimento italiano,* 97–103; Woolf, *History of Italy;* Anthony Cardoza, "Cavour and Piedmont," in Davis, *Italy in the Nineteenth Century,* 108–131; Rosario Romeo, *Vita di Cavour* (Rome-Bari: Laterza, 1984), 305–334; Adriano Viarengo, *Cavour* (Rome: Salerno Editrice, 2010); and Luciano Cafagna, *Cavour* (Bologna: Il Mulino, 1999), 179–185.

16. Mazzini's letter to Ronchi is quoted in Rossi, *Image of America,* 94. See also Eyal, *Young America Movement;* McDaniel, *Problem of Democracy,* 204; and Yonatan Eyal, "A Romantic Realist: George Nicholas Sanders and the Dilemma of Southern International Engagement," *Journal of Southern History* 78, no. 1 (2012): 107–130.

17. Giuseppe Mazzini to Nicola Fabrizi, 28 July 1856, quoted in Della Peruta, "Giuseppe Mazzini: Nota introduttiva," 256. See also Sarti, *Mazzini,* 208–212; Morelli, *Mazzini,* 73–83; Romani, "Reluctant Revolutionaries," 45–73; and Raimond Grew, *A Sterner Plan for Italian Unity: The Italian National Society in the Risorgimento* (Princeton, NJ: Princeton University Press, 1963).

18. Giuseppe Mazzini, "La situazione," in *GMD,* 740, 751. See also Mack Smith, *Mazzini,* 117–121; Berti, *I Democratici e l'iniziativa meridionale,* 646–648; Nello Rosselli, *Carlo Pisacane nel Risorgimento italiano* (Turin: Einaudi, 1932); C. Pascarelli, *Il Risorgimento incompiuto: La tensione rivoluzionaria e l'iniziativa di Carlo Pisacane nell'Italia meridionale* (Pavia: Iuculano, 2009); Fabio Bertini, "I moti del giugno 1857: Mazzini, Pisacane e il problema della democrazia," in Ceccuti, *Giuseppe Mazzini dalla Giovine Europa,* 99–110; Pier Ferdinando Giorgetti, ed., *L'arco latino e il Risorgimento: Realtà ed echi dei moti mazziniani del 1857* (Pisa: ETS, 2007); Luciano Perini, "Gli utopisti: Delusioni della realtà, sogni dell'avvenire," in *Storia d'Italia,* annali 4, *Intellettuali e potere,* edited by Ruggero Romano and Corrado Vivanti (Turin: Einaudi, 1981), 412–413; and Morelli, *Mazzini,* 84–85.

19. Della Peruta, "Giuseppe Mazzini: Nota introduttiva," 258. See also Sarti, "Mazzini and His Opponents," 101–102; Scioscioli, *Giuseppe Mazzini,* 231–279; and Bianca Montale, "Mazzini e le origini del movimento operaio," in Bonanni, *Pensiero e Azione,* 307–352.

20. See Bianco di Saint-Jorioz, *Della Guerra d'insurrezione per bande;* Luraghi, *Storia della Guerra Civile americana;* Giulio Schenone, "John Brown e il pensiero insurrezionale italiano," in *Atti del I Congresso Internazionale di storia americana: Italia e stati Uniti dall'Indipendenza americana ad oggi (1776–1976)* (Genoa: Tilgher, 1978), 356–360; Timothy M. Roberts, "The Relevance of Giuseppe Mazzini's Ideas of Insurgency to the American Slavery Crisis of the 1850s," in Bayly and Biagini, *Mazzini and the Globalization,* 311–322; and also Dal Lago, "Radicalism and Nationalism," 197–214.

21. On the comparison between Lincoln and Cavour, see Enrico Dal Lago, "Lincoln, Cavour, and National Unification: American Republicanism and Italian Liberal Nationalism in Comparative Perspective," *Journal of the Civil War Era* 3 (2013): 85–113.

22. The Republican Party's platform is quoted in Levine, *Half Slave and Half Free, 200;*

also 206. See also Sewell, *Ballots for Freedom,* 239–245; Wilentz, *Rise of American Democracy,* 701–702; Eric Foner, *Free Soil, Free Labor, Free Men: The Ideology of the Republican Party before the Civil War* (New York: Oxford University, 1990, 1st ed. published in 1970); and William E. Gienapp, *The Origins of the Republican Party, 1852–1856* (New York: Oxford University Press, 1987).

23. William Lloyd Garrison to James McKim, 18 October 1856, in *LWLG,* 4:407, 410; William Lloyd Garrison to Parker Pillsbury, 3 June 1859, in *LWLG,* 4:626; "a complexional party" quote in Wilentz, *Rise of American Democracy,* 700; Sewell, *Ballots for Freedom,* 340.

24. Abraham Lincoln, "House Divided Speech," in Michael P. Johnson, ed., *Abraham Lincoln, Slavery, and the Civil War: Selected Writings and Speeches* (New York: Bedford/St. Martin's, 2000). See also David Herbert Donald, *Lincoln* (New York: Simon & Schuster, 1995), 196–229; Eric Foner, *The Fiery Trial: Abraham Lincoln and American Slavery* (New York: Norton, 2010), 99–103; Allen C. Guelzo, *Lincoln and Douglas: The Debates that Defined America* (New York: Simon & Schuster, 2009); and David M. Potter, *The Impending Crisis, 1848–1861* (New York: Harper & Row, 1976), 328–356.

25. Mayer, *All on Fire,* 453, 510; William Henry Ashurst to William Lloyd Garrison, Jr., 18 August 1860, BPL; William Lloyd Garrison, "Anti-Slavery Progress," *Liberator,* 7 September 1860. See also Merrill, *Against Wind and Tide,* 274–275; Thomas, *Liberator,* 398–399; and George Fredrickson, *Big Enough to Be Inconsistent: Abraham Lincoln Confronts Race and Slavery* (Cambridge, MA: Harvard University Press, 2008), 43–84.

26. William Lloyd Garrison's quote in Thomas, *Liberator,* 399; William Lloyd Garrison, "Southern Desperation," *Liberator,* 16 November 1860.

27. *Liberator,* 4 January 1861. See also Stewart, *Garrison and the Challenge,* 172–174; Mayer, *All on Fire,* 514–516; Wilentz, *Rise of American Democracy,* 768–769; Orville Vernon Burton, *The Age of Lincoln* (New York: Hill & Wang, 2007), 118–119; and Doris Kearns Goodwin, *Team of Rivals: The Political Genius of Abraham Lincoln* (New York: Simon & Schuster, 2005), 211–236.

28. Wendell Phillips's quote in McDaniel, *Problem of Democracy,* 224; Merrill, *Against Wind and Tide,* 278; William Lloyd Garrison, "The War—Its Cause and Cure," *Liberator,* 3 May 1861. See also Burton, *Age of Lincoln,* 122–132; Thomas, *Liberator,* 402–408; Stewart, *Holy Warriors,* 181–183; Don E. Fehrenbacher, *The Slaveholding Republic: An Account of the United States Government's Relations to Slavery* (New York: Oxford University Press, 1999), 295–304; and Russell McClintock, *Lincoln and the Decision for War: The Northern Response to Secession* (Chapel Hill: University of North Carolina Press, 2008); Richard Carwardine, *Lincoln: A Life of Purpose and Power* (New York: Knopf, 2006), 249–297; Foner, *Fiery Trial,* 161–205; and Richard Striner, *Father Abraham: Lincoln's Relentless Struggle to End Slavery* (New York: Oxford University Press, 2006), 89–136.

29. Riall, *Risorgimento,* 29. See also Grew, *Sterner Plan for Italian Unity,* 101–123; Woolf, *History of Italy;* Candeloro, *Dalla rivoluzione nazionale all'unità,* 215–243; and La Puma, *Giuseppe Mazzini,* 91–110.

30. See Romeo, *Vita di Cavour,* 331–448; Banti, *Il Risorgimento italiano,* 107–109; Roberto Balzani, "Cavour e le vie della Guerra," in Isnenghi and Cecchinato, *Fare l'Italia,* 342–357; Alberto M. Banti and Marco Mondini, "Da Novara a Custoza: Culture militari e discorso nazionale tra Risorgimento e Unità," in *Storia d'Italia,* annali 18, *Guerra e Pace,* ed. Walter Barberis (Turin: Einaudi, 2002), 417–464; and Sarti, *Mazzini,* 218–222.

31. Giuseppe Mazzini, "La Guerra," in *GMD,* 768; Mazzini's motto in Monsagrati, *Giuseppe Mazzini,* 93. On Ricasoli, see Michele Puccioni, *L'Unità d'Italia nel pensiero e nell'azione del Barone Bettino Ricasoli* (Florence: Vallecchi, 1932). See also Denis Mack Smith, *Victor Emmanuel, Cavour, and the Risorgimento* (Oxford: Oxford University Press, 1971), 127–143.

32. Mazzini's quote in Sarti, "Giuseppe Mazzini and His Opponents," 104. See also Candeloro, *Dalla rivoluzione nazionale all'unità;* Romeo, *Vita di Cavour,* 449–470; and Morelli, *Mazzini,* 89–100.

33. Giuseppe Mazzini, "Programma del Popolo d'Italia," in *GMD,* 773. See also Mack Smith, *Mazzini,* 140–149; Christopher Duggan, *Francesco Crispi: From Nation to Nationalism* (Oxford: Oxford University Press, 2002); Riall, *Garibaldi,* 306–346; Denis Mack Smith, *Cavour and Garibaldi in 1860: A Study in Political Conflict* (Oxford: Oxford University Press, 1954); Alfonso Scirocco, *Democrazia e socialismo a Napoli dopo l'unità (1860–1878)* (Naples: Libreria Scientifica Editrice, 1973); and Eva Cecchinato, *Camicie rosse: I garibaldini dall'Unità alla Grande Guerra* (Rome-Bari: Laterza, 2007).

34. The first Mazzini quote is in Sarti, *Mazzini,* 231; Giuseppe Mazzini, "Doveri dell'uomo," in *EN,* 69:1. See also Sullam, "Moses of Italian Unity," 120–122; Vittorio Parmentola, *Mazzini e i Repubblicani italiani: Studi in onore di Terenzio Grandi nel suo 92o compleanno* (Turin: Istituto per la Storia del Risorgimento italiano, 1976), 355–420; and Sauro Mattarelli, *Dialogo sui Doveri: Il pensiero di Giuseppe Mazzini* (Venice: Marsilio, 2005).

7. POLITICAL STALEMATE BETWEEN OPPOSITE EXTREMISMS: GARRISON'S COMPROMISE AND MAZZINI'S DEFEAT, 1862–1870

1. See Michael L. Bush, *Servitude in Modern Times* (Cambridge: Polity, 2000), 193–196; Robert Gildea, *Barricades and Borders: Europe, 1800–1914* (New York: Oxford University Press, 1997), 213–243; and Dal Lago, *American Slavery,* 156–164.

2. Blackett, "'There Shall Be No More Sea,'" 35. See also Drescher, *Abolition,* 322–332.

3. "Emancipation of Serfs in Russia," *Liberator,* 19 April, 1861; Giuseppe Mazzini, "La Russia," in *EN,* 69:274. See also especially Peter Kolchin, "Some Controversial Questions concerning Nineteenth-Century Emancipation from Slavery and Serfdom," in *Serfdom and Slavery: Studies in Legal Bondage,* ed. Michael L. Bush (London: Longman, 1996), 58–77.

4. Giuseppe Mazzini to Jessie White Mario, 15 September 1861, in *EN,* 71:394; Giuseppe Mazzini all'"Unità Italiana," in *EN,* 73:201. See also Biagini, "Principle of Humanity," 77–82; and Axel Korner, "Uncle Tom on the Ballet Stage: Italy's Barbarous America, 1850–1900," *Journal of Modern History* 83, no. 4 (2011): 721–752. On the Union's offer of a high officer's post to Garibaldi in the summer of 1861, see especially Don H. Doyle, "Bully for Garibaldi," *New York Times,* 26 September 2011. To be sure, as Massimo Furiozzi has noted, at the start of the Civil War, Mazzini made a clear distinction between the cause of the Union and the cause of black freedom, and he hesitated giving his support to Lincoln, both because he veered naturally toward the Democrats and because he could not simply ignore the Confederacy's claim to act in the name of national self-determination. Only when Lincoln took decisive steps toward the abolition of slavery, "Mazzini decided to side not only with emancipation, but also openly in favor of the North" and the Union; see Massimo Furiozzi, *La "Nuova Europa" (1861–1863): Democrazia e Internazionalismo* (Milan: FrancoAngeli, 2008), 112.

5. McDaniel, *Problem of Democracy,* 232; Giuseppe Mazzini to William Malleson, 15 February 1864, in *EN,* 78:9.

6. *Liberator,* 13 December 1861; "Laus Deo" in Mayer, *All on Fire,* 527; "serious dereliction of duty" in Walter M. Merrill, "Secession and Civil War," in *LWLG,* 5:4. See also Burton, *Age of Lincoln,* 161–162; and Ira Berlin et al., *Slaves No More: Three Essays on Emancipation and the Civil War* (New York: Cambridge University Press, 1992), 21–41.

7. Brooks D. Simpson, *America's Civil War* (Arlington Heights, IL: Harlan Davidson, 2009), 89; Foner, *Fiery Trial,* 244; Abraham Lincoln, "Abraham Lincoln's Emancipation Proclamation (1863)," in Halpern and Dal Lago, *Slavery and Emancipation,* 380. See also Foner, *Fiery Trial,* 216–245, 258–261; Striner, *Father Abraham,* 170–182; Carwardine, *Lincoln,* 198–219; and Berlin et al, *Slaves No More,* 49–51, 71–75.

8. William Lloyd Garrison to Fanny Garrison, 25 September 1862, in *LWLG,* 5:114–115; *Liberator,* 2 January 1863; Nye, *Garrison and the Humanitarian Reformers,* 177; *Liberator,* 6 February 1863. See also Thomas, *Liberator,* 418–420; and Merrill, *Against Wind and Tide,* 282–284.

9. *Liberator,* 16 January 1863; William Lloyd Garrison, "Why a Prolonged War," *Liberator,* 30 January 1863; Stewart, *Garrison and the Challenge,* 182. See also Ralph Korngold, *Two Friends of Man: The Story of William Lloyd Garrison and Wendell Phillips and their Relationship with Abraham Lincoln* (Boston: Little, Brown, 1950); McDaniel, *Problem of Democracy, 232–237;* Steven Hahn, *A Nation under Our Feet: Black Political Struggles in the Rural South from Slavery to the Great Migration* (Cambridge, MA: Harvard University Press, 2003), 89–102; and Stephanie McCurry, "War, Gender, and Emancipation in the Civil War South"; and Michael Vorenberg, "Abraham Lincoln's 'Fellow Citizens': Before and After Emancipation," both in *Lincoln's Proclamation: Emancipation Reconsidered,* ed. William A. Blair and Karen Fisher Younger (Chapel Hill: University of North Carolina Press, 2009), 120–150 and 151–169.

10. *Liberator,* 5 February 1864; William Lloyd Garrison, "Defense of Lincoln," *Liberator,* 20 May 1864; "NATIONAL VERDICT" quote in Mayer, *All on Fire,* 567. See also Thomas, *Liberator,* 420–425; and Merrill, *Against Wind and Tide,* 284–291.

11. Abraham Lincoln's quote in Mayer, *All on Fire,* 568; William Lloyd Garrison to Helen Garrison, in *LWLG,* 5:212; William Lloyd Garrison, "Remarks on Abraham Lincoln, Especially regarding the Emancipation Proclamation, in an address to the Illinois House of Representatives," 26 November 1865, William Lloyd Garrison Papers, MHS. See also Donald, *Lincoln,* 541–542.

12. Nye, *Garrison and the Humanitarian Reformers,* 175.

13. Mazzini's phrase quoted in Sarti, *Mazzini,* 233. See also Galletto, *Mazzini nella vita,* 3:1018–1044; Raffaele Romanelli, *L'Italia liberale, 1860–1900* (Bologna,: Il Mulino, 1990); Salvatore Lupo, *L'unificazione italiana: Mezzogiorno, rivoluzione, guerra civile* (Rome: Donzelli, 2011); and Salvatore Lupo, "Il Grande Brigantaggio: Interpretazione e memoria di una Guerra Civile," in *Storia d'Italia,* annali 18, *Guerra e Pace,* edited by Walter Barberis (Turin: Einaudi, 2002), 465–504.

14. Giuseppe Mazzini, "Agli Italiani!" in *GMD,* 780. See also Mack Smith, *Mazzini,* 159–164; Riall, *Garibaldi,* 317–329; and Scirocco, *Garibaldi,* 303–322.

15. Mazzini, "Agli Italiani!" 784–785. See also Sarti, *Mazzini,* 242–243; Morelli, *Mazzini,* 111–129; and Roberto Martucci, *L'invenzione dell'Italia unita, 1855–1864* (Florence: Sansoni, 1999).

16. Giuseppe Mazzini, "Agli Editori del *Dovere,*" 18 August 1863, in *EN,* 76:33–34; Giuseppe

Garibaldi's "I drink to him" quote is in Sarti, *Mazzini,* 245. See also Rossi, *Image of America,* 128–129; Mack Smith, *Mazzini,* 167–169; Jasper Ridley, "Il mito di Garibaldi in Inghilterra e la visita del 1864," *Rassegna degli Archivi di Stato* 2–3 (1982); and O'Connor, *Romance of Italy,* 149–151.

17. Mastellone, *Mazzini scrittore politico in Inglese,* 12; Karl Marx's term in Mack Smith, *Mazzini,* 199. See also Scioscioli, *Giuseppe Mazzini,* 253–263; Sarti, *Mazzini,* 246–249; Francesco Fiumara, *Mazzini e l'Internazionale: Contatti, rapporti, polemiche* (Pisa: Nistri-Lischi, 1968); and Aldo Romano, *L'unità italiana e la Prima Internazionale, 1861–1871* (Rome-Bari: Laterza, 1966).

18. See Paolo Lingua, *Mazzini il riformista: Gli ultimi anni e la questione sociale* (Genova: ECIG, 2005), 41–62; and Rosselli, *Mazzini e Bakunin.* On Bakunin's influence on Italian radicals, see especially Lovett, *Democratic Movement in Italy,* 227–230.

19. Giuseppe Mazzini, "Intorno alla questione dei negri in America," in *Giuseppe Mazzini: Scritti politici,* ed. Terenzio Grandi and Augusto Comba (Turin: UTET, 2011), 986–987; McDaniel, *Problem of Democracy,* 260–261.

20. William Lloyd Garrison, "Laus Deo!—Hallelujah!" *Liberator,* 3 February 1865; "'We are all abolitionists'" in William Lloyd Garrison, "The Death of Slavery," 10 February 1865; *Liberator,* 7 July 1865. See also James McPherson, *Battle Cry of Freedom: The Civil War Era* (New York: Oxford University Press, 1988), 851–853; Goodwin, *Team of Rivals,* 738–743; and Michael Vorenberg, *Final Freedom: The Civil War, the Abolition of Slavery, and the Thirteenth Amendment* (New York: Cambridge University Press, 2001), 197–208.

21. William Lloyd Garrison, "Valedictory: The Last Number of *The Liberator,*" 29 December 1865. See also Mayer, *All on Fire,* 590–601; Stewart, *Holy Warriors,* 184–195; and Merton L. Dillon, "The Failure of the American Abolitionists," *Journal of Southern History* 25, no. 2 (1959): 159–177.

22. William Lloyd Garrison's quote in Stewart, *Garrison and the Challenge,* 185–186. See also Eric Foner, *Reconstruction: America's Unfinished Revolution* (New York: Harper & Row, 1988), 61–62.

23. William Lloyd Garrison to Wendell Phillips Garrison, 10 April 1866, in *LWLG,* 5:409; William Lloyd Garrison to Francis Jackson Garrison, 18 January 1867, BPL; William Lloyd Garrison to Francis Jackson Garrison, 5 March 1867, MHS. See also Foner, *Reconstruction,* 333–336.

24. Stewart, *Garrison and the Challenge,* 195. See also Thomas, *Liberator,* 441–447. On the second meeting between Garrison and Mazzini, on 3 August 1867, see Wendell Phillips Garrison and Francis Jackson Garrison, *William Lloyd Garrison, 1805–1879: The Story of His Life Told by His Children* (New York: Century, 1889), 4:227–229.

25. William Henry Ashurst Jr., to William Lloyd Garrison, 9 April 1877, BPL. See also especially Lois A. Brown, "William Lloyd Garrison and Emancipatory Feminism in Nineteenth-Century America," in Stewart, *Garrison at Two Hundred,* 41–76; and Ellen DuBois, *Feminism and Suffrage: The Emergence of an Independent Women's Movement in America, 1848–1869* (Ithaca, NY: Cornell University Press, 1985).

26. Cain, "Introduction," 55. See also Mayer, *All on Fire,* 613–617; and Stewart, *Garrison and the Challenge,* 195–198.

27. Giuseppe Mazzini to Clementia Taylor, 1 May, 1865, in *EN,* 80:283. See also Rossi, *Image of America,* 130–135; and Mack Smith, *Mazzini,* 83–84.

28. Mazzini's quote in Rossi, *Image of America,* 146.

29. On the Universal Republican Alliance, see Sarti, *Mazzini,* 249–250; and Duggan, "Mazzini in Britain and Italy," 196–197.

30. See Mack Smith, *Mazzini,* 175–177; and Galletto, *Mazzini nella vita,* 3:1069–1093. See also Marco Mondini, "La guerra perduta: Il 1866 e l'antimito della disfatta," in Isnenghi and Cecchinato, *Fare l'Italia,* 618–623; Banti and Mondini, "Da Novara a Custoza," 417–464; Mack Smith, *Victor Emmanuel, Cavour, and the Risorgimento,* 303–335; and Wolf Giusti, *Mazzini e gli slavi* (Milan: Istituto per gli studi di politica internazionale, 1940).

31. Giuseppe Mazzini, "Ai membri del Congresso della Pace," in *EN,* 86:84–85. See also Mack Smith, *Mazzini,* 180–181; Riall, *Garibaldi,* 350–352; Scirocco, *Garibaldi,* 335–354; and E. Curatolo, *Il dissidio tra Mazzini e Garibaldi* (Milan: Mondadori, 1928).

32. Giuseppe Mazzini's quote in Sarti, *Mazzini,* 258; Monsagrati, *Giuseppe Mazzini,* 109. See also Giorgio Candeloro, *Storia dell'Italia moderna,* vol. 5, *La costruzione dello stato unitario (1861–1870)* (Milan: Feltrinelli, 1966); Scirocco, *Democrazia e socialismo;* and Gadi Luzzatto Voghera, "La presa di Roma"; and Simon Levi Sullam, "Mazzini e i conflitti dell'unità," both in Isnenghi and Cecchinato, *Fare L'Italia,* 770–780 and 253–266.

33. Mayer, *All on Fire,* 379. See also Garrison, introduction to *Mazzini: His Life,* i–xxv.

CONCLUSION: DIFFERENT ENDS AND PARALLEL FAME OF TWO ICONIC RADICALS

1. Garrison, introduction to *Mazzini: His Life,* vii.

2. Wendell Phillips's quote in Stewart, *Garrison and the Challenge,* 196; Francis Jackson Garrison's Diary, 11 July 1877, quoted in Mayer, *All on Fire,* 622.

3. Lucy Stone, "Remarks of Mrs. Lucy Stone," in *Tributes to William Lloyd Garrison at the Funeral Services, May 28, 1879* (Boston: Houghton, Osgood, 1879), 17. See also Mayer, *All on Fire,* 627–631.

4. Andrea Costa, *Bagliori di socialismo: Cenni storici* (Florence: Casa Editrice Nerbini, 1900), 11. See also Sarti, *Mazzini,* 259–261; Mack Smith, *Mazzini,* 216–217; and Giovanna Angelini, *L'ultimo Mazzini. Un pensiero per l'azione* (Milan: FrancoAngeli, 2008).

5. Garrison, introduction to *Mazzini: His Life,* xvii. See also Sarti, *Mazzini,* 262–264; and Sergio Luzzatto, *La mummia della repubblica: Storia di Mazzini imbalsamato, 1872–1946* (Milan: Rizzoli, 2001). It is worth looking briefly at the story behind the 1872 publication of Mazzini's autobiographical writings in America. In the spring of 1872, shortly after Mazzini's death, Henry Oscar Houghton and Melanchton M. Hurd, in charge of the Hurd & Houghton publishing house of New York (soon to become the current Houghton & Mifflin), had the idea of releasing in English an edited collection of Mazzini's writings for the benefit of the American public, because, as they stated, "the death of Mazzini has awakened an interest in his life amongst many whose impressions concerning it have been indistinct, and often prejudiced." Ashurst Venturi, *Mazzini: His Life,* iii. The contents of the collection came from the first six of the seven volumes of the *Scritti editi ed inediti di Giuseppe Mazzini,* originally published in Italian by Mazzini himself and his friend Aurelio Saffi with Daelli in 1861–64, and translated for the first time into English by Mazzini's longtime friend Emily Ashurst Venturi. The 1872 American edition was, therefore, based on what later was published in Italian as Mazzini's *Note*

autobiografiche (Autobiographical notes). However, in editing the material, Ashurst Venturi grouped the shorter chapters of the *Note* in nine longer chapters and also stopped Mazzini's own account at the 1849 Roman Republic—leaving out the last five chapters of the *Note.* She, then added her own concluding section, with a brief summary of the post-1849 events in Mazzini's life and with revealing comments about his character, such as the following: "He was the most *tenacious* man I had ever met. . . . As the spiritual torchbearer of a great cause, he was unsurpassable" (345). This later comment could have been easily applied also to William Lloyd Garrison, whom Hurd and Houghton asked to write the introduction to the book. The title of the book became eventually *Joseph Mazzini: His Life, Writings, and Political Principles.* Doubtless, given his personal acquaintance, friendship, and collaboration with Mazzini, Garrison seemed to Hurd and Houghton the perfect choice to introduce the volume they intended to publish; when they asked him to do so, it was "with the confidence that it will serve partially to inform the public respecting a man who is destined to fill a larger space in history than is commonly understood" (iv).

6. See Garrison and Garrison, *William Lloyd Garrison;* Johnson, *Garrison and His Times;* Emily Ashurst Venturi, *Joseph Mazzini: A Memoir* (London: H.S. King, 1875); and Bolton King, *The Life of Mazzini* (London: J.M. Dent, 1902). On the phases of Garrison's historiography, see Stewart, *Garrison and the Challenge,* 201–207; on the phases of Mazzini's historiography, see Sarti, *Mazzini,* 307–314.

7. Francis Jackson Garrison to Frederick William Chesson, 17 June 1884, BPL. See also Garrison and Garrison, *William Lloyd Garrison;* and, on the transnational perspective, McDaniel, *Problem of Democracy.*

BIBLIOGRAPHY

PRIMARY SOURCES

Manuscript Collections

Boston Public Library, Boston
  Anti-Slavery Collection, Rare Book and Manuscript Division
Cornell University Library, Ithaca, NY
  Samuel J. May Anti-Slavery Collection
Houghton Library, Harvard University, Cambridge, MA
  Garrison Family Papers
Massachusetts Historical Society, Boston
  William Lloyd Garrison Papers
  Whitcomb Family Papers

Printed Primary Sources

Newspapers

Abolitionist. Boston.
Liberator. Boston.

Books, Articles, and Essays

Ashurst Venturi, Emily. *Joseph Mazzini: A Memoir.* London: H.S. King, 1875.

———, ed. *Joseph Mazzini: His Life, Writings, and Political Principles.* New York: Hurd & Houghton, 1872.

Bianco di Saint-Jorioz, Carlo. *Della Guerra d'insurrezione per bande applicata all'Italia.* Vol. 1. Malta, 1830.

Cagnacci, Carlo, ed. *Giuseppe Mazzini e i fratelli Ruffini: Lettere Raccolte e annotate.* Porto Maurizio: Tipografia Berio, 1893.

Cain, William E., ed. *William Lloyd Garrison and the Fight against Slavery: Selections from "The Liberator."* New York: Bedford/St. Martin's, 1995.

Della Peruta, Franco, ed. *Scrittori politici dell'Ottocento.* Vol. 1, *Giuseppe Mazzini e i democratici.* Milan: Feltrinelli, 1966.

Garrison, Wendell Phillips, and Francis Jackson Garrison. *William Lloyd Garrison,*

1805–1879: The Story of His Life Told by His Children. 4 Vols. New York: Century, 1885–89.

Garrison, William Lloyd. *Thoughts on African Colonization; or, An Impartial Exhibition of the Doctrine, Principles, and Purposes of the American Colonization Society, Together with the Resolutions, Addresses, and Remonstrances of the Free People of Color.* Boston: Garrison and Knapp, 1832.

[Garrison, William Lloyd]. *A Brief Sketch of the Trial of William Lloyd Garrison for an Alleged Libel on Francis Todd of Newburyport, Mass.* Boston: Garrison and Knapp, 1834.

———. "Constitution of the *New England Anti-Slavery Society* (1832)." In *First Annual Report of the Board of Managers of the New England Anti-Slavery Society,* by New England Anti-Slavery Society. Boston, 1833.

———. *Letter to Louis Kossuth concerning Freedom and Slavery in the United States on Behalf of the American Anti-Slavery Society.* Boston: R. F. Walcutt, 1852.

Grandi, Terenzio, and Augusto Comba, eds. *Giuseppe Mazzini: Scritti politici.* Turin: UTET, 2011.

Halpern, Rick, and Enrico Dal Lago, eds. *Slavery and Emancipation.* Oxford: Blackwell, 2002.

Heyrick, Elizabeth. *Immediate, Not Gradual, Abolition; or, An Inquiry into the Shortest, Safest, and Most Effectual Means of Getting Rid of West Indian Slavery.* London: Hatchard, 1824.

Johnson, Michael P., ed. *Abraham Lincoln, Slavery, and the Civil War: Selected Writings and Speeches.* New York: Bedford/St. Martin's, 2000.

Johnson, Oliver. *William Lloyd Garrison and His Times; or, Sketches of the Anti-Slavery Movement in America and of the Man Who Was Its Founder and Moral Leader.* Boston: B.B. Russell, 1879.

Kish Sklar, Kathryn, ed. *Women's Rights Emerges within the Antislavery Movement, 1830–1870.* New York: Bedford/St. Martin's, 2000.

Martineau, Harriet. *Harriet Martineau's Autobiography.* New York: Cambridge University Press, 2010. Originally published in 1877.

Mazzini, Giuseppe, and Aurelio Saffi, eds. *Scritti editi ed inediti di Giuseppe Mazzini.* Vols. 1–18. Bologna-Milan: G. Daelli, 1861–91.

Melegari, Dora, ed. *La Giovine Italia e la Giovine Europa dal Carteggio inedito di Giuseppe Mazzini a Luigi Amedeo Melegari.* Milan: Fratelli Treves, 1906.

Menghini, Mario, ed. *Edizione Nazionale: Scritti editi ed inediti di Giuseppe Mazzini.* Vols. 1–106. Imola: Galeati, 1906–43.

———, ed. *La Giovine Italia.* Vols. 1–6. Rome: Società editrice Dante Alighieri, 1902–25.

———. "Luigi Kossuth nel suo carteggio con Giuseppe Mazzini." *Rassegna Storica del Risorgimento* 8, nos. 1–2 (1921).

Merrill, Walter M., and Louis Ruchames, eds. *The Letters of William Lloyd Garrison.* Vols. 1–6. Cambridge, MA: Harvard University Press, 1971–81.

Redpath, James. *The Roving Editor; or, Talks with Slaves in the Southern States.* New York: A.B. Burdick, 1859.

Tributes to William Lloyd Garrison at the Funeral Services, May 28, 1879. Boston: Houghton, Osgood, 1879.

Villard, Fanny (Garrison), ed. *William Lloyd Garrison on Non-Resistance, Together with a Personal Sketch by His Daughter, Fanny Garrison Villard, and a Tribute to Leo Tolstoy.* New York: Haskell House, 1924.

SECONDARY SOURCES

Abzug, Roger H. *Cosmos Crumbling: American Reform and the Religious Imagination.* New York: Oxford University Press, 1994.

———. "The Influence of Garrisonian Abolitionists' Fear of Slave Violence on the Antislavery Argument, 1829–40." *Journal of Negro History* 55, no. 1 (1970): 15–26.

Adams, Alice Dana. *The Neglected Period of Antislavery in America (1808–1831).* Boston, 1908.

Alonso, Harriet Hyman. *Growing Up Abolitionist: The Story of the Garrison Children.* Amherst: University of Massachusetts Press, 2002.

Anderson, Bonnie S. *Joyous Greetings: The First International Women's Movement, 1830–1860.* New York: Oxford University Press, 2000.

Angelini, Giovanna. *L'ultimo Mazzini: Un pensiero per l'azione.* Milan: FrancoAngeli, 2008.

Aptheker, Herbert. *Abolitionism: A Revolutionary Movement.* New York: Twayne, 1989.

Arisi Rota, Arianna. *Il processo alla Giovine Italia in Lombardia (1833–1835).* Milan: FrancoAngeli, 2003.

———. *I piccoli cospiratori: Politica ed emozioni nei primi mazziniani.* Bologna: Il Mulino, 2010.

Arkin, Mark M. "The Federalist Trope: Power and Passion in Abolitionist Rhetoric." *Journal of American History* 88 (2001): 75–98.

Armitage, David, and Sanjay Subrahmanyam, eds. *The Age of Revolutions in Global Context, c. 1760–1840.* New York: Palgrave, 2010.

———. "Introduction: The Age of Revolutions, c. 1760–1840: Global Causation, Connection, and Comparison." In Armitage and Subrahmanyam, *Age of Revolutions,* xii–xxxii.

Ascoli, Albert Russell, and Krystyna Von Henneberg. "Introduction: Nationalism and the Uses of Risorgimento Culture." In *Making and Remaking Italy: The Cultivation of National Identity around the Risorgimento,* edited by Albert Russell Ascoli and Krystyna Von Henneberg, 1–26. Oxford: Berg, 2001.

Assereto, Giovanni. "Genova e la Liguria nella prima metà dell'Ottocento." In Bonanni, *Pensiero e Azione,* 11–28.

Audeh, Aida, and Nick Havely. *Dante in the Long Nineteenth Century: Nationality, Identity, and Appropriation.* New York: Oxford University Press, 1994.

Ayers, Edward L. "The American Civil War, Emancipation, and Reconstruction on the World Stage." In Reichard and Dickson, *America on the World Stage,* 125–137.

Bacarella, Michael. *Lincoln's Foreign Legion: The 39th New York Infantry, the Garibaldi Guard.* New York: White Mane, 1997.

Badaloni, Nicola. "La cultura." In *Storia d'Italia,* vol. 3, *Dal primo Settecento all'Unità,* edited by Ruggero Romano and Corrado Vivanti. Turin: Einaudi, 1972.

Bagnoli, Paolo. *L'idea dell'Italia, 1815–1861.* Reggio Emilia: Diabasis, 2007.

Balzani, Roberto. "Cavour e le vie della Guerra." In Isnenghi and Cecchinato, *Fare l'Italia,* 342–357.

———. "Il problema Mazzini." *Ricerche di storia politica* 8, no. 2 (2005): 159–182.

———. "Mazzini e la stampa democratica." In *Potere e circolazione delle idee: Stampa, accademie e censure nel Risorgimento italiano,* edited by Domenico Maria Bruni, 74–90. Milan: FrancoAngeli, 2007.

Banti, Alberto M. *Il Risorgimento italiano.* Rome-Bari: Laterza, 2004.

———. *La nazione del Risorgimento: Parentela, santità e onore alle origini dell'Italia unita.* Turin: Einaudi, 2000.

———. "Presentazione." In Banti et al., *Atlante culturale del Risorgimento,* v–xv.

———. "Sacrality and the Aesthetics of Politics: Mazzini's Concept of the Nation." In Bayly and Biagini, *Mazzini and the Globalization,* 59–74.

Banti, Alberto M., Antonio Chiavistelli, Luca Mannori, and Marco Meriggi, eds. *Atlante culturale del Risorgimento: Lessico del linguaggio politico dal Settecento all'Unità.* Rome-Bari: Laterza, 2011.

Banti, Alberto M., and Paul Ginsborg. "Per una nuova storia del Risorgimento." In Banti and Ginsborg, *Il Risorgimento,* xxiii–xli.

———, eds. *Storia d'Italia.* Annali 22, *Il Risorgimento.* Turin: Einaudi, 2007.

Banti, Alberto M., and Marco Mondini. "Da Novara a Custoza: Culture militari e discorso nazionale tra Risorgimento e Unità." In *Storia d'Italia,* annali 18, *Guerra e Pace,* edited by Walter Barberis, 417–464. Turin: Einaudi, 2002.

Barducci, Marco. "Giuseppe Mazzini e Thomas Carlyle." In *Mazzini e gli scrittori politici europei, 1837–1857,* edited by Salvo Mastellone, 2:29–42. Florence: Centro Editoriale Toscano, 2005.

Barnes, Gilbert H. *The Antislavery Impulse, 1830–1844.* New York: Classic Textbooks, 1933.

Bayly, C. A. "The Age of Revolutions in Global Context: An Afterword." In Armitage and Subrahmanyam, *Age of Revolutions,* 209–217.

———. *The Birth of the Modern World, 1780–1914: Global Connections and Comparisons.* Oxford: Blackwell, 2004.

Bayly, C. A., and Eugenio Biagini, eds. *Giuseppe Mazzini and the Globalization of Democratic Nationalism, 1820–1870.* Oxford: Oxford University Press, 2008.

Beales, Derek, and Eugenio F. Biagini. *The Risorgimento and the Unification of Italy.* London: Longman, 2002.

Belardelli, Giovanni. *Mazzini.* Bologna: Il Mulino, 2010.

Bender, Thomas, ed. *The Antislavery Debate: Capitalism and Abolitionism as a Problem of Historical Interpretation.* Berkeley: University of California Press, 1992.

———. *A Nation among Nations: America's Place in World History.* New York: Hill & Wang, 2006.

Berger, Stefan. "Germany: Ethnic Nationalism par Excellence?" In *What Is a Nation? Europe, 1789–1914,* edited by Timothy Bancroft and Mark Hewitson, 42–62. Oxford: Oxford University Press, 2006.

———. "National Movements." In *A Companion to Nineteenth-Century Europe, 1789–1914,* edited by Stefan Berger, 178–192. Oxford: Blackwell, 2009.

Berlin, Ira, Barbara J. Fields, Steven F. Miler, Joseph P. Reidy, and Leslie S. Rowlands. *Slaves No More: Three Essays on Emancipation and the Civil War.* New York: Cambridge University Press, 1992.

Berti, Giuseppe. *I democratici e l'iniziativa meridionale nel Risorgimento.* Milan: Feltrinelli, 1962.

Bertini, Fabio. "I moti del giugno 1857: Mazzini, Pisacane e il problema della democrazia." In Ceccuti, *Giuseppe Mazzini dalla Giovine Europa,* 99–110.

Biagini, Eugenio. "Mazzini and Anticlericalism: The English Exile." In Bayly and Biagini, *Mazzini and the Globalization,* 145–166.

———. "The Principle of Humanity: Lincoln in Germany and Italy, 1859–1865." In *The Global Lincoln,* edited by Richard Carwardine and Jay Sexton, 76–94. New York: Oxford University Press, 2011.

Biagini, Eugenio, David Blight, Carolyn P. Boyd, Richard Carwardine, Kevin K. Gaines, Vinay Lal, Nicola Miller, et al. "Interchange: Nationalism and Internationalism in the Era of the Civil War," *Journal of American History* 98, no. 2 (2011): 455–489.

Blackburn, Robin. *The American Crucible: Slavery, Emancipation, and Human Rights.* London: Verso, 2011.

———. *The Overthrow of Colonial Slavery, 1776–1848.* London: Verso, 1988.

Blackett, Richard J. M. "'And There Shall Be No More Sea': William Lloyd Garrison and the Transatlantic Abolitionist Movement." In Stewart, *Garrison at Two Hundred,* 13–40.

———. *Building an Antislavery Wall: Black Americans in the Atlantic Abolitionist Movement, 1830–1860.* Baton Rouge: Louisiana State University Press, 1983.

Blight, David. "William Lloyd Garrison at Two Hundred: His Radicalism and His Legacy for Our Time." In Stewart, *Garrison at Two Hundred,* 1–12.

Bonanni, Stefania, ed. *Pensiero e Azione: Mazzini nel movimento democratico italiano e internazionale.* Rome: Istituto per la Storia del Risorgimento italiano, 2006.

Bonazzi, Tiziano. "Postfazione: La guerra civile Americana e la 'nazione universale.'" In *La Guerra Civile Americana vista dall'Europa,* edited by Tiziano Bonazzi and Carlo Galli, 463–502. Bologna: Il Mulino, 2004.

Bonsanti, Marta. "Amore familiare, amore romantico e amor di patria." In Banti and Ginsborg, *Il Risorgimento,* 127–152.

Boylan, Anne M. *The Origins of Women's Activism: New York and Boston, 1797–1840.* Chapel Hill: University of North Carolina Press, 2002.

Brennan, Denis P. "The Printer's Stand: William Lloyd Garrison and *The Liberator.*" PhD diss., State University of New York, 2003.

Brewer, David. *The Greek War of Independence: The Struggle for Freedom from Ottoman Oppression and the Birth of the Modern Greek Nation.* London: Overlook Press, 2003.

Brown, Lois A. "William Lloyd Garrison and Emancipatory Feminism in Nineteenth-Century America." In Stewart, *Garrison at Two Hundred,* 41–76.

Browne, Patrick T. J. "'To Defend Mr. Garrison': William Cooper Nell and the Personal Politics of Antislavery." *New England Quarterly* 70, no. 3 (1997): 415–442.

Burin, Eric. *Slavery and the Peculiar Solution: A History of the African Colonization Society.* Gainesville: University Press of Florida, 2005.

Burke, Peter. "Mazzini and Brazil." In Bayly and Biagini, *Mazzini and the Globalization,* 347–354.

Burton, Orville Vernon. *The Age of Lincoln.* New York: Hill & Wang, 2007.

Bush, Michael L. *Servitude in Modern Times.* Cambridge: Polity, 2000.

Butler, Randall Richardson. "New England Journalism and the Question of Slavery, the South, and Abolitionism." PhD diss., Brigham Young University, 1980.

Cafagna, Luciano. *Cavour.* Bologna: Il Mulino, 1999.

———. *Dualismo e sviluppo nella storia d'Italia.* Venice: Marsilio, 1989.

Cain, William E. "Introduction: William Lloyd Garrison and the Fight against Slavery." In *William Lloyd Garrison and the Fight against Slavery: Selections from "The Liberator,"* edited by William E. Cain, 1–57. New York: Bedford/St. Martin's, 1995.

Candeloro, Giorgio. *Storia dell'Italia moderna.* Vol. 1, *Le origini del Risorgimento (1700–1815).* Milan: Feltrinelli, 1958.

———. *Storia dell'Italia moderna.* Vol. 2, *Dalla Restaurazione alla rivoluzione nazionale (1815–1846).* Milan: Feltrinelli, 1962.

———. *Storia dell'Italia moderna.* Vol. 3, *La rivoluzione nazionale (1846–1849).* Milan: Feltrinelli, 1970.

———. *Storia dell'Italia moderna.* Vol. 4, *Dalla rivoluzione nazionale all'unità (1849–1860).* Milan: Feltrinelli, 1964.

———. *Storia dell'Italia moderna.* Vol. 5, *La costruzione dello stato unitario (1861–1870).* Milan: Feltrinelli, 1966.

Candido, Silvano. "La 'Giovine Italia' a Montevideo (1836–1842): Contributo alla storia mazziniana nelle Americhe." *Bollettino della Domus Mazziniana* 21, no. 1 (1975): 53–76.

Capper, Charles. *Margaret Fuller: An American Romantic Life.* 2 vols. New York: Oxford University Press, 1994, 2010.

Capra, Carlo. *L'età giacobina e napoleonica in Italia, 1796–1815.* Turin: UTET, 1978.

Cardoza, Anthony. "Cavour and Piedmont." In Davis, *Italy in the Nineteenth Century,* 108–131.

Carton, Evan. *Patriotic Treason: John Brown and the Soul of America.* New York: Simon & Schuster, 2009.

Carwardine, Richard. *Lincoln: A Life of Purpose and Power.* New York: Knopf, 2006.

———. *Transatlantic Revivalism: Popular Evangelicalism in Britain and America, 1790–1865.* Westport, CT: Greenwood Press, 1978.

Castellano, Carolina. "Segreto e società segrete." In Banti et al., *Atlante culturale del Risorgimento,* 176–186.

Cazzaniga, Gian Mario. "Nascita del Grande Oriente d'Italia." In Cazzaniga, *La Massoneria,* 545–558.

———. "Origine ed evoluzione dei rituali carbonari italiani." In Cazzaniga, *La Massoneria,* 559–578.

———, ed. *Storia d'Italia.* Annali 21, *La Massoneria.* Turin: Einaudi, 2006.

Cecchinato, Eva. *Camicie rosse: I garibaldini dall'Unità alla Grande Guerra.* Rome-Bari: Laterza, 2007.

Ceccuti, Cosimo, ed. *Giuseppe Mazzini dalla Giovine Europa alla Lega Internazionale dei popoli.* Florence: Polistampa, 2008.

Chase, Malcolm. *Chartism: A New History.* Manchester: Manchester University Press, 2007.

Ciuffoletti, Zefiro. "Mazzini e la *Giovine Europa.*" In Ceccuti, *Giuseppe Mazzini dalla Giovine Europa,* 27–34.

Cleves, Rachel Hope. *The Reign of Terror: Visions of Violence from Anti-Jacobinism to Antislavery.* New York: Cambridge University Press, 2010.

Codignola, Arturo. *La giovinezza di G. Mazzini.* Florence: Vallecchi, 1926.

———. *Mazzini.* Turin: UTET, 1946.

Cohen, Deborah, and Maura O'Connor. "Introduction: Comparative History, Cross-National History, Transnational History—Definitions." In *Comparison and History: Europe in Cross-National Perspective,* edited by Deborah Cohen and Maura O'Connor, ix–xxx. London: Routledge, 2004.

Conti Odorisio, Ginevra. *Harriet Martineau e Tocqueville: Due diverse letture della democrazia americana.* Soveria Mannelli: Rubettino, 2003.

Costa, Andrea. *Bagliori di socialismo: Cenni storici.* Florence: Casa Editrice Nerbini, 1900.

Croce, Benedetto. *Storia d'Italia dal 1871 al 1915.* Bari-Rome: Laterza, 1928.

Curatolo, E. *Il dissidio tra Mazzini e Garibaldi.* Milan: Mondadori, 1928.

Curry, Richard O. "Romantic Radicalism in Antebellum America." *Reviews in American History* 1, no. 4 (1973): 524–530.

Dal Lago, Enrico. *Agrarian Elites: American Slaveholders and Southern Italian Landowners, 1815–1861.* Baton Rouge: Louisiana State University Press, 2005.

———. *American Slavery, Atlantic Slavery, and Beyond: The U.S. "Peculiar Institution" in International Perspective.* Boulder, CO: Paradigm, 2012.

———. "Lincoln, Cavour, and National Unification: American Republicanism and Italian Liberal Nationalism in Comparative Perspective." *Journal of the Civil War Era* 3 (2013): 85–113.

———. "Radicalism and Nationalism: Northern 'Liberators' and Southern Laborers in the USA and Italy, 1830–1860." In *The American South and the Italian "Mezzogiorno": Essays in Comparative History,* edited by Enrico Dal Lago and Rick Halpern, 197–214. New York: Palgrave, 2002.

D'Amelia, Marina. "Between Two Eras: Challenges Facing Women in the Risorgimento." In Patriarca and Riall, *Risorgimento Revisited,* 117–122.

Davis, David Brion. *Challenging the Boundaries of Slavery.* Cambridge, MA: Harvard University Press, 2003.

———. "Declaring Equality: Sisterhood and Slavery." In Kish Sklar and Stewart, *Women's Rights and Transatlantic Slavery,* 3–18.

———. "The Emergence of Immediatism in British and American Antislavery Thought." *Mississippi Valley Historical Review* 49, no. 2 (1962): 209–230.

———. *Inhuman Bondage: The Rise and Fall of Slavery in the New World.* New York: Oxford University Press, 2006.

———. *The Problem of Slavery in the Age of Revolution, 1770–1823.* Ithaca, NY: Cornell University Press, 1975.

———. *Revolutions: Reflections on American Equality and Foreign Liberations.* Cambridge, MA: Harvard University Press, 1990.

———. *Slavery and Human Progress.* New York: Oxford University Press, 1985.

Davis, John A., ed. *Italy in the Nineteenth Century.* Oxford: Oxford University Press, 2000.

Davis, Richard P. *The Young Ireland Movement.* London: Gill and MacMillan, 1988.

De Francesco, Antonino. "Ideologie e movimenti politici." In Sabbatucci and Vidotto, *Le premesse dell'unità,* 229–336.

Degler, Carl N. *One among Many: The Civil War in Comparative Perspective.* Gettysburg, PA: Gettysburg College, 1990.

Della Peruta, Franco. "Giuseppe Mazzini: Nota introduttiva." In Della Peruta, *Mazzini e i democratici,* 205–270.

———. "Giuseppe Mazzini dalla *Giovine Italia* alla *Giovine Europa.*" In Bonanni, *Pensiero e Azione,* 29–46.

———. "Giuseppe Mazzini dalla *Giovine Italia* alla *Giovine Europa*." In *Potere e circolazione delle idee: Stampa, accademie e censure nel Risorgimento italiano,* edited by Domenico Maria Bruni, 31–83. Milan: FrancoAngeli, 2007.

———. *I Democratici e la rivoluzione italiana: Dibattiti ideali e contrasti politici all'indomani del 1848.* Milan: Feltrinelli, 1958.

———. *Il giornalismo italiano del Risorgimento: Dal 1847 all'Unità.* Milan: FrancoAngeli, 2011.

———. "Il mondo latomistico della Restaurazione." In *La nascita della nazione: La Carboneria: Intrecci veneti, nazionali, internazionali,* edited by Giampiero Berti and Franco Della Peruta. Rovigo: Minelliana, 2003.

———. "La Giovine Italia in Lombardia." In *Mazzini e la Lombardia: Lo sviluppo dell'ideale unitario,* edited by Gianfranco De Paoli, 21–30. Pavia: Cardano, 1997.

———. "Le teorie militari della democrazia risorgimentale." In *Garibaldi condottiero: Storia, teoria, prassi,* edited by Filippo Mazzonis, 61–72. Milan: FrancoAngeli, 1984.

———. "Mazzinianesimo e democrazia nel Mezzogiorno (1831–1847)." In *Democrazia e mazzinianesimo nel Mezzogiorno d'Italia, 1831–1872,* edited by A.A.V.V., 6–27. Geneva: Librairien Droz, 1975.

———. *Mazzini e i rivoluzionari italiani: Il "Partito d'azione," 1830–1845.* Milan: Feltrinelli, 1974.

———. "Mazzini e la Giovine Europa." *Annali dell'Istituto Gian Giacomo Feltrinelli* 5 (1962): 11–147.

——— *Politica e società nell'Italia dell'Ottocento: Problemi, vicende e personaggi.* Milan: FrancoAngeli, 1999.

———. *Storia dell'Ottocento: Dalla Restaurazione alla "belle epoque."* Florence: Le Monnier, 1992.

Della Peruta, Franco, and Tiziano Tussi. *Mazzini.* Varese: Arterigere, 2007.

Demarco, Domenico. *Una rivoluzione sociale: La Repubblica romana del 1849 (16 Novembre 1848–3 Luglio 1849).* Naples: M. Fiorentino, 1944.

De Paz, Alfredo. *Europa romantica: Fondamenti e paradigmi della sensibilità moderna.* Naples: Liguori, 1994.

Dillon, Merton L. *The Abolitionists: The Growth of a Dissenting Minority.* New York: Norton, 1974.

———. *Benjamin Lundy and the Struggle for Negro Freedom.* Urbana: University of Illinois Press, 1966.

———. "The Failure of the American Abolitionists." *Journal of Southern History* 25, no. 2 (1959): 159–177.

Donald, David Herbert. *Lincoln.* New York: Simon & Schuster, 1995.

Doyle, Don H. "Bully for Garibaldi." *New York Times,* 26 September 2011.

———. *Nations Divided: America, Italy, and the Southern Question.* Athens: University of Georgia Press, 2003.

Drescher, Seymour. *Abolition: A History of Slavery and Antislavery.* New York: Cambridge University Press, 2009.

———. *The Mighty Experiment: Free Labor versus Slavery in British Emancipation.* New York: Cambridge University Press, 2002.

DuBois, Ellen. *Feminism and Suffrage: The Emergence of an Independent Women's Movement in America, 1848–1869.* Ithaca, NY: Cornell University Press, 1985.

Duggan, Christopher. *The Force of Destiny: A History of Italy since 1796.* London: Penguin, 2008.

———. *Francesco Crispi: From Nation to Nationalism.* Oxford: Oxford University Press, 2002.

———. "Giuseppe Mazzini in Britain and Italy: Divergent Legacies, 1837–1915." In Bayly and Biagini, *Mazzini and the Globalization,* 187–207.

Dumond, Dwight L. *Antislavery: The Crusade for Freedom in America.* New York: Norton Library, 1961.

Earle, Jonathan H. *Jacksonian Antislavery and the Politics of Free Soil, 1824–1854.* Chapel Hill: University of North Carolina Press, 2004.

Egerton, Douglas R. "Its Origin Is Not a Little Curious: A New Look at the American Colonization Society." *Journal of the Early Republic* 5 (1985): 463–480.

———. "Rethinking Atlantic Historiography in a Postcolonial Era: The Civil War in a Global Perspective." *Journal of the Civil War Era* 1 (2011): 79–95.

Epstein, Steven A. *Speaking of Slavery: Color, Ethnicity, and Human Bondage in Italy.* Ithaca, NY: Cornell University Press, 2001.

Eyal, Yonatan. "A Romantic Realist: George Nicholas Sanders and the Dilemma of Southern International Engagement." *Journal of Southern History* 78, no. 1 (2012): 107–130.

———. *The Young America Movement and the Transformation of the Democratic Party, 1828–1861.* New York: Oxford University Press, 2007.

Fairclough, Adam G. *To Redeem the Soul of America: The Southern Christian Leadership Conference and Martin Luther King, Jr.* Athens: University of Georgia Press, 2001.

Fanuzzi, Robert. *Abolition's Public Sphere.* Minneapolis: University of Minnesota Press, 2003.

Fehrenbacher, Don E. *The Slaveholding Republic: An Account of the United States Government's Relations to Slavery.* New York: Oxford University Press, 1999.

Filler, Louis. *Crusade against Slavery: Friends, Foes, and Reform, 1820–1860.* New York: Harper & Row, 1960.

Finelli, Michele. *"Il prezioso elemento": Giuseppe Mazzini e gli emigrati italiani nell'esperienza della Scuola Italiana a Londra.* Verrucchio: P.G. Pazzini, 1999.

Fiorentino, Daniele. "Il governo degli Stati Uniti e la Repubblica romana del 1849." In *Gli Americani e la Repubblica romana del 1849,* edited by Sara Antonelli, Daniele Fiorentino, and Giuseppe Monsagrati, 89–139. Rome: Gangemi Editore, 2000.

Fiumara, Francesco. *Mazzini e l'Internazionale: Contatti, rapporti, polemiche.* Pisa: Nistri-Lischi, 1968.

Fladeland, Betty. *Men and Brothers: Anglo-American Antislavery Cooperation.* Urbana: University of Illinois Press, 1972.

Fleche, André. *The Revolution of 1861: The American Civil War in the Age of Nationalist Conflict.* Chapel Hill: University of North Carolina Press, 2012.

Fogelman, Aaron Spencer. "The Transformation of the Atlantic World, 1776–1867." *Atlantic Studies* 6 (2009): 5–28.

Foner, Eric. *The Fiery Trial: Abraham Lincoln and American Slavery.* New York: Norton, 2010.

———. *Free Soil, Free Labor, Free Men: The Ideology of the Republican Party before the Civil War.* New York: Oxford University, 1990. The 1st ed. was published in 1970.

———. *Reconstruction: America's Unfinished Revolution.* New York: Harper & Row, 1988.

Forbes, Robert Pierce. *The Missouri Compromise and Its Aftermath: Slavery and the Meaning of America.* Chapel Hill: University of North Carolina Press, 2009.

Förster, Stig, and Jörg Nagler, eds. *On the Road to Total War: The American Civil War and the German Wars of Unification, 1861–1871.* New York: Oxford University Press, 1997.

Fournier-Finocchiaro, Laura. "Le paradoxe Mazzini: Ennemi et pére de l'Italie du Risorgimento." *Italies* 15 (2011): 357–379.

Francovich, Carlo. *Albori socialisti del Risorgimento: Contributo allo studio delle società segrete, 1776–1835.* Florence: Le Monnier, 1962.

Fredrickson, George. *Big Enough to Be Inconsistent: Abraham Lincoln Confronts Race and Slavery.* Cambridge, MA: Harvard University Press, 2008.

———. *The Black Image in the White Mind: The Debate on Afro-American Character and Destiny, 1817–1914.* New York: Ardent Media, 1971.

———. "From Exceptionalism to Variability: Recent Developments in Cross-National Comparative History." *Journal of American History* 82, no. 2 (1995): 587–604.

French, Scot A. *Nat Turner in History and Memory: The Rebellious Slave in the American South.* New York: Houghton Mifflin, 2004.

Friedman, Lawrence J. *Gregarious Saints: Self and Community in American Abolitionism, 1830–1870.* New York: Cambridge University Press, 1982.

Furiozzi, Massimo. *La "Nuova Europa" (1861–1863): Democrazia e Internazionalismo.* Milan: FrancoAngeli, 2008.

Gabaccia, Donna. "A Long Atlantic in a Wider World." *Atlantic Studies* 1 (2004): 1–27.

Galante Garrone, Alessandro. *Filippo Buonarroti e i rivoluzionari dell'Ottocento (1828–1837).* Turin: Einaudi, 1951.

———. "I giornali della restaurazione, 1815–1847." In *La stampa italiana del Risorgimento,* by Alessandro Galante Garrone and Franco Della Peruta, 1–246. Rome-Bari: Laterza, 1979.

———. *I radicali in Italia (1849–1925).* Milan: Garzanti, 1973.

———. *L'albero della libertà: Dai giacobini a Garibaldi.* Florence: Le Monnier, 1987.

Galasso, Giuseppe. *Da Mazzini a Salvemini: Il pensiero democratico dell'Italia moderna.* Florence: Le Monnier, 1974.

Galletto, Pietro. *Mazzini nella vita e nella storia: Nel secondo centenario della nascita (1805–2005).* Vols. 1–3. Padova: G. Battaglin, 2005.

Gamber, Francesca. "The Public Sphere and the End of American Abolitionism, 1833–1870." *Slavery and Abolition* 28, no. 3 (2007): 351–368.

Garvey, T. G. *Creating the Culture of Reform in Antebellum America.* Athens: University of Georgia Press, 2006.

Gemme, Paola. *Domesticating Foreign Struggles: The Italian Risorgimento and Antebellum American Identity.* Athens: University of Georgia Press, 2005.

Gentile, Emilio. *Politics as Religion.* Princeton, NJ: Princeton University Press, 2006.

Gentile, Giovanni. *I profeti del Risorgimento italiano.* Florence: Vallecchi, 1923.

Geyer, Michael, and Charles Bright. "Global Violence and Nationalizing Wars in Eurasia and America: The Geopolitics of War in the Mid-Nineteenth Century." *Comparative Studies in Society and History* 38, no. 4 (1996): 619–657.

Ghisalberti, Antonio. *Momenti e figure del Risorgimento romano.* Milan: Giuffrè, 1965.

Gienapp, William E. *The Origins of the Republican Party, 1852–1856.* New York: Oxford University Press, 1987.

Gildea, Robert. *Barricades and Borders: Europe, 1800–1914.* New York: Oxford University Press, 1997.

Ginsborg, Paul. "Romanticismo e Risorgimento: L'io, l'amore e la nazione." In Banti and Ginsborg, *Il Risorgimento,* 5–68.

Giorgetti, Pier Ferdinando, ed. *L'arco latino e il Risorgimento: Realtà ed echi dei moti mazziniani del 1857.* Pisa: ETS, 2007.

Giusti, Wolf. *Mazzini e gli slavi.* Milan: Istituto per gli studi di politica internazionale, 1940.

Gobetti, Piero. *Risorgimento senza eroi.* Turin: Edizioni del Baretti, 1926.

Goodman, Paul. *Of One Blood: Abolitionism and the Origins of Racial Equality.* Berkeley: University of California Press, 1998.

Goodwin, Doris Kearns. *Team of Rivals: The Political Genius of Abraham Lincoln.* New York: Simon & Schuster, 2005.

Gramsci, Antonio. *Il Risorgimento.* Turin: Einaudi, 1966. Written in the 1930s.

Greenberg, Kenneth. Introduction to *The Confessions of Nat Turner and Related Documents,* edited by Kenneth Greenberg, 1–34. New York: Bedford/St. Martin's, 1996.

———, ed. *Nat Turner: A Slave Rebellion in History and Memory.* New York: Oxford University Press, 2003.

Grew, Raymond. *A Sterner Plan for Italian Unity: The Italian National Society in the Risorgimento.* Princeton, NJ: Princeton University Press, 1963.

Guarneri, Carl. *America in the World: United States History in Global Context.* New York: McGraw-Hill, 2007.

Guelzo, Allen C. *Lincoln and Douglas: The Debates That Defined America.* New York: Simon & Schuster, 2009.

Gura, Philip F. *American Transcendentalism: A History.* New York: Norton, 2007.

Hahn, Steven. *A Nation under Our Feet: Black Political Struggles in the Rural South from Slavery to the Great Migration.* Cambridge, MA: Harvard University Press, 2003.

Hayes, Edward E. Y. *Mazzini and the Secret Societies: The Making of a Myth.* New York: P.J. Kenedy, 1956.

Hearder, Harry. *Italy in the Age of the Risorgimento, 1790–1870.* London: Longman, 1983.

Hinkley, Edyth. *Mazzini: The Story of a Great Italian.* London: Ayer, 1924.

Hinks, Peter P. *To Awaken My Afflicted Brethren: David Walker and the Problem of Antebellum Slave Resistance.* University Park: Pennsylvania State University Press, 1997.

Hobsbawm, Eric J. *The Age of Capital, 1848–1875.* London: Abacus, 1975.

———. *The Age of Empire, 1875–1914.* London: Abacus, 1983.

———. *The Age of Revolutions, 1789–1848.* London: Abacus, 1962.

———. *Nations and Nationalism since 1780.* Cambridge: Cambridge University Press, 1983.

Hogan, Lisa Shawn. "A Time for Silence: William Lloyd Garrison and the 'Woman Question' at the 1840 World Anti-Slavery Convention." *Gender Issues* 25 (2008): 63–79.

Honeck, Mischa. "Freemen of All Nations: Bestir Yourselves! Felice Orsini's Transnational Afterlife and the Radicalization of America." *Journal of the Early Republic* 30 (2010): 587–615.

———. *We Are the Revolutionists: German-Speaking Immigrants and American Abolitionists after 1848.* Athens: University of Georgia Press, 2010.

Howe, Daniel Walker. *"What Hath God Wrought": The Transformation of America, 1815–1848.* New York: Oxford University Press, 2008.

Isabella, Maurizio. "Exile and Nationalism: The Case of the *Risorgimento.*" *European History Quarterly* 36 (2006): 493–520.

———. "Freedom of the Press, Public Opinion, and Liberalism in the *Risorgimento.*" *Journal of Modern Italian Studies* 17, no. 5 (2012): 551–567.

———. "Italian Exiles and British Politics before and after 1848." In *Exiles from European Revolutions: Refugees in Mid-Victorian England,* edited by Susan Freitag, 59–87. Oxford: Oxford University Press, 2003.

———. "Mazzini's Internationalism in Context: From the Cosmopolitan Patriotism of the Italian Carbonari to Mazzini's Europe of the Nations." In Bayly and Biagini, *Mazzini and the Globalization,* 37–58.

———. "Nationality before Liberty? *Risorgimento* Political Thought in Transnational Context." *Journal of Modern Italian Studies* 17, no. 5 (2012), 507–515.

———. "Rethinking Italy's Nation-Building 150 Years Afterwards: The New *Risorgimento* Historiography." *Past and Present,* no. 217 (2012): 247–268.

———. *Risorgimento in Exile: Italian Emigrés and the Liberal International in the Post-Napoleonic Era.* Oxford: Oxford University Press, 2009.

Isnenghi, Mario, and Eva Cecchinato, eds. *Gli Italiani in Guerra: Conflitti, identità, memorie dal Risorgimento ai giorni nostri.* Vol. 1, *Fare l'Italia: Unità e disunità nel Risorgimento.* Turin: UTET, 2008.

Jackson, Maurice. "The Rise of Abolition." In *The Atlantic World, 1450–2000,* edited by Toyin Fayola and Kevin Roberts, 211–248. Bloomington: Indiana University Press, 2005.

Jeffrey, Julie Roy. *The Great Silent Army of Abolitionism: Ordinary Women in the Antislavery Movement.* Chapel Hill: University of North Carolina Press, 1998.

Johnson, Reinhard O. *The Liberty Party, 1840–1848: Antislavery Third-Party Politics in the United States.* Baton Rouge: Louisiana State University Press, 2009.

Kachun, Mitch. "'Our Platform Is as Broad as Humanity': Transatlantic Freedom Movements and the Idea of Progress in Nineteenth-Century African American Thought and Activism." *Slavery and Abolition* 24, no. 3 (2003): 7–9.

Kaye, Anthony E. "The Second Slavery: Modernity in the Nineteenth-Century South and the Atlantic World." *Journal of Southern History* 75, no. 2 (2009): 627–650.

Kennon, Donald R. "An Apple of Discord: The Woman Question at the World's Anti-Slavery Convention." *Slavery and Abolition* 5 (1984): 244–266.

Kerr-Ritchie, Jeffrey R. *Rites of August First: Emancipation Day in the Black Atlantic World.* Baton Rouge: Louisiana State University Press, 2007.

Kinealy, Christine. *Daniel O'Connell and the Anti-Slavery Movement: The Saddest People the Sun Sees.* London: Pickering & Chatto, 2010.

King, Bolton. *The Life of Mazzini.* London: J. M. Dent, 1902.

Kish Sklar, Kathryn. "Women Who Speak for an Entire Nation: American and British Women at the World Anti-Slavery Convention, London, 1840." In *The Abolitionist Sisterhood: Women's Political Culture in Antebellum America,* edited by Jean Fagan Yellin and John C. Van Horne, 301–311. Ithaca, NY: Cornell University Press, 1994.

Kish Sklar, Kathryn, and James B. Stewart, eds. *Women's Rights and Transatlantic Slavery in the Age of Emancipation.* New Haven, CT: Yale University Press, 2007.

Klooster, Wim. *Revolutions in the Atlantic World: A Comparative History.* New York: New York University Press, 2009.

Kolchin, Peter. "Some Controversial Questions concerning Nineteenth-Century Emancipation from Slavery and Serfdom." In *Serfdom and Slavery: Studies in Legal Bondage,* edited by Michael L. Bush, 58–77. London: Longman, 1996.

———. *A Sphinx on the American Land: The Nineteenth-Century South in Comparative*

Perspective. Baton Rouge: Louisiana State University Press, 2003.

Korner, Axel, ed. *1848—A European Revolution? International Ideas and National Memories of 1848.* New York: Palgrave, 2000.

———. "Uncle Tom on the Ballet Stage: Italy's Barbarous America, 1850–1900." *Journal of Modern History* 83, no. 4 (2011): 721–752.

Korner, Axel, and Lucy Riall. "Introduction: The New History of Risorgimento Nationalism." *Nations and Nationalism* 15, no. 3 (2009): 396–401.

Kornfeld, Eve. "Minerva and the Muse." In *Margaret Fuller: A Brief Biography with Documents,* edited by Eve Kornfeld, 1–76. New York: Bedford/St. Martin's, 1997.

Korngold, Ralph. *Two Friends of Man: The Story of William Lloyd Garrison and Wendell Phillips and Their Relationship with Abraham Lincoln.* Boston: Little, Brown, 1950.

Kraditor, Aileen S. *Means and Ends in American Abolitionism: Garrison and His Critics on Strategy and Tactics, 1834–1850.* Chicago: University of Chicago Press, 1969.

Kramer, Lloyd. *Nationalism in Europe and America: Politics, Cultures, and Identities since 1776.* Chapel Hill: University of North Carolina Press, 2011.

Krikler, Jeremy. "Lessons from America: The Writings of David Roediger." *Journal of Southern African Studies* 20, no. 4 (1994): 663–669.

Landogna, Francesco. *Giuseppe Mazzini e il pensiero giansenistico.* Bologna: Zanichelli, 1921.

Langley, Lester. *The Americas in the Age of Revolutions, 1750–1850.* New Haven, CT: Yale University Press, 1990.

La Puma, Leonardo. *Giuseppe Mazzini democratico e riformista europeo.* Florence: Olschki, 2008.

La Salvia, Sergio. "Mazzini, il partito e la rivoluzione." In Bonanni, *Pensiero e Azione,* 115–306.

Laurie, Bruce. *Beyond Garrison: Antislavery and Social Reform.* New York: Cambridge University Press, 2005.

———. "Putting Politics Back In: Rethinking the Problem of Political Abolitionism." In Stewart, *Garrison at Two Hundred,* 77–92.

Lee, Matthew. "Ashurst, William Henry." In *Oxford Dictionary of National Biography.* Oxford: Oxford University Press, 2004. Available at www.oxforddnb.com.

Levine, Bruce. *Half Slave and Half Free: The Roots of Civil War.* 2nd ed. New York: Hill & Wang, 2005.

Lingua, Paolo. *Mazzini il riformista: Gli ultimi anni e la questione sociale.* Genova: ECIG, 2005.

Logan, Deborah A. "The Redemption of a Heretic: Harriet Martineau and Anglo-American Abolitionism." In Kish Sklar and Stewart, *Women's Rights and Transatlantic Antislavery,* 242–265.

Loveland, Anne C. "Evangelicalism and 'Immediate Emancipation' in American Antislavery Thought." *Journal of Southern History* 32 (1966): 172–188.

Lovett, Clara M. *The Democratic Movement in Italy, 1830–1876.* Cambridge, MA: Harvard University Press, 1982.

Lupo, Salvatore. "Il Grande Brigantaggio: Interpretazione e memoria di una Guerra Civile." In *Storia d'Italia,* annali 18, *Guerra e Pace,* edited by Walter Barberis, 465–504. Turin: Einaudi, 2002, .

———. *L'unificazione italiana: Mezzogiorno, rivoluzione, guerra civile.* Rome: Donzelli, 2011.

Luraghi, Raimondo. "The Civil War and the Modernization of American Society: Social Structure and Industrial Revolution in the Old South before and during the War." *Civil War History* 18 (1972): 230–250.

———. *Storia della Guerra Civile americana.* Milan: Rizzoli, 1966.

Luzio, Alessandro. *Giuseppe Mazzini carbonaro: Nuovi documenti dagli archivi di Milano e Torino.* Turin: Bocca, 1920.

Luzzatto, Sergio. *La mummia della repubblica: Storia di Mazzini imbalsamato, 1872–1946.* Milan: Rizzoli, 2001.

Luzzatto Voghera, Gadi. "La presa di Roma." In Isnenghi and Cecchinato, *Fare l'Italia,* 770–780.

Lynch, John. *Simon Bolivar: A Life.* New Haven, CT: Yale University Press, 2006.

Mack Smith, Denis. *Cavour and Garibaldi in 1860: A Study in Political Conflict.* Oxford: Oxford University Press, 1954.

———. *Mazzini.* New Haven, CT: Yale University Press, 1994.

———. *Victor Emmanuel, Cavour, and the Risorgimento.* Oxford: Oxford University Press, 1971.

Mahin, Dean B. *The Blessed Place of Freedom: Europeans in Civil War America.* Washington, DC: Potomac Books, 2003.

Mannori, Luca. "Alla periferia dell'Impero: Egemonia austriaca e immagini dello spazio nazionale nell'Italia del primo Risorgimento (1814–1835)." In *Gli imperi dopo l'Impero nell'Europa del XIX secolo,* edited by Marco Bellabarba, Brigitte Mazohl, Reinhard Stauber, and MarcelloVerga, 309–346. Bologna: Il Mulino, 2008.

Martucci, Roberto. *L'invenzione dell'Italia unita, 1855–1864.* Florence: Sansoni, 1999.

Mason, Matthew. "Federalists, Abolitionists, and the Problem of Influence." *American Nineteenth Century History* 10, no. 1 (2009): 1–27.

Mastellone, Salvo. *Il progetto politico di Mazzini (Italia-Europa).* Florence: Olschki, 1994.

———. *La democrazia etica di Mazzini (1837–1847).* Pisa: Archivio Guido Izzi, 2000.

———. "L'europeismo democratico di Mazzini." In Bonanni, *Pensiero e Azione,* 85–114.

———. *Mazzini e la "Giovine Italia," 1831–1834.* 2 vols. Pisa: Domus Mazziniana, 1960.

———. *Mazzini scrittore politico in inglese: Democracy in Europe (1840–1855).* Florence: Olschki, 2004.

Mattarelli, Sauro. *Dialogo sui Doveri: Il pensiero di Giuseppe Mazzini.* Venice: Marsilio, 2005.

Mayer, Henry. *All on Fire: William Lloyd Garrison and the Abolition of Slavery.* New York: St. Martin's Press, 1998.

Maynard, Douglas H. "The World's Anti-Slavery Convention of 1840." *Mississippi Valley Historical Review* 47 (1960): 452–471.

McCarthy, Patrick, and John Stauffer, eds. *Prophets of Protest: Reconsidering the History of American Abolitionism.* New York: New Press, 2006.

McCarthy, Timothy P. "To Plead Our Own Cause: Black Print Culture and the Origins of American Abolitionism." In McCarthy and Stauffer, *Prophets of Protest,* 114–146.

McClintock, Russell. *Lincoln and the Decision for War: The Northern Response to Secession.* Chapel Hill: University of North Carolina Press, 2008.

McCurry, Stephanie. "War, Gender, and Emancipation in the Civil War South." In *Lincoln's Proclamation: Emancipation Reconsidered,* edited by William A. Blair and Karen Fisher Younger, 120–150. Chapel Hill: University of North Carolina Press, 2009.

McDaniel, W. Caleb. "'Our Country Is the World': Radical American Abolitionists Abroad." PhD diss., Johns Hopkins University, 2006.

———. *The Problem of Democracy in the Age of Slavery: Garrisonian Abolitionists and Transatlantic Reform.* Baton Rouge: Louisiana State University Press, 2013.

———. "Repealing Unions: American Abolitionists, Irish Repeal, and the Origins of Garrisonian Disunionism." *Journal of the Early Republic* 28, no. 2 (2008): 243–269.

———. "What Counts as Radical Abolitionism? A Reconsideration of Recent Scholarship." Paper presented at the annual meeting of the Organization of American Historians, Seattle, 27 March 2009.

McDaniel, W. Caleb, and Bethany L. Johnson. "New Approaches to Internationalizing the History of the Civil War Era." *Journal of the Civil War Era* 2 (2012): 145–150.

McDonagh, Oliver. *O'Connell: The Life of Daniel O'Connell, 1775–1847.* Dublin: Four Courts Press, 1991.

McFeely, William. *Frederick Douglass.* New York: Norton, 1991.

McInerney, Daniel John. *The Fortunate Heirs of Freedom: Abolition and Republican Thought.* Lincoln: University of Nebraska Press, 1994.

McKivigan, James R. *Forgotten Firebrand James Redpath and the Making of Nineteenth-Century America.* Ithaca, NY: Cornell University Press, 2008.

———. "James Redpath, John Brown, and Abolitionist Advocacy of Slave Insurrection." *Civil War History* 37, no. 4 (1991): 293–313.

McMenamin, Iain. "'Self-Choosing' and 'Right-Acting' in the Nationalism of Giuseppe Mazzini." *History of European Ideas* 23, nos. 5–6 (1997): 221–234.

McPherson, James. *Battle Cry of Freedom: The Civil War Era.* New York: Oxford University Press, 1988.

———. *The Struggle for Equality: Abolitionists and the Negro in the Civil War and Reconstruction.* Princeton, NJ: Princeton University Press, 1964.

Meriggi, Marco. *Breve storia dell'Italia settentrionale dall'Ottocento a oggi.* Rome: Donzelli, 1996.

———. *Gli stati italiani prima dell'unità.* Bologna: Il Mulino, 1997.

Merrill, Walter M. *Against Wind and Tide: A Biography of William Lloyd Garrison.* Cambridge, MA: Harvard University Press, 1963.

Minardi, Margot. *Making Slavery History: Abolitionism and the Politics of Memory in Massachusetts.* New York: Oxford University Press, 2010.

Mitton, Steven Heath. "The Free World Confronted: The Problem of Slavery and Progress in American Foreign Relations, 1833–1844." PhD diss., Louisiana State University, 2005.

Mondini, Marco. "La guerra perduta: Il 1866 e l'antimito della disfatta." In Isnenghi and Cecchinato, *Fare l'Italia,* 618–623.

Monsagrati, Giuseppe. *Giuseppe Mazzini.* Florence: Giunti, 1994.

———. "La Repubblica romana del 1849." In Isnenghi and Cecchinato, *Fare l'Italia.*

Montale, Bianca. "Mazzini e le origini del movimento operaio." In Bonanni, *Pensiero e Azione,* 307–352.

Montale, Bruno. *Maria Drago Mazzini.* Genova: Comune di Genova, 1955.

Morelli, Emilia. *Giuseppe Mazzini: Saggi e ricerche.* Rome: Edizioni dell'Ateneo, 1950.

———. *L'Inghilterra di Mazzini.* Rome: Istituto per la Storia del Risorgimento italiano, 1965.

———. *Mazzini: Quasi una biografia.* Rome: Edizioni dell'Ateneo, 1984.

Moya, José C. "Modernization, Modernity, and the Transformation of the Atlantic World in the Nineteenth Century." In *The Atlantic in Global History, 1500–2000,* edited by Jorge Cañizares-Esguerra and Erik Seeman, 176–198. Upper Saddle River, NJ: Pearson, 2007.

Murialdi, Paolo. *Storia del giornalismo italiano: Dalle gazzette a Internet.* Bologna: Il Mulino, 2006.

Murphy, Angela F. *American Slavery, Irish Freedom: Abolition, Immigrant Citizenship, and the Transatlantic Movement for Irish Repeal.* Baton Rouge: Louisiana State University Press, 2010.

Myers, John L. "Organization of 'The Seventy': To Arouse the North against Slavery." *Mid- America* 48 (1966): 29–46.

Myers, Jorge. "Giuseppe Mazzini and the Emergence of Liberal Nationalism in the River Plate and Chile, 1835–1860." In Bayly and Biagini, *Mazzini and the Globalization,* 323–346.

Nabulsi, Karma. "Patriotism and Nationalism in the 'Oath of Allegiance' to Young Europe." *European Journal of Political Theory* 5, no. 1 (2006): 61–70.

Nanni, Telesforo. "Mazzini nel giudizio di Gaetano Salvemini." In *Mazzini nella cultura italiana,* edited by Vincenzo Pirro, 39–54. Terni: Associazione mazziniana italiana, 2008.

Newman, Richard. "'A Chosen Generation': Black Founders and Early America." In McCarthy and Stauffer, *Prophets of Protest,* 59–79.

———. *The Transformation of American Abolitionism: Fighting Slavery in the Early Republic.* Chapel Hill: University of North Carolina Press, 2002.

Nye, Russell B. *William Lloyd Garrison and the Humanitarian Reformers.* Boston: Little, Brown, 1955.

Oakes, James. *The Radical and the Republican: Frederick Douglass, Abraham Lincoln, and the Triumph of Antislavery Politics.* New York: Norton, 2007.

O'Connor, Maura. *The Romance of Italy and English Political Imagination.* New York: Palgrave, 1998.

Ofele, Martin. *True Sons of the Republic: European Immigrants in the Union Army.* Westport, CT: Praeger, 2008.

Osborn, Ronald. "William Lloyd Garrison and the United States Constitution: The Political Evolution of an American Radical." *Journal of Law and Religion* 24 (2008–9): 65–88.

O'Tuathaigh, Gearoid. "Daniel O'Connell." In *Dictionary of Irish Biography Online,* edited by James McGuire and James Quinn. Cambridge: Cambridge University Press, 2009. Available at http://dib.cambridge.org.

Palmer, Robert R. *The Age of Democratic Revolution: A Political History of Europe and America, 1760–1800.* 2 vols. Princeton, NJ: Princeton University Press, 1959, 1964.

Parmentola, Vittorio. "Carlo Bianco, Giuseppe Mazzini e la teoria dell'insurrezione." *Bollettino della Domus Mazziniana* 5 (1959): 5–40.

———. *Mazzini e i Repubblicani italiani: Studi in onore di Terenzio Grandi nel suo 92o compleanno.* Turin: Istituto per la Storia del Risorgimento italiano, 1976.

Pascarelli, C. *Il Risorgimento incompiuto: La tensione rivoluzionaria e l'iniziativa di Carlo Pisacane nell'Italia meridionale.* Pavia: Iuculano, 2009.

Patriarca, Silvana. "Indolence and Regeneration: Tropes and Tensions of Risorgimento Patriotism." *American Historical Review* 110, no. 2 (2005): 380–408.

Patriarca, Silvana, and Lucy Riall. "Introduction: Revisiting the Risorgimento." In Patriarca and Riall, *Risorgimento Revisited,* 1–17.

———, eds. *The Risorgimento Revisited: Nationalism and Culture in Nineteenth-Century Italy.* New York: Palgrave, 2012.

Pease, Jane H., and William H. Pease. "Confrontation and Abolition in the 1850s." *Journal of American History* 58, no. 4 (1972): 923–937.

———. *They Who Would Be Free: Blacks' Search for Freedom, 1830–1861.* Urbana: University of Illinois Press, 1974.

Perini, Luciano. "Gli utopisti: Delusioni della realtà, sogni dell'avvenire." In *Storia d'Italia,* annali 4, *Intellettuali e potere,* edited by Ruggero Romano and Corrado Vivanti. Turin: Einaudi, 1981.

Perry, Lewis. *Radical Abolitionism: Anarchy and the Government of God in Antislavery Thought.* Ithaca, NY: Cornell University Press, 1971.

Pescosolido, Guido. "L'economia e la vita materiale." In Sabbatucci and Vidotto, *Le premesse dell'Unità,* 3–118.

Pesman, Ros. "Mazzini and/in Love." In Patriarca and Riall, *Risorgimento Revisited,* 97–114.

Pope Melish, Joanne. *Disowning Slavery: Gradual Emancipation and Race in New England, 1780–1860.* Ithaca, NY: Cornell University Press, 2000.

Potter, David M. "Civil War." In *The Comparative Approach to American History,* edited by C. Van Woodward, 135–145. New York: Oxford University Press, 1968.

———. *The Impending Crisis, 1848–1861.* New York: Harper & Row, 1976.

Puccioni, Michele. *L'Unità d'Italia nel pensiero e nell'azione del Barone Bettino Ricasoli.* Florence: Vallecchi, 1932.

Quarles, Benjamin. *Black Abolitionists.* New York: Oxford University Press, 1969.

Rao, Anna Maria. "Republicanism in Italy from the Eighteenth Century to the Early Risorgimento." *Journal of Modern Italian Studies* 17, no. 2 (2012): 140–167.

Rath, R. John. "The *Carbonari:* Their Origins, Initiation Rites, and Aims." *American Historical Review* 69, no. 2 (1964): 353–370.

Ravenna, Leone. *Il giornalismo mazziniano: Note ed appunti.* Florence: Le Monnier, 1967.

Recchia, Stefano, and Nadia Urbinati. "Introduction: Giuseppe Mazzini's International Political Thought." In *A Cosmopolitanism of Nations: Giuseppe Mazzini's Writings on Democracy, Nation Building, and International Relations,* edited by Stefano Recchia and Nadia Urbinati, 1–30. Princeton, NJ: Princeton University Press, 2009.

Reichard, Gary W., and Ted Dickson, eds. *America on the World Stage: A Global Approach to U.S. History.* Urbana: University of Illinois Press, 2008.

Reynolds, Amy. "William Lloyd Garrison, Benjamin Lundy, and Criminal Libel: The Abolitionists' Plea for Press Freedom." *Communication Law and Policy* 6 (2001): 577–607.

Reynolds, David S. *John Brown, Abolitionist: The Man who Killed Slavery, Sparked the Civil War, and Seeded Civil Rights.* New York: Knopf, 2006.

Riall, Lucy. *Garibaldi: Invention of a Hero.* New Haven, CT: Yale University Press, 2007.

———. "The Politics of Italian Romanticism: Mazzini and the Making of a Nationalist Culture." In Bayly and Biagini, *Mazzini and the Globalization,* 167–186.

——. *Risorgimento: The History of Italy from Napoleon to Nation State.* New York: Palgrave, 2009.

Richards, David A. J. *Disarming Manhood: Roots of Ethical Resistance.* Athens: Ohio University Press, 2005.

Richards, Leonard. *Gentlemen of Property and Standing: Anti-Abolitionist Mobs in Jacksonian America.* New York: Oxford University Press, 1970.

Ridley, Jasper. "Il mito di Garibaldi in Inghilterra e la visita del 1864." *Rassegna degli Archivi di Stato* 2–3 (1982): 270–284.

Roberts, Timothy M. *Distant Revolutions: 1848 and the Challenge to American Exceptionalism.* Charlottesville: University of Virginia Press, 2009.

——. "The Relevance of Giuseppe Mazzini's Ideas of Insurgency to the American Slavery Crisis of the 1850s." In Bayly and Biagini, *Mazzini and the Globalization,* 311–322.

Robertson, Stacey. *Hearts Beating for Liberty: Women Abolitionists in the Old Northwest.* Chapel Hill: University of North Carolina Press, 2010.

Rodgers, Daniel T. *Atlantic Crossings: Social Politics in a Progressive Age.* Cambridge, MA: Harvard University Press, 1998.

——. "Worlds of Reform." In Reichard and Dickson, *America on the World Stage,* 147–157.

Roediger, David. *The Wages of Whiteness: Race and the American Working Class.* London: Verso, 1991.

Roggero, Maria Pia. "L'emancipazione della donna nel pensiero italiano dai lumi a Mazzini." *Il Risorgimento* 35, no. 2 (1983): 149–164.

Rohrbach, Augusta. "'Truth Stronger and Stranger than Fiction': Reexamining William Lloyd Garrison's *The Liberator.*" *American Literature* 73, no. 4 (2001): 727–755.

Romanelli, Raffaele. *L'Italia liberale, 1860–1900.* Bologna: Il Mulino, 1990.

Romani, Roberto. "Reluctant Revolutionaries: Moderate Liberalism in the Kingdom of Sardinia, 1849–1859." *Historical Journal* 55, no. 1 (2012): 45–73.

Romano, Aldo. *L'unità italiana e la Prima Internazionale, 1861–1871.* Rome-Bari: Laterza, 1966.

Romeo, Rosario. *Dal Piemonte sabaudo all'Italia liberale.* Turin, 1963.

——. *Risorgimento e capitalismo.* Rome-Bari: Laterza, 1959.

——. *Vita di Cavour.* Rome-Bari: Laterza, 1984.

Rosen, Bruce. "Abolition and Colonization, the Years of Conflict: 1829–1834." *Phylon* 33, no. 2 (1972): 177–192.

Rosselli, Nello. *Carlo Pisacane nel Risorgimento italiano.* Turin: Einaudi, 1932.

——. *Mazzini e Bakunin: Dodici anni di movimento operaio in Italia, 1860–1872.* Turin: Fratelli Bocca, 1927.

Rossi, Joseph. *The Image of America in Mazzini's Writings.* Madison: University of Wisconsin Press, 1954.

Rugemer, Edward Bartlett. *The Problem of Emancipation: The Caribbean Roots of the American Civil War.* Baton Rouge: Louisiana State University Press, 2008.

Russi, L. *Carlo Pisacane: Vita e pensiero di un rivoluzionario senza rivoluzione.* Naples: ESI, 2007.

Sabbatucci, Giovanni, and Vittorio Vidotto, eds. *Storia d'Italia.* Vol. 1, *Le premesse dell'Unità.* Rome-Bari: Laterza, 1994.

Sacerdoti Mariani, Gigliola. "Fuller e Mazzini: Tra fede e fato." In *Mazzini e gli scrittori politici europei, 1837–1857,* edited by Salvo Mastellone, 95–116. Florence: Centro Editoriale Toscano, 2005.

Sagramola, Oreste. *Giuseppe Mazzini nel Risorgimento italiano: Pensiero, azione, educazione politica.* Viterbo: Sette Città, 2007.

Salvemini, Gaetano. *Scritti sul Risorgimento.* Milan: Feltrinelli, 1963.

Sarti, Roland. "Giuseppe Mazzini and His Opponents." In Davis, *Italy in the Nineteenth Century,* 74–107.

———. "Giuseppe Mazzini and Young Europe." In Bayly and Biagini, *Mazzini and the Globalization,* 275–291.

———. "La democrazia radicale: Uno sguardo reciproco tra Stati Uniti e Italia." In *La democrazia radicale nell'Ottocento europeo: Forme della politica, modelli culturali, riforme sociali,* edited by Maurizio Ridolfi, 133–158. Milan: Feltrinelli, 2005.

———. *Mazzini: A Life for the Religion of Politics.* Westport, CT: Prager, 1997.

Schenone, Giulio. "John Brown e il pensiero insurrezionale italiano." In *Atti del I Congresso Internazionale di storia americana: Italia e stati Uniti dall'Indipendenza americana ad oggi (1776–1976),* 356–360. Genoa: Tilgher, 1978.

Schoen, Brian. *The Fragile Fabric of Union: Cotton, Federal Politics, and the Global Origins of the Civil War.* Baltimore: Johns Hopkins University Press, 2009.

Scioscioli, Massimo. *Giuseppe Mazzini: I principi e la politica.* Naples: Guida Editori, 1995.

Scirocco, Alfonso. *Democrazia e socialismo a Napoli dopo l'unità (1860–1878).* Naples: Libreria Scientifica Editrice, 1973.

———. *Garibaldi: Battaglie, amori, ideali di un cittadino del mondo.* Bari-Rome: Laterza, 2001.

———. *I democratici italiani da Sapri a Porta Pia.* Naples: Edizioni Scientifiche Italiane, 1969.

———. *L'Italia del Risorgimento.* Bologna: Il Mulino, 1990.

Sellers, Charles. *The Market Revolution: Jacksonian America, 1815–1848.* New York: Oxford University Press, 1990.

Sewell, Richard R. *Ballots for Freedom: Antislavery Politics in the United States, 1837–1860.* New York: Norton, 1976.

Simpson, Brooks D. *America's Civil War.* Arlington Heights, IL: Harlan Davidson, 2009.

Spini, Giorgio. *Risorgimento e protestanti.* Milan: Il Saggiatore, 1989.

Stampp, Kenneth M. *America in 1857: A Nation on the Brink.* New York: Oxford University Press, 1992.

Staudenraus, P. J. *The African Colonization Movement, 1816–1865.* New York: Columbia University Press, 1961.

Stauffer, John. "Abolition and Antislavery." In *The Oxford Handbook of Slavery in the Americas,* edited by Robert L. Paquette and Mark M. Smith, 556–577. New York, 2010.

———. *The Black Hearts of Men: Radical Abolitionists and the Transformation of Race.* Cambridge, MA: Harvard University Press, 2002.

———. *Giants: The Parallel Lives of Frederick Douglass and Abraham Lincoln.* New York: Twelve, 2008.

Stewart, James B. *Abolitionist Politics and the Coming of the Civil War.* Amherst: University of Massachusetts Press, 2008.

———. "The Aims and Impact of Garrisonian Abolitionism, 1840–1860." *Civil War History* 15, no. 3 (1969): 197–209.

———. "From Moral Suasion to Political Confrontation: American Abolitionists and the Problem of Resistance." In *Passages to Freedom: The Underground Railroad in History and Memory,* edited by David Blight, 67–92. Washington, DC: HarperCollins, 2004.

———. *Holy Warriors: The Abolitionists and American Slavery.* New York: Hill & Wang, 1996. 1st ed. published in 1976.

———. "Humanitarian Reform and Antislavery." In *A Companion to Civil War and Reconstruction,* edited by Lacy K. Ford, 94–111. Oxford: Blackwell, 2005.

———. "Peaceful Hopes and Violent Experiences: The Evolution of Reforming and Radical Abolitionism, 1831–1837." *Civil War History* 17, no. 4 (1971): 293–309.

———. *William Lloyd Garrison and the Challenge of Emancipation.* Arlington Heights, IL: Harlan Davidson, 1992.

———, ed. *William Lloyd Garrison at Two Hundred.* New Haven, CT: Yale University Press, 2008.

Striner, Richard. *Father Abraham: Lincoln's Relentless Struggle to End Slavery.* New York: Oxford University Press, 2006.

Sullam, Simon Levi. "Costruire un nazionalismo e un 'gran convegno de' popoli: Giuseppe Mazzini tra Europa e Polonia." In *L'eredità di Giuseppe Mazzini: La democrazia tra coscienza nazionale e coscienza europea,* edited by Giampietro Berti, 49–64. Padova: Il Poligrafo, 2006.

———. "Dio e il popolo: La rivoluzione religiosa di Giuseppe Mazzini." In Banti and Ginsborg, *Il Risorgimento,* 401–422.

———. "'Fate della nazione una religione': Aspetti del nazionalismo mazziniano come religione politica." *Società e Storia* 106 (2004): 705–730.

———. *L'apostolo a brandelli: L'eredità di Mazzini tra Risorgimento e Fascismo.* Rome-Bari: Laterza, 2010.

———. "Mazzini e i conflitti dell'unità." In Isnenghi and Cecchinato, *Fare l'Italia,* 253–266.

———. "The Moses of Italian Unity: Mazzini and Nationalism as Political Religion." In Bayly and Biagini, *Mazzini and the Globalization,* 107–124.

Tatti, Silvia. "Ugo Foscolo." In *Vite per l'unità: Autori e scrittori del Risorgimento civile,* edited by Beatrice Alfonzetti and Silvia Tatti, 3–18. Rome: Donzelli, 2011.

Taylor, Clare, ed. *British and American Abolitionists: An Episode in Transatlantic Understanding.* Edinburgh: Edinburgh University Press, 1974.

Temperley, Howard. *British Antislavery, 1833–1870.* London: Longman, 1972.

Thom, Martin. "Europa, libertà e nazioni: Mazzini e Cattaneo nel Risorgimento." In Banti and Ginsborg, *Il Risorgimento,* 331–378.

Thomas, John L. *The Liberator: William Lloyd Garrison: A Biography.* Boston: Little, Brown, 1963.

———. "Romantic Reform in America, 1815–1865." *American Quarterly* 17, no. 4 (1965): 656–681.

Thompson, Dorothy. *The Chartists: Popular Politics in the Industrial Revolution.* New York: Pantheon, 1984.

Tomich, Dale. *Through the Prism of Slavery: Labor, Capital, and the World Economy.* Lantham, MD: Rowman & Littlefield, 2003.

Tomich, Dale, and Michael Zeuske. "Introduction: The Second Slavery: Mass Slavery, World- Economy, and Comparative Microhistories." *Review* 31, no. 2 (2008): 91–100.

Tramarollo, Giuseppe. "Il giornalismo di Mazzini." *Il Risorgimento* 29, no. 3 (1977): 113–126.

Turley, David. "Religion and Approaches to Reform: Boston Unitarians versus Evangelicals in the Context of the 1820s and 1830s." *American Nineteenth Century History* 10, no. 2 (2009): 187–209.

Tyrrell, Ian. *Transnational Nation: United States History in Global Perspective since 1789.* New York: Palgrave, 2007.

Urbinati, Nadia. "'A Common Law of Nations': Giuseppe Mazzini's Democratic Nationality." *Journal of Modern Italian Studies* 1, no. 2 (1996): 197–222.

———. "The Legacy of Kant: Giuseppe Mazzini's Cosmopolitanism of Nations." In Bayly and Biagini, *Mazzini and the Globalization,* 11–32.

Van Broekhoven, Deborah Bingham. "Perspectives on Slavery: Opposition to Slavery." In *Macmillan Encyclopedia of World Slavery,* edited by Paul Finkelman and Joseph Miller. New York: Macmillan, 1997.

Van Deburg, William L. "William Lloyd Garrison and the 'Pro-Slavery Priesthood': The Changing Beliefs of an Evangelical Reformer, 1830–1840." *Journal of the American Academy of Religion* 43 (1975): 224–237.

Varon, Elizabeth. *Disunion! The Coming of the Civil War, 1789–1859.* Chapel Hill: University of North Carolina Press, 2008.

Venturi, Franco. "L'Italia fuori d'Italia." In *Storia d'Italia,* vol. 3, *Dal Primo Settecento all'Unità,* edited by Ruggero Romano and Corrado Vivanti, 987–1481. Turin: Einaudi, 1973.

Verdecchia, Enrico. *Londra dei cospiratori: L'esilio londinese dei padri del Risorgimento.* Milan: Tropea, 2010.

Viarengo, Adriano. *Cavour.* Rome: Salerno Editrice, 2010.

Viroli, Maurizio. *Come se Dio ci fosse: Religione e libertà nella storia d'Italia.* Turin: Einaudi, 2009.

Von Frank, Albert J. "John Brown, James Redpath, and the Idea of Revolution." *Civil War History* 52, no. 2 (2006): 142–150.

———. *The Trials of Anthony Burns: Freedom and Slavery in Emerson's Boston.* Cambridge, MA: Harvard University Press, 1998.

Vorenberg, Michael. "Abraham Lincoln's 'Fellow Citizens': Before and After Emancipation." In *Lincoln's Proclamation: Emancipation Reconsidered,* edited by William A. Blair and Karen Fisher Younger, 151–169. Chapel Hill: University of North Carolina Press, 2009.

———. *Final Freedom: The Civil War, the Abolition of Slavery, and the Thirteenth Amendment.* New York: Cambridge University Press, 2001.

Voss Hubbard, Mark. "Slavery, Capitalism, and the Middling Sort: The Rank and File of Political Abolitionism." *American Nineteenth Century History* 4, no. 2 (2003): 53–76.

Walsh-Russo, Cecelia Catherine. "'The World Is My Country and My Countrymen Are All Mankind': Transnational Diffusion of Anglo-American Abolitionism, 1824–1839." PhD diss., Columbia University, 2008.

Walters, Ronald G. *American Reformers, 1815–1860.* New York: Hill & Wang, 1996.

———. *The Antislavery Appeal: American Abolitionism after 1830.* New York: Norton, 1978.

Watson, Harry L. *Liberty and Power: The Politics of Jacksonian America.* New York: Hill & Wang, 1990.

Wilentz, Sean. "Jeffersonian Democracy and the Origins of Political Antislavery in the United States: The Missouri Crisis Revisited." *Journal of the Historical Society* 4 (2004): 375–401.

———. *The Rise of American Democracy: From Jefferson to Lincoln.* New York: Norton, 2006.

Winch, Julie. *A Gentleman of Color: The Life of James Forten.* New York: Oxford University Press, 2002.

———. "Onward, Onward Is Indeed the Watchword: James Forten's Reflections on Revolution and Liberty." In McCarthy and Stauffer, *Prophets of Protest,* 80–89.

Woolf, Stuart J. *A History of Italy, 1700–1860: The Social Constraints of Political Change.* London: Routledge, 1979.

Yarema, Allan. *The American Colonization Society: An Avenue for Freedom?* Lanham, MD: University Press of America, 2006.

Yellin, Jean Fagan. *Women and Sisters: The Antislavery Feminists in American Culture.* New Haven, CT: Yale University Press, 1989.

Zaghi, Carlo. *L'Italia di Napoleone dalla Cisalpina al Regno.* Turin: UTET, 1986.

Zorn, Roman J. "*New England Anti-Slavery Society:* Pioneer Abolition Organization." *Journal of Negro History* 42, no. 3 (1957): 157–176.

INDEX